Sir John Fortescue's
The Bloodiest Folly

Sir John Fortescue's
The Bloodiest Folly
The British Army in Afghanistan 1837-42

J.W. Fortescue

Sir John Fortescue's The Bloodiest Folly
The British Army in Afghanistan 1837-42
by J. W. Fortescue

FIRST EDITION

Text taken from *A History of the British Army*

Leonaur is an imprint of Oakpast Ltd

Copyright in this form © 2016 Oakpast Ltd

ISBN: 978-1-78282-489-3 (hardcover)
ISBN: 978-1-78282-490-9 (softcover)

http://www.leonaur.com

Publisher's Notes

The views expressed in this book are not necessarily those of the publisher.

Contents

Preface	7
Lord William Bentinck Governor-General in India	9
Arrival of the Bombay Force in the Indus	37
The British Enter Kabul	86
Trouble with the Ghilzais	111
Unrest about Kandahar	140
Arrival of Shelton's Brigade	161
Sale Forces the Khurd Kabul Pass	186
Crisis at Kabul	194
The Retreat	223
Council of War at Jalalabad	240

Preface

This volume is concerned mainly with India; and unfortunately the original documents relating to the events therein narrated are, (at time of writing), preserved in India. The authorities at the Record Department of the India Office have been, as always, most courteous and helpful, but they could give me nothing except the collection known as the "Secret Consultations of the Governor-General and Council of India," which is quoted in my pages under the initials "I.O.S.C." It purports to contain transcripts of all the documents which came before the Governor-General in Council at each meeting, and it is, on the whole, the most disorderly and chaotic assembly of papers that I have encountered in more than thirty years of research. In the first place the volumes are so gigantic, heavy and unwieldy, that it is difficult to read them comfortably in any attitude. In the second, many of the documents before the Council (as is plain from internal evidence) have not been transcribed at all, while others have been copied two or three times over.

In the third the transcripts have not been checked, and contain many corrupt passages which cost me much trouble to emend. In the fourth, many of the clerks wrote vile hands, and occasionally one of the idler among them has filled up his exhausted ink-pot with water instead of ink, and has left writing so faint that it can only be read with much suffering to the eyes. In the fifth, there is no index, and, though the volumes are numbered, the pages are not, so that it is impossible to give an accurate reference to them. In the sixth, if the Governor-General happened to be closer to the scene of action than his Council, there is no reference to that scene of action at all. And, finally, the documents observe no kind of order, chronological or other, as may be seen by my note in chapter 6. Altogether the collection forms an appropriate monument to the administrative methods of the East

India Company. However, after toiling through several score of these volumes, I got something new out of them for the Afghan War. I wish that I could have paid a visit to the archives at Lahore, for I should not have grudged the fatigue and the labour, could I have afforded the time and the money; and, though this was impossible, I am not the less oppressed by a feeling of self-reproach that I have left an important source of information unexplored.

J. W. F.

CHAPTER 1

Lord William Bentinck Governor-General in India

With the fall of Bhurtpore India sank into the tranquillity of the overawed; and early in 1828 Lord Amherst resigned the Governorship-general and sailed for England. He was succeeded in July of the same year by Lord William Bentinck. This officer had been removed from the government of Madras in 1807 by the directors of the East India Company, who held him to be responsible for the mutiny at Vellore; and, feeling himself deeply aggrieved by this treatment, he was anxious to wipe off the stigma from his name by returning to India in the highest of all positions. He received his appointment in 1827 from Canning who had courted alliance with the Whigs and doubtless was not averse from conciliating the house of Portland; and he was allowed to retain it by the generous forbearance of Wellington. The duke, indeed, did not favour the distribution of great places according to the prejudices of party; and, since Bentinck had given him a good deal of trouble by his blunders in Spain, he would be the more anxious to show that he bore him no malice and was well content to see him elevated to high station.

A wiser man than Bentinck would have hesitated before accepting the place upon the terms imposed on him by the court of directors. The succession of costly wars conducted by the Indian government between 1814 and 1826 had involved it in financial difficulties which imperatively demanded economy; and it was natural and right that the court should prescribe reduction of the army and general diminution of military expenditure. But there was one detail of retrenchment which, to say the least, was of doubtful expediency. It had long been the practice to grant an allowance, known as *batta*, to officers of the army when serving in the field within the company's territories; which allowance was reduced to one-half when the officers were in cantonments and were furnished with quarters at the public expense.

In 1801, however, the government of Bengal granted full *batta* at all times, and threw upon the officers themselves the burden of providing themselves with quarters. This arrangement had never been sanctioned by the directors; and in 1814 they instructed that government to revert to the original plan of granting half-*batta* only, within the old territory of the company in that presidency. Moira, realising that such a regulation would be a great hardship, to officers and would provoke legitimate discontent among a body of men who were already none too well disciplined, refused to obey the court's orders and referred them back to it for reconsideration. He judged that the saving of a paltry £20,000 was not worth the risk of a possible mutiny. Amherst in his turn did likewise; and the directors, losing patience instead of learning wisdom, insisted that Bentinck must obey their commands as to half-*batta*, or resign. Being at the moment solicitous above all things for the vindication of his own good name, such as it was, Bentinck consented to obey; and on the 9th of November 1828, as one of his first measures of retrenchment, he issued the order which reduced the *batta* of officers by one-half.

He was obliged to do so mainly upon his own authority. Combermere, the commander in chief, flatly refused to be a party to the order and resigned his office. The two civil members of the council only with the greatest reluctance assented to it lest they should seem to defy their superiors in Leadenhall Street; and the abler of them, Sir Charles Metcalfe, recorded his opinion that the measure was unjust and unwise, and his consequent hope that the order might be rescinded. The regulation was at first made applicable to five stations only; but that was amply sufficient to raise a storm. As a matter of fact the officers were none too well paid even with full *batta*, and the halving of the allowance signified to them real privation and suffering. In high indignation they held meetings, passed resolutions and forwarded petitions to the Commander-in-chief and to the court of directors.

The *sepoys*, hearing of the reduction of their officers' pay, trembled lest the same misfortune should overtake them; and it seems to be no more than true that, if the officers had but lifted their fingers, the Bengal Army would have risen to a man. There were indeed rash spirits who proposed to turn the feelings of the soldiers to account in order to put pressure upon the government, but they were at once overruled by the majority, who took their revenge in a different fashion.

From the day when the order became known, the officers, to use an old phrase, sent the governor-general to Coventry. If they saw him approaching, they turned out of the way to avoid him. If he entered the park, not an officer would go near it while he was there. If he gave a ball, not an officer would attend it. Even commanding officers agreed to decline his invitations to dinner; and one of them, questioned by Bentinck himself, flatly avowed the fact. All this, though superficially it might seem unimportant, was bad for discipline at large. Bentinck was greatly hurt. It seems that in his heart he loved the new regulation as little as anyone, but that he felt himself bound to enforce it under the command of the directors. But no soldier who knew anything of soldiers would have pledged himself to do anything so foolish; for he would have divined that the mischief would not be limited to his own unpopularity. And it was not.

No sooner did the *sepoys* learn that their officers only were to be mulcted than "they twirled their moustaches with pride, strutted about with a lordly, swaggering air and gave every indication that they had formed an overweening estimate of their own importance," (Seaton, *From Cadet to Colonel*, i.). The directors, realising after a time that it was false economy to wreck the Bengal army for £20,000, forbore to extend their new regulation beyond the five stations first selected; but the evil in the ranks of the *sepoys* had been already done past recall.

Bentinck then proceeded to aggravate it by abolishing the lash in the Indian native regiments, though it was still retained in the British service. This was a combination of two gross stupidities. In the first place, flogging was absolutely necessary for the preservation of discipline among the native soldiery, and the fact was proved by the revival of the punishment within a very few years. In the second place, the native troops, observing that they enjoyed an immunity which was not accorded to their British comrades, naturally inferred that they were a superior people, and in fact that they, and they alone, constituted the military force upon which depended the British dominion in India. If it ever occurred to them that, without their British officers, they were naught, they could banish the idea by reflecting that those officers were no longer of worth, since their own masters had lately reduced their pay. If Bentinck can be excused for his action in the affair of *batta* by the plea that he was acting under orders, no such defence can avail him over the question of flogging. Therein he showed himself to be not only no statesman, but also no soldier.

In regard to relations with native states, Bentinck tried hard to reconcile Barlow's system of abjuring all intervention in their affairs with Hastings's principle that order must be maintained among the neighbours on the British frontier. The result was not very happy. More than once he was obliged to interfere at last when he had better have done so at first, or contented himself with temporary adjustments which only laid up trouble for the future.

The most serious of his interventions was the invasion of the territory of Coorg, on the west coast by the upper waters of the Cauvery, where the reigning *raja* had been guilty of the vilest cruelty and oppression. The total force employed included three regiments of the King's Infantry, the Thirty-Ninth, Forty-Eighth and Fifty-Fifth, and seven battalions of Madras Native Infantry, besides artillery, making a total of some six thousand men, under the command of Brigadier-General Lindesay of the Thirty-Ninth, a veteran of the Peninsula.

The country was wild, mountainous, forest-clad and pathless; and the main difficulties to be encountered were those of transport and supply. In the circumstances it was impossible to feed or to move any great number of men in a single body; so Lindesay distributed his force into four columns, which were to converge upon the capital, Mercara, from the north, east and west. The northern column, under Colonel Waugh, consisted of the Fifty-Fifth, two Madras battalions, with artillery. The eastern column, which was commanded by Lindesay himself, was made up of the Thirty-Ninth, two Madras battalions and artillery, and was based on Periyapatna; one western column, under Colonel Foulis, included part of the Forty-Eighth and two Madras battalions with artillery, with its base at Cannanore; and an auxiliary western column, based on Mangalore, under Colonel Jackson, had a detachment of the Forty-Eighth, one battalion of Madras Infantry, but no guns.

The whole of these columns crossed into the territory of Coorg on the 2nd of April 1834. One and all found themselves confronted by blind mountain-tracks, which were obstructed by felled trees, and defended by stockades. Waugh, being stopped by one such stockade, sent out parties to right and left to pass round it, unite in rear of it and take it in reverse; but the two detachments, turning inward too soon, joined together in front, instead of in rear, of the enemy's position, and rushing forward to storm it were beaten back after four hours' fighting with a loss of over one hundred and sixty killed and wounded, one hundred of them belonging to the Fifty-Fifth. Lindesay himself, who crossed the Cauvery at Hebhali, met with little opposition, and entered Mercara victorious on the 6th.

It was a secondary column, detached from his own, under Colonel Stewart, which did such little fighting as was to be done on that side. Foulis joined touch with the enemy on the 2nd, spent the 3rd and the 4th fighting his way through the Heggala Ghat over innumerable felled trees, and finally cleared it after storming two stockades and two breastworks at a cost of about fifty casualties. Jackson, learning of a stockade five miles ahead of him, pushed forward forty of the Forty-Eighth and about one hundred *sepoys* to reconnoitre it, with the result that the party walked into an ambush, and was only extricated after the loss of half of its numbers killed and wounded. The entire campaign lasted just five days, and cost in all the lives of five British officers and about forty British soldiers, with a total casualty list of over two hundred killed and wounded.

It is difficult to pronounce judgement upon little affairs of this kind. The work seems to have been similar to that of the Nepali War, though the enemy, albeit possessed of both matchlocks and cannon, was far less formidable. The difficulties were very great, for the artillery could generally be brought forward only by man-handling, the paths being impracticable for bullocks; and the fatigue thus caused to the men was aggravated by intense heat. Bush-fighting, where troops must depend upon native guides, always timid and often treacherous, must always be a hazardous matter. None the less, both Waugh and Jackson were much blamed, and, it should seem rightly, seeing that Foulis succeeded against as formidable resistance as had caused their failure, with the loss of but fifty men. Seniority too often in those days, and indeed many years later, placed commands which called for real skill and professional knowledge, in the hands of men who were not to be trusted in charge of a corporal's guard.

In regard to the remoter powers in the north-west of India—the Sikhs, the Amirs of Sind and the Afghans—Bentinck, in consequence of the steady advance of Russia eastward, took more definite and significant measures. In 1826 war between Russia and Persia again broke out, and England found herself, under the treaty of 1812, bound to heal their differences or, in default, to supply Persia either with troops or money. Canning refused to furnish either men or cash, preferring to spend the amount of the covenanted subsidy in purchasing the erasure of these awkward stipulations from the treaty. British media-

Colonel Stewart, charging with his column

tion, however, was forthcoming; and in 1828, Persia, having suffered many defeats, bought peace by the cession of further territory to Russia. Thenceforward British influence vanished from Tehran, and Persia became the tool of Russia. The Shah, naturally sore at seeing his western dominions shorn from him, conceived the idea that he might indemnify himself by encroaching upon his neighbours to eastward; and, as naturally, the Russians assured him that he could not do better. The arrangement did not promise peace on the north-western frontier of the British dominions.

Immediately to east of Persia lay Afghanistan, and eastward of her again Ranjit Singh and the Sikhs to north, and the Amirs of Sind to south. The relations of these three powers to each other and to the British were somewhat curious. In Afghanistan, since the flight of Shah Shuja, in 1809, events had tended steadily towards the supplanting of his dynasty—that of the Sadozais—by the chiefs of the rival tribe of Barakzais. As these chiefs included a score of brothers, each of them jealous and distrustful of the others, the change would have promised little improvement, had not one of them, Dost Mohamed, been a man of such clear intellect and strong character as to assure him ultimate pre-eminence.

But, while the strife in Afghanistan continued, Ranjit Singh took the opportunity to snatch away Mooltan in 1818 and Kashmir in 1819, losses which could not but rankle deep in the hearts alike of Sadozais and Barakzais. Ranjit, still insatiable, then meditated a descent upon the delta of the Indus, but here, as shall presently be seen, he was anticipated by the British. By 1826 not only had the rule of the Sadozais been extinguished in Afghanistan, except at Herat, where one of them, Khamran by name, still held his own, but Dost Mohamed, after many contests with his brothers, had made over Kandahar to one of them—Kohan Dil Khan—and reigned himself supreme at Kabul. None but a very strong and fearless man can govern those lawless and turbulent tribes; and he must add to his strength a sense of duty and a rude justice administered with inflexible severity. Such a combination of qualities is not common, but they were certainly found in Dost Mohamed.

Looking to the alarming advance of Russia and to the hold which she had gained upon Persia, the supreme government of India conceived that the wise course would be to seek the friendship alike of *amirs*, Afghans and Sikhs, and unite them, if possible, into a solid barrier against a Russian invasion from the west. Little was known about any

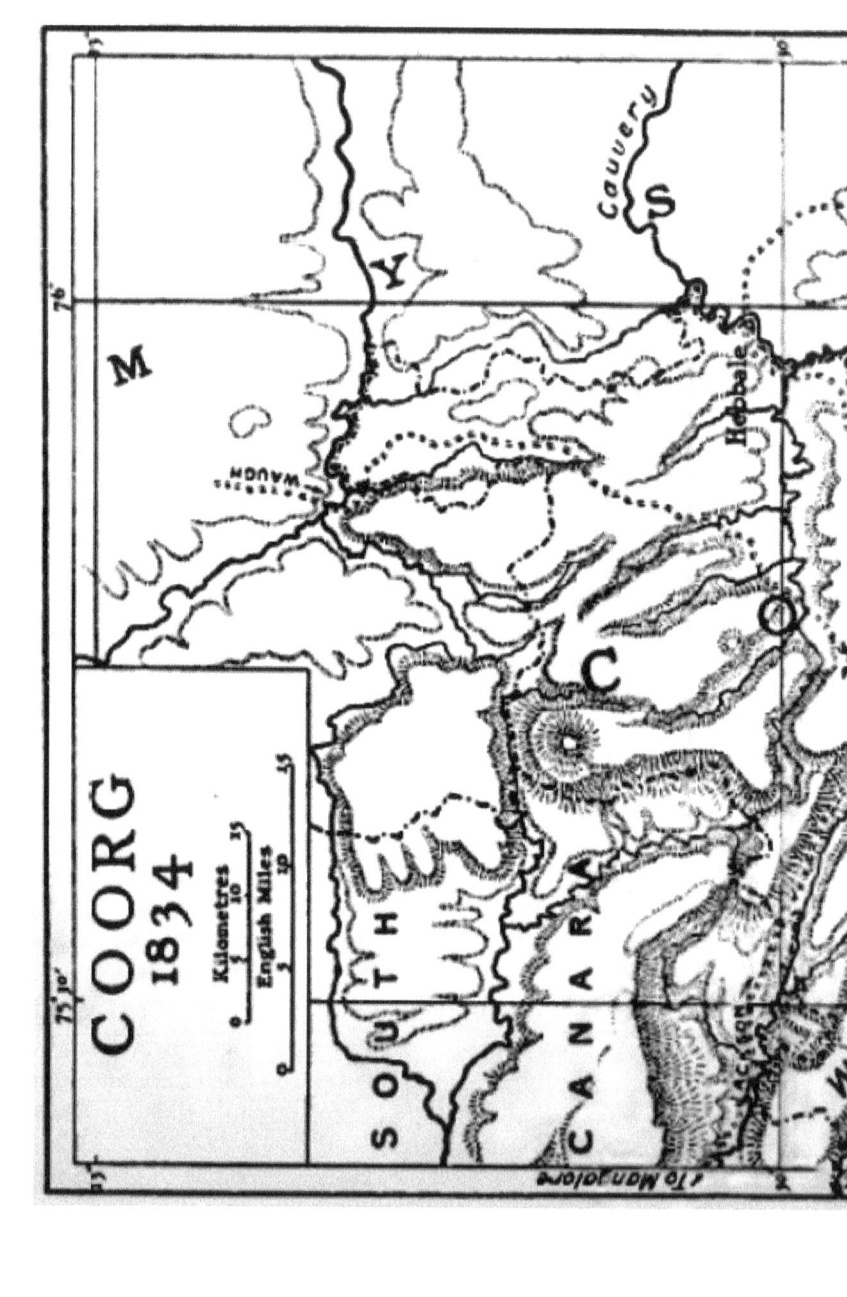

of the three; and their jealousies and rivalries were such as promised to baffle the most skilful diplomacy. In the first place, the Amirs of Sind were nominally dependent upon the court of Kabul, and tributary to it; but they were anxious to throw off that dependence, and paid little tribute unless it were collected by an Afghan army. With Ranjit Singh they had had little to do; but he was firmly established at Mooltan and casting greedy eyes down the stream of the Indus. With the British they had, in 1820, renewed their original treaty of amity and alliance; and it was not difficult to play upon their fears of a British agreement with Afghanistan and their hopes of British help for themselves against that country. By their friendship the most southerly outlet into India from the west—the Bolan Pass—might well be secured; but they were extremely jealous of any proposals of the Calcutta Government for opening the navigation of the Indus; and this was a matter which that government earnestly desired to accomplish.

As to Afghanistan, the situation was more complicated still. The original treaty negotiated with Shah Shuja by the British mission of 1809 had fallen to naught with the expulsion of that potentate in 1810. After being despoiled of his jewels by Ranjit Singh, he had managed to escape from the overpowering attentions of his protector to British territory, and had long been living at Ludhiana upon a pension granted to him by the Indian government. He dreamed, however, continually of the recovery of his lost empire with the help of Ranjit Singh, with the help of the British Government, with the help, in fact, of any one who for any consideration would replace him upon a throne which he was quite unfit to occupy. Ranjit Singh, who had already torn from his realm Kashmir and Mooltan, readily played with the poor creature's hopes, no doubt with the expectation of shearing away yet more of the Afghan dominions. There are no such dreamers as exiled princes; and it suited well the purposes of the crafty *Sikh* to have, as cat's-paw, so weak and foolish a dreamer as Shah Shuja.

As to the British sentiments towards Ranjit Singh himself, it seems hardly too much to say that the Calcutta Government was heartily afraid of him. Nor, perhaps, was this altogether unnatural, for the Sikh chief was hardly less than a man of genius, and he had a formidable disciplined army under his hand. British India needed peace after the exhaustion of the Nepalese, Pindari and Burmese campaigns. The Bengal Army had been reduced as a consequence of that exhaustion; and if, as seemed surely to be the case, the Russians were meditating an invasion of India, it was far more convenient that the task of

First Afghan War

repelling them should fall upon Ranjit Singh than upon the British. As Palmerston had tried to palm off upon Spain the military duties of England, so the Calcutta Government sought to some extent to palm off its military duties upon the Sikhs, the *amirs* and the Afghans; and of the three the Sikhs were decidedly the most powerful. Looking to the fact that the British were not only the most formidable neighbours of Ranjit Singh but most anxious to cultivate his friendship, it was thought that there should be no great difficulty in gaining his help, and in averting any danger of his conquest of Sind.

There remained the problem of inducing Afghanistan to work with the Sikhs and the *amirs*, which seemed not easy except upon one condition. The actual ruler of Afghanistan was an usurper, but nevertheless not likely to feel friendly towards the chief who had appropriated so much of his usurped kingdom. The legitimate ruler was a guest on British territory, who reposed his hopes of restoration mainly upon Ranjit Singh. Could he but be reinstated, and the usurper driven out, then, with a little tact and management, all differences between the three parties might be adjusted by a triple alliance, and an impassable barrier might be thrown up against the Russian armies. Such seem to have been the vague ideas, original or instilled into him by others, which possessed the imagination of Bentinck and were to be inherited from him by his successor. They were soon proved to rest upon false conceptions of fact, but, in default of better information, they were not in themselves absolutely unreasonable. Nevertheless it is curious that a Whig, who based all his political philosophy upon the glorious Revolution of 1688, should have favoured a legitimate sovereign of tried incompetence as against an usurper of proved ability.

However, in 1830 the first diplomatic step was taken. At the instance of Lord Ellenborough, President of the Board of Control, or in other words the chief director of Indian affairs in London, it was decided that a complimentary mission should be sent to Ranjit Singh, and that it should proceed to Lahore by water. The selected emissary was one Alexander Burnes, a young man of twenty-six, who having shown talent as a linguist and as a topographical draughtsman, had been transferred from military to political duties. Upon his entering the Indus he was stopped by the *amirs* and forbidden to proceed further; but after protracted negotiation he was allowed to ascend the river to Hyderabad, and finally arrived at Lahore in July. Here he delivered a present of English horses to Ranjit Singh and was received by the old warrior with open arms.

From Lahore he made his way to Ludhiana, where he met the exiled prince Shah Shuja, and thence to Simla, where Bentinck gave him leave to travel home overland. Starting at the beginning of 1832, Burnes travelled first by the Khyber Pass to Kabul, where he was hospitably entertained by Dost Mohamed; and during his stay he realised that his host was a man able and worthy to rule the Afghans and that Shah Shuja was not. From Kabul he journeyed over the Hindu Kush to the Oxus, thence to Bokhara, Tehran and Bushire and so back to Bombay and Calcutta. Early in 1833 he made his report to Bentinck, and was sent home to lay his information before the authorities in England. There, for the present, let us leave him, much sought after in London society for all that he had seen and could tell of lands so far almost unknown.

Meanwhile, events began to move with greater rapidity. In October 1831 the governor-general himself paid a visit to Ranjit Singh. The meeting took place at Rupar on the Sutlej, where a week was passed in ceremonial visits and military evolutions, Bentinck having brought with him a wing of the Sixteenth Lancers, a troop of horse-artillery, two squadrons of native horse and the Thirty-First Foot; while Ranjit had for escort six thousand of his best infantry and ten thousand cavalry. The display was significant and so also was the time; for Shah Shuja, after many attempts, was on the point of concluding a negotiation with Ranjit Singh for his restoration to the throne of Kabul. Bentinck was aware of the conditions; and it is hardly possible that the Sikh chieftain should not have referred to the subject and at least have attempted to ascertain the governor-general's views thereon; though it is not likely that Bentinck should have committed himself to any very definite expression of opinion. Certainly, when Shah Shuja asked him directly for aid, Bentinck refused to interfere in any way; but, whether he said so or not, Bentinck undoubtedly wished the fallen monarch success in his venture.

The next incident resulted immediately from Burnes's report upon the navigation of the Indus. In 1832 the East India Company presented to the Amirs of Sind the project of a treaty under which the river might be opened to the merchants and traders of Hindustan upon payment of fair and moderate duties. The Baluchi chieftains did not favour the proposal, which they regarded with suspicion, and only very reluctantly did they yield their consent to it, specially stipulating that in no case should military stores nor armed vessels enter the river. With true instinct they foresaw in the advent of the Europeans the passing of their own rule; but, with enemies on every side, they hoped by this concession at least to gain England for their friend. It is a curious complication in the whole of this intricate affair that the British rulers of India—at any rate in England—seem to have held access to the Indus more closely to their hearts than any other object, and that for commercial purposes only, without any reference to the eastward advance of Russia. It is more than likely that this confusion of purposes led to confusion of thought and of policy.

In January 1833 Shah Shuja, having obtained from the British four months' advance of the allowance granted to him by them, marched out of Ludhiana with a handful of followers, and moving slowly down the Sutlej and the Indus into Sind crossed the latter river to Shikarpur. By the time that he had arrived there, his army had swelled to thirty thousand men; and, as the *amirs* had received him with friendship and furnished him with supplies, he was in no great haste to proceed to the Bolan Pass. His exactions, however, became so intolerable that the Sindians rose against him, but, after defeat in a pitched battle in January 1834, were fain to submit. In due time, therefore, Shah Shuja continued his advance, and marching by the Bolan Pass appeared in the early summer before Kandahar. He laid siege to the city, but, before he could master it, Dost Mohamed swept down upon him from Kabul in all his wrath, completely defeated him and drove him in hopeless flight from the country.

This, however, was only the beginning of Dost Mohamed's troubles. By his treaty with Ranjit Singh Shah Shuja had agreed to deliver to him, upon his restoration, the district of Peshawar. The wily old chief, however, being in no mood to wait for Shah Shuja's success, which probably he considered very doubtful, seized the moment while Dost Mohamed's hands were full to snatch away his prize by treachery without further ado. Furious with rage, Dost Mohamed proclaimed a holy war. The tribes flocked by thousands to his banner, and, when he came before Peshawar, even Ranjit Singh quailed before the aspect of the Afghan host. But, once again, the cunning Sikh set treachery to work; and in a few hours Dost Mohamed's army had melted away. Peshawar was gone, gone, as it proved, for ever; and Dost Mohamed never forgot nor forgave the loss. Henceforward there could be no real peace between him and Ranjit Singh.

In the spring of 1835 Lord William Bentinck resigned the post of Governor-General and was succeeded in the autumn by Lord Auckland. The vacancy had occurred during the brief administration of Sir

Shah Shuja

Robert Peel from December 1834 to April 1835; and Lord Heytesbury, a man who had proved his ability during a long and successful diplomatic career, had been chosen to fill it. But it would have done violence to all sentiment and tradition of the Whigs that so rich a piece of patronage should pass out of their hands, so Lord Heytesbury's appointment was unceremoniously cancelled, and the better man was displaced to make way for the worse. Not that there was grave fault to be found in Auckland. On the contrary, he was a quiet, modest, diligent, conscientious man, with every desire to do good in an unobtrusive way, and no passion to make himself a resplendent name. In brief, he was conscious of his own mediocrity, which was so far in his favour; and this consciousness, as often happens, had gained him the reputation of being what is called a "safe" man.

Now a mediocre man, if he possess some measure of shrewdness, a sense of the ridiculous, and a certain degree of strength, may be trusted to ensure that description of "safety" which consists in placing present difficulties, so to speak, on deposit, to accumulate with compound interest for discharge by his successors. But Auckland, though a cultivated man, possessed little mother-wit, was painfully in earnest, and was both weak and irresolute. Being unmarried he was accompanied by his two sisters, ladies of unusual cleverness and accomplishments, but not on that account likely to be the wisest counsellors for an unambitious and hesitating man.

By an unfortunate coincidence it chanced that the Indian Civil Service was particularly rich at the moment in what were termed brilliant young men. Such persons generally attained to that reputation in India by the mastery of a number of Oriental languages. To the ordinary European, who turns in despair from any script, other than Roman or Greek, such an accomplishment appears marvellous; and certainly it does imply at least diligence and mental gifts of a certain kind. In the Indian climate, moreover, the mere fact that a man entered upon any serious intellectual labour, except under compulsion, avouched activity of mind and strength of character. Yet experience shows that astonishing proficiency in Oriental tongues can be acquired by men who live among the speakers of those tongues, but who in other respects are not remarkable for intellect.

In India, however, an accomplished linguist was sure of promotion, and no doubt rightly so, both in the administrative and the diplomatic service. The truth seems to be that any young man who possessed brains, lived steadily and was fond of work, was sure of advancement.

Any youthful subaltern who chose to spend his leisure hours—and those hours were very many in cantonments—in the acquisition of a new language was caught up, taken away from his military duties for administrative or diplomatic business, and became what was called a "political". If by chance he were sent to some country heretofore unvisited, he wrote a book about it and commenced author. If like, for instance, Alexander Burnes, he voluntarily accomplished some adventurous journey for purposes of intelligence and exploration, he might attain celebrity, not only in India but in London drawing-rooms. The field thus opened to enterprising young men was wide; and indeed it may be said that this period, when the consolidation of British power in the great peninsula was extending British interests westward to the Bosporus and the Nile and eastward to the Pacific Ocean, was the golden age of British youth in India.

None the less, the system had its dangers. In the first place it was a very grave evil that military officers should be not merely taught but encouraged to look outside the military service for advancement. This signified that the army was robbed of its best and most promising men, and was left with those who preferred an idle and easy life. If the latter devoted their leisure to sport with rifle, gun or hog-spear, little harm was done, for there could be no better training for active service; but if they fell back upon alcohol and pursuit of their neighbours' wives, or even upon nothing worse than the petty jealousies and squabbles of life in cantonments, they could be nothing save unprofitable. In any case the elimination of all who might raise the standard of cultivation and encourage a zest for intellectual pursuits among the younger officers, was most mischievous.

Moreover, the effect of their removal from the military sphere had a most pernicious effect upon these young "political" themselves. Distinguished above their fellow men in virtue of their linguistic gifts, often trusted, while yet immature, with a very large measure of independence whether for administrative or diplomatic duties, they readily formed an exaggerated estimate of their own ability and their own importance. The few really capable men in India were, from the nature of the case, scattered far and wide; and it was rare for them to meet their intellectual peers. Having never encountered any that they judged to be their intellectual superiors, they had a suspicion, sometimes amounting to a certainty, that such superiors did not exist. Among the British in India it is possible that they were supreme, and certainly they were honoured accordingly. Where, as about the headquarters of government, a few of them were gathered together, they formed a select society, not lacking mutual admiration. Everywhere they were encouraged in the worst and, apparently, the incurable vice of Indian administration—copious and interminable writing of minutes, memoranda and reports.

There is no one with much experience of Indian official records who has not longed to summon the writers before him, tear the documents asunder before their faces, and bid them compress their wordy effusions into a quarter of their original compass. No training can be worse for what is called a clever man than to suffer his prolixity with patience. Yet in India it was suffered with gladness, nay more, was accepted as a measure of efficiency. Such was the result of a lack of intellectual competition extending over many generations. Truly has it been said that nowhere is a great reputation so easily made as in India.

The group with which Auckland was chiefly concerned numbered three. The first was William Macnaghten, who had begun his service as a cadet in the Madras Cavalry in 1809, had become a civilian in Bengal five years later and by 1833 had risen to be the head of the "Secret and Political Department," that is to say of the department of Foreign Affairs, and later Chief Secretary to the government. He had a profound knowledge of Oriental languages and customs, with a considerable experience of administration, as carried out in India, and was an able and industrious public servant. The second was Henry Torrens, son of the Duke of York's military secretary, and himself at the outset a soldier who had keenly studied his profession. He was a more brilliant variety of Macnaghten, familiar with many tongues both European and Oriental, and possessed further a taste for letters, a quick intelligence and a dangerously facile pen. We are told:

> The airy grace with which he could throw off a French canzonet, was something as perfect in its kind as the military genius with which he could sketch out the plan of a campaign, or the official pomp with which he could inflate a state-paper.—Kaye, i.

The bare fact that such a sentence could be written of him by an Indian civil servant of no small reputation reveals the impression made by Torrens upon his fellows, who certainly were poor judges of a plan of campaign and probably possessed small acquaintance with the rules of French prosody. Such a man, full of vivacity and of miscellaneous information, would be a welcome addition to any government house, and might, if closely watched and tightly curbed, be an exceedingly valuable public servant. But he would need a chief of hard prosaic common sense, who would throw the canzonets into the waste-basket and incarcerate the effusions of military genius in those official dungeons from which there is no delivery except into the fire.

The third was John Colvin, a familiar name in the history of British India, who was Auckland's private secretary and official adviser. With less shining outward accomplishments than the other two, he possessed a stronger will and a sounder understanding. Though both loyal and patriotic, he nourished the ambition to guide and control with an unseen hand the policy and the actions of his chief; and he was troubled by no misgivings as to his competence for so high a task. Altogether each of the three would, in the hands of a wise, strong man, have made an excellent servant; but not one was qualified to be, what each felt sure that he should be, a master.

When Auckland reached India affairs in Persia had reached a very critical stage. The *Shah*, Futteh Ali, always the friend of England, died in the autumn of 1834; and with the cordial assent both of the Russian and of the British governments, his son Mohamed Shah reigned in his stead. Palmerston promptly sent a mission to congratulate the new monarch, and took occasion to warn him against allowing himself to be pushed into war against the Afghans. But such a war was precisely the measure upon which Mohamed Shah, under Russian advice, was intent, that he might indemnify himself in the east for losses in the west. Indeed, he had actually led an army to Herat and besieged it in 1833, but had been obliged to abandon the enterprise owing to internal troubles in Persia. He now announced that he claimed not only Herat, but Kandahar and even Ghazni, and that he would shortly set an army in motion to assert his right by force. The British Minister at Tehran offered to mediate between the incensed potentate and the ruler of Herat, but in vain; and he then bethought him that the wisest course would be to anticipate the designs of Persia in Afghanistan by sending a mission to Dost Mohamed at Kabul, and offering him the use of British officers to train the Afghan Army.

In Calcutta likewise the eyes of the government were already turned to the north-west; and it was considered advisable at least to gain some information of the countries through which Russia must pass if she intended to invade India. In the spring of 1836 Dost Mohamed addressed to Auckland a letter of congratulation upon his assumption of the Governorship-General, wherein he took occasion to complain of his own ill-treatment by the Sikhs and to beg, in a complimentary fashion, for Auckland's advice. The governor-general sent a becoming answer of goodwill, and expressed his hope that Dost Mohamed might be in favour of promoting the navigation of the Indus. He hinted that he might shortly send a mission to Kabul to discuss certain commercial topics, and, referring to the Sikhs, made the old declaration that it was not the habit of the British to interfere in the affairs of her independent neighbours. It is not quite clear how this admirable sentiment could be reconciled with the navigation of the Indus, nor how Dost Mohamed could be concerned with that matter, except as the nominal suzerain of the Amirs of Sind, with whom the British had concluded an alliance, or as the rightful owner of Mooltan and Peshawar, which had been wrested from the Afghan empire by the Sikhs.

Auckland's prime mistake seems to have been that he regarded the navigation of the Indus as a matter which could be arranged by diplomacy, whereas it could only have been permanently settled by actual, or threatened, force of arms. Some at least of his council seem to have realised this, and one of the most sagacious among them, Sir Charles Metcalfe, protested from the first against all of Auckland's measures with respect to the trade on that river, (Kaye, i.). As a matter of fact, we found ourselves within ten years engaged in desperate conflict with Afghans, Baluchis and Sikhs. If Auckland had seen his way more clearly he might, indeed, have been dragged into war with Baluchis and Sikhs, but need not have become entangled with the Afghans. If the Sikhs had been in the delta of the Indus instead of three hundred miles from it, there would have been far less talk about the navigation.

However, it was decided in the autumn to despatch a commercial mission to Kabul; and Alexander Burnes, who in the autumn of 1835 had been sent to the court of the Amirs of Sind, was selected to be the envoy. He had been very successful in Sind, had gained the consent of the *amirs* to a survey of the river, and could readily have made the British alliance with them more intimate, if the supreme government had been willing to take such a step. He sailed from Bombay for the Indus at the end of November, renewed his friendly but vague parleys with the *amirs*, by whom he was hospitably received, and passed slowly and deviously five hundred miles up the river to Dera Ghazi Khan, where he heard important news. In the spring of 1837, Dost Mohamed had sent an army through the Khyber Pass to lay siege to Jamrud, just at the mouth of the pass; and this force had defeated an army of Sikhs which had marched to the relief of the fort. The Afghan commander, in the first flush of success, spoke of a dash upon Peshawar; but the Sikhs soon reappeared in such strength that the Afghans were fain to retreat within their mountains. But they were full of exultation over their victory; and Ranjit Singh, one of whose dearest friends and best officers had fallen in the fight, never forgave Dost Mohamed for his loss.

Proceeding to Peshawar, Burnes was hospitably received by General Avitabile, an Italian in Ranjit Singh's service; and thence, passing through the still unburied dead at Jamrud, he entered the Khyber Pass. Friendly messages from Dost Mohamed met him as he journeyed; and on the 20th of September he was escorted with great pomp and splendour into Kabul, where the best accommodation had been prepared for the mission. Whatever his ostensible object, the envoy soon forsook commercial for political topics, and in no long time satisfied himself that Dost Mohamed honestly and whole-heartedly desired an alliance with the British and would have nothing to do with any other power.

Within two months of his arrival, Mohamed Shah fulfilled his long-standing threats; and on the 23rd of November a Persian army, equipped with powerful artillery and, in part, directed by Russian officers, laid siege to Herat. This fortress, it must be repeated, was the one fragment of the Afghan empire which remained under the control of a Sadozai chieftain, Khamran; and on this account the heads of the Barakzais, with one exception, applauded rather than otherwise the Persian menace to Herat. They had a blood feud with Khamran; they yearned to see the extinction of the last remnant of Sadozai dominion, and they hoped to see the principality of Herat transferred to themselves. Hence it was that Kohan Dil Khan of Kandahar, against the advice of his brother, Dost Mohamed, had sent one of his sons to the Persian camp to welcome the invaders.

For this action Kohan Dil Khan received warm commendation from the Russian agents who accompanied Mohamed Shah; but Dost Mohamed remained unmoved; and, even before the Persian host came before Herat, he offered, if Burnes approved it, to march an army against his brother. Burnes discountenanced any such measure, but he seconded Dost Mohamed's remonstrances with such effect that Kohan Dil Khan dismissed the Persian emissaries, and declared himself eager to act according to the advice of his brother and of the British government. Burnes replied, pledging himself to repair to Kandahar in person together with Dost Mohamed if the Persians should threaten that city, and even to pay the troops of Kohan Dil Khan. He sent, moreover, one of his officers to Kandahar to guard against the intrigues of the Persians and to give him the earliest information of their movements.

Herein, as was proved by later events, Burnes served his country well. It was no common good fortune to find so genuine a friend in the ruler at Kabul, particularly when that ruler was one of those rare strong men who really could control his turbulent and ungovernable subjects. Yet Dost Mohamed's inclinations towards the British were easily explained. Russian rule in Georgia had been calculated to alienate all good Mussulmans, and the demeanour of the Russians towards the conquered was the reverse of conciliating. Dost Mohamed's shrewdness may also have remarked that the Russians are essentially Orientals, more congenial in temperament than the Anglo-Saxons, but less thorough, less trustworthy, less stable to lean upon.

Be that as it may, he was not only ready but eager to work with the British; and Burnes, with true insight, recognised that such a friend at Kabul would be of priceless value, and, moreover, could be gained at little cost. Peshawar was always the sore point with Dost Mohamed; and, if the Calcutta government would consent to mediate with the Sikhs for its restoration, even if not on the most favourable terms, he would be won to the British side for ever. Burnes, having no powers to pledge his government to any such course, could only urge the point strongly upon Auckland and await his instructions.

Meanwhile, towards the end of December a rival negotiator, likewise concerned ostensibly with commerce only, arrived at Kabul in the person of a Russian officer, Captain Witkewitch. Upon hearing of his coming to Ghazni, Dost Mohamed at once approached Burnes, repeated that he wished to have no dealings with any power but the British, and declared his readiness either to delay Witkewitch on the road, or to turn him straight out of the country. Upon Burnes's advice the Russian envoy was permitted to enter the capital; but Dost Mohamed refused to admit him to more than a single formal audience and declined to notice any of his communications. So matters went on until the end of January 1838, when at last the governor-general's answer came to Burnes's hand. Auckland, who was on his way to Simla with Macnaghten, Torrens and Colvin, and without the members of his council, declined to mediate between Dost Mohamed and Ranjit Singh, censured Burnes for promising assistance to the Barakzai chiefs at Kandahar, and ordered him to revoke his pledges and to undeceive all parties. The fair structure which Burnes had reared, and which was awaiting only the coping stone, was shattered at a blow.

There was nothing left to the envoy but loyally to commend to Dost Mohamed advice which he thought wrong, and professions which he knew to be vain. Yet still for another month the Amir showed marked coldness to Witkewitch, and did his utmost to obtain some indication of warmth from the government of India; but Burnes, fettered by his instructions, could give none. Then came the turn of Witkewitch. He now received favourable audience and was publicly paraded as the friend of the *amir*, for he was ready to promise all that Auckland had denied. On the 26th of April, Burnes, with a heavy heart, left Kabul, and not long afterwards Witkewitch departed for Herat. He had already engaged himself to mediate with Ranjit Singh, and he was now to undertake to pay subsidies to Kohan Dil Khan. He, no less than Burnes, had served his country well, and foresaw not the bitterness of his coming reward.

Meanwhile, the siege of Herat was not going well for the Persians. It chanced that Lieutenant Eldred Pottinger of the Bombay Artillery had been sent by his uncle, then Resident in Sind, to gather, unofficially, information concerning Afghanistan. Disguised as a horse-dealer from Kach, he had made his way first to Kabul and then to Herat, where, after a time, he practically took charge of the defence. The operations of the Persians were feeble, but they violated the treaty under which Persia had pledged herself not to attack Afghanistan; and on the 6th of April the British Resident at Tehran, Mr. McNeill, presented himself in Shah Mohamed's camp and endeavoured to mediate between the contending parties.

But at the end of the month a Russian envoy from the Tsar likewise arrived in the camp, with officers who instructed the Persians in the raising of their batteries, and with money, which was freely distributed among the Persian soldiers. This was fatal to the influence of McNeill, who, after suffering more than one insult without redress, on the 7th of June broke off diplomatic relations with the Shah, and took his departure. Still Herat held out; but meanwhile, Palmerston at home and Auckland in India were losing patience. It was not at Herat only, but at Bushire also that a British Resident had been disrespectfully treated by the Persian authorities; and in May Auckland despatched a small naval and military expedition to the island of Karak, a little to north of Bushire, in the Persian Gulf. The squadron reached its destination on the 19th of June; the troops—detachments of Bombay native regiments—were landed, without opposition, and Karak was peacefully surrendered.

Five days later, on the 24th of June, the most formidable assault upon the walls of Herat was delivered, and, mainly through the energy and example of Eldred Pottinger, was repulsed. Mr. McNeill judged the moment favourable for a second summons to Mohamed Shah to withdraw the Persian army from before Herat. Rumour had magnified the strength and prowess of the expedition to Karak; and on the 9th of September Mohamed Shah raised the siege and marched back to his own place. The leaguer had lasted for ten months, and after all, despite of Russian generals and Russian engineers, had failed ignominiously. A British army would, in Pottinger's judgement, have mastered the fortress within ten days. Nesselrode, as has been told, disclaimed all responsibility for the Persian enterprise and drove Witkewitch to suicide. Whether Herat were taken, or whether, as the result of British intervention, England ceased to be on good terms with Persia, Russia was bound to reap advantage; and so far she was content. But to the Afghan chiefs the fact that the Persian army, with what seemed to be all the might of Russia at its back, had retreated at the bidding of Great Britain, could teach but one lesson.

It remained to be seen whether the supreme government of India would turn the situation to good account. The vague report of a mighty host advancing from beyond the great mountains had created unrest among all classes in India. The Mohammedans interpreted it as an army of the faithful moving towards the extirpation of all infidels in the plains; and on the frontier to north and north-east, Nepal and Burma, still sore from their recent chastisement, muttered menaces of their vengeance to come. In the face of such perils something must be done; and the obvious expedient was to maintain the independence of Afghanistan and cultivate friendship and alliance with its rulers.

But the policy of the British so far had been amazingly contradictory. In any case it was certain that, against the advice of Burnes, and not of Burnes only but of McNeill and of Captain Wade, the agent on the northwest frontier, the principal chiefs, Kohan Dil Khan and Dost Mohamed, had been either encouraged or forced to throw themselves into the arms of Persia, while at the same time Herat had been defended principally by a British officer—acting, it is true, without authority—and had been saved by the actual movement of a British expedition against a Persian possession.

The explanation of this wild behaviour is doubtless to be found in imperfect understanding between Downing Street and Calcutta, accentuated by the fact that Downing Street signified the resolution and high language of Palmerston, and Calcutta the halting caution and weakness of Auckland. Still, the close of events at Herat seems to have offered a chance for a reversal of former policy, of overtures to Dost Mohamed, and of an effort to make the various chiefs lay aside their jealousies for the moment, and look for help in their troubles and their quarrels to the might and arbitrament of Britain.

But it was not to be. While the siege of Herat was yet going forward and its fall seemed to be inevitable, Auckland was bound to devise some course of action, and could think of nothing better than to follow the line indicated by his predecessor. Bentinck, who, to do him justice, had never seen the reports sent by Burnes during his mission at Kabul, had tacitly favoured Shah Shuja's efforts to regain his kingdom with the help of Ranjit Singh. This was in reality no more than an attempt on the part of the Indian government to secure its desires through the agency of other parties, but was not likely upon that account to be the less favoured by Auckland.

Nevertheless, he guessed that a repetition of the experiment of 1833 might be unacceptable to Ranjit Singh without the moral support of the British; and that moral support he was now disposed to offer, if necessary, in the shape not only of pecuniary subsidies, but of the concentration of a British division at Shikarpur, off the eastern outlet of the Bolan Pass. When he came to this decision he was at Simla, with no counsellors but Macnaghten, Torrens and Colvin; and it seems to have been the last named who was principally responsible for the political side of it; military considerations being dealt with by the great strategist, Torrens. Thus at the end of May instructions were drawn up, and with these Macnaghten set out on a mission to Ranjit Singh.

The envoy was warmly received by the old Sikh chieftain, and proceeded to unfold his proposals. The first was that Ranjit Singh should act independently, as in 1833, in aiding Shah Shuja to recover his throne; and this, Macnaghten represented, was the course commended by Lord Auckland. Ranjit Singh declined even to listen to it. Then Macnaghten put forward the alternative, that the Indian government should become a party to the treaty between Ranjit and Shah Shuja, help the latter with money and with British officers to lead his soldiers, and possibly send troops to the Indus to repel any possible aggression in that quarter. He even went so far as to recommend that the Sikhs should invade Afghanistan by the Khyber Pass, moving on

Kabul, while the *Shah* should take the route on Kandahar.

This proposal Ranjit Singh accepted with avidity; but three anxious weeks were spent in haggling over the details of the agreement, each party being nervously anxious lest it should be saddled with the brunt of the work and denied its full share of the reward. At length, on the 26th of June, there was signed a treaty, commonly known as the tripartite treaty, between Ranjit Singh and Shah Shuja, with the approbation and under the guarantee of the Indian government. The principal points of this covenant were that Ranjit Singh should retain all the territory which he had already wrested from the Afghan dominions; that, if he assisted Shah Shuja with an auxiliary force, the Sikhs should receive one-half of the booty taken from the Barakzais; and that Shah Shuja, after the recovery of his kingdom, should pay Ranjit Singh two *lakhs* of *rupees* annually, the punctual discharge of which was guaranteed by the Indian government. The next step was to obtain the concurrence of Shah Shuja with the pledges that had been given in his name. With some reluctance, for he relished neither the cession of Peshawar nor the promise of the two *lakhs* of *rupees*, the exiled potentate, in the middle of July, signed the treaty; and the business was concluded. General Avitabile, when he perused the document, declared that it must have been dictated by Ranjit Singh; and the comment was by no means unreasonable.

The next step was to determine the action that should follow upon the treaty. Torrens, as military adviser, urged, unquestionably with good sense, that, if the expedition were left to Shah Shuja and Ranjit Singh alone, it was bound to fail. The Sadozai prince possessed neither strength nor ability; and, in Afghanistan itself, his name was associated with perpetual misfortune. The Sikhs, on the other side, were not only detested in Afghanistan but unwilling to enter it, having an almost superstitious dread of venturing within the Khyber Pass. The more the question was studied, the more plainly it became manifest that the work could not be done at all unless the British took a hand in it. No great insight was needed to perceive that a British division, immovable and passive at Shikarpur, would be of no real support to Shah Shuja in advancing over the three to four hundred miles that separated that place from Kandahar.

It was, therefore, suggested that two or three British regiments would suffice to escort the restored monarch into the recesses of his former dominions. This mad project was likewise abandoned; and now the commander-in-chief, Sir Henry Fane, arrived at Simla, and insisted, first, that if the British interfered at all it should be with such a force as must assure success, and secondly, that it was for himself to determine the strength of that force. Had Auckland then and there decided to abstain from intervention, it is not likely that Fane would have gainsaid him. But it must be remembered that the prospect at Herat was then as gloomy as ever. Something must be done; and there was no one except the British prepared to do it. Auckland yielded to Fane; and on the 3rd of August orders were sent out to sundry regiments, both in Bengal and Bombay, to prepare for active service.

On the 10th of September, Auckland directed the formation of an army for an expedition into Afghanistan. On the 13th Fane published an order for the organisation of the Bengal Army into brigades and divisions, and for its concentration at Kurnal, about eighty miles north of Delhi; and on the 1st of October Auckland issued a declaration of the motives which had led him to intervene by force of arms in the affairs of Afghanistan. These were set forth to be that Dost Mohamed had, without provocation, attacked Ranjit Singh, and that he had leagued himself with the Persians when they laid siege to Herat; the true facts being that Ranjit Singh had made an unprovoked seizure of Peshawar, which Dost Mohamed had tried to regain, and that Dost Mohamed had only joined the Persians, because Auckland, rejecting his friendly overture to himself, had literally forced him into Persia's arms.

These disingenuous details, however, were of small importance. The main reason for the enterprise was avowed to be the Persian attack upon Herat; and, not many days after the declaration had been published, came news that the siege of Herat had been raised and that the Persians had retreated. All pretext for war, therefore, seemed to have vanished; and the troops, in bitter disappointment, were the first to recognise the fact. Auckland had given no engagement to send a single soldier beyond the Indus. The immediate danger was past, and Shah Shuja and Ranjit Singh might be left to work out their plans unaided. It was practically certain that, abandoned to their own devices, they would do nothing; and the cause for all immediate action had disappeared.

Moreover, British might and ascendancy were plainly recognised when Persia, at the bidding of McNeill, had forfeited the labour and losses of ten months and withdrawn her armies from before Herat; and a mission to Kabul and Kandahar would almost certainly rally the Barakzai chiefs to the standard of Britain. Nothing could have fallen out more happily to save the government of India from the embarrassments raised by fate and its own blunders.

Yet, to the general surprise, Auckland, the timid, the cautious, the irresolute, on the 8th of November made proclamation that though Herat was now safe, the expedition was still to go forward:

.... with the view to the substitution of a friendly for a hostile power in the Eastern province of Afghanistan, and to the establishment of a permanent barrier against schemes of aggression upon our north-west frontier.

Practically, the proclamation signified that the Barakzais had ceased to reign, and that the exiled Sadozai, Shah Shuja, was to replace them. Could the appointed end of a permanent barrier against Russia have been assured by this expedient, it might have been justified, no matter how hardly the process might bear upon individuals; and the object would have been worth great sacrifices. But there was no security for anything of the kind. The experiment was, in fact, far more hazardous than that of displacing a Napoleon to restore a Bourbon in France. The Bourbons, if they had possessed some small allowance of common sense, might possibly have endured, for they had at least centuries of use and wont behind them.

But one who is to rule Afghanistan must be above all things a strong man, and such men are hard to find; even more, a succession of such men. Dost Mohamed, if Auckland had taken the advice of Burnes, might have fulfilled the British aspirations towards a permanent barrier in Afghanistan during his lifetime—perhaps for twenty years—after which the chances were in favour of a disputed succession and a period of anarchy. But to impose a man known to be feeble, such as Shah Shuja, upon the Afghans, was to court trouble. The British must either uphold him with their own bayonets, or submit to see him cast out. Yet this was the course chosen by Auckland, notwithstanding the military objections of the commander-in-chief, at the dictation of three men who abounded in cleverness, but had not found wisdom.

The First Afghan War had been set upon its inexorable course and not for nothing would that disastrous conflict also come to be known as "Auckland's Folly," since based upon the principle that the 'buck stops' with the person in overall authority, the causes of this catastophe must be laid squarely on that gentleman's shoulders.

CHAPTER 2

Arrival of the Bombay Force in the Indus

Auckland and his advisers now looked forward to the invasion of Afghanistan as a mere military promenade; and the "political" rejoiced in the prospect of conducting a harmless military operation. The governor-general wrote to Fane that Shah Shuja's force would lead the way, that the Bengal army would follow in rear, and that the reception of both would be "welcome with general gladness." Fane wrote with respectful sarcasm:

> I do not think that for this, my service is needed; and I consider Sir Willoughby Cotton quite competent to command. . . . I think, too, that your instructions to Sir William Macnaghten and to me are such as an officer of my rank could hardly submit to serve under.—*I.O.S.C.,* vol. 1 of 1839, Fane to Auckland, Nov. 2, 1839.

Fane had the better reason for renouncing the chief command since, in the change of circumstances, it had been decided that one only of the two divisions assembled at Ferozepore should advance, and that the other should stand fast, occupying that place and Ludhiana. Sir Willoughby Cotton was accordingly placed in charge of the division that was to cross the Indus, and the supreme command was reserved for Sir John Keane, who was to accompany the contingent from Bombay. Keane, however, even as Fane, had his misgivings. If the march to Kandahar was to be a mere military promenade, all might be well; but if it should prove otherwise, then the proportion of British soldiers in the force was small, he wrote:

Without any reflection upon the native troops, it remains to be seen how they will stand the fatigues and privations of a distant enterprise in a severe climate against a resolute and hardy race.—*I.O.S.C.*, vol. 1 of 1838, Keane's minute of Oct. 15, 1838.

Such warnings were thrown away upon Auckland and Macnaghten, the latter of whom had all the "political's" love of parading his authority with the pomp of a military demonstration.

Meanwhile Henry Pottinger, whose mission it was to make the British policy acceptable to the Amirs of Hyderabad, had discovered at once that the entry of the British troops into Sind was to the last degree distasteful to them. Auckland had instructed him to displace any of them that might show unwillingness; and in fact, on the 18th of October, Pottinger, having been publicly insulted and stoned by the populace, called upon the government of Bombay to embark at once the five thousand men that were held ready to sail to the mouth of the Indus. But, until these arrived, it was of the utmost importance to keep secret the intentions of the Indian government. For to provoke the immediate hostility of the *amirs* would be to neutralise the efforts of the political agents towards collecting supplies and transport for the expedition in its passage through Sind.

Auckland, however, had no notion of patience or conciliation in dealing with parties who seemed to be so weak as the *amirs*. It was important to secure the fort of Bukkur on the Indus, over against Shikarpur, as the spot where a bridge could most easily be thrown over the river; and Burnes was despatched to the Amir of Khairpur in Upper Sind to negotiate for the cession of the fort. He arrived at Khairpur on that same 18th of October, found the *amir*, Mir Rustam, who had heard of the retreat of the Persians from Herat, in a very complaisant mood, rushed to the conclusion that Mir Rustam was not acting in concert with the Amirs of Hyderabad, and hastened to bind him, as he hoped, to the British cause by a separate treaty. Pottinger, who knew that Mir Rustam was very unwilling to cede Bukkur, disapproved of this treaty as premature, and implored Burnes to be very wary in his negotiations with Mir Rustam, lest the Amirs of Hyderabad should get wind of them, and, realising the intentions of the Indian government to pass troops through their territory at any cost, should at once take measures of active enmity.

By a singular coincidence, on the very day when Pottinger was writing these instructions, Auckland, likewise, was writing direct to Burnes, empowering him to enter into a separate agreement with Mir Rustam. Thus, there was on one side Pottinger, the man on the spot, trembling for the wreck of the whole expedition if the *amirs* should be prematurely exasperated, and doing his utmost to stave off such a catastrophe; and on the other side the governor-general, hundreds of miles away, knowing nothing of the circumstances and supremely ignorant of all military matters, giving instructions to one of Pottinger's subordinates which were calculated to undermine Pottinger's authority, and to hasten the very misfortune which Pottinger was striving to avert.

On the 27th of November the first transports from Bombay reached the mouth of the Indus, and by the 30th the whole of the Bombay division, about fifty-six hundred strong under Major-General Willshire, was at anchor in the river.(See list following).

Cavalry.	2 squadrons 4th Light Dragoons.
	1st Bombay Light Cavalry.
	Poona Local Horse.
Artillery.	2 troops Horse Artillery.
	1 Field battery.
Infantry.	H.M. 2nd Queen's.
	H.M. 17th Foot.
	19th Bombay N.I.
	Bombay Sappers and Miners.

Some of the vessels had been towed by a steamer of seven hundred and fifty tons' burden with engines of one hundred and fifty horsepower, which, with three craft of one kind or another in tow, had made the creditable speed of nearly five knots an hour. Sir John Keane and his personal staff took their passage upon this steamer, which contained no other troops, while in the first vessel astern of her—a gun-brig of one hundred and seventy-five tons—were packed the principal medical officer and three more doctors, with servants and camp-followers, which, added to the numbers of the officers and crew, made up a total of one hundred and ninety-one souls. Contrary to the advice of Burnes, the armament made, not for Karachi, but for the Hajamro Creek, some seventy miles to south of it, where the vessels waited, some of them for a full week, in idleness, until the transport-agent arrived on the 30th. The disembarkation, which had so far been conducted fitfully according to the caprice of merchant-skippers or the urgency of commanding officers, was then at last taken seriously in hand. A camp was marked out; and by the 3rd of December matters were so far advanced that Keane left the steamer and took up his quarters ashore.

The general had been informed that the troops were to land with the concurrence of the Sind government, and that he was to consider himself in a friendly country. As a matter of fact, the Sindians had celebrated the arrival of the transports by firing a cannon-shot over Pottinger's tent; and the news that Pottinger had to give was not reassuring. No grain, no boats and no camels had been collected, and the *amirs* had done their best by intimidation to deter owners of camels and boatmen from engaging themselves to serve the British. The Amirs of Hyderabad had further ordered the Baluchi army to assemble at that city, and were endeavouring to persuade the Amir of Khairpur to join them in open war against the invaders. Keane was, in fact, in precisely the same situation as had been Archibald Campbell when he landed at Rangoon, during the First Burma War, absolutely powerless to move for want of transport and supplies. He was fain to pitch his camp at Vikkur and sit still, sending a member of his staff, Captain James Outram, by sea to Kach in the hope of procuring camels from that quarter.

In the meanwhile Pottinger was more than ever anxious to keep the *amirs* quiet, with the greater cause since, owing to the indiscretion of Burnes, they had discovered the negotiations that were going forward at Khairpur, and were increasingly suspicious. He therefore wrote to Burnes emphasising the importance of keeping the governments intentions still secret for a time, until Keane should be in a position to move and the Bengal Army should have approached the borders of Sind. But Auckland had in the interim granted Burnes independent powers to act at Khairpur without reference to affairs in Lower Sind; and Burnes was far too ambitious, conceited and short-sighted not to avail himself of his authority. He therefore tendered an ultimatum to the Amirs of Upper Sind, pointed out that the terms were more favourable than would be offered to their brothers at Hyderabad, and threatened that he would leave the country if they were refused.

Evidently Burnes wished to subdue the Sindians by force of arms before entering Afghanistan, and from a purely military standpoint he was perhaps right; for the conquest of Sind would have helped to make the British communications secure. But this was very far from the desire of the Indian Government, which contemplated a military promenade into Afghanistan and not a campaign in Sind; and, in any case, it was criminal to exasperate the Sindians into war while Keane lay helpless in the delta of the Indus. The Baluchis might not be very formidable against a mobile British force, but against five thousand isolated men, ill-provisioned, tied to the ground on which they lay, and subject to a blazing sun, endless clouds of dust and all the sickness incident to a tropical climate, they might by harassing tactics first weaken Keane, and finally overwhelm him.

As to the action of Auckland in thus setting up rival agents to tear each other's diplomatic work to pieces, it may be regarded, according to the reader's estimate of the man, with pity or with contempt; but it cannot escape damnation.

On the 10th of December Outram returned to report the success of his mission to Kach and the further discoveries that he had made on his journey. In the course of his return he had sailed to Karachi, then an obscure fishing village, spied out the land, sounded the disposition of the inhabitants, done a good stroke of work for the transport of the army, and finally returned overland, travelling ninety-five miles on camelback in twenty-seven hours. But the camels from Kach arrived not until the 19th, having been compelled by the hostile action of the Amir of Mirpur to fetch a compass round his territory. On that day Pottinger, after consultation with Keane, wrote to summon from Bombay to Karachi the reserve troops which, besides Willshire's division, had been prepared for service; for it was very evident that, even if the *amirs* should ultimately consent to allow Keane's force to pass quietly through their country, its base and communications could not be left unprotected. At last, on Christmas Eve, Keane was able to make his first movement northward, having during his stay at Vikkur buried one officer and eight privates.

At the close of the march on Christmas Day cholera made its appearance, but vanished again on the 29th after claiming no more than eight victims. On the 27th the force reached Tatta, where Keane, despite of the protests of his chief medical officer, (Kennedy, i.), marked out cantonments for a permanent garrison, and came to a halt. He was now in a better position to obtain supplies from the surrounding country, to watch the proceedings of the *amirs*, and to await, with safety to his communications, the arrival of the reserve from Bombay and the nearer approach of the Bengal Army. To the movements of that Bengal army it is now necessary to return.

By the 28th of November, the date fixed originally by Fane, the two divisions of Bengal troops had been duly assembled at Ferozepore, together with the six thousand half-disciplined men who had been raised, under British officers, in Hindustan for the service of Shah Shuja. With very doubtful wisdom, Fane had decided that the choice of regiments to proceed on the expedition should be determined by lot, and thus the Thirteenth, a weak regiment, was preferred to the Buffs, which were a particularly fine battalion. (See list following).

FIELD FORCE (Maj.-gen. Sir Willoughby Cotton)—
  Cavalry Brigade (Maj.-gen. Thackwell):
    H.M. 16th Lancers.
    2nd Bengal Light Cavalry.
    6th ,, ,, ,,
    4th Local Horse.
  Artillery:
    1 troop Horse Artillery.
    2 batteries Field Artillery.
    4 eighteen-pounder siege-guns.
  Infantry:
    1st Brigade (Col. Sale):
      H.M. 13th L.I.
      16th Bengal N.I.
      48th ,, ,,
    2nd Brigade (Maj.-gen. Nott):
      31st Bengal N.I.
      42nd ,, ,,
      43rd ,, ,,

Reserve Force at Ferozepore (Maj.-gen. Duncan):
  Cavalry:
    Skinner's Horse.
  Artillery:
    1 troop Horse Artillery.
    1 battery Field Artillery.
  Infantry:
    3rd Brigade
      H.M. Buffs.
      2nd Bengal N.I.
      27th ,, ,,
    5th Brigade
      5th Bengal N.I.
      20th ,, ,,
      53rd ,, ,,

The halt of the Second Division at Ferozepore was, however, in one sense a fortunate circumstance, for it did provide some small, though inadequate, protection of the base of operations against the Sikh army, forty thousand strong, which, under the orders of so doubtful an ally as Ranjit Singh and only four marches from Ferozepore, might at any moment turn against the British. And it must be pointed out that the nearest supports which could have been collected to reinforce this corps of observation, could have found no point of assembly less than two hundred and fifty miles from Ferozepore. Moreover, the commander-in-chief was left with very insufficient troops to guard his line of communications. Cotton's task in the first instance was to march and effect a junction with the Bombay division in the delta of the Indus, seven hundred and eighty miles away. Of that distance the first two hundred miles lay wholly at the mercy of the Sikhs; then for a short distance came the friendly territory of Bahawalpur, and then Sind, which, if it were not hostile, had every reason to become so.

Assuming that the Bombay division could advance as far as Shikarpur to meet the Bengal troops, then, roughly speaking, the former would have three hundred miles and the latter five hundred miles to guard, so far; after which there was a matter of another four hundred miles, one-fourth of them mountain-passes, to be traversed and made safe between Shikarpur and Kandahar. William Windham had projected, but fortunately had abandoned, the landing of five or six thousand men on the western coast of South America, with the design that it should march across the Andes and join another force that had been landed in the Rio de la Plata; and this, it might have been thought, was the extreme of reckless folly to which an English civil administrator could attain in the planning of military operations. But even Windham must yield the palm of imbecility to Auckland. If we imagine a German army marching through France to the invasion of Spain, and effecting, north of the Pyrenees, a junction with a weak force landed at the mouth of the Adour, we can take some measure of the hazard of the enterprise.

Things were not well at Ferozepore in those last days of December 1838, and Fane, who had been punctual in accomplishing his concentration, was very uneasy. Though he was not to command the army, he was to travel with it by water on his way to Bombay and to England, and he felt his responsibility for the preliminary arrangements. In his view—and he was quite correct—it was of vital importance that the troops should have passed through the Bolan Pass before the end of March, so as to escape any extreme heat in those parts. He had, therefore, fixed the day for leaving Ferozepore for the 2nd or 3rd of December at latest. Knowing, too, that supply would be the great difficulty, he had from the first urged the establishment of depots along the line of the river to Bahawalpur. Yet on the 1st of December he was greeted with a request that the march of the army should be delayed until the 10th, to enable fuel and forage to be cut for the army on its passage through Bahawalpur territory. Fane was furious. He wrote to Auckland:

> This staggers my confidence in the commissariat. . . . Even an hour's delay is serious . . . and it is a great evil to the army to be delayed by want of common foresight.

The truth was that the entire business of establishing supply-depots along the enormous line of the army's projected march had been committed to political agents. Having been originally of the military profession, these gentlemen bore military titles; but, though full of zeal and industry, they had no knowledge of the requirements of an army, and were already in difficulties over this vital matter. One of them, Lieutenant Mackeson, had seen to the cutting of a road through heavy jungle from Bahawalpur to the frontier of Sind, and could announce, on the 29th of November, that the magazines were ready for the *Shah's* contingent, as also, with the important exception of grain, for the British troops also. But Fane distrusted these reports from "inexperienced persons." He wrote to Auckland:

> If such matters are left to be settled by any subordinate civil officer, discord will inevitably ensue, and your expectations will be disappointed.

In Lower Sind matters were far more serious. Owing to a partial failure of the inundation of the Indus the last crops had not been too abundant, and a part of them had been exported to relieve famine in the north-west provinces of India. Burnes was obliged to confess on the 14th of November that depots of grain, promised by the *amirs*, at Shikarpur, Bukkur and Larkhana did not exist, though his agents were busy creating them. It was very evident that the expedition, dangerous even to madness in its mere conception, was to be made yet more hazardous by sheer mismanagement.

As Fane considered the situation, his anxiety was painfully increased. He had no great confidence in Cotton, who had served far too long in India, he wrote:

> I don't think that Cotton has a mind which carries away much of verbal instructions.

A delicate way of insinuating that he was both slow and stupid— and he accordingly addressed to him a few hints in such guarded language as his loyalty to Auckland permitted to him.

> The countries through which you pass on the way to the Indus are not supposed (by me) to be abundant in resources. Fuel and supplies will demand your constant attention. You are furnished with a commissariat which the Supreme Government deems ample.

The aposiopesis as to the commander-in-chief's opinion of the same being eloquent. But to Auckland he wrote far more openly and seriously.

I do hope that all circumstances that may happen to the army may be considered. The chance of any reverse in Afghanistan should be carefully weighed, for there is the Bolan Pass and Sind behind it in one quarter, and the Khyber Pass and Sikhs in another. The army will be placed in a position to be surrounded and annihilated unless due precautions be taken in time. Supposing a reverse—what is to be the army's line of retreat? Magazines should be collected beside it. The safety of the army should be placed beyond doubt.

Auckland, for his part, professed to share all of Fane's anxieties, agree with all of his recommendations and deplore with him all shortcomings. But he made the excuse for his agents that the people in territory not under British control were reluctant to act at their bidding, and, as a remedy for this failing, he empowered Cotton to requisition supplies by force in Bahawalpur and elsewhere, in case of real necessity.

But how such a measure was to render the British communications more secure he did not explain. Indeed the nature of the instructions which he wrote at this very time for Keane and Macnaghten show that Auckland had a very imperfect apprehension of the military risks that he was taking. The first and strongest point impressed upon both the general and the civilian was that Shah Shuja's progress should bear, if possible, the semblance of a peaceful march. His own detachment, therefore, was to be under Macnaghten's immediate control and was to move in advance of the British; and the *Shah* was to appear the undoubted chief of the enterprise, not, upon any account, a puppet dependent upon foreign power. If the *Shah* should encounter resistance in arms then Keane was to act with vigour, taking the *Shah's* troops as well as his own under his orders; in fact:

> Every military operation was to be under the unqualified direction of the general in command, and Macnaghten would require his concurrence in every measure upon which military operations might depend.

Further, Macnaghten, who combined the double function of envoy and minister to Shah Shuja, was to sanction no declaration of war, no new treaty and no correspondence with foreign powers, except in full concert and agreement with Keane. On the other hand, in all political proceedings and all matters concerning the *Shah's* court, government and proceedings, Macnaghten, though in communication with Keane, was to act upon his single responsibility. For, if the *Shah* were established at Kabul, Keane's work would be done, the British troops would be withdrawn, and Macnaghten would be left as sole Resident in Afghanistan. Meanwhile the *Shah's* disciplined force was not to be used to aid in the ordinary maintenance of internal tranquillity. (*I.O.S.C.*, vol. 2 of 1838, Fane to Auckland, Dec. 2. Memo, of Fane, Dec. 5. Auckland to Fane and Keane, Dec. 5; to Fane, Dec. 6; to Macnaghten, Dec. 8, 1838).

No sane man could issue such instructions as these except in the blindest assurance of a bloodless campaign; but, were such bloodlessness never so certain, they remain inexcusable. The *Shah* was to appear the undoubted head of the enterprise, but was actually to be a tool in Macnaghten's hands. His disciplined troops were to be under Macnaghten's immediate control, but were not to be used in Afghanistan for purposes of internal police; the inference being that this task must fall upon the British. Lastly, Macnaghten was to control the *Shah's* foreign policy, Keane's concurrence being required if such policy were likely to involve military operations. But what is a military operation? It was in Macnaghten's power to order a small detachment, or even the whole of the *Shah's* force, to march from some one point to some other. He might not consider this a military operation at all. He might regard it in much the same light as ordering a battalion of the Guards to march from London to Hounslow.

And yet, among turbulent tribes in a wild and mountainous country, the movement of a company or two over a distance of a few miles might prove to be a military operation, ultimately entailing a whole series of military operations in which Keane, though not originally consulted, might be bound by later events to take part. In other words Macnaghten, without the slightest military knowledge, was empowered to entangle himself and the *Shah* in military difficulties, and to require the military commander to extricate him. Such was the wisdom of Auckland under the guidance of Macnaghten himself, and of Macnaghten's peers.

However, on the 2nd of December, Shah Shuja's force marched from Ferozepore, and on the 10th the British started likewise. These latter moved off in five columns, which followed each other at one day's interval; headquarters, with the cavalry brigade leading the way, and after them in succession the infantry, artillery, supplies and stores. The victuals included thirty days' allowance of grain and slaughter-cattle "on the hoof" for two and a half months. For the supplies alone over fourteen thousand camels were required, besides a very large number for the ordnance-stores, for which it had been found impossible to collect water-carriage. From these figures alone some idea may be formed of the vast number of animals required for the army. But this was not all. Not only were the troops hampered by four times their number of followers, making altogether some fifty thousands souls; but the officers, true to the comfortable tradition of campaigns in the plains, had encumbered themselves with an extravagant quantity of baggage and endless retinues of servants. It was said that one brigadier had sixty camels to convey the various articles which he deemed necessary for himself alone. In this way the camels, public and private, attached to the army counted from twenty-five to thirty thousand. Such a number, if placed in single file with no interval from nose to croup, would extend from London to Reading and beyond it.

Fane, as became a veteran of the Peninsula, had not overlooked this difficulty but had tried to meet it. Thus he had ordered that the infantry should carry their packs instead of loading them, as was customary, upon animals hired by themselves; though officers with long experience of India judged that the additional fatigue, with its necessary accompaniment of sickness, thus caused to the troops was not worth the saving of transport and forage, (Havelock, i.). Further, Fane had cautioned the officers against bringing into the field large tents, large establishments and much baggage; but something more than advice was needed, (Hough), though possibly, remembering the retreat from Burgos, Fane may have counted upon the enemy to do the necessary work of thinning the baggage-trains. In any case the army set off on its two hundred miles' journey down the Sutlej to Bahawalpur with all the unwieldy bulk of a moving city.

Trouble with the transport and supply began directly. The general conditions were not unfavourable. The weather was cold, but the air was clear and healthy; the country was open, and the roads were good; but the *Shah's* contingent, arriving on the 15th within three marches of Bahawalpur, reported that it was already in difficulties over victuals, and that no supplies had been laid in within the territory of Bahawalpur for the British troops that were following in rear. Cotton, on the 19th, complained that at every stage the depots of grain had been found deficient. The commissariat also was bitterly bewailing the order of march, which condemned the supplies and stores to the rearmost place, and so to dearth of forage almost from the day of leaving Ferozepore. They left their camping-ground at daylight and were often halted for hours while the foremost columns defiled through some strait; and, when at last they reached their halting-place early in the afternoon, the camels were driven far afield to find fodder, and at nightfall were driven back after only two hours' grazing and little food.

Thus the beasts were overworked and underfed; and matters were not improved by the fact that the water was brackish and strongly saline all the way from Ferozepore to Rohri. After reaching the city of Bahawalpur, it was necessary to allow the commissariat to move off several hours in advance of the troops; but this gave facilities for another great evil. Already vast numbers of camel-drivers had deserted, carrying their camels with them, the Hindustanis from sheer terror of the strange land in which they found themselves, the Sikhs from resentment at being subjected to such a service. The loss of private baggage and of camp-equipment during the first six marches alone was very serious, and the trouble was not likely to be diminished by allowing the transport to take the lead of the army on the march. (*I.O.S.C.*, vol. 9 of 1840; *Report of Commissary-General Curtis*, Feb. 29, 1840; vol. 2 of 1839; Cotton to Auckland, Dec. 19, 1838; Havelock, i.; Hough).

At Bahawalpur, which was reached by headquarters on the 29th of December, the columns halted and closed up; and Fane, who had come down the river by water on his homeward journey, exchanged courtesies with the *khan*. On the 31st news came in from Burnes that the Amir of Khairpur had, with some difficulty, been persuaded to cede the island of Bukkur for the construction of a bridge over the Indus, but that the Amirs of Hyderabad were likely to offer resistance. He pressed, therefore, for the rapid advance of the army into Sind; and all ranks, fed with tales of fabulous wealth within Hyderabad, looked forward to a rich share of prize-money.

On the 1st of January 1839, the march was resumed; and the army moved by Ahmadpur to Khanpur, which was reached by headquarters on the 8th. Here, thanks to Mackeson, the political agent, there was a fresh supply of camels, which in some measure made good the losses of the four previous weeks. After one day's halt, headquarters continued the advance, and on the 14th reached the border of Sind. Burnes, who had arrived on the previous day, announced that the Sindians were still adverse to the passage of the British through their territory, and that, though they might be cowed into outward submission, they would lose no opportunity of throwing hindrances covertly in its way.

Headquarters seemed to realise that when once the Sindian frontier was crossed the major difficulties of the campaign would begin; but for the present all remained in suspense.

However, the columns marched on, slowly, for the camels, being ill-fed, were weak. Great numbers died and very many disappeared through the flight of their drivers; for the owners of the hired animals disliked the idea of their passing the Indus, and the nearer the army drew to the crossing-place, the more clearly that dislike expressed itself through desertion. On the 19th it was discovered that the mortality of the camels that carried grain was outrunning the consumption of their loads, (Hough), a fact which seems to point to extreme inefficiency on the part of the commissariat. Though the supplies collected on the line of march were not sufficient to feed the whole of the columns, yet they were enough to relieve at any rate a certain number of camels from carrying a load for a few days, which would have meant the saving of their lives. But it should seem that, in the general confusion, no unloaded camel could travel far without having a burden of some kind, private or public, laid upon his back, and that thus hundreds, if not thousands, were broken down by sheer mismanagement.

On the 24th of January the head of the column trailed into Rohri, opposite Sukkur, about two hundred miles up the river from Hyderabad; Fane, always pursuing his way down stream, having arrived there before it. Shah Shuja's force, having crossed the river in boats between the 11th and the 17th, was safely out of the way at Shikarpur; and the British engineers were making good progress with the construction of a bridge. But the latest news from Keane said only that the governor-general's treaty would shortly be despatched to the Amirs of Hyderabad, and that upon its acceptance or rejection depended peace or war. Fane interpreted the silence as to the issue in his own way. On the 26th he received a ceremonial visit from the Amir of Khairpur, who produced the separate treaty which he made with the British, duly ratified, and declared that he would insist upon the acceptance of the British terms by the chief of Hyderabad.

"I have wasted time enough in treating," answered Fane by the mouth of Burnes. "I will now march down and attack him." Curiously enough, this was precisely the movement which Keane at that moment was advocating.

We left the Bombay division halted at Tatta, where it commanded communication both with Vikkur and Karachi, pending the ultimate issue of Pottinger's negotiations with the Amirs of Hyderabad. On the

18th of January Pottinger at last ventured to lay before the *amirs* the terms which Auckland was resolved to impose upon them; and on the 23rd Keane advanced by the right bank of the Indus, and on the 25th halted at Jerrak, two marches from Hyderabad, to allow his supplies and stores to come up with him. The *amirs* rejected the treaty; and Keane at once wrote to Fane begging that a column might advance forthwith upon Hyderabad from the north.

Fane, having made up his mind, issued orders on the 26th for the cavalry brigade and two brigades of infantry to move on the following day. But meanwhile the Amir of Khairpur made difficulties about the cession of Bukkur. A very old man, he felt the humiliation of surrendering his fort, and, knowing that his brethren of Hyderabad had declined to yield, clung to the hope that some chance might deliver him from it. For two days Burnes cajoled and threatened, till at last on the 29th the keys of Bukkur were delivered to him, though even to the end it was doubtful whether the stronghold would be peaceably surrendered. However, upon the embarkation of a few companies of native infantry for the island of Bukkur, the garrison evacuated the place, and on the 30th Cotton marched south with some fifty-six hundred men upon Hyderabad.

Keane, meanwhile, remained at Jerrak and laid his plans for throwing his force across the Indus, under cover of his artillery, in the face of the entire Baluchi Army. The operation would have been extremely hazardous, for he had none but square-headed unmanageable boats; the stream was swift and a thousand yards broad; and the men must have landed as best they could on banks covered with jungle. It would have been, in fact, a disembarkation of the most dangerous kind; and, though Keane was confident of success, Fane was not so sanguine, and ordered the engineers at Bukkur to be ready to break up their nearly completed bridge, embark engineers, gunners and artillery, and drop down the river to the neighbourhood of Hyderabad.

But meanwhile the *amirs*, having news of Cotton's march, grew nervous, and, reopening negotiations, agreed on the 1st of February to accept Pottinger's terms. On the 5th Cotton received Keane's original message asking for his help, but on the night of the 6th a messenger came into Kandiaro, sixty miles south of Rohri, to report that the *amirs* had agreed to the treaty; and after three days' halt the column began its journey back to Rohri. The march had been absolutely unopposed, but forage had been scarce, and the loss of camels had in consequence been very serious.

Thus, owing to the military incapacity of the *amirs*, Keane's isolated force was delivered from all danger of destruction, and the arrival of the Bombay Reserve Force—H.M. 40th Foot. 2nd Bombay Grenadiers. 22nd and 26th Bombay N.I.—under Major-General Valiant, at Karachi, on the 3rd of February relieved him from the protection of his base on the sea.

There was, indeed, some show of resistance to the disembarkation at Karachi, but the Sindian forts were silenced by a single broadside from the line-of-battle-ship, *Wellesley,* and the troops then landed without molestation. Keane, however, was by no means easy about the future, and was quite as distrustful as Fane of the competence of political officers to collect supplies for the army. Moreover, he was in grave difficulties for transport, having no more than twenty-four hundred camels, despite of all Outram's efforts, for the five thousand men of the Bombay division. Auckland, it is true, had written in an airy way that the Bengal commissariat had thirty thousand camels; but the commissary-general reported that he had only half of that number, and there was no prospect that Burnes, or any other political agent, could make good the deficiency.

As it happened, too, just at this time there were two awkward complications. The chief minister, Yar Mohamed Khan, of the ruler of Herat had at the end of 1838 picked a quarrel with the English mission in that place, and had ordered the two members, Eldred Pottinger and Colonel Stoddart, to leave it forthwith. Burnes at once detected the hand of Russia in this incident, and declared that the army must be prepared to advance to Herat and secure it for Shah Shuja. He therefore recommended that Duncan's division should move across the Punjab upon Kabul, being replaced by another division at Ferozepore, while the existing army of the Indus should move upon Kandahar and Herat. The bare news of the expulsion of Pottinger and Stoddart, without any details, reached Keane in the third week of January, adding a new element of uncertainty to a situation which was already sufficiently anxious.

Then Macnaghten, who was at Shikarpur with Shah Shuja and knew not the course of Pottinger's negotiations with the *amirs*, became nervous lest active hostilities with Sind should delay the grand enterprise against Afghanistan for a whole season; and on the 6th of February he urged an immediate advance upon Kandahar. His idea was that one brigade of infantry, one regiment of native cavalry and a proportion of artillery added to Shah Shuja's contingent would suffice for the purpose, since the resistance offered would be very inconsiderable. It was true that the *Shah's* force was in want of eight thousand more camels, but Cotton would furnish a thousand, he wrote cheerfully:

> . . . . and with this addition, we shall be able to scramble on somehow.

He therefore ordered Cotton on the 7th to throw the detachment above named across the Indus forthwith, so as to prosecute the advance into Afghanistan without further delay.

Macnaghten was pressing, and Cotton was not a strong man; but Cotton at least knew his duty well enough to decline to obey Macnaghten's orders without the sanction of Keane. Thereupon Macnaghten addressed himself directly to Keane, and apparently suggested as an alternative that Shah Shuja's contingent, taking with it all the artillery of the Bengal column, should advance first, leaving the British troops to follow in rear, and that Keane should decide for himself whether he should accompany the Shah in person.

To this Keane replied with a very decided negative. The *Shah's* troops, as he truly said, were only half-disciplined; and it would be too perilous to risk failure at the outset, much more to hazard the whole of the British artillery. Any reflections on the impudence of Macnaghten in thus attempting to take the commander-in-chief under his orders—for it must be remembered that Macnaghten's control of the *Shah's* force was absolute—Keane kept to himself. (*I.O.S.C.*, vol. 2 of 1839; Burnes to Indian Government, Dec. 28, 1838; Keane to Auckland, Jan. 22, 1839; vol. 5, Commissary Johnson to O.C. Shah's contingent, Jan. 14, 1839; Macnaghten to Pottinger, Feb. 6; to Cotton, Feb. 7; to Keane, Feb. 11; Keane to Cotton, Feb. 23, 1839).

Meanwhile the conveyance of stores across the Indus in barges had begun on the 9th of February, and the bridge of boats over the river had been completed. This latter work was most creditable to the chief engineer, Major Thomson, and his subordinates, for they had been very ill-provided with materials. They had no regular pontoons and could only with difficulty obtain native craft; they had to make their own ropes, fell and saw up most of the timbers and improvise anchors for themselves; they had no sappers trained to such operations and no boatmen except Sindians, whose language they did not understand; and finally, they had to deal with a swift and treacherous stream, subject to sudden rises and falls and encumbered by floating boughs and snags. Yet by sheer perseverance and resource they overcame all difficulties, putting to utter shame the inefficient departments which had sent them forth to so arduous a task without a thought for their requirements, (Durand).

On the 15th Cotton's column returned to Rohri, and by the 18th every man and beast had passed the river without a single accident of any kind. A native battalion was left to garrison the fort of Bukkur; the heavy baggage of the cavalry brigade was deposited with it; a hospital was established at Sukkur; and orders were issued for the longer section of the bridge to be broken up, and for the boats to be employed as ferries at Ferozepore and Rohri. On the 18th Fane took leave of the army and pursued his way down the river to Bombay, and Keane assumed the supreme command. The cavalry of both presidencies was now united, for purposes of organisation, into a division under Major-General Thackwell; the Bengal infantry became the First Division under Cotton, and the Bombay infantry the Second Division under Major-General Willshire. Until Keane should come up, Cotton retained command of the Bengal troops, the whole of which marched, between the 17th and the 20th, into Shikarpur.

Meanwhile, the Bombay column had moved northward from Jerrak to Kotri, a little to the south-west of Hyderabad, whence after four days' halt it resumed its march northward. Heavy dust-storms on the 12th and 13th caused two days of misery to the troops; but, travelling by way of Manjhand, Sann and Amri, they came on the 16th to Laki, where the mountains then abutted on the river. Here it was suddenly discovered that the pass between the high ground and the Indus was impracticable for artillery, and two days were occupied in improving the road; though why this obstacle had not been reconnoitred and penetrated before the troops reached it is not explained.

However, having at length surmounted it the column pursued its way by Sehwan, where it entered the fertile district known as the Garden of Sind, up the river to Larkhana, about forty miles south-west of Shikarpur, where for nine days, from the 3rd to the 11th of March, it remained stationary. Keane, during the halt at Laki, had pushed on with an escort to Sehwan to take leave of Fane; and it is absolutely inexplicable why he did not go straight on to Shikarpur, where three-fourths of his army was assembled and where his presence was urgently needed. Want of transport had compelled him to waste two whole months in carrying the Bombay column over the eighty miles from his landing-place to Jerrak; the same trouble added to the attitude of the *amirs* had detained him at Jerrak for some ten days more; and this was no fault of his. But, when once the *amirs* had accepted Pottinger's treaty, there was no reason whatever why he should not have joined his principal force at once; and his failure to do so, which led to most serious consequences, was quite inexcusable.

On the 22nd of January Keane wrote to Auckland that he could not hear of any great amount of supplies collected at Shikarpur by Burnes or by his political brethren, and that it was extremely doubtful whether further advance could be hazarded unless a very large magazine were formed either there or in some neighbouring place. The commissary-general was likewise anxious, (Hough), to halt for three weeks at Shikarpur, in order to collect the greatest possible quantity of victuals, and to that end had at once detached to the rear four thousand camels. But now again the impatient Macnaghten intervened. According to his intelligence (which was invariably wrong), the Bolan Pass was about to be occupied by the enemy, and the passage of the defile, unless accomplished at once, would be contested. He urged, therefore, immediate advance; Burnes, who had persuaded himself of a fresh attempt of the Persians upon Herat, seconded Macnaghten; and Cotton, instead of insisting that he must first obtain Keane's sanction, too quickly gave way.

It must be said in his excuse that he had already had an unpleasant controversy with Macnaghten. The envoy had demanded a thousand of Cotton's camels for the *Shah's* contingent, and Cotton, declaring this to be civil encroachment upon military authority, had declined to give them without Keane's consent. Macnaghten rejoined that the march of the Shah's contingent was a political matter of the first importance, that it could not be accomplished without transport, and that he should refer the matter to the governor-general. The two men had the good sense not to lose their tempers; but Cotton was sensitive in the matter of transport, for he had been lately warned that his commissariat must provide for the Bombay troops as well as for his own, and he had therefore some reason to resent the claim of a thousand camels for a force of very doubtful value.

On the other hand, he had written a month before to Auckland expressing on other grounds the hope that Keane would not keep the Bengal force long at Shikarpur; and it was very certain that, if Keane were not on the spot, Cotton could leave orders to allot both to the Bombay troops and to the Shah's contingent such animals as he could with least reluctance spare. It is in fact impossible to ascribe to Cotton purely military or patriotic motives when, on the 21st of February, he issued orders for his troops to advance on the morrow.

The distance to be traversed from Shikarpur to Dadhar, at the eastern end of the Bolan Pass, was one hundred and seventy miles, of which about one hundred miles was practically desert, the villages being few and far asunder, water scanty and bad, and forage barely procurable. The length of the marches was definitely fixed by the distance from group to group of wells; but, though the *Shah's* contingent had lain idle at Shikarpur for a full month, no attempt had been made by its commander, Macnaghten, to form any depots of grain upon the line of route, to collect supplies of forage at the halting-places, nor to improve the facilities for obtaining water. Moreover, Cotton had allowed the number of the army's followers to swell unchecked; the followers of the *Shah's* force had likewise increased considerably; and altogether the commissariat was charged with the business of maintaining some eighty thousand souls, barely one-fifth of them combatants.

Since no large body could pass over such a district at one time, Cotton distributed his force into seven columns, which were to follow each other upon consecutive days; the engineers and their escort leading the way, followed in succession by the cavalry brigade, two infantry brigades, the park of artillery, the stores, and a third infantry brigade, with which last travelled Shah Shuja, though his contingent was not to start until the 7th of March. At the second stage outward from Shikarpur there were already difficulties over water and forage, and the Sixteenth Lancers were obliged to move in two detachments. The longest tract of absolutely waterless country was twenty-six miles, and at Barshori, which marked its northern extremity, the water was so noisome that no human being could touch it, and even the horses refused to drink.

It was questioned whether it would not be expedient to countermarch; but a messenger, sent forward to inquire from the engineers as to the prospects further on, brought word from Thomson that the cavalry must advance at all hazards, since a retrograde movement at this time would be the ruin of the expedition, and that the engineers would go forward whether the cavalry followed them or not. The Sixteenth, therefore, pursued their way to Mirpur, fourteen miles west of Barshori, where water, though brackish, was more abundant; and another fourteen miles northward brought them to Usta, where was a lake of sweet water, with fields of green corn, which were instantly devoured by the starving cattle. The next halting-places were Bagh, where a small quantity of grain was procured, Makesar, on the Bolan River, which set at rest any further anxiety as to water, Naoshera, and finally Dadhar, which was reached by headquarters on the 10th of March, the seventeenth day after leaving Shikarpur.

A movement, conducted with so little foresight that it narrowly missed failure at the outset, could not fail to be costly. The horses suffered severely, first from want of forage and water, and then from a sudden supply of green fodder, which lowered them still further in strength and condition. Nott severely condemned Cotton for sending the cavalry ahead of the infantry, instead of allowing it to follow in rear at such speed as the water-supply permitted; but Cotton was not a man capable of much thought. The camels, disabled by heavy loads and want of food, dropped down by hundreds; and, from the moment when the columns entered Baluchistan at Barshori, the predatory mountaineers swooped down upon them, cutting down followers, carrying off camels and cattle, and causing general alarm and confusion.

That such things should occur in the open plains was discreditable, and promised ill for the time when the troops should enter the passes; but the fault lay not chiefly with the military authorities. The political agents deprecated effective measures for protecting the line of march, lest the Baluchi tribes should be stirred into active hostilities. An attack upon a hospital-waggon and the wounding of some sick provoked orders to the leading detachment that the soldiers covering the line of march were to use force against marauders; but the only result was a complaint from Burnes to Cotton that such instructions were "bloodthirsty and calculated to bring on a blood-feud," (Durand). Keane wrote to Auckland, three months later:

> The political officers led me—and I suppose you—to believe that we should find the country friendly from Shikarpur to Kandahar. . . . There was no hint that it was full of robbers, plunderers and murderers, brought up to it from their youth.—
> *I.O.S.C.,* vol. 14 of 1839, Keane to Auckland, June 3, 1839.

Such men as Burnes, blind with the infatuation of their own conceit, would not allow such trifles as the slaughter of a few sick soldiers to upset their cherished theories.

However, Dadhar was reached; but now again the question of victuals became pressing. Despite of all previous losses of cattle, Cotton, when he started from Shikarpur, had still transport for six weeks' supplies. Kandahar was reckoned to be thirty-two marches, making no allowance for halts, from Shikarpur; and the margin was therefore, for practical purposes, on the wrong side. But Cotton's commissary counted upon finding ten days' victuals at Dadhar and twenty days' more at Quetta, on the other side of the Bolan Pass. Dadhar, however, could produce only one day's supplies; and on the 8th of March it was necessary to place the followers upon half-rations, as the grain could not be brought forward with sufficient rapidity to feed them. Unless, therefore, Quetta should fulfil its promise better than Dadhar, Cotton had practically but one month's victuals to carry him to Kandahar, a distance of some two hundred miles, of which sixty lay through the Bolan Pass.

In the circumstances it might have been expected that Cotton would have cut down the number of the followers to the lowest possible figure and reduced the baggage to the utmost; but nothing of the kind occurred to the good, easy man. He had the foresight to push forward a reconnoitring party under a good officer, Major Cureton of the Sixteenth Lancers, into the pass; and under this escort Burnes started on a mission to the Khan of Kalat, while the indefatigable engineers under Major Thomson began the work of rendering the track through the defile practicable for the troops. Cotton was urgent that he should find a better road than that from Bagh to Dadhar; and, when it was represented to him that the Bolan was a mountain-pass, choked with boulders and rough shingle, which could not easily be cleared away, he answered, with touching simplicity, that "the stones might be broken." Even now, he could not wean himself from the traditions of an old-fashioned campaign in the plains.

Cureton entered the pass on the 11th, while the main body remained halted for the columns to close up. Reports from the rear announced constant attacks of Baluchis upon camp-followers; and round Dadhar itself the foragers were not exempt from the same danger. On the other hand, Burnes succeeded in persuading the neighbouring Baluchi tribes not to impede the progress of the main body through the pass, which was a valuable service; and Cotton ordered the march to be resumed on the 15th. It was postponed for a day owing to the desertion of one complete party of regimental litter-bearers; but these recalcitrant men were headed off and hounded back; and on the 16th the head of the column entered the gorge. Observant officers, noting how admirably the defile lent itself to defence against an invading army, were thankful that they

BOLAN PASS

were not called upon to force a passage, (Havelock, i.).

The depth of the mountain-barrier at this point is about one hundred and twenty miles, one-half of which is pierced by the single pass of the Bolan. The path followed closely on the bed of the Bolan River, which during the rains or the melting of the snow becomes a raging torrent, sweeping all before it and flooding the camping grounds on its banks. These camping grounds were few, limited in area and always foul, the Bolan being, after the Khyber, the most important commercial route between Afghanistan and India. The Oriental is not remarkable for cleanliness in camp; but, even if he were subject to the sanitary laws of Moses, he would often find it difficult to fulfil them in this pass, the soil being frequently so thin that it would not hold a tent-peg, much less afford space for the burial of foul matter or of dead animals. The track was so stony as to be very trying to the feet of horses or camels, and absolutely fatal to the feet of bullocks, which were soon worn to the quick by constant attrition; and it crossed the water as often as sixteen to twenty times in a single day's march. Finally, though water was plentiful, there was complete dearth alike of forage and of fuel.

Since immunity from attack was by no means assured, Cotton broke up his force into small columns of all three arms, each with its own proportion of supplies, which were to follow each other in succession. The weather was not unfavourable, though upon one day heavy rain so swelled the torrent that the camp of the engineers was swept away. The temperature was moderate, the cold before dawn not sinking to freezing-point, and the heat at noon not exceeding that of an English summer. At Dozan, near the western outlet of the pass, the engineers had blasted out a road over the hills to the north, in order to save the labour of following the existing more circuitous track to the west. The guns of the horse-artillery, despite of eight horses and a number of men to each piece, were only with great difficulty brought to their halting-place, and the destruction of camels was very great.

However, by great exertion the leading column reached Sar-i-Bolan on the 20th, debouched from the pass to the plain on the 21st, and halted at Sar-i-ab, ten miles south of Quetta, to allow the rear columns to close up. Every one of them reported heavy loss of transport-animals and of baggage, including the men's quilts. The Fourth Brigade alone lost close upon two hundred and fifty camels in four days from starvation; and at every ten yards in the pass lay a dead camel or a dead bullock or a broken-down cart. Marauders, too, had carried off many living animals with astounding audacity. General Nott himself, with an escort of four troopers, had ridden down one such band of camel-robbers; and one of his battalions had been obliged to clear a horde of sharpshooters from the outlet of the pass before it could emerge from the defile. However, notwithstanding cruel casualties among beasts and followers, the Bengal division traversed the Bolan Pass with little molestation; and on the 26th Cotton moved on to the wretched mud village of Quetta and halted, in obedience to orders, to await the further directions of the commander-in-chief.

He now found himself in a very anxious situation. Keane, very angry with him for having advanced from Shikarpur without orders, had censured him severely, and peremptorily forbidden him to leave Quetta until he himself should come up. But this was not the worst. Cotton had counted upon finding twenty days' supplies at Quetta, and he found practically none. His commissary, on the 28th of March, reported one-third of his camels to have perished, and the survivors to be in such wretched condition as to be unfit to carry more than half-loads. Only ten days' victuals were left for the cavalry and for the First Infantry Brigade, with no prospect of obtaining more; and there was only two days' store of grain for the horses of the cavalry and artillery. Kandahar was one hundred and fifty miles ahead, with the Khojak pass, a most difficult obstacle, on the way. Shikarpur was two hundred miles in rear, and not to be reached without retraversing the whole length of the Bolan Pass. Cotton could move neither forward nor back; and to this dilemma he had been reduced by his disloyalty to his military chief, and his ready acceptance of the promptings of two so vain and shallow men as Macnaghten and Burnes.

The only thing to be done immediately was to place the troops upon half-rations and the followers upon quarter-rations, but Cotton hesitated to take even this step lest he should rouse discontent among the fighting-men, until Thomson, the engineer, fairly forced him to a decision. As a more practical measure he sent Burnes on a mission to Mehrab Khan of Kalat, to induce him, if possible, to furnish supplies, which as the *Khan* had already failed to fulfil his undertaking to collect depots of grain at Dadhar and Quetta, seemed not very promising. Burnes was well received; but Mehrab Khan told him some unpleasant truths; complaining justly that his territory had already suffered much from the passage of the British force, declaring truly that a bad harvest had left little grain in his country, and predicting the ultimate failure of the enterprise.

In return, however, for the promise of an annual subsidy of £15,000 he agreed to pay homage to Shah Shuja, whom he disliked and distrusted, to do his best to provide victuals, and to give safe passage to the British convoys from Shikarpur through the mountains. Of the promised subsidy, Burnes paid to Mehrab £2000 on the spot to conciliate him, and, having done so, proceeded to insult him, thus increasing the *Khan's* suspicions at the very moment when it was most desirable to allay them, and furnishing him with the funds to raise and pay the tribes if he designed to incite them against the British. Altogether Burnes's diplomacy at Kalat was wholly unprofitable to the British Army, and was the beginning of troubles which were to prove fatal to Mehrab Khan.

Therewith Cotton's efforts to extricate himself from his troubles were practically exhausted. As the commissariat could supply no grain for the horses of the cavalry and artillery, he gave commanding officers liberty to make their own arrangements—a simple device which, as only green growing corn was procurable, could do little to fill the animals' bellies or improve their condition. He seems to have made an appeal to Keane for permission to advance, for Keane; on the 27th of March, (*I.O.S.C.*, vol. 8 of 1838, Keane to Cotton, March 27, 1839), refused it, saying that there April, was no object in leaving Quetta until Shah Shuja should come up to lead the movement upon Kandahar.

At length, in despair, Cotton appears either to have resorted to the political agents for advice or to have received it from them unasked, for Captain Leech, one of Burnes's underlings, pointed out that there were three courses open to him, namely, to march at once upon Kandahar notwithstanding Keane's prohibition; to make a foraging expedition towards Kalat; or to retreat at once upon Shikarpur, leaving a detachment at Quetta. He adopted not one of these measures, keeping Leech's counsel entirely to himself; and indeed the incident might never have become known had not a copy of Leech's letter—probably torn from the body of some hapless murdered messenger—been picked up in the Bolan Pass and carried to Macnaghten. There was a fourth course open, namely, to move on very slowly and by easy marches, so as to husband provisions and forage to the utmost, and lead cavalry and followers over fresh ground, where at least they might find something to eat. But having flouted Keane once, by advancing wrongly and without orders from Shikarpur, Cotton dared not flout him a second time, when Keane was wrong and he himself right.

And so the unhappy man sat still at Quetta, consuming the supplies

of his fighting-men, and starving both his horses and his followers. Symptoms of the unfriendliness of the tribes now became frequent. Cotton had issued strict orders to prevent plunder and to ensure respect for the women and for the religious feelings of the people, hoping to conciliate them and to obtain from them food. But the predatory instincts of the tribes were too strong to be overcome by blandishment; and on the 31st of March a party of robbers swooped down from the hills and carried off two hundred camels in a body.

Such thefts now became frequent, and with good reason, for the starving followers, despite of all orders and the severest punishments, were perpetually stealing food and forage, whereupon the tribesmen retaliated not only by slaying them without mercy, but by carrying off every camel that they could appropriate. Very soon the followers were living on fried sheepskins and congealed blood; and Cotton sat still bemoaning his hard fate, until all ranks from the general to the drummer were discussing but one topic, the miserable outlook for the army and the certain prospect of starvation.

Through most of this time Keane, though fully warned by Fane of Cotton's incapacity, was dawdling far away with the Bombay division. Not until the 12th of March did this division, now reduced to eighteen hundred Europeans and as many native soldiers, break up from Larkhana, whence it marched, through hot and sultry weather, across the desert to Shadihar and by Jhal upon Gandava, which was reached on the 21st. It had been Keane's idea that he might find the pass from thence to Kalat practicable for his column; and the plan was not a bad one, for the Bombay division in such a case might have reached the highlands of Afghanistan nearly as soon as Cotton. Two days were spent in reconnaissance of the pass, after which Keane decided that it would be better to make for the Bolan; and on the 23rd, leaving the Bombay troops to follow him on the 31st, he at last rode forward to join the Bengal column.

On the 26th Keane met Shah Shuja at Naoshera, and on the following day moved on with him to Dadhar. Here he took measures to establish a magazine of supplies, and inquired as to the transport provided for the Bombay troops by the Bengal commissariat. The result was not satisfactory. Cotton had undertaken to leave two thousand camels for them at Shikarpur, but two-thirds of these were still on the east bank of the Indus. He had promised a thousand camels to Shah Shuja, but only five hundred were forthcoming. The truth was that the whole arrangement of the transport had been utterly confounded, because the Bengal commissariat had been called upon without warning to find carriage for the Bombay division.

The consequence was that the Bengal troops were crippled, the Bombay troops were not half equipped, and the inevitable jealousy between the two was greatly embittered. It was with no very amiable feelings that Keane, in company with Shah Shuja and Macnaghten, entered the Bolan Pass. On the 4th of April he rode into Sar-i-ab, whither Cotton had come back to meet him; and here his camp was attacked by plundering tribesmen, of whom eleven were taken and at once shot. On the 6th, at last, he rode into Quetta, to find the Bengal troops, from highest to lowest, sunk in utter gloom and despondency.

For this Keane had no one to thank but himself; but it is fair to say that when at last he did assume personal command, he showed energy and decision. Realising that it was hopeless to look for supplies from Kalat, he turned a deaf ear to all croaking and gave orders to advance on the morrow. Cotton reverted to the divisional command of the Bengal infantry, Willshire was set over the whole of that of Bombay; and Nott, to his great indignation, was left at Quetta with only one battalion of his own brigade, another of the Shah's infantry, and detachments of cavalry, to guard the lines of communication. The commissariat departments of both presidencies were placed under a single head. The engineers were sent forward to prepare the road over the Khojak pass, fifty miles to the north-west; and on the 7th of April the march began. It was ominously heralded by a patter of musketry, signifying the execution of sixty unfortunate horses which could drag themselves no further.

The way lay over an elevated plateau some fifty miles in breadth intersected by low ranges of minor hills and a few inconsiderable streams, with rare villages and still rarer little towns, and presenting general dearth of food, forage, fuel and water. Since resistance might be expected from the wild predatory tribes, it was ordained that all baggage and camp equipment should move in rear of the columns, which, as the heat was steadily increasing, signified considerable discomfort for the troops. But this was a small matter compared to the scarcity of food and forage. The cavalry horses continued to die, and the survivors were in such wretched condition that they were unfit for real work.

Worse still, a commissariat officer, who was bringing forward a much-needed convoy through the Bolan, reported that he had been obliged to fight his way through the most difficult portion of the defile, and had lost, through fatigue and bad forage, eight hundred camels, with their loads, between the Indus and Sar-i-ab. However, there was nothing for Keane but to struggle on, repelling the occasional onslaughts of plunderers; and on the 14th of April he began the ascent of the Khojak pass. Three tracks had been prepared, more or less, for traffic by the engineers, that in the centre for the guns, that on the left for camels, that on the right, which was roughest of all, for bullocks, ponies and men. Both the ascent to the summit and the descent from it were extremely steep and difficult, and on no one of the tracks was there room for camels to pass except in single file. Yet, through the mismanagement either of Keane or of his staff, three regiments of infantry, as many of cavalry and two batteries of horse-artillery, together with the baggage of general headquarters, divisional headquarters and of the infantry brigade, besides the field-commissariat and grain-cattle, were all expected to pass through the defile and make a march of five miles on either side of it within twenty-four hours.

The result was dire confusion. The infantry-brigade and the baggage marched at 3 a.m. and were soon in difficulties. The steep ascent daunted many riders, and the descent even more. Camels fell and blocked the way, until they could by some means be removed. The defile, after twelve hours of desperate exertion, was hopelessly choked, and orders were sent back to the cavalry not to leave camp. But their baggage was already in the pass, and belated efforts to turn their camels back increased the anarchy and the chaos. Night closed upon a seething mass of men and beasts, without food or water, pent close along four miles of narrow track.

On the 15th the cavalry brigade marched at 3 a.m., and, to its consternation, came unexpectedly upon the tail of the infantry-brigade's baggage, still stuck fast. Thousands of animals, hardly able to move after thirty-eight hours of standing or crawling, were jammed hopelessly together; and the baggage-officers, some of whom had been on duty for twenty-six hours without food or drink, were wearied out. The troopers, dismounting, hove some of the worse obstructions out of the road. The press from the rear was stopped; the wretched camels and drivers ahead were goaded on with the lance; and then the whole of the Sixteenth Lancers, dismounting, set themselves to bring the first battery of horse-artillery to the summit.

The poor, weak, exhausted horses by some means or another were forced up; and, though one gun went over the edge of the road, and rolled, team, drivers and all over a low precipice, the only damage done was the smashing of one wheel, which was presently replaced. Stripped to their shirts, the men toiled on unceasingly, and at length, after nine hours of cruel work, the cavalry-brigade descended into the plain, near the foot of the pass. But there the only water offered to them was so foul that the horses would not touch it; and Brigadier Arnold, representing that at all risks he must move on, obtained from Keane permission to march again on the morrow, (Fane, i.). Accordingly, on the morning of the 16th the cavalry brigade started off, and after a long and distressing march struck a tank and a little cultivated ground fed by the River Kadanai, where it halted in comfort at Dandi Golai.

Keane, meanwhile, was tied to his headquarters at Chaman, near the foot of the pass, until the rest of the Bengal division should have passed through the defile of the Khojak. On the 16th every man of the First Infantry Brigade that could be spared was sent to fatigue-duty at the pass, and on the 18th the Fourth Brigade took its place to help in bringing over the siege-train. With all their labour they could pass but one eighteen-pounder and two large mortars over the precipitous hills in the course of the day, and it was not until the 21st that the rear of the Bengal division at last came down into the plain. No accurate account of what it lost in the defile could ever be compiled, but it included vast quantities of baggage, tents and camels, fourteen barrels of powder, twenty-seven thousand rounds of musket ammunition, and unknown quantities of supplies.

On the 18th, however, Keane advanced his headquarters to Dandi Golai, and on that same evening the water-supply fell short, the tribesmen having built a dam across the upper waters of the Kadanai to intercept it. A party was sent up to turn the water back into its own channel; but it occurred to no one to place a guard so as to prevent the water from being cut off. Indeed, the tribesmen seem to have done very much what pleased them with the Bengal division. They carried off five of the headquarters' camels during the march of the 18th, and on the 19th they murdered twelve followers and stole two elephants belonging to Shah Shuja and Macnaghten. On the 20th the water-supply was again cut off, again reopened and once more cut off; and on the 21st Keane moved forward ten miles with the cavalry brigade and Second Infantry Brigade to Kila Fathulla. There no water but a salt spring was to be found, and, the thermometer standing at noon at over one hundred degrees Fahrenheit, the distress among men and cattle was very great.

Troops emerging from Khojak Pass

On the 22nd Keane pushed on another twelve miles to Mel Manda, where, after a time, plenty of good water was discovered. None, however, was at first offered to the cavalry brigade but a little foul stuff which the horses could not touch; and Brigadier Arnold, representing the matter to Keane, obtained his leave to move on at any cost. He therefore led his brigade in advance for twelve more terrible miles. Men and animals were hardly able to drag themselves on from thirst, and the Sixteenth Lancers travelled afoot, goading their horses forward with their lances. At last a patch of cultivated ground came into view along the banks of the River Dori; and at the sight of the water men and horses made one mad rush into it and drank and drank insatiably.

Fortunately, the river was everywhere at least three feet deep, so that there was enough for all, (Fane); but it may be doubted whether any discipline could have withstood the test to which these men were subjected. They had been practically without water for two days, and without food for one day, and they had marched for hours under a burning sun. Fifty-nine horses were reported dead at the close of the march, while many more were unfit to go further, and no fewer than ninety men of one regiment went into hospital. In fact, this march gave the finishing stroke to the starved horses and overworked men of the cavalry brigade.

On the next day the Second Infantry Brigade and the artillery moved to Takht, encamping by the bank of the Dori, where they were joined by the cavalry brigade before 4 a.m. on the 24th, for there were reports that the chiefs of Kandahar were coming out to fight. On the 23rd, however, a deserter from among those chiefs came to make his submission to Shah Shuja and to report that the rest had fled; and therewith Macnaghten, without a word to Keane, (*I.O.S.C.*, vol. 9 of 1839, Keane to Auckland, April 26, 1839), hurried Shah Shuja forward to Kandahar. The *Shah's* reception was not cordial, for it was realised at once that he was a mere puppet in British hands, and that the advent of the British host must cause scarcity and raise the price of provisions.

However, the childish vanity of Macnaghten in parading himself as the person nearest to the king, was duly gratified, since for two whole days he had His Majesty all to himself. On the 26th Keane and the troops with him entered the city; and the Fourth Infantry Brigade and the siege-artillery came in four days later. The long journey was over, and the Bengal division had reached its goal at last, with just two days' supply of half-rations in store. They had marched, since they left

Ferozepore on the 10th of December, just over one thousand miles in one hundred and thirty-seven days. The troops had been on half-rations for the past twenty-eight days, and the horses had subsisted on green forage, always scanty and often very bad, for twenty-six days. The health of the men had suffered from their great exertions at the Khojak pass, from the subsequent heat, from inadequate nourishment and from bowel-complaints, due to the enforced drinking of saline water.

If the Barakzai chiefs had offered resistance before or near Kandahar, Keane must have met them with the enfeebled men of his infantry and artillery only, for his cavalry was, for the time, absolutely unfit for service. And even now, neither men nor horses could count upon sufficiency of food. There was indeed a good crop of corn, ripening but not yet ripe, and there was great plenty of fruit and vegetables, which were the more welcome since many soldiers were sick of scurvy; but fruit in large quantities is not the best diet for half-starved men. There was also sound abundance of green forage, but this again is not the best food for exhausted animals, and, since barley and grain were scarce, the horses were little better off than before.

As to the camels, their numbers had been so much reduced that none could be spared from the army to fetch provisions from Dadhar. Altogether the prospects at Kandahar were not of the brightest. The only remedy that Keane could think of was to take the whole business of supply out of the hands of the political agents, who after spending enormous sums had failed along the whole line of one thousand miles to collect adequate magazines, and to place it in the charge of his far more efficient commissaries. This was the first step towards the emancipation of the army from the paralysing incubus of political control. (*I.O.S.C.*, vol. 9 of 1839, Keane to Auckland, April 19, 1839).

Meanwhile the Bombay division, after receiving its supplies at Gandava, had marched thence for Dadhar, where it arrived on the 5th of April, not without loss of camels by theft on the way. The heat at Dadhar was by this time extreme, and there was consequently much sickness. On the 9th, the artillery and the Seventeenth Foot entered the Bolan Pass and found both water and air unspeakably poisoned by the thousands of rotting carcases that encumbered the defile. The remainder of the division followed, and, though not seriously attacked, lost camels at every stage by theft. Between the 15th and 20th the column reached Quetta, and pressed on with the least possible delay to the Khojak pass. Two days were needed to carry the artillery through

Keane approaching Quetta

that obstacle; and on the 4th of May the division entered Kandahar, having lost one-fifth of its horses dead, a vast number of camels worn out or stolen, and some hundreds of camp-followers murdered. In actual fighting the casualties in both divisions did not exceed forty killed, most of these being officers and men who had been reckless in wandering far from camp alone or in small parties. The losses of the marauding tribesmen of all descriptions was set down at about five hundred killed between the Indus and Kandahar.

The heat was now very great, and, with the reaction of rest after many weeks of toil and hardship, sickness increased among the troops at large, and among the British in particular. There was some effort to make good the casualties among the troop-horses with native animals, and to gather in fresh camels for transport; but camel-stealing soon began round Kandahar, and when some of the thieves—Afghans—were caught and sentenced to be hanged, Macnaghten, on behalf of the *Shah*, intervened to protect them. Moreover, the marauders who stole camels were quite ready to murder unwary individuals, as one or two British officers discovered to their cost. Keane wrote:

> The country round Kandahar is as full of robbers as Kach Gandava; and the king's name goes for nothing outside the palace gates, unless backed by an overwhelming force. Robberies and murders go on daily and nightly, and, as my correspondence with Mr. Macnaghten will show, I am precluded from doing justice to those who look to me to protect them and the property of the government.—*I.O.S.C.*, vol. 14 of 1839, Keane to Auckland, June 23, 1839.

The question of supplies, again, was still urgent. There was none too much grain to feed both the inhabitants and the army, which of course tended to raise the price. Shah Shuja, thereupon, against all Macnaghten's remonstrances, fixed the cost of corn by his arbitrary will, whereupon the price instantly rose to more than double of its former rate. Frightened by this result, he revoked the order, but too late. (I.O.S.C., vol. 9 of 1839, Macnaghten to Indian government, May 2, 1839).

On the 11th of May some of the followers broke into riot and plundered the merchants in the bazaar; and, though the ringleaders were sternly punished, the incident did not endear the expedition to the Afghans. The transport of provisions from the base was also unsatisfactory. On the 7th of May a convoy, nominally of two thousand camels, came in from Shikarpur, purporting to carry nearly three hundred tons of grain; but, owing to mismanagement and the rascality of the native agents, not above one-fifth of that quantity reached Kandahar. And meanwhile Auckland in India was calmly writing instructions that Kandahar must not be left with less than six months' provisions for troops and followers, and that no movement from thence must be undertaken with less than six weeks' full rations at starting. To do the governor-general justice, he was sedulous in ordering convoys of provisions to proceed to the front, but he did not realise that to start a convoy on the plains was one thing, and to bring it safely through the passes was another. He was an excellent, but simple gentleman. (*I.O.S.C.*, vol. 9 of 1839, Auckland to Keane, June 3, 1839; Keane to Auckland, June 26, 1839).

Military operations of any serious kind were for some time impossible. The Barakzai chieftains, upon leaving Kandahar, had fled to Girishk, seventy miles to westward; but, though Shah Shuja was urgent that they should be pursued, it was not until the 11th of May that a mixed column of seventeen hundred men could be sent thither under the command of Sale. Even this small force could not be collected without taking detachments from seven different units, including a few heavy cannon from the siege-train, nor could it carry more than twenty days' victuals at half-rations. Happily the chiefs had taken flight from Girishk before the arrival of Sale; and, having left some of Shah Shuja's contingent to occupy the fort, he returned with the remainder of the column before the end of May to Kandahar. The army was destined to linger there for yet another month before it could find means to move.

Meanwhile, there was much trouble on the lines of communication. When Keane advanced from Quetta there was what Auckland described as an "uncontrolled rush" of officers from the plains to the hills. Everyone wanted to be at the front and no one to stay behind. A major of the Thirty-Seventh Native Infantry, who had been left with three companies at Dadhar, boldly brought them forward without orders, and was promptly sent back with public rebuke; and, to show that he was no respecter of persons, Keane deliberately set down Colonel Dennie at Shikarpur and Nott at Quetta, each with no very important body of troops under his command.

At Sukkur was Brigadier-General Gordon, who held the chief command in Upper Sind; but everywhere there was some political officer to help or to interfere. One of them, Lieutenant Eastwick, at Khairpur, early in May wrote alarming accounts of the defencelessness of the lines of communication. There were, he said, too few troops at Shikarpur, none at Bagh, only two companies at Dadhar; in fact the whole line from Shikarpur to Quetta was unoccupied—all of which stirred frantic agitation in the breast of Auckland, and drew from him such a letter to Keane as nearly caused a rupture between them. (*I.O.S.C,* vol. 11 of 1839, Eastwick to Indian government, May 8, 1839).

Keane had told off two brigades of infantry to guard his immense lines of communication, but, as he truly said, if he had been able to add a third brigade to them, the route from Shikarpur to Quetta could never have been secured against the attacks of the marauding tribesmen, who, as was suspected, rightly or wrongly, were hounded on by the Khan of Kalat. The remedy adopted by the political agents—and there was some sense in it—was to enlist the marauders themselves as police; but the agents marred all their services by interfering with the military officers. Thus Eastwick quarrelled with a captain for marching up to a marauders' fort and, upon being fired upon, storming it out of hand; Eastwick's argument being that the real offenders might have fled, and the occupants of the fort might have been harmless individuals. This tendency of political agents to prescribe to military officers the manner in which they should perform their duties led to a good deal of friction; and a battle royal between Mr. Ross-Bell, the political agent for Upper Sind, and Brigadier Gordon, who declined to take military orders from him, was decided by Auckland in favour of Gordon. (*I.O.S.C.,* vol. 9 of 1839, Gordon to Mil. Sec, May 14, 1839; vol. 12 of 1839, Correspondence of Gordon and Ross-Bell, July 18, 1839).

All this made for insecurity on the lines of communication; and another great difficulty was that, owing to the calls for transport at the front, few of the standing posts had camels enough to enable them to move even for a short distance to punish or overawe marauders. There was, moreover, always uncertainty as to the fidelity of the Amirs of Sind to their engagements. At the beginning of June it seemed very probable that they would rise, in which case every British post in Sind, with the exception of Sukkur, would have been in the greatest peril, and all irregular troops raised by the British among the Baluchis would certainly have joined their countrymen. (*I.O.S.C.,* vol. 9 of 1839, Ross-Bell to Indian government, June 9, 13).

A terrible factor in Sind was the heat, which was telling with frightful effect upon the detachments and convoys that passed up from Bukkur to Dadhar. The latter place was such a furnace that there was a Mohammedan saying, "Oh *Allah!* Wherefore make hell when thou hast made Dadhar?" yet it was inevitably the halting-place for troops after traversing one hundred and fifty miles of burning desert. Even at Shikarpur Colonel Dennie complained that in his tent—the best and largest in the camp—the thermometer rose to one hundred and twenty degrees Fahrenheit; and this was only in April. At the end of that month he moved up to the Bolan Pass and arrived there safely; but two British officers, who followed him, died of heat in their tents, "their bodies turning as black as charcoal."

On the 3rd of May he started to escort two batteries of Shah Shuja's artillery and six or seven hundred camels through the pass, and had to fight his way in intense heat for ten consecutive days along the whole length of the defile. Having with him but four companies of native infantry, he could not spare the men for continuous flanking-parties, and would hardly have brought his convoy through without the timely, though accidental, reinforcement of three companies more. The exertions of the *sepoys* in dragging the guns through the pass were beyond all praise, for their sufferings from want of water were extreme. Many died, and under an officer less able and inspiring than Dennie, the whole might have abandoned work and hope, and perished under the knives of the tribesmen. (Dennie's *Personal Narrative*).

Further to the rear, a convoy of treasure and stores, under escort of a wing of native infantry and of detachments, marched from Shikarpur on the 23rd of May and lost six out of fourteen European officers dead from heat. Two only were fit to proceed beyond Quetta, and they left behind them one hundred *sepoys* and at least three hundred camp-followers dead. Cholera, as well as heat and thirst, attacked this unhappy escort; and the memory of the sun, "turned to a ball of red-hot copper" by the dust of the desert, seems to have haunted the memory of the survivors to the day of their death, (Seaton's *From Cadet to Colonel*, i.). In the first week of June a native officer and nine *sepoys* died in one day at Mirpur, while on the march across the desert; and, of a party of fifty Europeans under an officer, which started from Bukkur for Shikarpur, the officer and nine men died outright within two days, and many others collapsed under the sun.

And the heat spared men as little in camp as on the march. In the middle of June Ross-Bell reported the detachments at Sukkur, Shikarpur, Bagh and Dadhar as fourteen hundred and thirty *sepoys* strong, nine-tenths of them unfit for duty; and this was at a moment when the Amirs of Sind threatened to rise. Beyond all question some at least of these tragic details must have been reported to the Indian government, yet so little was June, the truth realised that we find Auckland writing, as late as the 3rd of June, that the route by Shikarpur would soon be closed by heat and that he was looking for another. There was honest zeal, goodwill and loyalty in the poor man, but not a vestige of that essential quality in one who makes war—imagination. (*I.O.S.C.*, vol. 9, Auckland to Keane, June 3, 1839).

Meanwhile at Kandahar things went on as before. Money was scarce, grain was scanty, and only sickness and theft of camels abounded. The *Shah's* pardon of the robbers who had been condemned by Keane to be hanged produced its natural effect; and the men who guarded the camels were slack and unwatchful, (Hough). On the 8th of June a convoy of treasure arrived; and on the 10th Keane issued orders to march on the 15th. Macnaghten had long been urgent for an advance, and on the 7th of June he advised Keane to leave the whole of the Bombay division at Kandahar and take only the Bengal troops to Kabul; setting forth that trouble might indeed arise at Kalat or Herat, but that no opposition was to be anticipated at Kabul, nor on the road thither.

Keane at first assented to this proposal; but, thinking over it again, consulted the shrewd and sensible engineer, Thomson, who reminded him that the general and not the envoy would be held responsible for any military mishap, and put the pertinent question whether the information hitherto furnished by Macnaghten and the political agents had proved trustworthy or not. This touched Keane on a tender point, for the political agents had failed him throughout both as intelligencers and as commissaries, as he had predicted that they would. He now not only changed his intention concerning the Bombay division, but informed Macnaghten that he meant to form an intelligence department of his own. He wrote, in effect:

> There is no such thing at present, I have never seen the like in any army. The Indian Government differs from others, and tries to do more by policy and negotiation than by the sword. You have given me every assistance, but, after I leave this, I feel it will be proper for me to have my own intelligence department.

Macnaghten, to his credit, readily acquiesced; and a second step was thus taken towards delivering the military from political bondage.

(*I.O.S.C.*, vol. 10 of 1839, Macnaghten to Keane, June 7, 10; Keane to Macnaghten, June 10, 1839).

Before the 15th, however, arrived Auckland's letter, already mentioned, forbidding the army to start from Kandahar with less than six weeks' full rations in hand. It was, therefore, necessary to await the arrival of a convoy of about four thousand camels, carrying grain, which had passed through Dadhar on the 24th of May. Keane had sent back two parties to help to speed it on its way; the second of which, under a native leader of irregular cavalry named Azim Khan, had with great zeal and resolution defended it against several attacks in the Bolan and Khojak passes. On the 23rd of June some three thousand camels toiled safely into Kandahar.

Their load amounted to about one month's supply for the army on half-rations (no one ventured to think in terms of full rations for this luckless army), and as Keane had not at Kandahar transport sufficient to carry more than five weeks' victuals at full rations for the Europeans and half-rations for *sepoys* and followers, this reinforcement of camels was very welcome. He ordered the army to march on the 25th; but now came a sudden and, to the political gentlemen, wholly unexpected difficulty. The merchants who had brought the convoy refused to proceed further. Macnaghten, after much pressure, persuaded them to sell him two thousand camels at a high price; but the merchants backed out of the bargain at the last moment; and the camel-drivers, without whom the camels were useless, on their part, declined to accompany their animals, whether purchased or not. Thus, after losing twelve days, Keane was fain after all to store the newly-arrived grain in Kandahar, and to march off without it. (Durand; Hough; *I.O.S.C.*, vol. 14 of 1839; Keane to Auckland, June 26, 1839).

The garrison left at Kandahar consisted of two batteries of artillery, a battalion of Bengal native infantry, in all about eight hundred strong, and a battalion, a squadron and a horse-battery of Shah Shuja's contingent. In Kandahar also were deposited the four eighteen-pounders which had with such enormous labour been brought through the Bolan and Khojak Passes, and which formed the sole and entire battering-train of Keane's army. How the general was brought to commit this blunder, it is difficult to divine. The chief of the artillery did indeed urge that the bullocks were unequal to the labour of dragging these pieces; but this, in face of the fact that the guns had already travelled from Ferozepore to Kandahar, was ridiculous. Macnaghten, again, represented that Ghazni, the only fortress on the way to Kabul, was weak and could be breached by field-guns; but Keane knew perfectly well that Macnaghten's information was nearly always incorrect and valueless. The probability is that Keane gave way to a fit of temper, having just about this time received Auckland's upbraiding letter concerning the lines of communication, which irritated and hurt him exceedingly. But to account for a very grave mistake is not to excuse it.

★★★★★★

I have been unable to find Auckland's letters of the 27th, 28th and 29th April, and know their dates and the purport of their contents only from Keane's answers. The order to leave the siege-guns at Kandahar was issued on June 1. (Hough) Keane's first angry answer to Auckland is dated June 3.

★★★★★★

On the 27th accordingly, Keane marched for Kabul, with the native troops still on half-rations and the followers upon quarter-rations. The army moved in three columns at one day's interval; the first consisting of head-quarters, with the cavalry division, three batteries of artillery and one brigade of infantry; the second of the remainder of the Bengal troops; and the third of the Bombay force; the whole amounting to about seven thousand eight hundred fighting-men. The moon being favourable the troops started soon after midnight. No enemy was encountered, though two bodies of mounted Ghilzai tribesmen hung about both flanks of the columns throughout the ninety miles from Kandahar to Kalat-i-Ghilzai, which was reached by the leading column on the 4th of July.

After one day's halt there, Keane continued his advance with little incident beyond the occasional theft of a camel until the 17th, when, grain being abundant, the soldiers actually received full rations. On the 19th, when approaching Ahmed Khel, the advanced guard met a small party of hostile horse, whereupon Keane ordered the rear columns to close up by forced marches; and on the 20th the entire host was assembled at Nani, within one day's march of Ghazni. It numbered, besides the Queen's and Company's troops, two thousand of Shah Shuja's contingent and two thousand undisciplined Afghans levied by him, or about twelve thousand combatants in all, with forty guns.

On the 21st the army advanced in three parallel columns, the artillery on the road in the centre, the cavalry in open column of troops on its right, the infantry in column of companies on the left, and Shah Shuja's cavalry thrown out wide to the right of all. Macnaghten persisted that there would be no resistance at Ghazni nor elsewhere,

Ghazni

and Burnes, just as the fortress came into sight, reported to Keane, upon the information of an Afghan, that the place had been evacuated. Keane, who was riding ahead of his troops, therefore pushed on, until a few shots from some gardens within half a mile of the walls warned him that the suburbs were occupied. After some skirmishing the enemy was dislodged from the gardens, but a fire of cannon from the walls showed that Ghazni was held; and, after the staff and engineers had made their reconnaissance, the horse-artillery meanwhile plying the battlements with shrapnel, Keane withdrew his men out of range and encamped.

The works were now seen to be far more formidable than had been reported. Ghazni was a fairly regular quadrilateral, with sides about five hundred yards long, broken by a number of circular bastions of the usual Oriental type. The walls had been repaired, and the gates, so far as could be seen, had been built up. Light artillery could produce no effect on them, and, as Keane's battering guns had been left behind, a regular attack was out of the question. An escalade was, likewise, impracticable, the parapet being sixty to seventy feet above the plain. Mining, once again, could not be thought of, because there was a wet ditch before the parapet. Indeed, no operation that required the least time was feasible, for Keane had no more than three days' food left with him. Unless the army was to perish, Ghazni must be taken somehow and taken at once.

The situation was very grave, and Keane had only himself to thank for it. But Afghanistan is the land of treachery, and thereby Keane was saved. A nephew of Dost Mohamed, who had recently through disaffection deserted his cause, gave information that the Kabul Gate on the north side had not been built up, and his report was confirmed by the sight of a horseman entering it from the Kabul road. Thomson, therefore, presented to Keane two alternatives. Dost Mohamed and his army were represented to be only five or six marches to north of Ghazni; and, if the general advanced and beat him in the field, it was tolerably certain that the fortress would open its gates. If this could not be, then the only chance was to blow in the Kabul Gate and carry Ghazni by surprise, an extremely hazardous enterprise, and likely, even if successful, to be very costly. Unable to make even four marches from want of supplies, Keane was driven to adopt the more desperate course, (Durand).

Accordingly at 4 p.m., he set his troops in motion to circle round by the east from the southern to the northern side of the fortress,

Ghazni

executing the movement in two columns for greater expedition. Practically, however, the manoeuvre resolved itself into a night march, which is not generally a rapid one, particularly when men and beasts, both alike for months underfed, have already traversed several miles of rough ground. The result was that, after much confusion, the troops took up their position on a line of heights to north of the city between 10 p.m. and midnight, and there bivouacked, hungry, weary and shivering; while the sick, the baggage and the supplies, after long and helpless floundering in the dark, settled down wherever they found themselves for the night. Such was the disorder that the baggage did not reach its appointed place until noon of the 22nd; and it should seem that this ill-advised and hasty scramble was due to Macnaghten's intelligence—as usual incorrect—that Dost Mohamed had started from Kabul on the 16th, and on the 22nd would be within a day's march of Ghazni.

All through the night there was a dropping fire from the ramparts of Ghazni, with flickering blue lights and answering flickers from the hills to eastward. The enemy was evidently on the alert, and had good reason to be. Keane, never dreaming that the secret would be divulged, had imparted his plans to Macnaghten, who promptly passed them on to the *Shah's* army, so that already on the evening of the 21st they were the common talk of the *Shah's* camp, (Durand).

At 11 a.m. on the 22nd, bodies of Ghilzai horse and foot began to stream down the hills on the east, and the whole of Keane's cavalry division was turned out to meet them. Had the enemy been permitted to come down well into the plain they might have been severely punished; but, being checked too soon by fire of shrapnel and by the charge of a few squadrons, they took to flight before they had suffered serious loss. But for this trifling affair, the Afghans gave no further trouble that day; and Keane, after personal reconnaissance of the gate and walls, was able to perfect his plans, as follows.

The horse- and field-batteries were to move forward at midnight and take up, before dawn, positions within three hundred yards of the Kabul gateway, and from thence along the north-eastern front of the fortress. Three companies of native infantry and a regiment of native cavalry, were at the same time to make their way to the southern face, where the infantry were to make a demonstration of a false attack. For the true attack, the storming-party was composed of the light companies of the Queen's, Seventeenth and Hundred and Second, and a flank company of the Thirteenth, the whole, two hundred and forty men strong, under Lieutenant-Colonel Dennie.

It was to be followed by the main attacking column of the Queen's and the Hundred and Second, with the rest of the Thirteenth deployed as skirmishers upon both flanks and with the Seventeenth in support, the whole under Brigadier-General Sale. The skirmishers above mentioned were to be in position and under shelter by 12.30 a.m., so as to keep down any fire upon the engineers who were charged with the duty of blowing in the gate. The remainder of the infantry were formed into a reserve under Cotton. All troops were to assemble and move to their posts in dead silence. The assault and the false attack were designed to take place at 3 a.m. and the signal for the onslaught was to be the bugle-call "Advance," sounded by order of the chief engineer as soon as he could ascertain that the entrance was practicable.

The preliminary movements went forward without a hitch of any kind. The weather was highly favourable, with a high and gusty wind which helped to drown the noise of tramping columns and rumbling guns; and, by a singular chance, the Afghans, lulled into false security because disappointed of the assault that they had expected on the previous night, took no notice of any sounds. This was but one of an incredible series of accidents. The first streak of dawn had barely showed itself when Captain Peat and Lieutenants Durand and Macleod, with a few engineers, moved quietly with bags of powder towards the gate. Within one hundred and fifty yards of it their approach was discovered; blue lights were burned, and a heavy fire was opened from the upper ramparts. They had to cross a bridge of masonry over the ditch, which was commanded by low outer works.

Had these been occupied, not a man of the party could have reached the gate. But not a shot was fired; and they passed over unchecked and unhurt. Peat with a few men occupied a sally-port, until that moment unknown, which gave them shelter, and Durand and his men quietly laid three hundred pounds of powder in twelve bags against the gate, and edged their way back, hugging the foot of the wall, as they had come. The skirmishers of the Thirteenth on the other side of the ditch were meanwhile answering the musketry which had begun from the upper ramparts; the British batteries had opened fire, and along the whole circumference of the fortress the defenders showed their alertness and bewilderment by continuous flashes of flame.

Amid all this hubbub, Durand and Sergeant Robertson coolly uncoiled the hose—a cloth tube full of powder—which was attached to the lowest bag of powder, and which, once again by the merest accident, proved long enough to reach to the sally-port, where both of them took shelter. Fortunate it was for them, for the Afghans by this time had leaped on to the parapet, and were not only shooting straight down to the foot of the wall but hurling bricks, stones and every kind of missile also; and, by a strange fatality, Durand and his sergeant only with difficulty and delay were able to kindle the slow-match. At last it burned steadily, and the two slunk away to be out of reach of the explosion.

Meanwhile Peat, fearing that both of them had been killed—as but for the length of the hose and the shelter of the sally-port they must have been—came up to see what had happened, when the whole charge exploded, throwing him down so violently as for a time to stun him. Recovering himself, with superb coolness he went into the gateway to see if it were clear, but failed to perceive the sky through it, and before he could make closer examination, he was driven out by swordsmen. Durand, confident that the gate must have been demolished, tried to find a bugler to sound the advance; but Peat's own bugler had been killed, and Durand asked in vain for one from the nearest parties of infantry. In despair he hastened to the storming column, but tripped and fell so heavily over a grave of masonry that, being weak from illness, he could hardly move when he rose. Now fortunately he met a brother engineer, Broadfoot, who had been sent forward by Thomson; and Broadfoot, hearing from him that all was well, hurried back to Dennie, who at once led forward his four companies to the gate.

Meanwhile Peat, staggering back towards the main column, had collapsed on the way, and, being there found by Thomson, reported that he had been unable to see daylight through the gateway. Sale, who was close by, overheard the conversation, and, before Thomson could correct him on the strength of Broadfoot's report, ordered his bugler to sound the retire. The call was caught up by the whole length of the column in rear, and Keane, in deep anxiety, sent an *aide-de-camp* to ascertain the cause. Before this messenger had gone far, however, Thomson had made Sale understand his mistake; the bugles sounded the advance, and the main column rushed on.

By that time Dennie's four companies were practically masters of the place, and Sale on entering the gate met the full tide of fugitives from Dennie's bayonets. In the first rush these desperate men checked the main column for a few minutes. Sale himself was overthrown and only narrowly escaped with his life. But the men quickly recovered themselves and pressed on; the reserve followed them; and, though there was still some little resistance from a few brave and resolute men, it was easily overcome. In a very short time city and citadel alike were in the hands of the assailants, and Ghazni, by native tradition impregnable, had fallen.

The casualties did not exceed seventeen killed and one hundred and sixty-five, including eighteen officers, wounded. The brunt of the loss naturally fell upon the British, and chiefly upon the few companies of the storming-party; the light company of the Hundred and Second counting four officers and twenty-seven wounded out of sixty-two of all ranks present. But the truth is that as soon as the red-coats were fairly inside the fortress, resistance, as usual, collapsed; and if Sale had not been so hasty in sounding the retreat—a proceeding which seems absolutely unpardonable—but had followed the storming-party up closely, the success would have been even less costly than it was.

However, Dennie had given great offence to Keane at Shikarpur by protesting against the withdrawal of his transport for the Bombay division; and Keane, who seems to have been very remote from an amiable character, gave, in his official despatch, all the credit to Sale. He magnified the exploit to the utmost, devoting to it many more words than Wellington had found sufficient to describe the Waterloo campaign; and Sir Robert Peel, later on, characterised it as "the most brilliant achievement of our arms in Asia." Allowance must be made for the enthusiasm as well as for the ignorance of politicians when they speak of military matters, but this eulogy is quite ridiculous. The British had been accustomed to walk into Indian fortresses as a matter of course for more than a century and a half; and before Bhurtpore alone had they recoiled in permanent defeat. Only for the weary march of twelve hundred miles that preceded it did the storming of Ghazni deserve commemoration by a medal.

None the less, it is not pleasant to contemplate the probable fate of Keane's army if the attack had failed; and he deserves credit at least for the promptitude with which he accepted the risk of what certainly seemed a desperate venture. On the whole, accidents turned in his favour. The shameful indiscretion whereby Macnaghten imperilled the success of the enterprise actually turned to Keane's advantage by kindling a false alarm among the garrison on the night of the 21st, and lulling them into a false security on that of the 22nd. There was good luck, too, in the facilities, unforeseen in any way, which the engineers found ready to their hand when preparing to blow up the gate.

On the other hand, the precipitate and wholly unjustifiable retreat of Sale might have wrecked everything; but this is only the first of many instances in which Sale, notwithstanding his general reputation as a hero, showed himself a thoroughly bad officer. We may sum up the whole incident by pronouncing that Keane was very fortunate in escaping, with a blaze of triumph, the consequences of his gross blunder in leaving his siege-guns at Kandahar. The storm of Ghazni cannot excuse him for deliberately and unnecessarily hazarding disaster to his army, and therewith the stability of British rule in India.

CHAPTER 3

The British Enter Kabul

The capture of Ghazni, (July 1839), to all outward appearance, accomplished the object of the British expedition at a stroke. Afzul Khan, son of Dost Mohamed, who was in command of the Afghan troops that had menaced Keane on the morning of the 22nd, took to flight immediately upon hearing of the fall of the fortress, abandoning his elephants and camp-equipage. Within twenty-four hours Dost Mohamed himself received the news at Kabul, and took his measures for the defence of the capital. By an extremely fortunate coincidence Colonel Wade, with his native levies and Sikh allies, had advanced from Jamrud to enter the Khyber Pass on the very day of the assault on Ghazni. He had at first made no very great progress, not mastering Ali Masjid, the key of the defile, until the 25th, at a cost, during the three days, of some two hundred casualties. Dost Mohamed's main army, under his son Akbar Khan, was prepared to resist Wade further within the pass; but, after the fall of Ghazni, Akbar Khan received orders from his father to evacuate Jalalabad, and fall back at once upon Kabul, leaving Wade free to pursue his way through the defile unmolested.

On the 28th an emissary came in from Dost Mohamed to Ghazni tendering his submission to Shah Shuja on condition that he should hold the office, hereditary in his family, of chief adviser to the new sovereign. The proposal was at once rejected by Macnaghten, who would grant no more favourable terms than "honourable asylum in the British dominions," or, in other words, dignified captivity in India. The Afghan negotiator, refusing even to listen to such a suggestion, took his leave and rode back to Kabul, where Dost Mohamed, having his army by that time under his hand, took up a position at Argandeh, a few miles to west of the city and astride the road from Ghazni.

Keane, meanwhile, halted for a week after his success; and, since the fortress was found to be fully provisioned for a siege, was relieved of further anxiety as to supplies. The troops actually received full rations; and, heartened by this unwonted luxury, they marched on the 30th for Kabul, the Bengal division leading, and the Bombay force and Shah Shuja's contingent following one day in rear.

On the 1st of August Keane reached Haidar Khel; and here came to him the momentous news that Ranjit Singh had died on the 27th of July. On the 3rd he halted at Sheikhabad to allow the rear to close up, where he received authentic tidings that Dost Mohamed had fled from Kabul, heading westward over the mountains for Bamian. Treachery had shown itself in the Afghan chief's camp; and, after a lofty but vain appeal to his perfidious followers, he had dismissed them with contempt and ridden off with a handful of true men to await better times.

Keane at once sent a party of native horse, with twelve British officers under the supreme command of Outram, in pursuit. Beyond doubt these would have overtaken and captured the fugitive Amir, had they not been thwarted continually by the wiles of a traitorous guide; but on reaching Bamian on the 9th of August, they found that their quarry was thirty miles ahead of them, and were fain to abandon further chase.

Keane, meanwhile, had at once pushed a detachment of cavalry upon Kabul; and on reaching Maidan on the 4th, these found large numbers of Afghans drawn up to salute Shah Shuja. Another day brought him to Argandeh, where Dost Mohamed's guns, twenty-three in number, lay still in position but abandoned; on the 6th August the army encamped three miles west of Kabul; and on the 7th Shah Shuja made his formal entry into the city. Vast crowds were present to witness the spectacle, but there was no demonstration of welcome, much less of enthusiasm. There, for the present, he was established on the throne of Afghanistan. The British troops, after a weary march of fifteen hundred miles, had reached their goal at last; and Keane could assume with some justification that the object of their enterprise had been attained. (*I.O.S.C.*, vol. 9 of 1839, Keane to Auckland, Aug. 8, 1839).

Food was abundant and cheap at Kabul; and, both troops and followers being at last properly nourished, matters became more cheerful. On the 3rd of September Wade's column, escorting the Shahzada Timur, after a bloodless march from Ali Masjid through the Khyber

Pass, entered the city with pomp and display; and on the 17th Shah Shuja held a durbar, which all British officers off duty were required to attend. The poor creature, at the instance, presumably, of Macnaghten, but certainly of some member of the British mission, had been persuaded to institute an order of the Durani Empire, graduated, like the Order of the Bath, into three classes; and this distinction he was pleased to bestow upon some sixty officers of all ranks from the commander-in-chief to the subaltern. It is humiliating to record that many welcomed the grant of this miserable bauble, while not a few took offence because it had been denied to them. For the rest, the British officers, as is their wont, got up a race-meeting which lasted for five days; and so lightly passed the first six weeks of the army's stay at Kabul.

Auckland in his manifesto, published before the war, had pledged himself that when once Shah Shuja had been secured in power, and the independence and integrity of Afghanistan had been established, the British should be withdrawn. According to the reports of Macnaghten, Shah Shuja was a mild, humane, intelligent, just and firm man, whose only faults were a pride that made him pompous and inaccessible, and parsimony, which is seldom an endearing virtue. Moreover, his reception by the Afghans at Kabul had been, if the same authority were to be believed, "with feelings nearly amounting to adoration." (*I.O.S.C.*, vol. 10 of 1839, Macnaghten to Indian government, June 6, 1839; Durand).

This being so, the obvious conclusion would have seemed to be that the British should presently evacuate Afghanistan. The *Shah* had his own disciplined force, well armed, under British officers; the occupation of Kabul, Ghazni and Kandahar gave him a very firm hold on the country; and the not remote approach of winter, which practically forbade all armed unrest, promised him time to conciliate the most powerful of the subordinate chieftains. For the *amir* was not and could never be an absolute autocrat. He was rather the head of a group of semi-independent nobles, of a proud and turbulent aristocracy, which could only be kept in loyalty and obedience by a mixture of tact, firmness and, at times, ruthless severity. Whether Shah Shuja possessed this rare combination of gifts was another question; but if, as Macnaghten averred, he were both able and popular, then the sooner that he were left to stand by himself the better.

One thing at least was certain—that he could not be supported for ever by British bayonets. The number of troops required for effective military occupation of Afghanistan was far greater than India could spare, for not only was anarchy in the Punjab inevitable, now that Ranjit Singh was dead, but the state of affairs both in Nepal and in Burma was by no means free from menace. Again, communication with Afghanistan was both difficult and uncertain, looking to the doubtful friendship of both Sikhs and Sindians and the assurance of attack upon all convoys by the wild, plundering tribes of the mountains.

Lastly, the cost would be prohibitive and the waste necessarily enormous. Left to himself at once, Shah Shuja might possibly maintain his rule unaided. But, if he leaned wholly on the British battalions, and governed wholly by the advice of a British envoy who knew nothing of the country and of the people, then it was certain that his rule would be hateful to the Afghans, that his popularity, if it existed at all, would be short-lived, that if British troops remained in the country they must be too few to repress a general insurrection, and that when they were withdrawn, as sooner or later they must be, the whole fabric of Shah Shuja's domination must come down with a crash.

Macnaghten, however, could not or would not perceive these things. Over many good and commendable qualities his vanity and visionary ambition reigned supreme. Practically, he felt himself a king, and a king with an armed force under his command; and an armed force was to him a plaything as irresistible as is his first pocket-knife to a schoolboy. The whole of Central Asia lay before him with unknown possibilities, and even provocations, that he should do great things. At Herat, as has been already told, there had been a rupture between the British residents and the principal minister, Yar Mohamed, at the end of 1838; and though Pottinger, the chief resident, was presently invited to return, the other member, Colonel Stoddart, had proceeded on a mission to Bukhara.

It was not long before Pottinger was again insulted; and Yar Mohamed began then to intrigue both with Persia and with the Afghans of Kandahar. The British occupation of Kandahar, however, had so wrought upon him that he had sent a friendly mission to Macnaghten while the army was halted there. Thereupon Macnaghten had despatched a new envoy to Herat in the person of Major Todd, (May 15), with instructions to negotiate a subsidiary treaty of the usual kind, and to offer money, of which Yar Mohamed was prepared to absorb any amount, in furtherance of the same. But Yar Mohamed was not to be trusted; and Macnaghten was never quite free from the idea that a garrison ought to be sent to Herat to secure it against Persian aggression. (*I.O.S.C.*, vol. 9 of 1839, Macnaghten to E. Pottinger, May 3; to Todd, May 15, 1839).

Next, there was the question of Kalat. As to this, Macnaghten had made up his mind on the march from Kandahar to Ghazni. The political agents agreed with one accord that Mehrab Khan was responsible for the innumerable robberies, murders and raids suffered by the British on the march from Shikarpur and Quetta, and Macnaghten decreed that he should be punished by the annexation of Shawal, Mastung and Kach Gandava (or in other words, of most of the country west of a line drawn from Shikarpur to Quetta), to the dominions of Shah Shuja, and that, unless he came to Kabul to pay homage to the *Shah*, he should be deposed. The enforcement of this measure, if necessary, could be left to any troops that might be returning to the Indus; but the annexation would, of course, widen the bounds of Macnaghten's own dominion as adviser to the *Shah*. (*I.O.S.C.*, vol. 12 of 1839, Macnaghten to Indian government, July 6, 1839; Ross-Bell to *ditto*, Aug. 31, 1839).

This, however, was a small matter compared to three events which turned Macnaghten's eye in deep apprehension towards the Oxus. In the first place, Colonel Stoddart had been imprisoned at Bukhara upon his arrival there in December, 1838, and some measures must be taken not only to effect his release, but to vindicate the insulted honour of Britain. Next, Dost Mohamed himself had fled in that direction, and the neighbouring chieftains must be stirred up against him and warned against harbouring him. Lastly, it was reported by Pottinger from Herat that a Russian force was assembling at Orenburg for a march upon Khiva; and this might mean a Russian advance upon Turkestan or upon Herat.

Indeed the British *chargé d'affaires* at Erzeroum had written to Palmerston that a Russian occupation of Khiva would be a deep injury to England, and would bring Bukhara, Balkh, Badakshan, and the whole line of the Oxus under Russian domination, thus drawing British and Russian territories so close together that the Hindu Kush would become the natural boundary between Russia and Afghanistan. Altogether the peril to the newly-won realm of Shah Shuja seemed to be great upon every side, and Macnaghten, as envoy and minister to that forlorn potentate, could not but accept the responsibility also of guardian and protector. (I.O.S.C., vol. 14 of 1839, Justin Skeil to Palmerston, July 17; Macnaghten to Indian Government, Aug. 24,

1839. The first news as to the Russian advance came in a letter from Pottinger at Herat, July 2, 1839).

In the circumstances, Macnaghten and Keane decided that upon military and political grounds a brigade of regular British troops should be kept at Kabul, and detachments at Kandahar and Mastung, while the *Shah's* troops should hold Ghazni and Girishk; allowing three battalions of Bengal infantry, three of cavalry, and the whole of the Bombay troops to return to India. This was approved by Auckland upon the condition that Nott should command the troops at Kandahar, Quetta and Mastung. The Governor-general judged Kandahar to be the most important military post in Afghanistan, and, though Keane had humiliated and disparaged Nott, he himself recognised Nott as a strong and capable officer.

This was the more creditable to Auckland since Nott was a cantankerous man who abhorred political agents and all their ways, and was, on that account, naturally unacceptable to the circle dominated by Macnaghten. Had Auckland possessed the strength to follow his instincts, he might, as shall be seen, have averted many evils; but at least he insisted that the line from Quetta to Kandahar be under the control of Nott. (*I.O.S.C.*, vol. 13 of 1839, Keane and Macnaghten to Auckland, Aug. 24; Auckland to Keane and Macnaghten, Sept. 12, 1839).

This arrangement as to the troops had hardly been decided before it was overset. Macnaghten, being now practically in supreme control of all affairs, was obliged to scatter his political agents far and wide, in order to carry out his policy and to keep him in touch with the march of events all over the dominions, real or nominal, of Shah Shuja. The first thing to be done was to drive Dost Mohamed as far as possible from the border; and to this end Macnaghten borrowed Dr. Lord, a medical officer attached to Wade's staff, and sent him on a mission to Morad Beg, chief of Kunduz. Lord was instructed to intimate that, in a general way, Morad Beg might feel assured of peaceable retention of his territory, but that, if he allowed Dost Mohamed to remain in or near them, Shah Shuja's army might be compelled to march into Kunduz to expel the dethroned Amir by force, in which case the *Shah's* officers might find it hard to distinguish friends from foes.

It is somewhat singular that the political agents, who were always trying to conciliate robbers and marauders on the line of march by bribes, leniency and soft words, were very free with threats to the rulers of neighbouring states; and it is still more remarkable that the governor-general should have encouraged them in this policy. (*I.O.S.C.,* vol. 14 of 1839, Macnaghten to Indian government, Aug. 25; Auckland to Macnaghten, Sept. 19, 1839).

Lord started accordingly, but, when still within thirty-six miles of Kabul, returned hastily with the report that all the country before him was in rebellion, and that Dost Mohamed, with all the peoples west of the Hindu Kush at his back, was marching to the reconquest of his kingdom. The whole story was a fiction invented by Lord's Afghan escort, who felt disinclined to the hardship of facing the mountain-passes at a time when the snow of an early winter had already begun to fall; and Macnaghten, when he discovered this, was somewhat annoyed. But Lord, when he set out again, made amends for this little lapse. He boldly pressed for the re-annexation of all the country between the Hindu Kush and the Oxus to the kingdom of Kabul, an enterprise which even Macnaghten hesitated to undertake without reference to the governor-general.

When, however, Lord, having arrived at Bamian, declared that Khulm had been made a focus of agitation by Dost Mohamed and that it was essential at once to push troops on thither, within fifty miles of the Oxus, Macnaghten readily opened his ears. His idea was to send two battalions of Bengal native infantry and a regiment of native horse to Khulm, whence they should pursue Dost Mohamed, liberate Stoddart from Bukhara, forestall the Russian battalions on the Oxus, and make themselves, in a word, generally useful in forwarding Macnaghten's wild schemes. It is said that when he submitted this plan to Keane, the general would not trust himself to write his answer, but sent a verbal message declining to have anything to do with it, (Durand).

Later, however, he did condescend to give Macnaghten some reasons. Without mentioning that it was a serious operation to penetrate some fifty miles of mountain-range by passes rising to ten thousand feet and more above the sea, he pointed out that those passes would be open for only two months longer, and that any troops sent over them would be isolated for six or eight months, without any certainty of being fed, since it was impossible at the moment to send victuals for that period with them. He also objected to despatching British troops over the Hindu Kush at all, stating that the *shah's* troops, if any, were those that should undertake the duty; and finally he contended that if it were absolutely necessary for British troops to go so far north, they must wait until the following spring, and then march in respectable strength. (*I.O.S.C.*, vol. 15 of 1839, Macnaghten to Indian government, Sept. 3; vol. 1 of 1840, Macnaghten to Keane and Keane to Macnaghten, Sept. 29, 1839).

Macnaghten, however, was not to be defrauded of his military experiments by any such considerations as these. By alarming Keane with the spectre of Dost Mohamed, he obtained his consent to the detention of the whole of the Bengal division in Afghanistan, and then set about a little operation of his own. If he could not push British troops on to Khulm, he could at any rate order some of the Shah's contingent to join Lord at Bamian; and accordingly, on the 10th of September, he issued instructions to Captain Hay to march for that place on the morrow with one of the *Shah's* Gurkha regiments, two hundred of the *Shah's* horse, three thousand irregulars and a troop of Bengal horse artillery, and on arriving at his destination to place himself under the orders of Lord. As the route prescribed to him included the traversing of two passes, each over twelve thousand feet above the sea, an officer suggested two days' delay to await the return of an engineer who had been sent to report upon it; to which Macnaghten replied loftily that he did not like the raising of difficulties. After this it was hard to put forward any further objection.

Hay's detachment at Bamian was supposed to depend upon Kabul for its supplies, although the passes would be closed by snow during the winter months, already not far off; but if Macnaghten chose to believe that they would be open, there was nothing more to be said. So Hay marched on the 11th, as the great Macnaghten had ordained, and after a month of desperate toiling and fatigue covered the hundred miles to Bamian, in order, as an officer, then at Kabul, has recorded, "to lodge an excellent battery of artillery in a place where it could not be of any use." (*I.O.S.C.,* vol. 15 of 1839, Macnaghten to Hay, Sept. 10, 1839).

Having thus taken his measures to "drive Dost Mohamed beyond the Oxus"—for in this light Hay's march was represented to Auckland, and not only accepted but heartily approved by him, (*I.O.S.C.*, vol. 15 of 1839, Auckland to Macnaghten, Oct. 30, 1839)—Macnaghten turned his mind to the castigation of the principal offenders who had, or were asserted to have, impeded the progress of the army from the Indus to Kabul. Sept. The first and less important of these were certain refractory Ghilzai chiefs between Ghazni and Kandahar, against whom Outram marched from Kabul on the 7th of September with a mixed force of the Shah's contingent and Abbott's field-battery.

The second and great culprit was Mehrab Khan of Kalat. The original idea had been to entrust the attack upon him to Nott, then commandant at Quetta, whose force had by this time been increased to three native battalions, a few troops of cavalry and sixteen guns; and Nott had made every preparation for it. But this plan was overset by Macnaghten and Keane, who appointed General Willshire and the Bombay division to deal with Mehrab Khan on their homeward march to the Indus, (Stocqueler, *Life of Sir William Nott*, i.).

Leaving Kabul on the 18th of September, Willshire marched by way of Ghazni and thence by a new route due south, (2 squadrons. H.M. 4th L.D.; det. 1st Bombay L.C.; 4th Local Horse; 2 troops of Horse Artillery; 1 field-battery; H.M. Queen's; H.M. 17th Foot; 31st Bengal N.I.). On the 8th of October he approached the country in the vicinity of Lake Ab-i-Istadu, where Outram was conducting his operations against the Ghilzais, and left with Outram a small detachment of all three arms. From this day forward the two worked more or less together against the Ghilzais, and on the 31st the troops of both marched into Quetta.

Nott, fortunately, was no longer there. On the 13th he had received an intimation from Keane that he was to place his troops under Willshire's orders for the expedition against Kalat; and being a substantive major-general, whereas Willshire held only local rank, he had written a violent letter flatly declining to take any orders from Willshire. Had he been still at Quetta on the 31st, it is certain that, if any critical situation had arisen, he would not have co-operated heartily with Willshire, having already a grievance against Keane, and being encouraged in recalcitrance by a sympathetic political officer, (Stocqueler, *Life of Sir William Nott*, i.). However, on the 25th he had received a second message from Keane, bidding him move to Kandahar forthwith with half of his brigade, and, having marched on the 26th, he was safely out of the way.

Arrived at Quetta, Willshire found the place absolutely bare. Nott had in fact been greatly neglected. Though winter was approaching, there was no material to build huts for the troops, no straw for their bedding and very little fuel. There were no shoes to replace those worn out in service, no medical stores and no spare ammunition. Lastly, forage was so scarce that the camels, with their escorts, had to travel afield twelve miles to graze. In the circumstances, Willshire decided to send his cavalry and much of his artillery straight back through the Bolan Pass to Gandava, keeping only his three weak battalions, six horse-artillery guns and a detachment of irregular horse for the march on Kalat. On the 4th of November he set out, striking south-westward by way of Mastung, and by the 11th he was within two marches of his destination. A message had been sent beforehand to Mehrab Khan setting forth the terms upon which his submission would be accepted, and he had answered with defiance. In fact, he had called upon Willshire either to halt, pending further negotiations, or to meet him and his tribesmen in full force on the field of battle.

On the 12th Outram, who had now joined Willshire's force as a volunteer, led out an advanced party which struck against the enemy's vedettes; but the progress of the main body was practically unopposed, and on the 13th the column came within sight of Kalat about a mile away. The enemy's cannon opened fire; and upon reconnaissance, Willshire perceived that three hills to the north-west of the fortress were crowded with hostile infantry, which were sheltered by three redoubts and supported by five guns in position behind breastworks. Halting the column until the baggage had closed up, Willshire placed the latter under guard of his irregular horse, meanwhile clearing some gardens on his left and dispersing, with a few rounds of shrapnel, a body of hostile cavalry which was hovering in the same direction. He then formed three columns of attack, each of four companies, from the Queen's on the left, the Seventeenth in the centre, and the Thirty-First Bengal Native Infantry on the right, which were to assault the three redoubts, and, if possible, to enter the fortress on the backs of the fugitives. Willshire had about a thousand bayonets, and the Baluchis altogether numbered about twice as many; but it never occurred to him to hesitate in storming Kalat out of hand in broad daylight.

All was soon ready. The guns were unlimbered in rear of the centre; the reserve was formed in rear of them, and presently the little six-pounders opened a very accurate fire of shrapnel at a range of about seven hundred yards. The assaulting columns advanced steadily, and so searching was the practice of the guns that the enemy, unable to bear it, retired to the fortress, endeavouring to drag their cannon with them. Willshire thereupon ordered the Queen's and Seventeenth to make a rush for the Kandahar Gate, at the northern angle, and to enter it, if possible, with the enemy. The rush was duly made, but the enemy made haste to abandon the guns and to secure the gate; whereupon Willshire brought up two companies from the garden towards the same gate, and bade the assaulting columns take such cover behind walls and ruined buildings as they could, until the artillery could ad-

Storming of Kalat

vance. The battery was soon at the crest of the heights, and unlimbered in three divisions along the northern face of the fort.

A few rounds sufficed to blow in half of the Kandahar Gate; the storming columns dashed in despite of a gallant resistance by the defenders; and Willshire sent a detachment of his reserve round the western face of the fort to secure the heights on the southern side and cut off all retreat. These troops managed to enter the southern gate before the enemy could fasten it; and then the whole assaulted the citadel, where Mehrab Khan was leading the defence most bravely, sword in hand. He was overpowered and slain; and though isolated parties in isolated buildings held out until late in the afternoon, the enemy lost heart at length, and surrendered on condition that their lives should be spared. But the fate of Kalat had been sealed within two hours of the firing of the first shot.

This was a smart little affair, which cost Willshire thirty-one killed and one hundred and seven wounded, twenty-two of the former and forty-seven of the latter belonging to the Queen's. As this battalion numbered no more than two hundred bayonets, it may be said to have suffered heavily; and indeed, being exposed to a very sharp fire with very little shelter in the interval between the first rush to the walls and the blowing in of the gates, it underwent a trial which might have been too hard for a native regiment. On the whole the capture of Kalat was a more brilliant little success than that of Ghazni, where the number of men engaged was four times as great and the casualties only fifty more; though neither is really worth commemoration on regimental colours.

Having sent Outram to bear the news of his success to Bombay, Willshire returned by way of the Gandava pass and arrived at Larkhana on the 18th of December. His cavalry, meanwhile, had traversed the Bolan Pass without molestation, but upon emerging from it found cholera raging at Bagh, and lost nearly sixty of its European soldiers before, on the 30th of November, it reached the Indus. A week after his arrival at Larkhana Willshire received orders to break up his division, which henceforward disappears from the main scene of operations.

Thus the question of Kalat was, for the time being, settled; and the provinces of Shawal, Mastung and Kachhi were thereupon annexed to Shah Shuja's dominions. Having so dealt with foreign affairs to north and south, Macnaghten was at liberty to turn his attention to domestic matters. He had already blamed Shah Shuja's haughty bearing towards

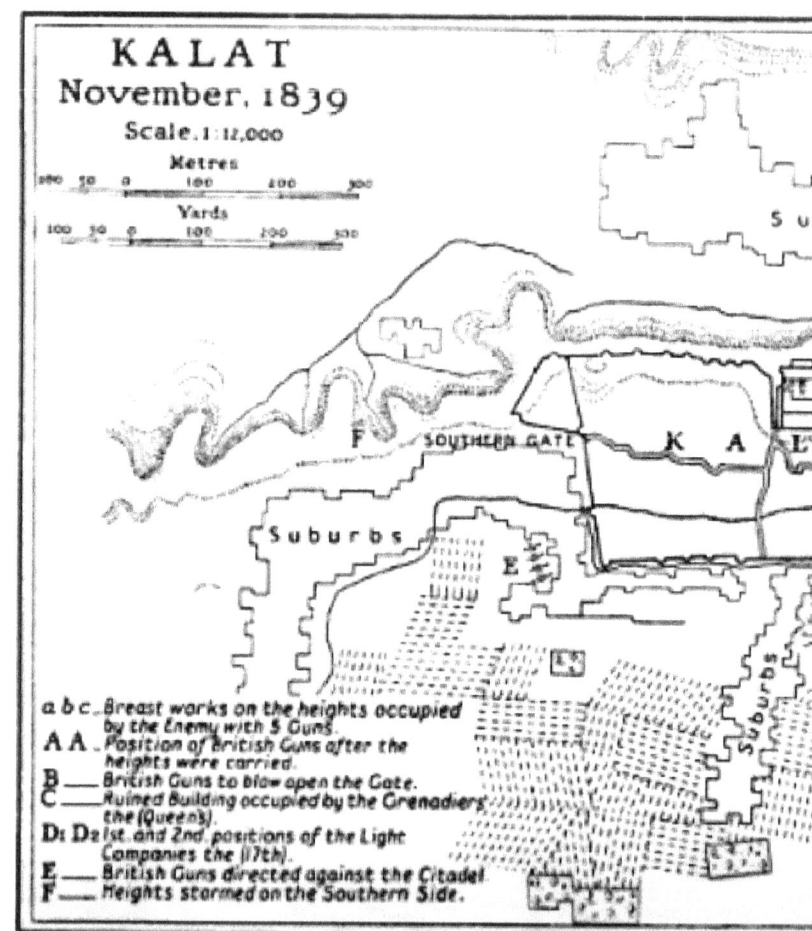

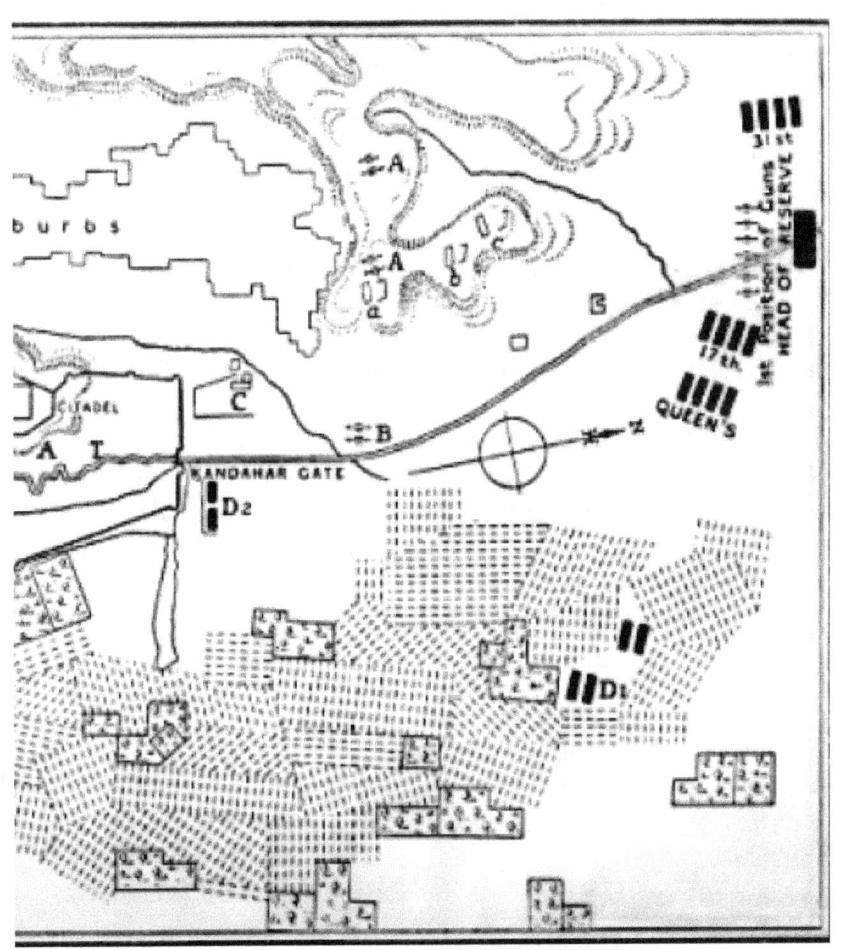

the Afghan nobles, and trusted that it might be replaced by greater condescension. Instead, however, of pursuing a policy of conciliation towards them, Macnaghten sought to repress them by raising levies of various tribes, which, as they were to be under the supervision of British officers and paid by the royal treasury, would, as he fondly supposed, be devoted to the *Shah's* cause. Thereby he alienated the nobles without gaining the attachment of the levies, who disliked the rigour of British discipline and were offended by subordination to foreign and *infidel* officers. This was in fact an experiment so dangerous that only an administrative pedant, wholly ignorant of the people with whom he was dealing, would have ventured upon it; for, whereas the weakness of the nobles was that they were at perpetual feud with one another, this oppressive measure tended to unite them in resentment against a common grievance.

To pay these mercenary levies it was of course necessary to raise money; and here Macnaghten, in his endeavour to prove that Shah Shuja was a king and no puppet, made a very fatal division of administrative authority. He left to the *Shah* the entire business of civil and criminal justice, and of the settlement, collection and appropriation of the revenue, but kept all that related to foreign affairs, and to independent or revolted chieftains, in his own hands. Above all, he retained supreme command of the *Shah's* armed force; and he alone ordered expeditions, settled the strength of detachments and gave instructions to their commanders as to what they were expected to do, and how they were expected to do it. To all intent, therefore, he gave the Shah all the powers of government except the employment of the police; with the result that the *Shah* was free to squander money upon favourites and to exert or authorise oppression as he wished, while the British, represented by Macnaghten, having alone power to enforce his will, had to bear the odium of his acts. The whole arrangement, in fact, was contrived to make both the *Shah* and the British as distasteful to the Afghans as possible, and to render the puppet only less odious to them than the power that pulled the strings.

There was another matter which kindled among the chiefs a burning hatred. Macnaghten sent for Lady Macnaghten to join him, and some military officers did likewise; but not a few of the British were better content to set up domestic establishments of a different kind in Kabul. The Afghan ladies, who pride themselves upon being fair, were, owing to other peculiar circumstances, very far from being inexorable to the strangers; and the fact was very quickly discovered. Burnes, in fact, during his first mission had given considerable offence by taking advantage of this failing; and, as he had not changed his character before his second visit to Kabul, his example was very readily followed. There was therefore great demand for houses in the capital; and the Shah confiscated and gave away the dwellings of absent nobles right and left, without a shred of compunction or a thought of the future. Already in the autumn there was hidden, but none the less perilous, fury in the city; and Keane, himself not the most delicate of men, was shrewd enough to note it. (Authority for last three paragraphs, Durand; *From Sepoy to Subadar*)

He said to Durand, who was returning to India:

> I cannot but congratulate you on quitting the country, for, mark my words, it will not be long before there is here some signal catastrophe.

While thus provoking the wrath of every class of the Afghans, Macnaghten took long before he would decide where the British troops at Kabul were to be lodged for the winter. The engineer, Durand, to whom the choice of a suitable place had been mainly committed, was strong for the military occupation of the Bala Hissar, or upper fort, which commanded the city, and whereof the citadel, if placed in a proper state of defence with a garrison of a thousand men and a few guns, could defy all the power of Afghanistan.

The *Shah*, however, upon various pretexts, objected, and Macnaghten, while recognising the absurdity of the *Shah's* arguments, weakly gave way. Durand then appealed to Sale, who was to command the garrison at Kabul, and pointed out that, while it would be impossible to construct barracks outside the Bala Hissar before winter, there was cover enough within it to make the construction of good quarters easy. In the face of Sale's representations, the *Shah* reluctantly yielded, and Durand at once set to work to make the citadel impregnable. But again the *Shah* intervened, alleging that the measure would make him unpopular, and again the foolish Macnaghten bowed to his will.

Durand then proposed that Macnaghten, who occupied two houses of Dost Mohamed within the Bala Hissar, should give them up to the European troops, since the envoy was intending to spend the winter with the *Shah* in the milder climate of Jalalabad. But Macnaghten had no idea of sacrificing his own importance and his private comfort for so trivial a public purpose as the lodging of a mere battalion of the line, and rejected the proposal with displeasure. Durand, therefore, suggested that the native troops should be housed in the *Shah's* stables, and the Thirteenth under temporary cover upon adjoining ground; and so the matter was arranged, Durand flattering himself that, once the troops were settled somewhere in the Bala Hissar, the repair and occupation of the citadel would follow as a matter of course. He reckoned without the vacillation of Macnaghten, though for the present the envoy was in full accord with his projects. Macnaghten's political designs for the government of Afghanistan were fatuous to the last degree, but his mistakes, if they showed him to have little insight or common sense, reflected no evil on his character. In the matter of the occupation of the Bala Hissar, however, he deliberately sinned against such poor light as was in him, (Durand).

So the autumn wore on. October came, and with it the time approached for Keane to withdraw from Kabul, with such few troops of the Bengal division as were not to remain in Afghanistan. This raised immediately the question as to his successor. Cotton was the officer next senior to Keane, who, together with Macnaghten, assumed as a matter of course that Cotton would take his place, and gave him instructions accordingly, emphasising the fact that Shah Shuja's army was absolutely under the envoy's command. The Indian government, however, went further and was careful to point out that Cotton's position and powers, now that the *Shah* was established on the throne, would be totally different from Keane's. The substance of the new instructions was as follows. The new commander-in-chief would be uncontrolled in the exercise of discipline and good order, but "the disposal and employment of the force would be under political direction."

The military authorities would, of course, be consulted in both matters; and "in the moving and cantonment of the troops, both military and political considerations would be attended to." It was therefore essential for the two departments to work cordially together, in respect not only of these points, but also of the employment of the troops in any military operations. As to these last, however, it was for the political officer to decide whether they should be undertaken, and for the Commander-in-chief to give his opinion whether they were practicable, and what would be the means required for their execution. As to the Shah's force, the envoy alone could be the channel for conveying to them the *Shah's* orders.

When the *Shah's*, Queen's and Company's troops were working together, the senior British officer was to command the whole; and the envoy would naturally communicate with him before issuing orders on the part of the *Shah*. But it should seem, though it is not expressly so stated, from the tenor of this last sentence that at any moment the envoy could overrule the orders given by any British commander to any of the *Shah's* contingent when actually in the field. (*I.O.S.C.*, vol. 1 of 1840, Indian government to Macnaghten, Oct. 28, 1839).

The purport of this astonishing document has been given at some length, because it contains within itself the explanation of all our disasters in Afghanistan. Keane had been more than a little hampered by the encroachment of the political agents upon his authority, and, under the stress of active operations, had actually thrown off a shackle or two which they had imposed upon him; but now when, according to Macnaghten's delusions, the sovereignty of Shah Shuja had been joyfully accepted in Afghanistan, and all was peace, the military commander-in-chief was deliberately shorn of all independent authority, and placed, together with his troops, under the heel of the civilian. How any self-respecting officer could have been content to accept the command upon such terms is not easy to understand; and indeed there seems to have been some difficulty about it.

Auckland himself had no doubt that, after Keane's departure, Nott was the right man to succeed him in command of all the troops in Afghanistan; and he went so far as to write privately to Cotton, urging him to return to India and take charge of the forces in the Upper Provinces. Cotton took the hint, left Kabul on the 16th of October, and had actually proceeded as far as Ali Masjid when he received a second letter from Auckland which, as he put it, seemed to leave him no alternative but to offer to remain where he was. He made his offer accordingly, which was readily accepted, and he presently returned as commander-in-chief in Afghanistan. (*I.O.S.C.*, vol. 2 of 1849, Keane and Macnaghten to Indian government, Oct. 14; Auckland to Keane, Nov. 4, 1839; vol. 8 of 1849, Keane to Auckland, Nov. 5, Nov. 6—enclosing letter from Cotton of Nov. 5—, Nov. 15; Auckland to Keane, Nov. 15, 1839).

The whole transaction is obscure, but Auckland's sudden change of mind as to replacing Cotton and keeping Nott in subordination to him admits of but one explanation—that Macnaghten was intent on holding the military commander in subjection to himself, and knew that Nott would not endure such a position.

★★★★★★

Many essential portions of the correspondence are, as usual, wanting in the minutes of the Supreme Council of India. The preceding paragraph shows how the letters concerning a single subject are scattered about whole volumes apart. In vol. 2 of 1849 it is recorded that Cotton is returning to India; in vol. 3, that he is conducting operations in Afghanistan; in vol. 4, that he has left Kabul, reached Peshawar and turned back to Kabul.

✶✶✶✶✶✶

Possibly he may have been influenced by Keane, who had treated Nott ill and therefore hated him; possibly one or other of the clever young men about Auckland may have warned him that Nott was a difficult man and not likely to brook interference; possibly Nott's refusal to take orders from Wiltshire may already have become known to the governor-general; by no possibility could the government of India have been unaware that Nott hated "political" with his whole soul. Be that as it may, Cotton was sent back to Kabul, and Nott was left as his inferior at Kandahar. Auckland made no more fatal blunder than this, which, tragically enough, was against his own better judgement.

✶✶✶✶✶✶

The following incident shows that Nott had good reason for his hatred. On October 23, 1839, the resident at Quetta, a certain Captain Bean, ordered Nott to march to Kalat with a battalion, some local horse and three guns. Nott flatly refused to do anything of the kind, giving conclusive military reasons. Thereupon Bean complained to his immediate superior, Ross-Bell, and to Macnaghten in the following terms: "The responsible position I hold and the power delegated to me authorise (in my humble opinion) my calling for the aid of troops to effect any measure that may appear to me to be of importance to the State, and in this case I consider I was acting according to the views of the Right Hon. The Governor-General." This is a good specimen of the pompous and inflated style in which young political captains set forth their pretensions to give orders to generals; and it is no wonder that the generals found it insufferable. There were many as foolish and self-important as Bean, and there were some even worse. (*I.O.S.C.*, vol. 3 of 1840, Bean to Nott, Oct. 23; Nott to Bean, Oct. 24, etc., 1839.)

✶✶✶✶✶✶

It had been arranged that Keane should leave Kabul on the 15th of October, making his return journey through the Khyber Pass, from the mouth of which the Sikhs had agreed to give his troops free transit across the Punjab. His force consisted chiefly of cavalry—the Sixteenth Lancers, Third Bengal Light Cavalry and a battery of horse-artillery—with no more infantry than two companies of sappers and miners and four of *sepoys*, besides invalids and drafts, both European and Indian; and it was expected that there would be no trouble with the tribesmen on the march. The Khyberris, indeed, were friendly to Shah Shuja, having helped him in the past, and welcomed his return; and the *Shah*, without consulting Macnaghten, had in gratitude promised them the handsomest scale of the blackmail which was paid by all *amirs* to these tribes for safe passage through their defile.

For the regular settlement of this matter the chiefs applied themselves to Wade, who had left Kabul on his return to Peshawar on the 5th of October; but Wade, having no instructions from Macnaghten, referred them to Captain Mackeson, a political officer, who, he said, would meet them at the eastern mouth of the pass and there arrange everything. Having seen Wade advance to Kabul at the head of an armed force with the Shahzada Timur under his protection, the chiefs took it ill that the satisfaction of their demands should be delayed and turned over to an inferior officer; and therewith they resolved to seize Ali Masjid and to close all traffic through the pass.

The garrison of Ali Masjid consisted of two companies of *sepoys*, reduced by sickness to five men fit for duty, and some irregular infantry, most of whom were in an outlying post which was in every way an ill-chosen position. Upon these last unfortunate isolated men the Khyberris descended, swept them away, despite of a stout resistance, with a loss of three hundred killed and wounded, and then assaulted Ali Masjid. They were beaten back, however; and then, hearing of the approach of Keane, they hastened away to a safe distance. Keane duly approached with a vast train of baggage, which, being loaded on bullock-carts and worn-out camels, crept slowly and painfully in a long straggling line through the defile, and offered an easy prey to the tribesmen had they dared to attack.

But they were awed by the fame of the conqueror of Ghazni and allowed him to pass unmolested to Ali Masjid, where he halted on the 3rd and 4th of November to allow his column to close up. Mackeson, meanwhile, had begun his negotiations with the tribesmen; but the subsidy tendered by Macnaghten fell short of that promised by Shah Shuja, and the Khyberris waited only for Keane to make his way to Peshawar, before they again closed in upon Ali Masjid. It was imperative to throw a supply of victuals and ammunition into the fort; but this seemed to be no very difficult matter, for Keane was at hand at the mouth of the pass, and Shah Shuja and Macnaghten had recently moved, with two battalions of British and two of Afghan troops, for the winter to Jalalabad.

On the 10th of November, therefore, Keane detached half of his *sepoys* and fifty sappers, with eight hundred Sikhs, lent by General Avitabile from Peshawar, in support, to escort a convoy of stores to Ali Masjid. The column reached its destination, after some slight skirmishing, on the 11th. On the following morning the Khyberris tried to drive off the British camels while at graze, and were pushed back by the detachment; but, as this was not effected until the afternoon, the commanding officer decided not to return until next day. Mackeson thereupon went out with the fifty sappers to inflict further punishment on the marauders, and had thrust them back some distance from camp, when it was observed that the commanding officer, without a word of warning, had set the main column on march to Peshawar.

With some difficulty the sappers fought their way back to the rear-guard, which was also engaged, and then the two together retired, fighting steadily, upon the support of the Sikhs, who were in position in the pass. The Sikhs, however, no sooner saw them retreating than they were seized with panic and took to their heels, firing blindly at their friends, at anything and at nothing, and stabbing the camels that obstructed their flight. The entire convoy was thrown into confusion. The rear-guard and sappers only with difficulty extricated themselves, and the detachment returned, with no greater casualties, indeed, than twenty two killed and wounded, but with the loss of over four hundred camels slain or carried off.

The tribesmen were naturally much encouraged by their success; and Keane judged it prudent to throw the whole of his infantry, except his sappers, into Ali Masjid until they could be relieved by troops from Jalalabad. The detachment marched accordingly on the 14th, overcame all resistance with little difficulty and occupied the fort; while Mackeson, arriving a few days later, renewed his negotiations with the tribesmen, who continued to beleaguer the post, and varied the monotony of the parleys by firing occasional shots into the British camp. Such was the state of affairs when Colonel Wheeler appeared upon the scene with two battalions from Jalalabad, and told Mackeson plainly that he would not endure such insulting behaviour on the part of the Khyberris but would attack them at once. This was just what was wanted at the moment, and Mackeson knew it; but having been charged by Macnaghten with the task of coaxing the tribesmen to complaisance, he obtained from Wheeler twenty-four hours' respite, and in the course of the night brought them to terms by promising an annual subsidy of £8000, or just four times more than Dost Mohamed had ever consented to pay.

Accordingly, on the 22nd, Keane's detachment marched for the last time for Peshawar, escorting, with the help of Wheeler's battalions, a convoy of two thousand camels. The sight of the animals was too much for the Khyberris. Forgetting the newly concluded treaty, they swooped down from two lateral ravines upon the main defile and carried off a large number of them. But they had reckoned without Wheeler, who drove them off with considerable loss and recovered every camel that had not been hamstrung.

The fact was that it was hopeless to think of controlling the Khyber Pass by payment of blackmail only, for the money was necessarily made over to the chiefs, who kept most of it for themselves and left their followers to indemnify themselves by plunder. The alternative was coercion, but for this there were not sufficient troops; and, moreover, both Macnaghten and Mackeson were anxious, if possible, not to resort to force, if they could by any other means secure safe communication through the pass, because the operations would be very difficult, their success rather doubtful, and their failure, if misfortune should overtake them, most detrimental. Altogether, Macnaghten's first experiment in the handling of the mountain-tribes was not very encouraging. (Durand; *I.O.S.C.*, vol. 3 of 1840, Keane to Auckland, Nov. 10, 1839; vol. 6 of 1840, Macnaghten to Indian government, Dec. 2, 1839; to Mackeson, Mar. 10, 1840; Mackeson to Macnaghten, Mar. 3, 1840).

However, Keane was now at last free to leave Peshawar with the few troops that had marched with him from Kabul to return to Bombay; and henceforward he disappears from this history. It is not easy to make a just summary of his work in a campaign which he had no share in planning, and hardly a full share in directing. His worst blunder was his failure to join the Bengal troops and take the command out of Cotton's hands at the earliest possible moment; and, though many have pointed this out, not one has attempted to account for it. He was so unpopular that if there were some scandalous reason for his clinging so long to the Bombay division, some or other of the narrators of the First Afghan War would certainly have hinted at it; but I can

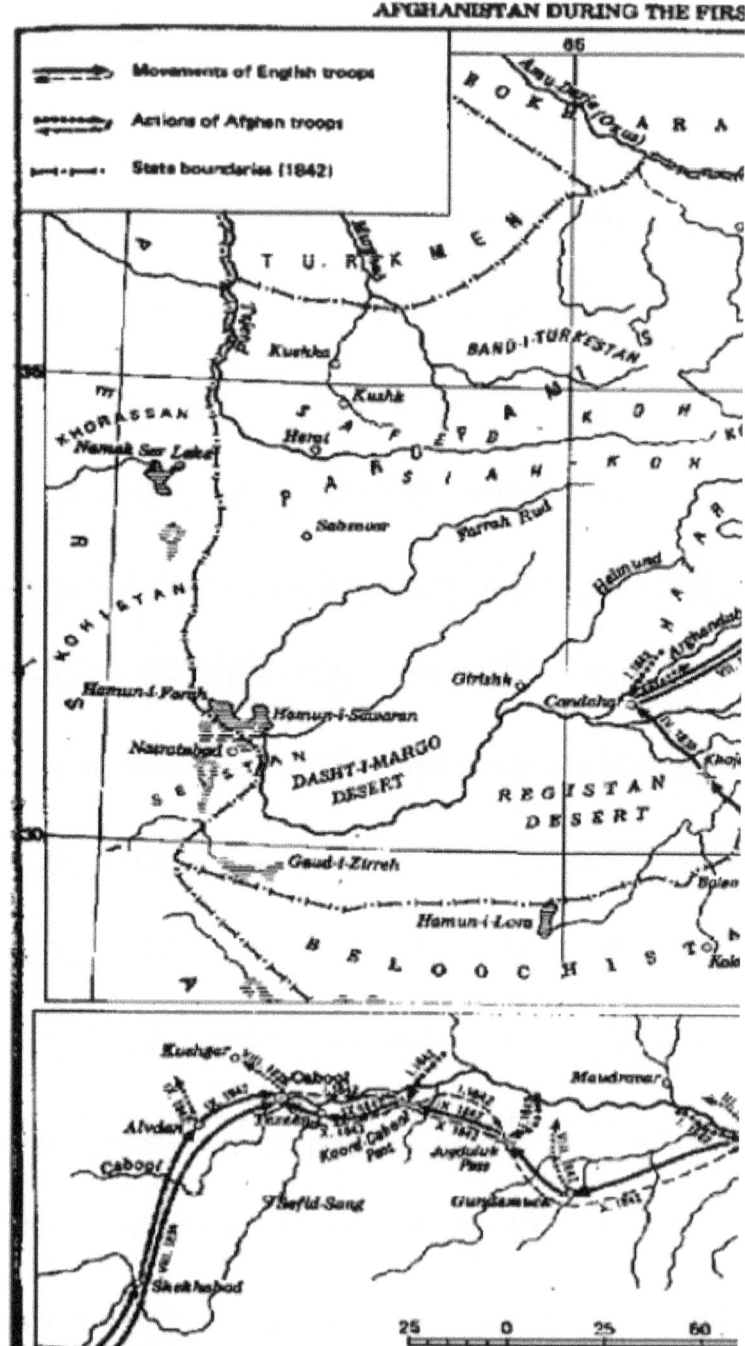

FIRST ANGLO-AFGHAN WAR, 1838-42

discover nothing of the kind. Probably, therefore, it is to be explained by sheer laziness and shrinking from discomfort, for it was said by Keane's enemies that he appropriated no fewer than two hundred and sixty public camels for the use of himself and staff, (Kennedy i.).

His peremptory orders to Cotton not to advance from Quetta were also ill-judged, and show some sign of petulance; and his final mistake in leaving his siege-guns at Kandahar was very serious. Any one of these three errors—and they were something worse than errors of judgement—might easily have wrecked the entire enterprise committed to him. On the other hand, no one can deny to him character, moral courage and resolution. He could have enriched himself and endeared himself to the whole army by forcing a quarrel upon the Amirs of Hyderabad and storming their city, and he might honestly have justified himself by pleading the danger of his communications through Sind. Yet, in loyalty to his civil chiefs, he was moderate and forbearing, and incurred no small odium with his troops. Again, when he joined the Bengal force at Quetta he found discipline slack and a discreditably querulous and despondent spirit abroad. In a day or two he restored obedience by a few severe examples, and cheerfulness and content by his own active influence. Lastly, by swift and unhesitating decision, he made good his culpable lack of siege-guns before Ghazni.

It must be said, further, that he behaved well to Macnaghten under exceedingly trying conditions. The Supreme Government of Calcutta, anxious to make the envoy the chief figure, hardly excepting Shah Shuja, in Afghanistan, had surrounded him with a pomp and circumstance which must have been galling, (See Kennedy's account of the gorgeous mounted messengers in the retinue of Macnaghten), to a commander-in-chief who, after all, bore the chief weight of responsibility. Yet Keane showed uniformly both loyalty and patience alike on the march to Kabul and during his stay there, curbing Macnaghten's eager ambition with firmness and tact, and gently putting aside the wildest of his extravagant schemes with a joke. More he could not do, looking to the limitation of his powers, though he clearly foresaw that disaster was inevitable. Upon the whole, though his mistakes disentitled him to the peerage which he received for this campaign, he proved himself worthy of his command.

CHAPTER 4

Trouble with the Ghilzais

Keane having withdrawn from Afghanistan, Macnaghten was left with authority practically unfettered except by the distant governor-general. Settled at Jalalabad with Shah Shuja for the winter, 1840, with military operations stopped for the present by the snow, he was at liberty to work out his great schemes for carrying the threads of his diplomacy from end to end of Central Asia, using his armed force, where necessary, for a needle. It is true that the said force was somewhat scattered, Jalalabad being the only station where as many as three regular battalions were collected together; but the envoy, as he had shown when he sent a battery to Bamian, believed in sowing the country with small detachments.

******

The distribution of the troops was as follows: Kabul, H.M. 13th L.I., 35th Bengal N.I., 3 field-guns; Ghazni, 16th Bengal N.I., 1 squadron Skinner's Horse; Bamian, Shah Shuja's Gurkha battalion, 1 battery Horse Artillery; Jalalabad, 1st Bengal Europeans (101st), 37th and 48th Bengal N.I., 2nd Bengal Cav., Shah Shuja's 1st, 2nd and 3rd Cav., Khyberri Corps; Dakka, Ghilzai Corps; Kandahar, 42nd and 43rd Bengal N.I., Shah Shuja's 2nd troop H.A., 2nd Cav., 2nd, 5th and 6th Inf.; Quetta, 1 battalion Shah Shuja's infantry, 2 guns. (*I.O.S.C*, vol. 4 of 1840, Jan. 11, 1840.) This list differs slightly from that printed in Durand, who places the 31st N.I. and a detachment of the *Shah's* artillery at Kalat, and a battalion of the *Shah's* infantry at Girishk, these troops being in the above list assigned to Kandahar.

******

Moreover, the raising of irregular Afghan levies was going forward with apparent success. Leech and Bean, the residents at Kandahar, and at Quetta, acting upon the principle that a reformed poacher makes the best gamekeeper, had enlisted some of the predatory tribes as police to guard the communications from the Khojak pass to the eastern mouth of the Bolan; and Mackeson was doing the like with the Khyberris. All seemed to be going well. The *Shah's* troops, owing to the resignation of General Simpson, had passed to the command of Brigadier-General Roberts, father of a little boy who was later to become famous, and himself a very capable officer, if Macnaghten would have deigned to consult him.

The only jarring note came from Nott at Kandahar, who reported that one of his two regular regiments was very sickly, that the cavalry and infantry of the *Shah's* contingent which were with him were totally disabled by illness, and that, in the event of trouble, he would have only fourteen to fifteen hundred men at his disposal. He did not say that he expected such trouble, though he did add the warning that Shah Shuja's government at Kandahar was absolutely inefficient. But Nott was always finding fault, and neither the envoy nor the governor-general thought his representations worthy of notice. (*I.O.S.C.*, vol. 1 of 1840, Leech to Macnaghten, Sept. 21, 1839; vol. 2 of 1840, Macnaghten to Mackeson, Oct. 12; Lieut. Bosanquet to Macnaghten, Oct. 1, 1839; vol. 4 of 1840, Nott to Macnaghten, Nov. 19; Indian govt, to Macnaghten, Dec. 1, 1839; Macnaghten to Mackeson, Jan. 9, 1840).

Meanwhile, Macnaghten did not forget the defences of Kabul, but sent to Auckland an estimate of the cost of a thorough repair of the citadel. There was, he explained, no assault by a foreign enemy to be dreaded; but the measure was recommended by Cotton upon military grounds, and, from a political standpoint, was calculated to produce a good effect throughout Shah Shuja's dominions. Auckland, however, did not consider the need for these repairs so urgent as to justify the expense. The governor-general was already alarmed at the enormous cost of the expedition, what with the huge loss of transport animals, the extravagance of the political agents and the incessant calls of Shah Shuja, which Macnaghten found it hard to refuse, for pecuniary aid. Auckland was so far justified in his decision that Macnaghten's glowing reports of Shah Shuja's popularity seemed to render the fortification of Kabul against internal enemies absolutely superfluous. None the less, this petty economy was a most fatal blunder. (*I.O.S.C.*, vol. 3 of 1840, Macnaghten to Indian govt., Jan. 11; Indian govt, to Macnaghten, Feb. 17, 1840).

The Lahore Gate of the Bala Hissar

Unfortunately at this same time Macnaghten must needs seize an opportunity for displaying his talent as a military commander. The presence of British troops at Jalalabad had induced nearly all of the neighbouring chieftains to pay homage to Shah Shuja; but there was one among them, the chief of Kunar, who refused to do so. The valley where he ruled runs into the main defile of the Kabul River a little below Jalalabad, and is of considerable extent, running, indeed, up to Chitral and beyond it, but it was so wretchedly poor as to be valueless; and it really mattered very little whether the chief were nominally dependent or independent. Macnaghten, however, thought differently.

The Indian government, at the beginning of the trouble with the Khyberri tribes, had pronounced that, if there were troops sufficient for the purpose, it would be well to send a punitive expedition, like that of Outram against the Ghilzais, to reduce them to obedience. As has been told, Macnaghten judged it more prudent to pay blackmail to the Khyberris, but he may well have thought that a little demonstration of his military power might have a wholesome effect upon them, and he accordingly decided to send a column to chastise the refractory chief of Kunar.

As the whole of the proceedings are instructive as an illustration of Macnaghten's military methods, they may be told in some slight detail. First, he wrote to Cotton, asking him what force he deemed adequate for the purpose, offering the use of some of the *Shah's* troops and sending a political agent, Captain Macgregor, to give information to the general and to the officer who was to command the expedition. It so happened that Cotton had sent most of his camels down the pass to Dakka, some thirty miles east of Jalalabad, to bring in grain; and he was now obliged to recall them, which meant, of course, dislocation of plans, waste of camels' strength and three days' delay.

However, the force was prepared; Lieutenant-Colonel Orchard was placed in nominal command, with orders "to attend to all the instructions" of Macgregor, who was to accompany him; and the column, (three nine-pounder guns, 20 sappers, 80 men of the 101st, 1 wing 37th N.I., 1 battalion *Shah's* infantry, Christie's Irregular Horse), marched off, its objective being Pashat, a paltry fort not more than one hundred and fifty yards square, where the chief of Kunar bade the *Shah* defiance.

The weather was unfavourable, rain being almost incessant; but after a march of fifty miles Orchard came before Pashat at dawn of the 18th of January, and with his guns battered down the outer gate of

The Bala hissar and city of Kabul from the upper part of the citadel

the fort. There was, however, an inner gate against which an engineer, Lieutenant Pigou, three several times lodged charges of powder to no purpose, the rain always weakening the explosion. Having expended the whole of the ammunition for his guns and lost sixty-eight killed and wounded, Orchard was fain to fall back, whereupon the chief quietly evacuated the fort and fled away.

The whole affair was, in fact, a failure, and, though this result was chiefly due to the weather, it was not the less serious upon that account. It must be noted that the military commanders had no voice as to the expediency, or otherwise, of despatching the expedition at all. That was the affair of Macnaghten, whom they were bound to obey. As a matter of fact, the weather was at this time so appalling that the country became impassable, and a convoy on its way to Orchard was stopped for at least twenty-four hours within two miles of Jalalabad. The probability, therefore, is that the men suffered considerable hardship, which meant sickness, and that the loss of camels from exposure must have been serious, which meant inconvenience, more work for the remaining camels, more losses and more expense. Auckland, upon hearing the particulars of the expedition, deprecated the employment of British troops except for objects of permanent advantage, he wrote:

> It is important that you should not seem to rely, for assertion of Shah Shuja's rights, upon the British Army.

But, unfortunately, Macnaghten, whatever the fair words that he sent to Calcutta, had nothing else to rely on. This was his first essay towards the two results which he finally accomplished, namely, to break the hearts and ruin the confidence of the military officers, and to teach the Afghans that the British might be resisted with success. (*I.O.S.C.*, vol. 2 of 1840, Macnaghten to Cotton, Jan. 11, 1840—enclosing instructions to Macgregor—;Cotton to Indian govt., Jan. 10; to Auckland, Jan. 22, 1840; Durand).

But, if Macnaghten plumed himself upon his military talents, much more so did Dr. Lord, his agent at Bamian. Upon the arrival of Hay's force at that place Lord had discovered—what might have been ascertained before—that forage was scarce in the winter, and had sent back all his cavalry; but with the *Shah's* battalion of Gurkhas and his battery of horse-artillery he at once became busy. His first step was to intervene in a local quarrel between two petty chieftains in the valley of Saighan, and to displace, with little bloodshed, one whom he conceived to be in the interest of Dost Mohamed. This was at the end of November, 1839; and a week or two later came in news that Dost Mohamed had taken refuge in Bukhara, which was true, and that the ruler of Bukhara intended to help him to recover his lost kingdom, which was false, for that potentate had, as a matter of fact, thrown him treacherously into confinement. Lord, however, at once begged for a reinforcement of four companies to march over the passes in midwinter; and not content with three very defensible forts, in which his troops were housed at Bamian, he began to throw up an entrenched position.

This done, he became dissatisfied with Bamian, and marching with a small detachment to Saighan, took over the fort in which he had lately installed his friend, and garrisoned it with two companies of Gurkhas. This fort, it should be added, was effectually commanded by a hill within musket-shot; so that even as an advanced post it was valueless, and as an isolated stronghold simply a trap. Finally, Lord became dissatisfied with the whole position unless it should prove to be the first step towards an advance into Turkestan. For that object Bamian, in his view, presented unexampled facilities, and, as he pointed out, the territory to south of the Oxus was the most valuable part of Shah Shuja's dominions.

It is a grave reflection upon the depth of Macnaghten's intelligence and the sanity of his judgement that he took all the foolish outpourings of this conceited and self-important doctor with the utmost seriousness. Dost Mohamed and the Russian advance upon Khiva possessed his brain to the exclusion of all other matters, save the extension of Shah Shuja's realm. When rumours came in that the Khan of Bukhara contemplated making Balkh over to Dost Mohamed, he trembled for the consequences without questioning the truth of the report. When Lord wrote grandiloquently that the choice lay between bounding Russian influence by the Oxus, or allowing it to reach within a few years to Bamian, it never occurred to him that from Orenburg to Khiva is eight hundred miles as the crow flies. Far from that, he deliberately wrote a letter advising an advance beyond the Hindu Kush for three principal objects, namely, to push the Khan of Bukhara out of all territory south of the Oxus, to compel him to liberate Colonel Stoddart, and—evidently as a sop to soothe Auckland's just alarm as to the cost—to pay the expenses of the expedition to Afghanistan.

Auckland, upon the first receipt of Lord's extravagant letters, had expressed anxiety, and, upon hearing of his raid upon Saighan, had written mildly that Dr. Lord's zeal needed moderation by Macnaght-

Shah Shuja

en's judgement; but Lord was only another Macnaghten in little, and the governor-general was obliged to affirm roundly that he had no desire to assert Shah Shuja's rights in Turkestan, and declined to do so. (*I.O.S.C.*, vol. 5 of 1840, Lord to Macnaghten, Jan. 6; Macnaghten to Indian Govt., Jan. 15, Feb. 25; Indian Govt, to Macnaghten, Feb. 17, 1840).

With the return of spring, Lord again launched out into military operations. Forage for his horse-artillery battery could only be obtained from the Hazaras, who, though freely paid for it, naturally grudged the drain of the supplies which they had laid up for their own live stock. At length they refused to furnish more; and Lord sent a force against one of their strongholds, one tower of which was defended so desperately that it was only mastered by the slaying of every man within it. This, of course, bred ill-will not only among the Hazaras but among the neighbouring tribes; and Lord seemed bent upon multiplying opportunities for them to wreak their vengeance in the future. He had already split up his little detachment between Bamian and Saighan, and he now found a pretext for dividing it still further. Dost Mohamed, when he fled to Bukhara, had left his family at Khulm under the charge of his brother, Jabar Khan; and Macnaghten, wishing to hold hostages against Dost Mohamed's designs, was trying to persuade Jabar Khan to throw himself upon the protection and generosity of the British.

Lord, thinking to hasten Jabar Khan's decision by showing him that Khulm was no secure resting-place, ordered a reconnaissance to northward, in the course of which a local chief offered to make over to him the little fort of Rajga, at the mouth of the defile beyond Kamard, some twenty-five miles north-east of Saighan. As a military post Rajga was faulty, but Lord, jumping at the occupation of any forward position, good or bad, at once accepted it, and urged Macnaghten to occupy it permanently. Macnaghten agreed; and three hundred Afghan levies, under Captain Hopkins, were sent up to reinforce Lord, who now pushed forward five companies of the *Shah's* Gurkhas to Rajga, leaving two at Saighan and one at Bamian. General Roberts was not consulted in the matter, for Macnaghten pressed his authority in command of Shah Shuja's regular troops to the utmost, and would suffer no interference from any one with the irregular corps. The envoy, indeed, seems to have become positively intoxicated by the joyful knowledge that he could send armed men whither he would to enforce his august will.

Apart from the vicious disposition of the troops, however, Lord's military promenades produced precisely the opposite effect to that which Macnaghten desired, by alarming every native chief between Bamian and the Oxus. The Khan of Kokan remonstrated with his brother of Bukhara against his treatment of Dost Mohamed, who had resisted the British aggressor that now threatened them all, with the result that Dost Mohamed before long effected his escape. The Wali of Khulm, being nearer to Lord, was even more frightened, and, as a natural result, even more sympathetic with Dost Mohamed. These petty potentates, who might have been secured as friends, were converted into enemies; and endless dangers were laid up for the future because a handful of political agents, headed by Macnaghten, could not deny themselves the pleasure of that delightful game which is known as "playing at soldiers."

During this time Cotton and Nott were corresponding amicably and soberly about the Russian advance upon Khiva, neither of them anticipating any movement of the Russians beyond the Oxus, but both dreading the effect of their approach upon unquiet spirits in Afghanistan. Cotton was for concentrating as large a force as possible at Kabul in readiness to seize, if matters should come to the worst, the passes of the Hindu Kush. Nott, with more sober judgement, doubted whether without strong reinforcements it would be possible to hold even Kabul and the Khyber Pass against a Russian army backed, as he believed it would be, by the majority of the Afghans, (Stocqueler, *Life of Sir W. Nott*, i.).

Both generals, however, found that they had plenty of work in their hands without the Russians. The Ghilzais, that fierce and untameable race, whose country, following the line of the River Tarnak, ran from Kandahar almost to Kabul, had forgotten the sharp lessons that they had received the day before the storm of Ghazni and later at the hands of Outram; and in April they were busy on the road between Kandahar and Ghazni, intercepting the posts and wounding or slaying the messengers. Nott sent out a party of two hundred horse in the hope of seizing the leaders; but it was found that these leaders had assembled a considerable force about Kalat-i-Ghilzai, in order to sever communication permanently between Kandahar and Kabul; and Macnaghten realised the unpleasant fact that the Ghilzais, who at the best of times had never acknowledged the authority of any sovereign, whether at Kandahar or Kabul, were in open rebellion.

Accordingly, on the 7th of May, he called upon Cotton to furnish troops to aid Shah Shuja's levies in restoring order. Characteristically enough, he gave no information as to the nature of the service, and Cotton was obliged to ask for details as to the probable numbers of the enemy, the strength of their forts, the prospect of finding supplies in the country, and the means of feeding the troops if it were judged necessary to follow the tribesmen into the hills. In reply Macnaghten forwarded a memorandum from one of his underlings, Captain Peter Nicholson, who had been one of Auckland's *aides-de-camp*; and this officer, having been entrusted by Macnaghten "with the settlement of the Ghilzai tribes" (as he modestly styled it), was prepared to co-operate with Nott in a spirit of gracious patronage and high condescension. (See his very ridiculous letter to Nott of May 13, 1840. Stocqueler, *Life of Sir W. Nott*, i.).

The memorandum set forth that the tribesmen numbered twelve thousand but probably could not put more than six thousand into the field, that their forts were so strong as to require siege-artillery, but that upon the mere demonstration of force the Ghilzais would probably submit without firing a shot. Finally, Nicholson averred that supplies and forage were abundant in the plain, a statement which experience proved to be false, and that there would be no occasion to follow the enemy into the hills.

It is worthwhile to give these details, for the whole transaction is typical of the casual fashion in which Macnaghten and his minions approached military operations, and, by initiating them with the Shah's troops, forced the British officers to co-operate with them. Cotton could only reply that since Macnaghten's information was better than his own, he bowed to his decision, and would furnish a battalion of *sepoys* and two siege-guns; but he begged that Nott might take personal command of the whole. (*I.O.S.C.*, vol. 9 of 1840, Macnaghten to Cotton, May 7, 8; Cotton to Macnaghten, May 8, 9; Captain Anderson to Fort Adjutant, Kandahar, May 17, 1840. Nicholson's Memo, is printed in Stocqueler's *Life of Sir William Nott,* i.).

But while Macnaghten was thus elaborating his preparations, Nott, learning from his cavalry of the real state of affairs, on the 7th of May sent them reinforcements of a battalion of the *Shah's* infantry and four horse-artillery guns under the leadership of Captain Anderson. On the 16th of May Anderson, having his infantry and artillery on the road and his cavalry pushed out wide to right and left to feel for the enemy, came upon the Ghilzais, from two to three thousand horse and foot, well posted in a strong position at Tazi on the left bank of the

Kandahar City

Tarnak. Feeling no great confidence in his foot, which was new and untried, Anderson decided to stand upon the defensive, and, choosing his ground with skill, plied the Ghilzai horse with an accurate fire of shrapnel until, unable to endure the torment longer, they advanced and swooped down upon his left flank. Twice they charged up to the bayonets, but the *Shah's* battalion, under three good English officers, stood creditably firm, while the grape-shot from the guns played havoc among the tribesmen.

Before Anderson's cavalry could return, the fight was over and the Ghilzais had fled, leaving two hundred dead behind them; whereupon Anderson moved forward to Ulan Robat and there sat down in a strong position dominating the valley of the Tarnak. This was a sharp little affair and timely, for Nott discovered that in another two days the Ghilzais would have numbered ten thousand instead of three thousand, and that there was a plot at Kandahar to overwhelm the garrison as soon as Nott should have marched out, as it was considered certain that he must, with his two regiments of regular *sepoys*. The truth was that the Durani chiefs, who had expected much from the restoration of Shah Shuja, had realised that all power and influence was in the hands of the British, and were by this time thoroughly and permanently disaffected.

But, though Nott was fully persuaded of this, Macnaghten would never have believed it; and the news of the action at Tazi seems to have come to Cotton as an unpleasant surprise, for, according to Macnaghten's intelligence, the country was quiet, or, according to Nicholson's opinion, would sink into repose at the first demonstration of force. Though, therefore, Nott had done already all that was immediately necessary, Macnaghten, thoroughly scared, insisted on sending out his detachment from Kabul and on dragging Nott from Kandahar to Ulan Robat to command it.

With this force Macnaghten sent the heir-apparent, the Shahzada Timur, presumably with the object of conciliating the loyal affections of the people; but this prince brought with him a rabble of followers who fell upon the unfortunate inhabitants, robbing and plundering them with hideous cruelty, and, as Nott wrote, "doing all in their power to goad the people into open rebellion." As this oppression was exercised under the protection of Nott's troops, the sufferers naturally appealed to him, and Nott instantly made an example of some of the troops from Kabul who had caught the infection of rapine.

But with the Shahzada's own people he prudently declined to deal, bidding the complainants carry their grievance to Nicholson, who, apparently unwilling to trench upon the august privileges of royalty, took no steps to obtain for them redress. So matters went on for a short time until Nott, dreading the effects of this lawlessness upon his own troops, after due warning took matters into his own hands, soundly flogged a dozen of the Shahzada's followers, and restored the property that they had stolen to its owners. It does not appear that the prince objected in the slightest degree to this action; but the ridiculous political agent, Peter Nicholson, construed it as an affront to his petty dignity and complained to Macnaghten.

Macnaghten, taking up Nicholson's quarrel with childish readiness, referred the matter to Auckland. Cotton thereupon took up the cudgels for Nott, gave him the whole weight of his support and justified his conduct in every particular. Finally, Auckland, while unable to deny that the conduct of the Shahzada's people had been atrocious, was weak and foolish enough to write that he had "observed Nott's conduct with great regret and displeasure," and to hint that he was unfit for his command. In such infatuated fashion did governor -general, envoy and political agents labour strenuously for disaster. (See Stocqueler's *Life of Sir William Nott,* i.).

However, for the moment the Ghilzais were overawed into the semblance of tranquillity. Nott sent a detachment to occupy Kalat-i-Ghilzai and to destroy petty strongholds between Kandahar and Ghazni, thus rendering communication safer; and by the third week in July he had returned to Kandahar. Soon afterwards Macnaghten fell back upon his usual method of securing peace upon the highways by paying the chiefs £3000 a year to abstain from troubling them; thus confirming the saying which had already become proverbial in Afghanistan, that the British rewarded their enemies and oppressed only their friends, (Durand; Kaye, i.).

Almost simultaneously with the rising of the Ghilzais, there was a dangerous menace to the British line of communications between Shikarpur and Kandahar. Captain Bean, the political agent at Quetta, had, as has been told, enlisted some of the tribesmen, namely the Kachhis, to east and south-east of the Bolan Pass, to guard the line, while to westward it was hoped that all was made safe by the installation of Shah Nawaz Khan, as successor to Mehrab, at Kalat. With the political agent's usual conceit of his own influence and his own achievements, Bean, confident that all was well, had sent the Thirty-first Native Infantry back to India, without a word to Nott, retaining only two hundred and thirty bayonets of the *Shah's* infantry and two guns as the garrison at Quetta.

There was, however, another tribe, the Marris, east of the road from Shikarpur to the mouth of the Bolan, which could not resist the temptation of plundering convoys; and to curb them Mr. Ross-Bell decreed that their principal fort at Kahan, about eighty miles east and north of Bagh, should be permanently occupied. Accordingly on the 2nd of May, Captain Brown, with three hundred *sepoys*, fifty horse, one twelve-pounder howitzer and from seven to eight hundred camels, marched from the advanced post of Pulaji, some thirty-five miles north-east of Bagh.

The heat was intense, the route was circuitous, and the difficulties of the Nafusk pass into the hills were so great that Kahan was not reached until the 11th. The fort, an irregular hexagon, was deserted, but the walls were so ruinous and weak that the defence depended mainly upon the six towers at the six angles. However, Brown strengthened the wretched place as best he could, unloaded the four months' provisions that he had brought with him, and sent his camels back for more. Since it had pleased Ross-Bell to place a handful of men in isolation at a distance of at least a week's march from any support, it was essential that the post should at least be well furnished with food.

On the 16th of May, therefore, Lieutenant Clerk started from Kahan to escort seven hundred camels back to the plain with one hundred and sixty bayonets and fifty horse. Being unopposed in the Nafusk pass and mindful of the weakness of Brown's garrison, he ordered half of his infantry back to Kahan; but no sooner was this party beyond reach of Clerk than it was surrounded by superior numbers and annihilated, one camp-follower alone escaping to carry the news to Kahan. Emboldened by this success the Marris set themselves next to intercept Clerk, who, being a gallant officer, attacked them without hesitation. But the odds against him were too great. He himself fell fighting hand to hand; seventy of his eighty *sepoys* were killed; and the Marris could boast that they had cut off one hundred and fifty regular troops and captured seven hundred camels.

The news spread like wildfire among the tribes. Even the Kachhis, for generations at blood feud with the Marris, rejoiced over their success against the aliens, and, while planning the destruction of Bean and his garrison, were careful to persuade him that more than ever they hated the Marris and were attached to the British. Nasir Khan, son of the slain and dethroned Mehrab, and his followers likewise saw visions of the recovery of Kalat and the deposition of Shah Nawaz, who, without influence of his own, leaned wholly on the detested political agent Loveday, and his paltry garrison of sixty *sepoys*.

Bean, however, in his innocence reported to his political superiors that the Kachhis were assembling to attack the Marris, and assured Brown, who fortunately was far too sensible to believe him, that he might expect aid at Kalat from his Kachhi allies. A little earlier he had been blind enough to order Loveday to send twenty of his sixty *sepoys* from Kalat to Mastung, halfway between Kalat and Quetta, and Loveday had been mad enough to obey him. The sight , of this isolated handful of men was too much for the tribesmen. They rose and cut them to pieces, and then the entire province north and south of Kalat rose in revolt.

The Kachhis now threw off the mask and claimed the right to attack Quetta, which they did very feebly on the 23rd of June, and were easily repulsed. It should seem that Bean, though a large amount of treasure had been placed under his custody, had not thought it necessary to stow it in the citadel of Quetta, where a handful of *sepoys* could have beaten off any number of tribesmen; and, being thoroughly frightened, he shrieked for reinforcements, demanding a battalion of *sepoys*, four guns and three hundred horse from Kandahar.

Meanwhile he drew in the detachment of the *Shah's* troops which had been stationed at Kila Abdullah to keep open the Khojak pass, and having thus doubled the strength of his garrison, awaited events. The Kachhis, on their side, called to their aid the insurgents under Nasir Khan, and on the 9th of July again beleaguered Quetta. But after lying before the place for a week they fell asunder through internal dissension, and on the 17th retired to Mastung. Bean, though strong enough to pursue them and to reopen communication with Loveday at Kalat, omitted to do so; and the tribesmen were able to mature their designs for an attack upon Kalat.

Aware of the danger, Shah Nawaz Khan called in such tribes as were loyal to him, to the number of some seven hundred men, which, with Loveday's forty *sepoys*, and plenty of powder and lead, should have sufficed to repel the twelve hundred with which Nasir Khan finally besieged the place. But Loveday showed neither energy nor ability; and, although one assault was repelled, treachery within the walls constrained Shah Nawaz to open negotiations for the surrender of Kalat to Nasir Khan and for his own peaceful withdrawal together with Loveday and his party of *sepoys*. Loveday, however, seems to have taken complete leave of his senses. Chance had given him a loyal colleague during the siege in the person of the traveller Masson, but he had chosen to quarrel with him; and now, in the face of Masson's entreaties, he was not content with the engagement which Shah Nawaz had made for him, but must needs enter into parleys with Nasir Khan upon his own account.

The wily chief gladly played with him for a short time and then seized him, shackled him, and carried him off as an object of derision on a triumphal march to Mastung. Thus Kalat was lost; a British officer was prisoner in the hands of a semi-barbarous chief; and there was confusion and dismay along the whole line of the Bolan Pass. Nott alone kept his head, while all the political agents were crying out for a detachment here and a detachment there. He pointed out that from the Bolan to Ghazni there were only two regular regiments of *sepoys* and six guns, and he declined to break them up and allow them to be destroyed piecemeal by "a set of political boys." (*I.O.S.C.*, vol. 17 of 1840, Masson to Bean and to Torrens, Sept. 25, 1840; Stocqueler's *Life of Sir William Nott*, i.; Durand).

More trouble was at hand above the Bolan Pass. The post at Kahan, useless and isolated, was in need of supplies, and on the 12th of August a convoy of twelve hundred camels and half as many bullocks started from Sukkur to re-victual it, escorted by five hundred infantry and three howitzers under the command of Major Clibborn. The heat was appalling, but, the marches as far as Pulaji being accomplished at night, the troops suffered less than might have been expected. From that point the difficulties of the track through the mountains compelled all movements to be made by day, and the escort was strengthened by the addition of two hundred sabres. On the 31st of August the convoy reached the foot of the ascent to the Nafusk pass at 10 a.m., having taken eight hours to cover seven miles. So far it had been unmolested; but the heat of the morning had been overpowering, and both men and cattle were suffering from want of water.

Misled by his guides, Clibborn determined to force the pass, which was occupied by tribesmen, and push on to water on the side of Kahan; and at 2 p.m. two companies and fifty dismounted troopers, covered by fire from the howitzers, advanced to the attack. The road had been destroyed, and breastworks and other obstacles had been thrown up by the enemy, but these were carried, not without loss; and the assailants reached the crest of the ridge triumphant, but disordered, breathless and spent by heat and thirst. The Baluchis seized the moment to counter-attack, and cut down the storming-party right and left. The supports fell back in panic upon the main body, and the Baluchis made a gallant attempt to overwhelm the whole force. But the main body stood firm, and their musketry, added to the steady fire of the guns, swept the tribesmen back with heavy loss to the crest of the pass. They retreated, however, no further, and Clibborn's men were so much exhausted that pursuit was out of the question.

The distress of the troops from thirst was such that Clibborn was fain to send parties in search of water, which was found within a mile and a half of his position. But instead of marching to it with all his force, Clibborn sent only his water-carriers and the gun-teams, with an escort of irregular horse. Having with them no infantry, these were easily dispersed by the Baluchis, and thus all the water-vessels were lost. The news reached Clibborn at sunset, but still he hesitated to march to the water, and finally at 10 p.m. he decided to retreat, abandoning guns, stores and convoy; uncertain whether even so he might not have to fight his way through fresh bands of enemies. Having spiked his guns and taken a few camels to carry his wounded, he slunk away quietly at 11 p.m., and, passing over the scene of Clerk's disaster without opposition, reached water.

There, however, the Baluchis overtook the rear, cutting up numbers of camp-followers; and only after a sharp engagement with the rear-guard were they beaten off. When morning broke Clibborn found that he was without provisions of any kind. He had ordered the *sepoys* to carry four days' flour, but they were too much fatigued to obey. He was therefore obliged to make a forced march of fifty miles to Pulaji, which was fatal to many of his men. His casualties in action alone numbered two hundred and seventy, so that his total loss must have amounted to over two hundred *sepoys* dead, besides the whole of his bullocks and over one thousand camels lost.

Brown, thus left in hopeless isolation at Kahan, still showed so bold a front that on the 23rd of September the Marri chiefs offered to let him march away unmolested if he would give up the fort; and accordingly on the 28th Brown marched out. Though his sick numbered forty, and the men who could march were weak and faint from hunger, he brought away not only every man but also his gun, and after three days of exhausting march came safely on the 30th into Pulaji.

Such a mishap as Clibborn's following upon the previous misfortune of Clerk was alike serious and discreditable. The Marris alto-

The Wild Pass of Siri-Kajoor

gether had actually destroyed at least five hundred *sepoys* and carried off over seventeen hundred camels and six hundred bullocks, and all because an ignorant civilian had chosen to place a garrison in a post where it was absolutely useless. A court of inquiry condemned Clibborn and all the superior officers who had been responsible for sending him out; and it does not appear that Clibborn's handling of his command was altogether happy.

But it is easy to condemn an officer after the event, not so easy to imagine his difficulties in passing an unwieldy convoy over sixty to seventy miles of appalling country, at the rate of one mile an hour, with a burning sun overhead, rocky hills baked into a furnace all round him, men and animals frantic from thirst, and a wary and bold enemy lying in wait to take advantage of every weakness and every false step. All present testified at least to Clibborn's unshakable courage and self-possession throughout.

The man really responsible for these disasters was Ross-Bell, and the Supreme Government at Calcutta, arriving at this just conclusion six months after the event, passed upon him the gravest censure. But the worst offender of all was that same Supreme Government, with the governor-general at its head, which had initiated and upheld the system of placing civilians in charge of military operations. (Stocqueler, *Life of Sir William Nott*, i.; Durand; *I.O.S.C.*, vol. 13 of 1840; Brown—political agent at Sukkur—to Outram, Sept. 5, 1840; vol. 1 of 1841, Captain Lewis Brown to Ross-Bell, Dec. 9, 1840; vol. 5 of 1841, Indian govt, to Ross-Bell, April 12, 1 841).

Immediately after the first reverses in the Nafusk pass the political authorities had pressed urgently for reinforcements, and by the second week in August a wing of the Fortieth Foot was already on its way to the front from Karachi. Meanwhile, affairs along the whole line from Sukkur to Kandahar were in a most uncertain state; and, had there been less disunion among the tribes, the consequences might have been most serious. But Nasir Khan had no great resources at his back and, being weary of war, opened negotiations with Bean, through his prisoner Loveday, for a peaceful settlement. Bean replied by demanding that Kalat should be surrendered, and that Nasir Khan should do homage to Shah Shuja and accept his sovereignty.

This perfectly fatuous message from Bean was rejected with indignation, and naturally so, for its acceptance would have cost Nasir Khan his life at the hands of his chiefs; and the only result was to irritate the Brahuis beyond endurance. Loveday then urged that Masson should be sent to Bean to advise the offer of more moderate and less repellent terms; and Masson very generously undertook the mission. Upon his arrival at Quetta, however, he was placed under arrest by Bean and forcibly detained. The political agents, from Macnaghten downward, had been struck by the fact that Masson was suffered to go at large in Kalat, whereas Loveday had been seized and treated with ignominy; and the true explanation of the fact never occurred to them, namely, that Masson was a gentle creature, well known and respected, whereas Loveday had been overbearing, harsh and brutal. However, though Masson returned not, his companions carried back the news of his arrest, with the further information that the British had resolved to recover Kalat.

Thereupon Nasir Khan determined upon war to the knife, left a slender garrison at Kalat, and entering the Bolan Pass with the main body of his warriors prepared to join the Marris in assailing the British advanced posts in Kachhi. (Durand; *I.O.S.C.*, vol. 17 of 1840, Bean to Macnaghten—enclosing correspondence with Masson—Sept. 26; Masson to Torrens, Sept. 26; Macnaghten to Sec. of Govt., Oct 8; Nott to Ross-Bell, Nov. 3, 1840).

On the 29th of October he attacked Dadhar but was beaten off by a headlong charge of one hundred and twenty *sowars* of Skinner's Horse, a fine feat of arms, in which the leader, Captain Macpherson, and all of his native officers were wounded. On the two following days Nasir Khan assaulted two other posts without success; and then learning that reinforcements—a wing of the Fortieth under Major Boscawen—were approaching Dadhar, he withdrew, not omitting first to cut Loveday's throat and leave his body for his British countrymen to find in the deserted encampment.

Meanwhile Nott, under the orders of Macnaghten, had moved up to Quetta on the 9th of September with a small escort, leaving two siege-guns to follow him, for he had orders from Macnaghten to take over reinforcements which were expected from Karachi, and with them to recover Kalat. These reinforcements were not forthcoming, and Nott was obliged to wait until a battalion of *sepoys*, which the political agent at Kandahar dared not at first spare from that garrison, was able to join him. Having obtained it, together with his two siege-guns, he, at Bean's urgent entreaty, marched first to Mastung where he found that Nasir Khan had moved, as above related, to Kachhi, and thence proceeded to Kalat, which he reached on the 3rd of November. He found the place undefended and abandoned; and learning that

Loveday had treated the inhabitants very cruelly, he promised them protection.

With this object he sent forward four companies to occupy the town, giving strict orders that no individual was to enter it without his permission. Thereupon a certain Lieutenant Hammersley, who had begun the campaign as Nott's *aide-de-camp* but had since joined the political service, at once tried to gain entrance and was very properly turned back. Galloping up to Nott, he addressed him rudely before all his staff with the words, "What right have you to order *me* not to enter the city?" Nott silenced him by threatening to put him under instant arrest; but Hammersley wrote and complained to Macnaghten; and Nott was actually called upon to defend himself because he, a general, had refused to endure insult and accept orders from a lieutenant.

Such were the conditions under which military officers in high command were expected to conduct a campaign under the government of Auckland and Macnaghten. (Stocqueler, *Life of Sir William Nott*, i. & ii.) Having placed one of his own officers, whom he could trust, in political charge of Kalat, with the Forty second Native Infantry and fifty horse for garrison, Nott on the 7th set out for Quetta; and having left the Second Queen's and fifty horse at Mastung, marched for Kandahar. In the course of these fatiguing operations he had suffered hardly a casualty, and had lost not a single camel nor an ounce of baggage; and when he left Kalat the whole population lined the road uttering lamentations over the departure of the just man who had treated them humanely and shielded them from oppression. But he did not deceive himself as to the general aspect of affairs in Afghanistan. He wrote on the 29th of September:

> All goes wrong here we are become hated by the people, and the English name and character, which two years ago stood so high and so fair, is become a by-word. (Stocqueler, *Life of Sir William Nott* ii.; *I.O.S.C.*, vol. 1 of 1841, Nott to Ross-Bell, Nov. 7, 1840).

In the course of November the long-expected reinforcements from Karachi gradually reached Sind, and a very capable officer, General Brooks, assumed command on the line of communications west of the Indus. The Marris and Kachhis had fallen off from Nasir Khan, who, with his own followers only, from two to three thousand strong, had taken up a position at Kotra, a little to south-west of Gandava, on the western flank of the British line of communications. At the end of November Brooks organised a force of about nine hundred men, (25th Bombay N.I., detachments of 2nd and 21st Bombay N.I.), and two guns under Colonel Marshall, with orders to fall upon Kotra by surprise. Ross-Bell, the political agent, could not refrain from supplementing Brooks's commands with voluminous instructions of his own, enjoining in particular that Marshall should take with him no guns. Fortunately, Marshall was strong enough to disobey this particular order, and at daybreak on the 1st of December he fell upon Nasir Khan's people, completely defeated them after a stout resistance, with a loss of four hundred killed and over one hundred prisoners, and drove the *Khan* away in headlong flight, at no greater cost to himself than thirty-nine casualties, one-third of them killed. It was a timely little success which, as Marshall was careful to inform Ross-Bell, could never have been accomplished without artillery. (*I.O.S.C.*, vol. 1 of 1841, Ross-Bell to Colonel Marshall, Nov. 28; Colonel Marshall to Ross-Bell, Dec. 2, 1840; Durand).

Thus, after six months' hard work, Nott's line of communications between the line of the Indus and Kandahar was for the time secured. But it was not in this region only that there was trouble, for affairs had taken an equally unpleasant turn to north of Kabul. The Russian advance from Orenburg upon Khiva was, by the summer, known definitely to have broken down under difficulties of transport and supply and of sickness. This signified one anxiety the less; but Dr. Lord's feverish activities in the wrong direction were beginning to produce their inevitable results.

In June that busy projector was still advocating the advance of a brigade to Bukhara; but at the beginning of August he found danger menacing his own posts which he had so recklessly established in isolation beyond Bamian. Captain Hay, who commanded the station at Rajga, finding armed men hovering about him and being himself sick, summoned a European brother officer to march to him with one company from Saighan, and sent out a British sergeant, Douglas by name, with two companies of Gurkhas of his own garrison to meet them and help them on their way.

One of Lord's subordinate agents, however, forbade the march of the detachment from Saighan; and Douglas, not finding it at the appointed place, and supposing that it must have been delayed, bivouacked for the night, by permission of the native Usbeg chief, under the walls of a native fort at Kamard. The whole district, however, was about to rise against Lord's unprovoked aggression, and the chief summoned his own people and a neighbouring tribe to fall upon the two companies and make an end of them. At dawn, therefore, Douglas was surprised by a sudden attack, but keeping his men together he prepared to fight his way back to Rajga. For some miles he held his own with great skill and gallantry, notwithstanding heavy losses, and was fortunately rescued just as his ammunition was failing by two more companies which Hay, at the sound of the firing, had sent out from Rajga. It was no fault of the political agent that Douglas's two companies were not annihilated.

None the less, the Usbegs and their neighbours considered that they had been victorious; and now Dost Mohamed, who had escaped from Bukhara, was in the field, rallying, with the full support of the chief at Khulm, all malcontents to his standard. Lord promptly wrote the disquieting news to Macnaghten, and declared that there was no alternative but to send a brigade against Khulm at once. This was rather too much even for Macnaghten, who answered that so large a force could not be spared, and that the autumn was too far advanced to send troops across the Hindu Kush. Towards the end of August the Usbegs again threatened Rajga, and Lord was fain to evacuate the post and fall back first upon Saighan, which was held by some of Shah Shuja's newly raised native levies, and finally upon Bamian. In the retreat to this latter place Captain Hopkins's regiment of Afghan infantry distinguished itself by plunder of the baggage, and, upon arrival at Bamian, by the desertion of a complete company, with its arms and ammunition, to Dost Mohamed.

These same men had behaved badly on their way up to Bamian, and had showed suspicious goodwill to one of Dost Mohamed's sons while quartered in that district; and General Roberts had carefully reported the circumstances to the envoy. Macnaghten at the time treated the affair as of no consequence, but now he was frightened, for there could be no question of Dost Mohamed's advance with a mass of the Usbeg tribes at his back. He therefore sent Colonel Dennie with a battery of horse-artillery and the Thirty-Fifth Native Infantry to take command at Bamian.

Dennie reached his destination on the 14th of September, where he promptly disarmed the rest of Hopkins's Afghans, and so banished one danger. On the 18th, having intelligence of parties of horse in the valley, he sallied out with five hundred infantry, three hundred cavalry and two guns, drove in the enemy's outposts and found himself face

Kandahar City

to face with Dost Mohamed's entire host of Usbeg horse and foot. Without hesitation he attacked. His two guns soon shook the irregular undisciplined mass, which would not await the onset of Dennie's Gurkhas and *sepoys*; and the whole fled away, offering an easy prey to the sabres of the cavalry. Dost Mohamed contrived to escape; but the chief of Khulm hastened to make his peace with Dr. Lord, and the fugitive Amir was fain to seek new refuge among the none too friendly tribes of Kohistan.

Uncertain of Dost Mohamed's movements, but aware that his intrigues were at work in the capital itself, Macnaghten recalled Dennie with his battery and the Thirty-Fifth Native Infantry to Kabul; and, since the chiefs of Kohistan had belied their simulated allegiance to Shah Shuja by banding themselves in secret to overthrow him, Macnaghten despatched Sale and Burnes with a small force, (two companies each of H.M. 13th, 27th and 37th N.I.; two squadrons 2nd Light Cavalry; 5 guns), to punish them. They accordingly marched from Charikar on the 29th of September, destroyed a little fort or two, and then, receiving intelligence of Dost Mohamed at divers places, made unsuccessful attempts to overtake or surprise him. After a month of such work, with no result but the defection of Shah Shuja's Kohistani levies, Sale at last had definite information that Dost Mohamed was at Parwan a little to north-east of Charikar on the right bank of the Ghorband; and he marched for that place on the 2nd of November.

The advanced guard—seven companies of infantry, two squadrons of the Second Light Cavalry and two hundred Afghan horse, with two guns, under Colonel Salter—duly caught sight of the enemy near Parwan, evacuating the plain and taking to the hills. At Lord's suggestion Salter pushed forward his cavalry right and left to cut them off from the high ground; and so it was that the Second Light Cavalry found themselves confronted with a party of Afghan horse of inferior strength. And then followed one of those incidents which after endless explanations remain always mysterious. The commanding officer gave the word to charge, and he and all the Europeans with him galloped headlong into the Afghan horse.

But their men hesitated, fell back, and finally took to disgraceful flight. Two of the five Europeans engaged were slain, Dr. Lord being one of them, and two others were desperately wounded. The advance of the infantry and guns drove the enemy from the hills and recovered the bodies of the fallen; but Dost Mohamed, who commanded the Afghan horse in person, and should either have been killed or taken, es-

Kandahar City

caped without difficulty. The Second Light Cavalry was a good corps with good officers; but such misconduct could not be overlooked, and the regiment was with ignominy disbanded, (Durand; *Life of George Broadfoot*).

This disgraceful reverse was a severe blow to Macnaghten. Even before the tidings reached him, he had been much shaken by the revolt of the Kohistanis in Dost Mohamed's favour and by his intrigues at Kabul. He wrote gloomily to Auckland of the possibility of having "to submit to the disgrace of being shut up in Kabul for a time," and went so far as to prepare the citadel against a siege and mount guns to command the city. On the 3rd of November, while riding in the evening round the outskirts of Kabul, he received a letter from Burnes reporting the disaster, and urging immediate concentration of all troops at the capital.

Before he could reach his quarters, a horseman rode up to him and announced that Dost Mohamed was at hand. The *amir* then rode up, dismounted and tendered his sword to the envoy. Macnaghten courteously returned it, and the pair rode together into Kabul. What motives may have induced Dost Mohamed to surrender just at this juncture it is impossible to say. It has been said that the gallantry of the five British officers, who charged home into the Afghan horse while all of their own men galloped away, made him despair of triumph over such a foe.

More probably he was weary of being hunted and of having to elude not only the pertinacity of his foreign enemies but the treachery of his own countrymen. In any case he had abandoned the struggle, and the only formidable rival to Shah Shuja was a prisoner in Macnaghten's hands. Such a stroke of good fortune, coming at a most critical moment, was almost overwhelming. It remains to be seen to what end it was turned by the confident and ambitious envoy.

Dost Mohamed and Macnaghten

CHAPTER 5

Unrest about Kandahar

At this point it will be well to review briefly, by the light not of later events, but of contemporary documents, the general situation in Afghanistan at the end of 1840. Macnaghten's policy, it will be remembered, was to give Shah Shuja a free hand in the matter of administering justice, and of collecting and appropriating revenue, but to keep all foreign affairs and all control of the *Shah's* military forces strictly to himself. He had also sought to curb the turbulent Afghan nobles by raising native levies of every description; and lastly he had resorted to bribes in order to persuade the Khyberris on one side and the Ghilzais on the other to leave unmolested the British lines of communication.

Let us glance first at foreign affairs. Still dreading the advance of the Russians from Orenburg, Macnaghten had in May projected the despatch of two political officers to Khiva with orders to follow the Russian army, without protest or interference, to Bukhara. Authentic intelligence of the collapse of the Russian expedition had caused him to abandon this idea; but Major Todd, the political agent at Herat, had in December 1839, sent of his own motion a colleague, Captain Abbott, to Khiva, who had gone so far as to draw up a draft treaty of defensive and offensive alliance between England and Khiva, and to send it to Auckland for approval.

This, as Macnaghten could not but confess, was rather an extreme measure, but he pleaded for a lenient view of Abbott's mistaken zeal, which Auckland, while rejecting the treaty, was gentle enough to concede. For the rest, the withdrawal of the troops from Bamian was a first step towards allaying the irritation aroused at Kunduz and Khulm by the foolish aggression of Lord. (*I. O. S. C.,* vol. 9 of 1840, Macnaghten to Indian government, April 24; Indian government to Macnaghten,

May 25, 1840; Durand).

The other foreign relations of Shah Shuja were confined mainly to Herat on the one side and to the Sikhs on the other; and it is hard to say which gave the more trouble to Macnaghten. At Herat that extremely dexterous scoundrel, Yar Mohamed, was perfectly clear as to two principal objects, that the British must not take possession of the place, but that they must none the less be induced to fill his pockets with gold. To this end he was on the one hand perpetually stirring up both his near neighbours, as in the district of Kandahar, and the remoter chiefs, as at Bukhara and Khiva, to steady hostility against the foreign invaders, and on the other, intriguing with Persia, so that the British might give him a subsidy to keep the Persians at a distance. First and last, he wheedled out of the British political agents some £200,000, and was still intent on obtaining more.

Macnaghten became frantic with impatience, and in August he pressed for an advance upon Herat, which August, should end the difficulty once for all. Indeed, at the very moment when chaos was at its worst on the line of communication between Sukkur and Quetta, Macnaghten instructed Bean to keep negotiations moving as to Kalat, since any disturbance there would be a sufficient plea for an advance on Herat. Where the troops for such an advance were to be found, he did not say; but such details never troubled Macnaghten. The project came to nothing, for Auckland was firmly determined against it. (I.O.S.C., vol. 14 of 1840, Macnaghten to Indian government, Aug. 10; vol. 13, Macnaghten to Bean, Aug. 12, 1840).

The Sikhs were even more exasperating, for they were perpetually stirring up rebellion against Shah Shuja and in favour of Dost Mohamed. One such rebellion which took place at Bajaor, a valley some fifty miles north-west of Peshawar, in May 1840, drove a sad thorn into Macnaghten's side. The heat was too great for active operations, and, apart from this difficulty, there were no troops to spare. The political agent made a vain effort to compose matters by negotiation, but in vain. The *Shah's* levies, endeavouring to intervene by force, were discomfited and left a gun in the hands of the insurgents. It was very evident that only regular troops could deal with the situation; and the regular troops had their hands full already.

Beginning in May with a mild complaint that the outstanding details unsettled between the Indian government and the Sikhs caused great inconvenience, Macnaghten, by August, was urging that the Sikhs should "by vigorous policy be deprived of the means of molesting us."

The Afghan Revolt, the citadel of Herat

Auckland, however, was not inclined to make war upon the Sikhs when so many troops were already fully occupied with hostilities in Afghanistan. Both he and Macnaghten should have remembered at first, instead of at last, that the whole power of the Sikhs lay between the British Army beyond the Indus and its reserves in Hindustan.

******

I.O.S.C., vol. 9 of 1840, Macnaghten to Indian Government, May 11; vol. 11 of 1840, E. B. Conolly to Macnaghten, June 2, 1840; Durand. Mr. Clerk, the very able resident at Lahore, doubted whether the Sikhs had actually aided Dost Mohamed with funds, and he even urged the employment of Sikh troops in the interest of Shah Shuja. Macnaghten took great offence at this. *I.O.S.C.*, vol. 17 of 1840, Macnaghten to Indian government, Oct. 14, 27, Nov. 19, 1840.

******

Practically, therefore, Macnaghten's foreign policy on Shah Shuja's behalf amounted to war with his neighbours both to east and west. His domestic policy was no more successful. In August, Burnes summarised the position with creditable sincerity and force. There could be no doubt as to Shah Shuja's unpopularity, which, considering the conduct of his allies, the Sikhs and the British, was not surprising. His chief native adviser was imbecile, corrupt and oppressive. The collectors of the revenue were the *Shah's* soldiers. They received assignments on certain districts for their pay, and lived at free quarter until that assignment was paid. Necessarily this signified extortion and illusage towards the unfortunate inhabitants; but the British protected the Shah against the consequences. A system of revenue which was neither British nor Afghan could not fail to be vicious, and should be amended.

At Kandahar the Duranis complained that they had suffered from the coming of the British, and the tone of the people generally was unfriendly. The Ghilzais were discontented. The Kohistanis, who were handed over to Shah Shuja as subjects, had been alienated by misrule and had become enemies. Lastly, all confidence in British protection had been shaken by the late events in Shawal and in Kalat, where Macnaghten had set up Shah Nawaz Khan and had allowed him to be driven out. Next, the condition of Shah Shuja's military forces was most unsatisfactory. The only really serviceable portion of it was that raised in India and paid by the British, the remainder being simply the Shah's plaything. Thus his household artillery had been left throughout the past winter without pay, and had consequently sold their arms and clothing and had mutinied. Ultimately they had been paid by Macnaghten's order from the British funds at Kabul, and had then returned to duty. But there had been another mutiny in a Hindustani regiment of infantry; and altogether the outlook was most unpromising. Burnes's conclusion was:

> We shall make nothing of Afghanistan unless we change our ways.—*I.O.S.C,* vol. 14 of 1840, Burnes to Macnaghten, Aug. 7, 1840.

That Burnes, the visionary and optimist, should have written in such a strain was significant; but Macnaghten, when forwarding it to Auckland, made light of Burnes's opinion, and Auckland agreed to treat it as of little importance. Yet every word of it was true, and even fell short of the truth. The state of affairs about Kandahar, as shall presently be seen, had grown steadily worse since August. The system of collecting revenue was utterly vicious. The policy of raising native levies to check the Afghan nobles had resulted only in mutiny on the one side and bitter discontent on the other; while a succession of military reverses and mishaps testified eloquently to the fatal consequence of entrusting military operations to the supreme control of civilians. Among those civilians the very worst offender was Macnaghten himself.

Nominally, General Roberts was in command of Shah Shuja's forces, or at any rate of such part of it as had marched into Afghanistan from India; but Macnaghten insisted on keeping every detail of control in his own hands. He would not allow Roberts to have anything to do with the local corps, denying him even the opportunity of seeing them, and would listen to no representations from him concerning their misbehaviour. He kept from him all knowledge of the movements of troops on the frontier; he intercepted from him the reports even of regiments which were unquestionably under Roberts's command; he would listen to no warnings of the danger of isolated posts, and heed no entreaties for sufficient protection of important stations; he promoted officers according to his arbitrary preference, ignoring alike the personal recommendations of Roberts and the established rule of military practice, thereby giving deep offence to all, and ruining the spirit of his officers as a body.

He, like his august master, His Majesty Shah Shuja, looked upon his soldiers as playthings, some to be petted, others to be destroyed.

Alexander Burnes

He worked one battalion so unmercifully and subjected it to such hardship that he fairly wore it out and was obliged to disband it. He complained that he had not a moment to himself; and it is true that he gave himself no rest from the writing of interminable and unnecessary letters, but he always found time to do work which should have been left to General Roberts. In vain Roberts remonstrated and protested. Macnaghten, who was more than a match for the general with the pen, answered him with petulance, or forwarded his letters with sneering comments. Finally, at the end of 1840, growing weary of Roberts's pertinacity, he ousted him from his command and set up a new general, Anquetil, in his place, little guessing that he was ensuring long life to Roberts and speedy death to his successor. (*I.O.S.C.*, vol. 17 of 1840, Roberts to Macnaghten, Sept. 30; vol. 18 of 1840, same to same, Oct. 26, Nov. 8; Anquetil to Indian government, Dec. 2, 1840).

A yet more fateful military blunder had been made, chiefly through Macnaghten's weakness, in the course of the year at Kabul itself. Though fully alive to the importance of holding the Bala Hissar in some strength as a military post, and though at a critical moment ready to occupy it, he had yielded to the wishes of the *Shah*, who desired to keep the whole building for his family, which was now on the way to join him. In the course of this summer, therefore, the construction of cantonments was begun on the plain to north of the city, of which it is necessary to say no more at present than that they combined every possible defect of design and position.

For this very serious blunder Cotton alone must be held responsible, though it is difficult to judge how far he was really a free agent in the matter. It does not appear that the ground occupied by the cantonments was purchased, and it is certain that a very large proportion of it was given over to the envoy and his immense retinue. It is possible, therefore, that this was the only site that Shah Shuja was prepared, or even able, to grant, that Macnaghten accepted it, and that Cotton took it over as a matter of course, (see Hough, *Review of the Operations at Kabul*).

Cotton would have been the more willing to do so, first because, no matter how he might differ from Macnaghten on military questions, he considered himself bound by his instructions to obey him; secondly, because he considered the stables in the Bala Hissar, which had been of necessity occupied by the native infantry during the first winter, quite unfit for that purpose; and thirdly, because he had caught from Macnaghten the infection of unwillingness to disoblige Shah

Kabul

Shuja. Though often differing in opinion from Macnaghten he had contrived to work with him without serious friction, though always by the simple expedient of yielding to Macnaghten's will. He had, in October, resigned his command and was about to return to India on account of ill-health, and he may, therefore, have been unwilling to raise difficulties just before his departure, the more so since, according to the envoy, the troops were as safe at Kabul as at Calcutta.

Not that Cotton himself was so sanguine as Macnaghten concerning the future. He was under no illusions as to the instability of Shah Shuja's rule, and reported definitely and decidedly his own view that, if the British troops were withdrawn, the Shah would be unable to hold his crown. With this fact before us, his approval of the new cantonments is a fault that cannot be forgiven him; and it is only one more testimony to the demoralisation wrought among military officers by their enforced subservience to political masters.

★★★★★★

I. O., Cotton's Letter Book, Cotton to Auckland, Oct. 25, Dec. 5; to Sir J. Nicolls, Nov. 2, 1840. I have searched in vain for any light upon the inception of these cantonments either in manuscript or in print; but I find in Cotton's Letter Book a letter to the Indian government of Feb. 1, 1841, in which he speaks of "the new cantonments," which proves that they must have come into existence in the summer of 1840.

★★★★★★

As regards the British troops, hard work was beginning to tell upon them severely. The Hundred and Second could not produce two hundred effective men on parade, and at least one of the Bengal native battalions—the Forty-Eighth—was reduced to impotence by sickness. For this, once again, Macnaghten was in some degree responsible, because he insisted upon driving the soldiers into petty expeditions in the field when the general required them to build huts for their shelter during the winter. There were so many important posts to be held that the force at disposal for active operations was insufficient, and therefore was inevitably overworked. In fact, there was hardly a battalion at Kabul that did not require immediate relief; and, though Colonel Shelton of the Forty-Fourth had received orders in October to lead a brigade from Kurnal through the Khyber Pass to reinforce Cotton, he could not hope to accomplish the long march in less than four months.

Incidentally, it may be mentioned that the transport-department of the Bengal Army was in a hopeless state. Experience had shown that camels from India were useless in Afghanistan. They would not face steep ascents, showing terror at the prospect, nor go up a hill to graze; and they had not learned, as had the Afghan camels, to avoid poisonous herbs. In fact, as General Elphinstone tersely put it, they were purchased, apparently, only to be buried; but the transport-officers, hide-bound by tradition, would not resort to the use of mules, native ponies and asses. As with the troops, therefore, so with the transport; all the work was thrown upon a few creatures which were thereby the more speedily worn out. (*I.O.*, Cotton's Letter Book, Cotton to Auckland and to Sir J. Nicolls, Oct. 12; to Auckland, Oct. 25, Dec. 15, 1840; *I.O.S.C.*, vol. 9 of 1 841, Minutes of Court of Enquiry into the mortality of camels at Kabul, Sept. 9, 1841).

So much for the troops at Kabul and of the Bengal Army generally. Let us now turn to those of the Bombay Army, which by the end of 1840 had taken over the entire line of communication between Sukkur and Quetta. Here a principal difficulty was lack of a zealous and efficient staff. The spirit among the officers was, in fact, very bad. They jumped at staff-appointments in time of peace, when these signified ease and emolument, but could not be induced to accept them in the field, where they meant hard work. The result was that the Commissariat department, in spite of the experience of the past campaign, was in a very defective state. Extravagant contracts were made; and regiments were sent to the front without any record of the rate of hire agreed upon for their transport. And the Bombay Government increased rather than allayed the difficulties of the unfortunate general in command. If he persuaded officers to undertake duties with the commissariat, they threw up the task after a very brief trial.

If he recommended the removal of one who had proved himself inefficient, the Bombay Government left him for weeks without a reply. If he found a capable man to accept the post of baggage-master, the Bombay Government refused to appoint him, and substituted an incapable man of their own. If, remembering the hordes of followers that had encumbered the advance of Cotton, he chose a strong man to limit strictly the number of his own followers, the Bombay Government declined to confirm his choice. Whether all this were due to sheer neglect on the part of the authorities in Bombay, or to the spirit of jobbery which was quite as rife among Indian civilians as among their compeers in England, or whether intriguers were at work to harry General Brooks out of his command so that he might give place to some favourite of their own, is now of no great consequence. The result was in any case to increase friction, waste and extravagance, to paralyse the commander and to demoralise the troops. And this was a serious matter, for things were not secure between the Indus and Quetta.

Despite of the surrender of Dost Mohamed, of the crushing defeat of Nasir Khan by Marshall, and the reoccupation of Kalat by Nott, both General Brooks and Ross-Bell agreed that the situation in Upper Sind was no easier, and that not a single soldier could with safety be withdrawn. The truth was that the dismembering of Kalat and the annexation of Shawal and Mastung to Shah Shuja's dominions, hastily accomplished by Macnaghten against the opinion of Ross-Bell and—though he could not venture to undo it—of Auckland himself, had been a great political blunder; and, whether the Bombay Government cared to face the fact or not, had stirred up permanent discontent in the district. (*I.O.S.C.,* vol. 16 of 1840, Ross-Bell to Indian government, Sept. 24; Auckland's minute, Oct. 19; vol. 1 of 1841, General Brooks's Diary, Dec. 6-19, 1840).

And everywhere, at the risk of tedium it must be repeated, there was the same revolt of military officers against their domination by the political agents. Nott had spoken his mind freely about the "political boys." Ross-Bell had carried his arrogance so far as to have twice incurred censure from Calcutta for his interference with military matters, but he had done his best to wreck Marshall's enterprise against Nasir Khan, and was still harassing Brooks, and meant to harass him more. The evil must have been very great when Cotton, who had loyally given way himself to Macnaghten upon all points, spoke his mind at length to Auckland as the very last act of his command. He wrote:

> Some check must be imposed, or the whole system must be altered as regards young political officers assuming the authority they do when sent to accompany regular troops. Much disgust has arisen from this; and it is absurd that old experienced military men should be under the orders of lieutenants merely because they place after their names 'Acting-Assistant Political Agent.'—*I.O.*, Cotton's Letter Book. Cotton to Auckland, Feb. 1, 1841.

Meanwhile, ever since the autumn of 1840 there had been searchings of heart at Calcutta. Auckland, in October, had reviewed without flinching, though not without bitter disappointment, the reverses upon all sides; and early in November shrewd old Sir Jasper Nicolls took pen in hand and not only stated facts but drew conclusions. It was evident, he wrote in effect, that Shah Shuja, even with a force commanded by European officers (who could ill be spared), would never be independent King of Afghanistan. After all that had been done, it was, perhaps, impossible consistently with good faith to withdraw him from Afghanistan, and equally impossible to displace him. It was therefore inevitable for the British to continue to rule in his name, bearing the cost of his establishments, personal, civil and political, without prospect of reimbursement. Already a large portion of the army was in Afghanistan, where native corps suffered from the climate and should be relieved after two years.

The country could not be held with fewer than three European and ten native regiments, regular troops. Communication with it from India was always difficult and sometimes impossible. The Sikhs would not long permit the passage of our troops through their territory, and would choose their own time to force war upon us. The attitude of Nepal was also uncertain, if not menacing. We ought to be strong enough to fight Sikhs and Nepalis simultaneously, and therefore the army should be at once increased by the raising of additional regiments. (*I.O.S.C.*, vol. 3 of 1841, Minute of Sir Jasper Nicolls, Nov. 10, 1840).

Such a cold marshalling of unpleasant but undeniable truths was very distasteful to Auckland, who kept the document for two months, dismayed at the financial prospect which it opened up. But in January 1841 he laid it gently aside. The surrender of Dost Mohamed had, he said, changed the whole outlook, and there was now probability that troops might shortly be withdrawn from Afghanistan. He had no intention of sending a force to Balkh or Bukhara, nor even, if it could be avoided, to Herat.

In the Punjab the British were more likely to be called in by one faction of Sikhs against another than to have to contend with them united. The strain was no doubt considerable, for the occupation of Aden and Karak had been added to the military burdens of India, and, moreover, hostilities had recently broken out with China. Still, the increase of establishment during the past two years amounted to forty-five thousand native and six thousand European soldiers; and therefore there seemed no necessity for further augmentation of the army. (*I.O.S.C.,* vol. 3 of 1841, Auckland's Minute of Jan. 15, 1841).

It seems strange that Auckland should have misread the situation so completely as he did. In October, a he had reviewed the whole series of reverses along the lines of communication with dismay; and Macnaghten's confession—for it amounted to little less—that only the conquest of Herat and war against the Sikhs could enable him to hold his own in Afghanistan, should have shown him that the situation was most dangerous and that he could not too soon withdraw his troops from the country. Since then, any immediate danger of a Russian advance had come to an end.

Dost Mohamed had surrendered and was on his way to honourable captivity in Ludhiana. Kalat had been recovered, Nasir Khan had been heavily defeated and his levies dispersed, and Nott's communications with the Indus had been re-established. Now was the moment when, Shah Shuja's archenemy having been removed, the British troops might have marched out of Afghanistan with honour, and a mistaken policy might have been abandoned with a flourish of trumpets.

It is true that at Kandahar there were dangerous symptoms of unrest. There, since July, a new political agent had replaced Leech, namely, Major Henry Rawlinson, whose fame rests upon the deciphering of the cuneiform inscriptions, and who was then known in some measure already as an Oriental scholar, but chiefly as a good soldier and a very shrewd and sensible administrator. While Nott was on his return march to Kandahar early in December 1840, Rawlinson was stirred by the deepest anxiety over a rising in the district of Zamindawar, some fifty miles to north-west of the city.

The leader was one Akhtar Khan, a bold ambitious man, whose expectations of obtaining charge of Zamindawar had been baffled by the minions of Shah Shuja. His followers were not at the moment numerous; but Rawlinson saw, quite correctly, in the movement not a mere tumultuary rising of oppressed peasants but an organised conspiracy against the *Shah's* government. During Nott's absence he had borrowed two guns from the garrison and sent them out with some native levies under a native leader against Akhtar Khan. He duly reported this to the general upon his return to Kandahar, who answered with the chilling comment, "Well, then, you have lost your two guns." Nott proved to be right. The native levies fled before Akhtar and left their artillery in his hands. Rawlinson was fain to press for the employment of regular native troops to crush the insurrection before it should become more formidable; and Nott, fully alive to the danger, made no difficulty about compliance.

GENERAL NOTT

Accordingly, on the 23rd of December, Captain Farrington sallied out with the Second Bengal Native Infantry, two horse-artillery guns, a squadron of regular native cavalry and a party of Afghan horse. The cold was intense and the march was most arduous; but the *sepoys* faced all hardships without a murmur, and Farrington, having crossed the Helmand at Girishk, turned northward, and on the 3rd of January 1841 came up with his enemy, defeated them with a loss of sixty killed, and recovered the lost guns. Disheartened by this check and oppressed by the severity of the weather, the insurgents dispersed; and Farrington returned to Kandahar.

But neither Rawlinson nor Nott flattered themselves that the trouble was over; and Rawlinson wrote very strongly to Macnaghten in condemnation of the whole system of revenue. He also affirmed boldly that the policy of paying blackmail to the Ghilzais might have done some good but had done more harm, since it only spread wider over the land the impression that the British practice was to reward enemies and neglect friends.

Fortunately the malcontents were divided into two hostile camps, for the Durani chiefs and the Ghilzais loathed each other with mortal hatred; but it was as plain to Rawlinson as to Nott that the rule of the British was abominated by both. Nott, in September 1840, had in a private letter set down his opinion in strong language:

> The conduct of the one thousand and one politicals has ruined our cause, and bared the throat of every European in this country to the sword and knife of the revengeful Afghan and the bloody Belooch, and unless several regiments be quickly sent, not a man will be left to note the fall of his comrades. Nothing but force will ever make them submit to the hated Shah Shuja, who is most certainly as great a scoundrel as ever lived.

These words naturally had not come to Macnaghten's eye; but Rawlinson had conveyed the same idea in softer language, not omitting his suspicions that Shah Shuja had countenanced the revolt of Akhtar Khan, and that His Majesty's hand could be traced making serious and dangerous mischief. (*I.O.S.C.*, vol. 4 of 1 841, Rawlinson to Macnaghten, Jan. 17, 20, 1 841; *Life of Sir William Nott*, i.; Durand).

To all this Macnaghten replied that he would advise Shah Shuja to remove the minister who had abused the administration of the revenue, and to reform the system; but that, for the rest, he differed from Rawlinson upon every point. He communicated to the Shah the accusations brought by Rawlinson, and the monarch was, or pretended to be, well nigh frantic in affirming his innocence. Macnaghten accepted his assurances without question, and informed Rawlinson that in this case "the king could do no wrong." Auckland, of course taking Macnaghten's view, pronounced that Rawlinson's misgivings as to the general discontent and disloyalty about Kandahar was exaggerated; and so matters went on as before.

The obnoxious minister was indeed removed, and orders were given for juster collection of the revenue; but this was a matter which could only have been taken in hand when all disorder had ceased. In the midst of disturbance and rebellion there was no leisure for serious administrative change. Moreover, the Shah was always impecunious. He was expecting his harem—a trifling establishment of some eight hundred souls—at Kabul, which would add to his expenses. Unless Macnaghten were prepared to advance more funds from the Indian revenue—and the Indian government already stood aghast at the enormous cost of its Afghan venture—money must be wrung out of the Afghans by some means. And it was so wrung by the old condemned expedients. (Durand; *I.O.S.C.*, vol. 4 of 1841, Macnaghten to Rawlinson—letters—Jan. 30, 1841; Indian government to Macnaghten, Mar. 15, 1841).

It was perhaps natural that Macnaghten should discredit all reports of serious trouble about Kandahar, for by the end of January he was once more intent upon the capture of Herat. Reports had come in that Persia was again contemplating an advance upon that place; the explanation of which was that Yar Mohamed, with a view to extracting further subsidies from the British resident, Major Todd, had suggested to the Persians the expediency of such a movement, well knowing that there was no probability of their undertaking it. To his great disgust, however, the resident not only declined to pay him additional money, but on the 1st of February cut off his regular monthly allowance pending reference to Calcutta. Thereupon, Yar Mohamed, recovering himself, suggested that, if two *lakhs* of *rupees* were immediately made over to him, he would assent to the admission of a British force into Herat.

Todd, who had long been working for this very object, jumped at the offer, but was cautious enough to require first that Yar Mohamed should send his son, as a pledge of his good faith, to conduct the British troops into Herat. Yar Mohamed, who had no intention at heart of admitting troops willingly at all, thereupon drew back, declined to furnish the guarantee, and demanded either immediate payment of the money or the withdrawal of the mission from the city. He reckoned that the disturbances about Kandahar would keep the British troops fully employed and make Todd averse from a rupture with Herat; but, to his consternation, Todd took him at his word, removed the mission, and with it banished all immediate prospect of the two *lakhs* of *rupees,* (Durand).

The ultimate consequence of this very comical incident was the recall of Todd in disgrace and disavowal of his measures by Auckland, who wrote conciliatory letters to Yar Mohamed, and, as may be supposed, found no difficulty in restoring friendly relations. But the immediate result was, for a short time during February and March, feverish activity in preparing a march upon Herat. Captain Saunders of the Engineers, being consulted as to the force and artillery that would be required, named twelve thousand men, twelve heavy guns and as many mortars; whereupon Macnaghten, on the 25th of March, wrote urgently to Outram at Hyderabad bidding him hasten guns and ammunition to Sukkur, while Rawlinson addressed Ross-Bell at Quetta, pleading for immediate advance of Bombay troops through the passes to Kandahar.

But Ross-Bell had his own opinions upon this subject, and wrote them very plainly to the chief authorities both at Calcutta and at Bombay. He represented that the situation between the Indus and Quetta was still very uncertain, and in the Kandahar provinces decidedly bad. If the expedition to Herat were to take place, therefore, reinforcements of at least five battalions, one-third of them European, and a European battery must be sent forward to Quetta at once. Macnaghten, he added, was hurrying his preparations so as to reach Herat early in July, in time to save the harvest. But this was out of the question. Neither sufficient infantry, nor sufficient artillery, nor sufficient transport and supplies could be ready before October without dangerous weakening of the force in the Kandahar provinces; and even in that case there would be no siege-train. And to advance upon Herat without ample means to ensure success would be to court serious danger. Ross-Bell's apprehensions were very soon laid to rest, for, by the end of March, the whole project was abandoned, and Herat need for the present concern us no longer.

But the incident reveals the confusion which reigned among the British authorities in Afghanistan. Here were Rawlinson pressing for the advance of troops from Quetta and Macnaghten ordering the collection of a siege-train at Sukkur, both hot for the capture and occupation of Herat, while Ross-Bell, in his commanding position at Quetta, objected strongly to either measure, and would do nothing to further them without reference to Calcutta. Not only did the political authorities claim sole direction of the military operations, but each several political agent aspired to be an independent commander-in-chief within his own sphere. It is obvious that in such a condition of affairs the man who ruled on the lines of communication could neutralise all the efforts of his superiors at the front by undertaking little enterprises of his own, and then declaring that he could spare no troops. (*I.O.S.C.*, vol. 4 of 1841, Macnaghten to Ross-Bell, Jan. 28; vol. 6 of 1841, Rawlinson to Captain Saunders, Feb. 24; to Ross-Bell, Mar. 15; Macnaghten to Outram and to Dep. Comm. General Parsons, Mar. 15; Ross-Bell to Indian government and Bombay government, Mar. 29; vol. 7 of 1841, Ross-Bell to Rawlinson, April 11, 1841; Durand; Kaye, i.).

It was at this juncture, in the spring of 1841, that the government in Downing Street suddenly intervened in the Afghan war, being alarmed by all the numerous reverses of the summer and autumn of 1840, and as yet uninformed of the more favourable events of the close of the year. The Ministry attributed the various mishaps to the recall of too many troops at the end of 1839, and the resistance to Shah Shuja's government to want of energy in reforming the civil administration. They represented the financial embarrassment that had arisen from the cost of the Afghan venture, and foresaw no decrease of it, since it was evident that, without the support of a considerable British force for a considerable time, the rule of Shah Shuja could not be maintained.

They therefore concluded that the time was come to decide definitely whether Afghanistan should be evacuated forthwith, or whether the British should take the government into its own hands and uphold its position there at all costs. The Indian Government must choose between these two alternatives, and, if it should choose the latter, must act with energy. (I have been unable to find the original letter of the Secret Committee, but an abstract is given in Durand).

This letter appears to have reached Auckland in the second week in March, and, being a conscientious man, he reviewed the situation with sincerity, he wrote:

The result by which I *am* discouraged is that even for the support of the *Shah's* ordinary authority no reliance whatever can apparently be yet placed on his own establishments. Whether it be to quell an insurrection in the Durani districts or to repress the predatory habits of the Khyberris, the sole dependence of the authorities in Afghanistan seems to be on the British troops.

One of his council, Mr. Prinsep, took an even stronger line. It was, he wrote in effect, monstrous that Shah Shuja, a mere cipher in the first essentials of sovereignty, should be upheld by Macnaghten in irresponsible appropriation of every rupee of revenue, and suffered to make grants, aggressions and usurpations without any reference to the general welfare. If the British broke down the independence of the tribes by military force and brought a country into subjection, it was nothing less than their bounden duty to see that the revenue was properly collected and spent, and that justice was equitably administered. Practically, these few sentences, absolutely true in every respect, amounted to condemnation by both Auckland and Prinsep of Macnaghten's policy from beginning to end, and should have taken logical effect either in his immediate recall or in the evacuation of Afghanistan. (*I.O.S.C.*, vol. 4 of 1841, Auckland's minute of Mar. 19; Prinsep's of Mar. 21, 1841).

The moment was not unfavourable, if any moment could be called favourable, for such evacuation. All was, for the moment, quiet. On the side of Kabul, Shelton's brigade had reached Jalalabad and had made its presence felt, as shall presently be told, by a punitive march against one of the predatory tribes in a valley adjoining the Khyber Pass. On the side of Kandahar a timely display of force by Nott had overawed a fresh gathering of the tribes under Akhtar Khan, and that chief himself had received a dress of honour in token of his reconciliation to the rule of Shah Shuja and of the full pardon granted to him on his return to his allegiance, (Stocqueler, *Life of Sir William Nott*, i.; Kaye, i.).

Thus, there had been sufficient success to vindicate the honour of the British arms, and a sufficient manifestation of their power to show that they were irresistible. It was of course arguable that, if the British troops were withdrawn, Shah Shuja might very soon find his throat cut; but he certainly felt the indignity of the tutelage under which he reigned, and, by Rawlinson and Nott at any rate, he was suspected of endeavouring to shake it off by treachery. It would not, therefore, have been unreasonable to tell him that now he could stand without support, and that the British were content to leave him to himself with their best wishes.

But Auckland, whether from false shame, or unwillingness to wound Macnaghten, could not bring himself to acknowledge that his policy was mistaken. He was honest enough to admit all the difficulties, embarrassments and dangers that beset the position in Afghanistan, but none the less he persisted that without any change of system all would yet be well. He had even some warrant of military opinion in support of his view, for Cotton, upon Shelton's arrival, had informed Sir Jasper Nicolls that there was now no reason why the Thirteenth, three native battalions and two batteries of artillery should not return to India. (*I.O.*, Cotton's Letter Book, to Sir Jasper Nicolls, Feb. 1, 1841).

It is true that for purely military reasons—namely, for preserving the efficiency of these corps—it was urgently necessary that they should be withdrawn from Afghanistan as soon as possible. It is true also that Cotton was wholly dependent upon Macnaghten for his intelligence as to the feeling in the country, and that he shrank from any controversy with him even upon strictly military questions. He cannot have been wholly ignorant of Nott's apprehensions, but Nott had at his elbow Henry Rawlinson, who saw with him eye to eye, whereas Macnaghten derided the views of both. And it must be added that Cotton was no time-server to gain credit by belittling his own officers and adulating those of Macnaghten, for he held Nott's opinion in high respect, and had supported him loyally in the bitterest of his quarrels with the politicals. Cotton was, in fact, simply deceived by Macnaghten, or, if he was not, thought it better to keep his ideas to himself.

And Macnaghten, face to face with unpleasant and unanswerable criticism, had taken refuge in bold assertion which was almost bluster. He could not now deny Shah Shuja's unpopularity, but he was vehement as to his personal merits and as to the actual if not apparent success of his rule, he wrote:

> All things considered, the present tranquillity of this country is to my mind perfectly miraculous. Already our presence has been infinitely beneficial in allaying animosities and pointing out abuses. . . . We are gradually placing matters on a firm and satisfactory basis.—Durand.

When such was the language of the man on the spot, Auckland gladly set aside the warnings of Nott and of Rawlinson. He was indeed so much alarmed by the financial outlook that he demanded an early report upon the revenues of Afghanistan; but he shut his ears to the mutterings of the coming storm, and decided to continue his progress along the road that led to destruction.

CHAPTER 6

Arrival of Shelton's Brigade

On the 1st of February, 1841, Cotton definitely relinquished the command in Afghanistan, having by that day reached the River Ravi on his homeward journey. His last weeks in the country, spent with Macnaghten and Shah Shuja at Jalalabad, were not the pleasantest of his sojourn. Shelton's brigade, after a march of nearly three months, was approaching Peshawar towards Christmas 1840, and all the political agents were wild to make immediate use of it against the rebel chief, still unsubdued, of Bajaor. Mackeson in fact begged that the brigade might be halted for a season at Jamrud to give weight to his negotiations with the aforesaid rebel; and Cotton was justly apprehensive as to the result.

Dost Mohamed, proceeding under strong escort to India, was expected to reach Peshawar at about the same time; and such a concentration of troops, as Cotton wrote, was far more likely to give umbrage to the Sikhs than to frighten a barbarian in the mountains a hundred miles away. Trembling for his communications, Cotton protested so strongly that Macnaghten for the moment gave way. Cotton, moreover, was anxious not only to avoid friction with the Sikhs but to give Shelton's brigade time to construct huts for themselves at Jalalabad before the wet season should set in. But neither communications nor dwellings for the soldiers were matters that appealed to Macnaghten. He had in fact banished all consideration for the shelter, health and comfort of the men in the previous year when he ordered troops away on the abortive march to Pashat. He insisted that Shelton should halt at Jamrud, and Cotton was fain to yield. Cotton wrote:

> I think the measure in every way objectionable, but my instructions oblige me to comply.

His last letter to Nicolls adjured him to permit no expedition to Bajaor without proper reconnaissance. The political agents, he said, were bent upon it; but nothing was known of the country except that the roads were infamous, that one fort at least was so strong as to call for siege-artillery, and that supplies were not to be found in it. With this final warning and the protest, already quoted, against the subordination of generals to political lieutenants, Cotton leaves the stage of this history. (*I.O.,* Cotton's Letter Book, to Sir Jasper Nicolls, Feb. 1, 1841).

His successor, General Elphinstone, was at this time not far advanced on his journey from Meerut; and when Shelton at last reached Jalalabad in January, there was no commander-in-chief to give even nominal trouble to Macnaghten, while there were three new battalions and a new battery for him to play with. Shelton, colonel of the Forty-Fourth, was a veteran who had joined the Ninth Foot in 1805, seen his first service with Moore in the advance to Sahagun and retreat to Coruña, had then served at Walcheren, returned to the Peninsula in 1812, and, fighting there till shipped off to Canada in 1814, had since gone through the awful campaign in Arakan. His personal courage and fortitude were, even in those days, exceptional. He had lost his right arm at the storm of St. Sebastian; and it was said that he had stood up outside his tent, unmoved, while the surgeons took the limb out of its socket. He had not only great experience but had keenly studied his profession, and was by no means lacking in brains.

In fact, he had many of the qualities which go to make up a fine soldier, but undid them all by a morose and uncertain temper. As a regimental commander he was what is called a martinet, which may be defined as one who insists upon obedience but cannot evoke it willingly, and lacks sense of proportion in the enforcement of discipline. As a man he was difficult, contradictious and disposed to nurse grievances, yet not without latent generosity and power of appreciation. His defects being very real and very conspicuous, he was generally, and with good reason, disliked, and even hated. This type of officer is by no means extinct, though less common than it was in high place, experience having taught adjutants general that his shortcomings outweigh his merits. In Shelton's case, as in many others, it can never be known how far incessant physical pain, due to the rough surgery of those days, may have embittered his character.

★★★★★★

William Napier's intellect was completely unbalanced by the

General Elphinstone

pain of an old wound. Lord Anglesey, though he never uttered a sound, would lock himself into his room, and roll on the floor in agony. Sir Hugh Palliser's quarrel with Keppel admits of this explanation likewise.

******

Such was the man who marched into Jalalabad in January 1841, and found himself, after years of work with Moore and Wellington, under the orders of a Macnaghten. The envoy soon supplied work for him. A tribe called the Sanga Khels had lately given much trouble by making raids upon convoys in the Khyber Pass, and required to be brought to reason. The entrance to their valley, called the Nazian valley, was some four miles from the post of Pesh Bolak, which itself lies about fifteen miles east of Jalalabad; and there ran from its head a narrow pass, debouching on the Khyber at Landi Khana, eight miles to the southeast of Dakka, through which they carried off their plunder. They were a formidable folk who had repelled many great warriors, including Nadir Shah, and so far had held their valley intact against all invaders.

On the 21st of February Shelton marched from Jalalabad with a sufficient force to ensure success, and took the business scientifically in hand. The valley was twenty-five miles long, and was one series of formidable defiles, the breadth in many places not exceeding that of the stream which wound through it, and the cliffs being frequently so high and perpendicular as to shut out the sun for more than twenty hours out of the twenty-four. Shelton, recalling his studies of Alpine campaigns, made it his principle always to get above his enemy, no matter by what exertion, dislodged them thus with ease, and took most of their petty forts, or *sangars*, in reverse. Two strongholds only needed to have their gates blown in; and by the 13th of March he had penetrated to the very last dwelling at the foot of the snowy range, subdued the Sanga Khels completely and destroyed one hundred and forty-four of their petty strongholds, all at a cost of nine killed and twenty-nine wounded.

Such methods contrasted very favourably with those of stupid, blundering old Sale, who, near Charikar, had thrown away as many casualties, two-thirds of them in his own regiment, in a single unsuccessful and quite unnecessary assault upon some trifling fort. For this service Shelton, who had not a ribbon to wear on his coat, received from the Shah the ridiculous order of the Durani Empire, but from the Indian government no word of acknowledgement, which, to such a mind as his, of course constituted a grievance.

✶✶✶✶✶✶

I gather the foregoing details, as well as the situation of the Nazian valley, from a very brief scribbled memorandum in Shelton's hand, which was most kindly sent to me, with others of Shelton's papers, by Captain C. B. Norman. As to Sale in Charikar, see *I. O.*, Cotton's Letter Book, to Auckland, Oct. 6, 1840.

✶✶✶✶✶✶

The next incident was the arrival at Kabul at the end of April of the new commander-in-chief, Major-General Elphinstone. He had begun life in the Guards, but had seen no active service until he went with Graham to the Low Countries in command of the Thirty-third, in which campaign, as also in that of Waterloo, he had done extremely well. He was in fact a good soldier who knew his profession thoroughly, though a stranger to Eastern warfare; but he was so infirm, so much crippled by gout, and in such miserable health that he was quite unfit for any kind of work. He suffered intense and constant pain, and was, to all intent, a dying man. Knowing his weakness, he had not desired the command, and indeed had only accepted it after much and repeated pressure from Auckland, because he thought it wrong in a soldier not to go where he was ordered. Cotton, who had known him for five and thirty years, but had not lately seen him, warmly approved the appointment, evidently from esteem of the man; but the plain truth is that Elphinstone was chosen in order that Nott might be excluded, for it was expected that Elphinstone would obey Macnaghten, while it was quite certain that the other would not.

Elphinstone had hardly arrived before he found himself at variance with Macnaghten. The huge cumbrous convoy of Shah Shuja's *zenana* had marched across the Punjab under the escort of George Broadfoot in safety as far as the Indus, when it was threatened by a mob of mutinous Sikh soldiery who declared that they would stop it and plunder it. The political agent on the spot at once cried out for troops, and Macnaghten demanded the immediate despatch of Shelton's brigade by forced marches to Peshawar. To this Elphinstone strongly demurred.

The brigade should long since have been at Kabul; but the political agents had been playing with it ever since it had come within their reach, first halting it at Jamrud, then detaining it at Jalalabad, then sending it to the Nazian valley, and never allowing it to settle down. Now they wished to hurry it through the Khyber Pass to Peshawar, where it would arrive to meet the full heat of June and almost certainly smallpox as well, and thence back to Kabul, a march of at least two hundred miles—all on account of a pack of women. However, as usual, the envoy prevailed.

The brigade marched to the Sikh frontier; the mutinous Sikh soldiers decided to leave Broadfoot's convoy alone; and on the 10th of June Shelton at last led his men into Kabul, with their health fortunately unimpaired. After them the six hundred females and their attendants likewise trailed into the capital, and within six weeks Shah Shuja was applying to the bankers of Kabul for loans to enable him to support them. The general may be pardoned for his profound dissatisfaction with the whole proceeding. (*I.O.S.C.*, vol. 9 of 1841, Elphinstone to Auckland, May 30; Macnaghten to Indian government, June 19; vol. 16 of 1841, Macnaghten to Indian Government, Aug. 4, 1841; Broadfoot's *Life of Major George Broadfoot*).

Elphinstone was not better pleased by other things which he saw about him. The cantonment had been set down in the plain about a mile to the north of the city, and was of simple oblong outline, one thousand yards long and six hundred broad, protected by a low rampart and a narrow ditch with circular bastions at the four angles. At the northern end it was prolonged for about three hundred yards by a further enclosure containing the quarters of the envoy and of his very numerous staff and attendants. Everywhere it was hemmed in by fenced plots and gardens; and it was commanded upon three sides by a number of little forts, many within musket-shot, and on the fourth or west side by a low eminence, known as the Behmaru Hills, within long range of cannon.

Not an inch of ground outside the cantonment was under the control of the military commander, and there was no place whatever for exercising the troops. But Cotton had hired one little fort about five hundred yards south of the north-west angle and had there, with culpable carelessness, lodged his supplies, though the access to it was flanked along the whole length of the road by a walled garden and an unoccupied fort. The whole arrangement was as foolish and as vicious as it could be, and Elphinstone seems to have recognised the fact at once. There was really but one place where the victuals and the reserve of stores should have been lodged, and that was the Bala Hissar, where a sufficient guard at least should have been established for their protection.

The engineer, Lieutenant Sturt, seems to have plotted quietly and silently for some such arrangement, for in the very days when Shah Shuja's six hundred women were entering the city, he reported that he had nearly completed barracks within the Bala Hissar sufficient to house the European garrison and its native attendants. (*I.O.S.C.*, vol. 7 of 1841, Report of Lieutenant Sturt, Jan. 13, 1 841).

The moment might not have been the happiest for reopening a question which had already been settled, with fatal weakness and perversity, by Macnaghten; but a strong man in Elphinstone's place would have accepted no denial, and thereby would have simplified his whole task immensely.

It must, however, be admitted that the general was in a most difficult position. He had to take over a bad state of affairs as he found it, with the further disadvantage that there was a poor prospect of obtaining any money to amend it. The cost of the Afghan war was causing to the Indian revenue an annual deficit of a million and a half sterling; and the Supreme Government, naturally alarmed, was pressing upon Macnaghten the need for the strictest economy. If Elphinstone had insisted upon moving the cantonment to another site, the question of the Bala Hissar must inevitably have been raised anew; and in any case the new ground must have been bought, the cost of the old cantonment must have been thrown away, and it was doubtful whether the work could have been completed before winter.

Even in the existing cantonment there were not barracks enough to hold the troops, and the building of them was being urgently hurried forward. In a new cantonment, self-contained and self-dependent, as it ought to have been, very substantial structures would have been required for the housing of supplies and stores, to say nothing of barracks and defensive works. Moreover, there were already far too few officers of engineers in Afghanistan for all the tasks that were set to them in Quetta, Kandahar and Ghazni. It is more than doubtful whether such a new cantonment could have been completed before the winter, even with lavish profusion of money. The *Shah* would certainly have viewed the project with disfavour; and the Oriental is a past master in the arts of obstruction and delay.

In the circumstances Elphinstone took a middle course. It had been laid down as a principle in the occupation of Afghanistan that there should be both at Kandahar and at Kabul a brigade at disposal for work in the field at any moment. At Kandahar Auckland himself had ordered the construction of a fortified magazine, or citadel, which could be held by a small force so that the rest of the troops might be set free. Laying hold of this fact, Elphinstone reported that a like citadel to overawe the city of Kabul would be very desirable; and meanwhile, as a step towards that end, he urged Macnaghten to buy ground enough, close outside the south side of the cantonment, for the erection of a small fort which would hold all his ordnance and be defensible by two companies. Thereby several points would be gained. The garrison would be liberated for the field; the entrenchment would be strengthened by a flanking work on the side of the city; and the access to the fort—the Commissariat fort as it was called—where the supplies were lodged, would be to some extent guarded and covered.

Elphinstone even hoped that it would answer, in some degree, the purpose of a citadel. Macnaghten, to his credit, at once assented; the work was begun forthwith, and the circumstance was duly reported to Auckland. The sequel may as well be told at once. After some delay the Supreme Government wrote, in June, that it would not sanction the expenditure of so large a sum as £2400 upon such an object, and the work upon the fortified magazine was abandoned. (*I.O.S.C.*, vol. 8 of 1841, Elphinstone to Macnaghten, May 9; Macnaghten to Elphinstone, May 10; Indian government to Macnaghten, June 28; vol. 9 of 1841, Elphinstone to Auckland, May 30, 1841).

What further recommendations, if any, the unfortunate Elphinstone may have made, it is impossible to discover; but there can be no doubt as to their almost inevitable fate, if they involved the spending of money. One thing only is certain, that he felt and did not conceal from his superiors a sense of military insecurity; and this should not be forgotten. Meanwhile, it must be noted that, when Shelton's brigade arrived, it was placed in camp on the Sia Sang hills, some two miles to eastward of the cantonments, and separated from them by a canal and by the Kabul River. Both of these obstacles were bridged in two places, on the roads which led to the Bala Hissar and on that which led to the hills; but it does not appear that Elphinstone took any measures for the protection, by even the smallest permanent work, of any of these bridges; and this omission seems hardly in accord with sound military principle.

It is, however, impossible to find out what he may or may not have suggested to Macnaghten. Any application for money was not likely to be favourably received; and any hint of necessary precaution would have been scouted on the ground that Kabul was as safe as Calcutta. Upon that postulate was built the whole of Macnaghten's policy, and he could hardly be expected to admit, even by implication, that it was false.

For the rest Elphinstone complained bitterly of his transport-service which, in his view, required radical reform. Indeed, the mortality among the camels grew steadily all through the summer until it amounted, during the five months from April to August, to over twelve hundred out of the forty-five hundred at Kabul and Jalalabad. (*I.O.S.C.*, vol. 11 of 1841, Report of Court of Enquiry into mortality of camels, Sept. 9, 1841).

Moreover, there was dearth of officers in other departments besides the engineers. The medical staff was so deficient that, when Shelton marched to Peshawar, the only assistant surgeon who could be furnished to accompany him was the medical store-keeper; and, until his return, the medical stores had to look after themselves. Again an officer of experience was required to take charge of the ordnance, but the only one furnished was a young subaltern of artillery, named Vincent Eyre, who, though an absolute novice, was duly nominated commissary. Altogether Cotton had not left things in a satisfactory condition at Kabul.

Matters were little better at Kandahar and on the lines of communication through Sind. In the very first days of April, General Brooks had arrived at Quetta with a small field-force of about seventeen hundred men from the Bombay Army; (4th troop of Horse Artillery, 1 troop of Skinner's Horse, detachment of Pioneers, H.M. 10th Foot and 21st Bombay N.I. The two battalions had each a strength of about 750 rank and file), and the protection of Shawal and Kalat was supposed to be wholly under the charge of Bombay troops. When, however, Brooks was directed to send the one Bengal regiment with him—the Forty-Second Native Infantry—to escort treasure from Quetta to Kandahar, he answered that he was unable to spare it. The truth was that Ross-Bell had once again initiated military operations upon his own account. A petty Brahui chief, named Fazil Khan, had attacked another petty chief who was, or was supposed to be, friendly to the British; and Ross-Bell must needs step in to protect his ally.

The scene of action was Nushki, some seventy-five miles, as the crow flies, south-west of Quetta; and for thirty-four miles the road was one continuous defile, more formidable than any part of the Bolan Pass. Brooks, conceiving that he had no power to object, sent off the detachment of troops required by Ross-Bell without a word, though inwardly furious at the whole proceeding. Soon afterwards, however, he discovered that his instructions from the Supreme Government authorised him at any rate to give an opinion upon projected military operations, and that these instructions had been for months in the hands of Ross-Bell, who had omitted to forward them.

Then, not unnaturally, Brooks wrote to Ross-Bell pointing out the absolute futility of sending troops to Nushki at all. In the first place, it was doubtful whether the British ought to take any share whatever in the internal feuds of the wild tribes; in the second place, it was certain that Fazil Khan's people would disperse as soon as the British troops arrived, and reassemble as soon as they went away; and, in the third place, if the British troops were maintained at Nushki they must be fed, which signified the constant despatch of convoys under strong escorts, he concluded:

> Thus, we are incurring immense expense in loss of camels by transporting supplies, and risking the health of the men in order to give protection to sixty or seventy tents.

And in actual fact, Ross-Bell advanced this expedition to Nushki as a reason for declining to send reinforcements from Quetta to Kandahar, since he could spare none of his already weak, overworked camels to carry victuals through the Bolan Pass. (*I.O.S.C.*, vol. 8 of 1841, Ross-Bell to Rawlinson, May 2; Brooks to Ross-Bell, May 11, 15; to Indian government, May 20, 22, 1841).

Here, therefore, was another instance of the extreme danger of making every petty political agent an independent commander-in-chief; and Brooks, having once discovered that he had the right to give his opinions upon military matters, proceeded to deliver them very forcibly, not only to Ross-Bell but to the Supreme Government. What garrison, he asked, did the government intend to keep at Quetta for the winter, for the troops must positively be protected from the weather? To this the governor-general answered, after much correspondence and six weeks' delay, that he could not say at present but would inform the Bombay Government as soon as he had made up his mind. Probably anticipating some such reply, Brooks meanwhile addressed the military authorities in Bombay and pointed out, first, that it was useless to keep troops at Quetta in the winter since cold and snow forbade military operations altogether; and, secondly, that he could obtain no workmen to build barracks, as all were already taken up to construct a fortified magazine at Kandahar.

The Bombay Government meanwhile had already found it necessary to remove Brooks from his command for other reasons, and so was delivered from the need of answering his troublesome questions.

But, whatever the merits or demerits of this particular officer, it is evident from his correspondence that the Commander-in-chief in Afghanistan could not count upon the slightest control over the troops, nominally under his orders, between Sukkur and Kandahar. (I.O.S.C., vol. 7 of 1841, Bombay Government to Supreme Government, May 7; vol. 9 of 1841, Brooks to Q.M.G., May 11; vol. 10 of 1841, Brooks to Q.M.G., Bombay, undated (May or June) 1841).

About Kandahar the temporary suppression of the Durani rising had been immediately followed by unrest among the Ghilzais in the valley of the Tarnak, to curb which it had been resolved to restore the fortifications of Kalat-i-Ghilzai and to establish there a strong post. The inception of this work increased the excitement among the tribes; and in the middle of April Rawlinson, with Nott's concurrence, obtained Macnaghten's leave to send a strong detachment to Kalat-i-Ghilzai to guard the working-parties. On the 30th of April, Major Lynch, the political agent, having, as he said, information of a concerted plan of the Ghilzai tribes to besiege Kalat-i-Ghilzai, rode with an escort of two hundred troopers near the petty fort of one of the chiefs.

The Ghilzais, as he passed, rode out brandishing their swords; and thereupon Lynch summoned more men and stormed the fort out of hand. Macnaghten and Rawlinson admonished Lynch to be careful in future, and deplored the incident; but the mischief was done. The Ghilzais in that quarter began to assemble, and presently surrounded the works at Kalat-i-Ghilzai as if to isolate the post completely. (*I.O.S.C.*, vol. 7 of 1841, Rawlinson to Macnaghten, April 16; Lynch to Rawlinson, May 1, 8; Rawlinson to Macnaghten, May 4; Macnaghten to Rawlinson, May 8, 9, 1841; Durand).

Macnaghten, upon learning of this, suggested to Elphinstone a movement of British troops in cooperation with Shah Shuja's towards the threatened point, writing a typical letter which practically forced the general into compliance. But Nott, having occasion to send stores to Kalat-i-Ghilzai, took care to provide an escort of four hundred bayonets, a detachment of horse and two guns, under a good officer, Colonel Wymer, which should be strong enough to deal with any trouble. As Wymer drew near to the post, the Ghilzais broke up from before it and marched to meet him, followed for a short distance by Captain Macan, who was in command of the garrison. Macan, however, remembering the censure of Lynch for venturing to take the offensive, thought himself debarred from attacking them, and on the evening of the 29th of May the Ghilzais fell upon Wymer in force.

Though heavily punished by the guns, they assailed him with good courage, manoeuvred to take him in flank and, when Wymer made a change of disposition to meet these tactics, charged boldly to the bayonets. For five hours they persisted, being reinforced till their numbers were swelled from two to four thousand in the course of the combat; until at last, disheartened by heavy losses, they drew off and left Wymer to pursue his march. His casualties did not greatly exceed thirty, of which two only were killed; but if his *sepoys* had been less steady, or some misfortune, such as is common in war, had befallen him, Macan's unwillingness to attack would have been the determining cause of any mishap. Macnaghten's system of paying blackmail one day and fighting on the next was bound to throw everything into confusion. (*I.O.S.C.*, vol. 9 of 1841, Nott to Elphinstone—enclosing Wymer's report—June 1, 1841; Durand).

The check to the Ghilzais was not decisive. On June, the day after the action Rawlinson reported that Akhtar Khan had taken the field again in force, with the avowed intention of capturing the fort at Girishk; and a few days later he added the intelligence that the lesser Durani chiefs had joined the Ghilzais, in spite of their inveterate hatred of each other. This, commented Rawlinson, showed the intensity of dislike and jealousy with which the British were regarded by the Duranis. Macnaghten was deeply hurt, especially resenting the phrase "intensity of dislike," which, as he contended, there was no evidence to prove and much to refute.

However, the insurrection spread steadily; and Macnaghten felt himself bound to detach from Kabul a regiment of cavalry, a battalion of infantry and four of the Shah's guns, which, together with another battalion from Kandahar, were to take post at Mukur, on the upper waters of the Tarnak, to overawe the Ghilzais. As to Akhtar Khan, the envoy's irritation found vent in the offer of a large reward for that leader's head, and in the threat that he should be hung as high as Haman when caught. But Macnaghten still declined to admit that the situation was the least serious; and, when frankly informed by Rawlinson that things were growing worse every day, he rebuked his subordinate with considerable temper, he wrote:

> These idle statements may cause much mischief, and, often repeated as they are, they neutralise my protestations. I know them to be utterly false as regards Kabul, and I have no reason to believe them true as regards the country about Kandahar.

There is something almost pathetic in this outburst of childish petulance over facts that refused to be done away with by protestations. (*I.O.S.C.*, vol. 9 of 1841, Rawlinson to Macnaghten, May 30, June 3; Macnaghten to Rawlinson, June 7; vol. 10 of 1841, Rawlinson to Macnaghten, June 17, 28, 1841; Durand).

Something, however, had to be done about Akhtar Khan; and the task of dealing with him fell, of course, upon Nott. Auckland had long urged the employment of the *Shah's* troops only for the quelling of internal insurrections, and with the greater insistence since Sir Jasper Nicolls lost no opportunity of pointing out that, unless propped by British bayonets, Shah Shuja's throne must certainly fall. Elphinstone, when the point was pressed upon him, answered that the Afghans drew no distinction between the *Shah's* troops and the British—doubtless because both were commanded by British officers—and that the defeat of the one had as bad a moral effect as of the other. However, Macnaghten, being bound in policy to show that British troops could be dispensed with, had furnished Rawlinson with a body of a thousand Durani horse, and had recently added to these two more Afghan regiments known as Jan Baz horse, under Captain Hart.

These Rawlinson now purposed to send to the relief of Girishk; but, having some doubts as to their efficiency, he begged Nott to send also a battalion of the *Shah's* infantry, under Captain Woodburn, and a couple of horse-artillery guns. Against his will, and against his better judgement, for this detachment reduced his own garrison at Kandahar to a battalion and a half and four guns, Nott complied. Rawlinson represented that Akhtar Khan had only fifteen or sixteen hundred men; and it was certainly an important object, if it could be accomplished, to suppress that insurgent leader for ever.

Accordingly, at the end of June, Woodburn marched westward from Kandahar for the Helmand. The first incident was that the Durani horse failed to put in an appearance at all; but Woodburn, pursuing his way without them, on the 3rd of July reached the river opposite Girishk, and found the fords there in possession of the enemy, with the current running so rapidly as to be impracticable for infantry. He therefore sent Hart three miles up the stream where there was a ford which could be crossed by cavalry, and himself essayed to pass the water lower down. He failed, however; and Hart, who had succeeded in crossing, turned back, little pressed by the enemy, and forded the river again July 3. to rejoin him. Woodburn moved up the left bank to meet him; and at 8 a.m., his *sepoys* being much exhausted by heat and fatigue, he halted and pitched his camp.

At 4.30 p.m. he observed that the enemy was in motion, and sent Hart with his cavalry to oppose his passage of the river. But the Jan Baz were not anxious for a fight, and Akhtar Khan succeeded in crossing before Hart could prevent him; whereupon Hart was fain to fall back upon Woodburn, who formed his line of battle in the old-fashioned way with infantry and guns in the centre and cavalry upon either flank. The enemy, who were six thousand strong, promptly assailed him, but being repulsed in two attacks upon the centre, swept round Woodburn, right flank, put to flight the Jan Baz which were there stationed, and fell upon his rear.

The rear rank of the infantry on the left, with creditable steadiness, faced about and checked the assailants by their fire; but the panic and confusion of the horsemen had necessarily thrown those on the right into disorder, and for a time the situation was very critical, until Woodburn, moving a gun from his front, cleared the enemy away from his rear with a few rounds of grape. Akhtar Khan then drew off, but Hart could induce few of his Jan Baz to follow in pursuit, and Woodburn's men were too weary to give them support. Woodburn, therefore, took up a defensive position in an enclosure, against which Akhtar Khan, returning, delivered several half-hearted attacks without success, till at last, at 11 p.m., he recrossed the river and retreated. Woodburn then occupied the fort at Girishk, but felt himself too weak to advance further, unless Nott should send him reinforcements.

Nott, for his part, while full of praise for Woodburn, was perfectly furious when he heard the details of the action. Rawlinson had stated the enemy's numbers as only one-fourth of their real strength; and, of the *Shah's* levies, the Durani horse were strongly suspected to have fought on Akhtar Khan's side after nightfall, and the Jan Baz had not only run away, but plundered the baggage of Woodburn's infantry, being, as Woodburn reported, better fit for that work than for any other. Marshalling all these facts in telling sequence, Nott wrote to headquarters at Kabul that he would listen to no further requisitions from Rawlinson for troops, unless he were strong enough to detach a force that could hold its own without assistance from Duranis and Jan Baz. The former, he advised, should be disbanded forthwith; the latter he accused both of cowardice and of treachery.

It is pitifully ludicrous to add that the Supreme Government at Calcutta, upon reading this letter, expressed its resentment against the unnecessarily harsh terms in which Nott had criticised the Jan Baz.

AKHTAR KHAN

(*I.O.S.C.*, vol. 11 of 1841, Nott to A. A. G., Kabul, July 7; Indian government to Elphinstone, Aug. 11, 1841; Stocqueler, *Life of Sir William Nott*; Durand).

Weak though his garrison was, Nott had such confidence in Woodburn that he sent a strong force of infantry, a party of cavalry and two guns, under Captain Griffin, to Girishk; and at about the same time he despatched also another force under Captain Chambers against the Ghilzais. Chambers came upon the Ghilzais on the 5th, but they made no stand, and fled before the cavalry, or ever the infantry and guns could come up. Griffin was more fortunate, for Akhtar awaited him on strong ground, sheltered by walls and gardens, confident in his superiority of numbers. Attacking without hesitation, on the 17th of August, Griffin, with three hundred and fifty bayonets, drove the insurgents from their position and forced them into the open, where Hart's Jan Baz partly redeemed their character by charging home and dispersing the enemy with great loss.

The action was sharp, costing Woodburn rather over one hundred casualties, but it was decisive. Both Duranis and Ghilzais were disheartened by the sequence of defeats; and Macnaghten, who had reported the suppression of the Durani rebellion to Calcutta a full fortnight before it was accomplished, was exultant, for it seemed that his work was done. He was now under recall upon promotion to the government of Bombay, and counted upon quitting Afghanistan with honour to fill a great position which might, in its turn, lead to something greater still.

Ever since July he had been busy arranging with Elphinstone, or rather dictating to Elphinstone, his plans for the withdrawal of the Thirteenth and five native regiments to India on the 1st of November; and Elphinstone, cheerfully accepting the dictation, had rejoiced that there was nothing to prevent the return of these corps, since "it would have the worst possible effect on them and on those that were left behind, if they were detained later than that date." Macnaghten, however, was urgent that the government should send a strong brigade to Kabul by way of Peshawar, and two more battalions of *sepoys* by Shikarpur to Kandahar, which did not suggest great confidence in the situation; and, as Elphinstone mildly remarked, the participation of Herat in the Durani rebellion certainly called for the reinforcement of Kandahar, while the behaviour of the Khyberris also required a demonstration in some strength.

But Macnaghten hoped to quiet Herat altogether by offering Yar

Mohamed three *lakhs* of *rupees* annually to abstain from further trouble; and, though there was unrest among the Urakzais and the Afridis to south of the eastern end of the Khyber Pass, yet they were far more likely, if properly handled, to fight each other than combine against the British. By the middle of September Macnaghten had convinced himself that all was going as well as possible. The subjugation of the Duranis was complete; the Ghilzai insurrection had been totally suppressed; the country between Kandahar and Kabul was perfectly tranquil, and the fort at Kalat-i-Ghilzai, which was now nearly completed, would control any tendency to turbulence. Between Kabul and Jalalabad all was equally quiet. Far to north, Bukhara, Khulm and Kunduz were inclined to court British friendship.

Only in the Charikar district was Shah Shuja's authority still defied; but the people there could easily be subjugated if necessary. Altogether there was no occasion for large reinforcements, except for their moral effect, the present strength of the troops being ample for the maintenance of the British position. Such was the envoy's glowing report in the autumn of 1841, and Elphinstone was bound to accept it. So Macnaghten made his preparations to return to India; Elphinstone, who was resigning his command owing to ill-health, and indeed had the home-sickness of the dying strong upon him, prepared to start with him; Sale's brigade rejoiced in the prospect of a speedy retirement from the bleak mountains into the plains; and Burnes, who was to succeed Macnaghten as envoy, hugged himself over the great chance that was to assure for him a famous career. There were high hopes and joyful expectations in those September days at Kabul. (*I.O.S.C.,* vol. 11 of 1841, Macnaghten to Elphinstone and Elphinstone to Macnaghten, July 22; vol. 12 of 1841, Macnaghten to Indian government, July 31; vol. 15 of 1841, Macnaghten to Indian government, Sept. 15, 1841).

And yet there were warnings which only a wilfully blind man could have ignored. Rawlinson, in these very days, reported that to west of Kandahar the districts of Nish, Tirin and Derawat still, as ever, abjured allegiance to Shah Shuja, and had joined in the recent rebellion of Akhtar Khan, and that they must be reduced to obedience before any British troops could be withdrawn from Kandahar to India. In Zurmat, to east of Ghazni, a troublesome robber -chief had proved himself too strong to be dealt with by irregular levies, and needed regular troops and guns for the capture of his fort. From Charikar Henry Pottinger sent news of an aggressive movement so menacing as to demand the instant march of reinforcements.

Finally, in the Khyber Pass the eastern Ghilzais were assembling with hostile intent. In response to Auckland's urgent orders for economy, Macnaghten had summoned the Ghilzai chiefs and informed them that their subsidy would be reduced by £3000 a year; and the chiefs, accepting the situation without protest and indeed with cheerfulness, had gone to their own place and quietly taken measures to indemnify themselves in their own way. (*I.O.S.C.*, vol. 15 of 1 841, Rawlinson to Macnaghten, Sept. 11; H. Pottinger to Macnaghten, Sept. 18; Macnaghten to Elphinstone, Sept. 22; vol. 16 of 1 841, Macnaghten to Indian Government, Oct. 26, 1841).

On the 2nd of October it was known that the passes to Jalalabad were blocked up; and Shah Shuja sent emissaries to conciliate the eastern Ghilzai chiefs, without success. On the 4th a British officer, Captain Gray, who was returning to India with a small escort, was hotly opposed, and was obliged to take unfrequented paths to reach some native levies which were under orders to protect him. The loyal chief, who guided him, warned him plainly that all Afghanistan, even Kabul itself, was ready to break out, the whole country having made common cause to expel the British. Gray reported this incident on the 7th to Burnes; but, none the less, the leading detachment of Sale's brigade, namely, the Thirty-Fifth Native Infantry under Major Monteith, was ordered to march for Jalalabad on the 9th, as though the road had been as safe as from London to Portsmouth.

An officer, George Broadfoot, who commanded a body of sappers of Shah Shuja's army with great efficiency, has left us an account of his proceedings on these days, which will show how military matters were carried on under Macnaghten at Kabul. Broadfoot received orders on the 7th to proceed on field-service with one hundred sappers, and to take his orders from Major Monteith. Since another detachment of his corps had been sent, with all the tools at disposal, to accompany a small expedition to Zurmat, he set the armourers and smiths in Kabul to make tools. They refused to take orders from the British; whereupon Broadfoot sent down a party of men to give each smith his work and keep him at it until it was done.

Thus, by next day, the 8th, the tools were ready, and Broadfoot went to Major Monteith for orders. The major said that he could give none because he had received none, except that he was to move towards Jalalabad; and he declined to apply to Macnaghten for instructions, knowing by experience that it was not the envoy's custom to consult, much less to instruct military officers. It was the custom of the political agents, said Monteith, to send troops on "wild-goose chases," take the credit for any successes, and let the military officers bear the blame for failures; and he knew better than to ask Macnaghten for any information.

Proceeding next to the Commissary of Ordnance, Broadfoot found that he, too, had received no orders. He therefore sought out Elphinstone, who was in bed, but insisted on rising at once, though he could not walk into another room without assistance and was for a time quite exhausted by the effort. Courteous and cheerful, in spite of pain and infirmity, the general said that he knew nothing of the service on which Monteith was starting, having received no instructions from Macnaghten, except to send the major off with a given number of men. He had received no information as to the forts, if any, that might be encountered; he could not say if any engineer was accompanying the expedition; he had not even been apprised whether Monteith's mission was one of hostility or of precaution, and he could only leave it to Broadfoot to decide what tools and stores he should take with him. In fact he could give no orders, and, like Monteith, shrank through bitter experience not less than through a sense of indignity, from asking any questions of Macnaghten.

With great difficulty Broadfoot extorted from Elphinstone a private note to Macnaghten, begging him to give that officer a hearing, and to let him know definitely whether there were to be hostilities or not, and if so where, against what enemy, and in what probable strength. In particular he desired to be informed whether forts were to be taken and destroyed. With this note Broadfoot approached Macnaghten, who received him ungraciously.

The envoy averred that, being no prophet, he could not tell whether there would be hostilities or not, but that he would find out about the forts and would sanction whatever the general proposed; and with a private note to that effect, he sent Broadfoot back to Elphinstone no wiser than he had come. Deeply hurt, the general complained bitterly of this insulting treatment; but, fully alive to the injustice of allowing a junior officer to be held responsible for a possible failure in the field simply because the political agents declined to inform him of the nature of the service, he consented at last that Broadfoot should again apply to Macnaghten.

The envoy this time was peevish, and, with very questionable taste, declared that the general was fidgety; but Broadfoot stuck to his point that he could make no preparations unless he knew what he was expected to do. Then at length, with much irritation, Macnaghten produced his intelligencers, so that Broadfoot might examine them himself upon the question of the forts. They could give no information of the slightest value; but, when Broadfoot pointed this out, Macnaghten interrupted him impatiently. He said that Monteith should start on the morrow for Butkhak, nine miles east of Kabul on the northern road to the Khyber Pass, as a demonstration; that there would be no fighting; that the rebels would certainly submit before evening; and that then Monteith should proceed to Jalalabad. Broadfoot asked whether, if the rebels did not submit, Monteith should return; to which Macnaghten replied that Monteith should remain at Butkhak until the expedition lately sent to Zurmat, which had absorbed all the public transport at Kabul, should return. Broadfoot rejoined that in this case so small a force as Monteith's, encamping near all the outlets from the hills, would invite attack, the more so as his halting there would be ascribed to fear.

Thereupon Macnaghten lost his temper and said that he had given his orders; and that, as to Broadfoot and his sappers, twenty men with pick-axes would suffice, since they were wanted only to pick stones from under the gun-wheels for a peaceable march to Jalalabad. Broadfoot at once caught him up.

"Are those your orders?" he asked.

"No," answered Macnaghten, recovering himself, "it is only my opinion, given at the general's request and yours. The general is responsible and must decide as to the number of sappers and tools that must go."

With this Broadfoot returned to Elphinstone; and presently there arrived a note from Macnaghten, ordering the immediate march of Monteith, and containing almost the identical words that he had spoken to Broadfoot about the sappers and the enemy, but throwing all responsibility on the general. The unhappy Elphinstone, still strongly and rightly objecting to the movement, appealed to his chief staff-officer, one Captain Grant, upon whom the general, in his weak state, leaned wholly, and who responded to this confidence by bullying his chief. Grant abused the envoy, spoke insolently to Broadfoot, advised Elphinstone to have nothing to say to Macnaghten, or as to any part of the question, and, declining to discuss the matter further, retired with a newspaper to the window. Weak and shattered, Elphinstone still made one more effort, and sent Broadfoot back to Macnaghten to urge anew his reasons for objecting to Monteith's march.

The envoy refused to hear the reasons, saying that he had given his opinion and that the general was responsible; and, forgetting himself completely, he told Broadfoot that, if he thought Monteith's movement likely to bring on an attack, he need not go—he was not wanted, or, if he were, there were other officers. Therewith Broadfoot respectfully declined to hear more and took his leave. Macnaghten presently had the grace to follow him and to shake his hand, but made no other apology for an inexcusable insult.

These incidents, which, as a rule, would not deserve to be recounted at length, are here set down as the best means of illustrating Macnaghten's methods, and showing the utter demoralisation which they had wrought among the officers. It does not appear that Macnaghten's manners were always as offensive as upon this occasion. Indeed, he was habitually courteous; but he had a bad temper, which occasionally got the better of him, and then he revealed the fact that at bottom he was ill-bred. But it is the principle and not the manner with which we are here concerned, namely, that the political agents claimed the right to dictate military movements to military officers, taking the credit if all went well, and disclaiming responsibility for any military mishap. It may with reason be urged that no self-respecting general should have consented to serve upon such conditions. But too much must not be expected from poor human nature. Roberts had fought against the system and had been sent back to India. Nott had fought against it, and, though he had not been recalled, had been subjected to humiliating censure and insult, and had for months expected his recall daily.

The road to advancement lay in submission to the political agents; and only those who were content, whether through weakness or through time-service, to walk it, could hope for high command in Afghanistan. There is no reason to believe that either Cotton or Elphinstone were timeservers. They were selected because they were judged likely to be subservient, Cotton being weak and stupid, and Elphinstone, though by no means incapable, naturally of charming manners and ready tact. Both, however, resented their position bitterly, and both, after less than a year of command, took refuge in sick leave.

Meanwhile, the result of the system upon all ranks had been disastrous. The political agents made a point of concealing from the military officers the nature of any expedition upon which they sent them, partly because they wished to avoid awkward questions, but chiefly because they could themselves give no information and were quite content to dispense with it. The military chiefs, to guard themselves against any disaster, therefore made a point of sending a force which should be, so far as they could judge, of overwhelming strength—possibly greater than was necessary—and which invariably included British regular troops.

Thus Macnaghten, when applying to Elphinstone for the numbers that he could furnish for an expedition to Zurmat, gave the following particulars only: An officer of Shah Shuja's levies had by Macnaghten's desire attempted to take the stronghold of a robber chieftain, and had failed; it was necessary to make an example of this chieftain; the numbers of his followers were unknown, but were probably not formidable; and the area of his country was perhaps two hundred square miles. Upon information so vague it was impossible to judge whether five hundred or five thousand men might be necessary; but Elphinstone named about a thousand British regular troops, with ten pieces of artillery, and a thousand irregulars. (*I.O.S.C.*, vol. 15 of 1 841, Macnaghten to Elphinstone and Elphinstone's reply, Sept. 22, 1841).

The use of British troops for such service was of course deplored by Auckland; but, since the general was to have no say as to the policy of undertaking the operation at all, and yet was to bear the responsibility of any miscarriage, he naturally did his best to make himself safe against mischance.

The movement of these bodies of men naturally required transport for their supplies and stores, and possibly even of their forage, for this last was a matter seldom considered by the political agents. But there was also considerable work for the transport in bringing in supplies from time to time to feed the various garrisons; and the consequence was that the unfortunate animals were worked to death. Every expedition signified inevitably a certain number of casualties among them, and some expeditions a great many; and so their numbers steadily dwindled. It mattered not upon what service the transport might be employed at the moment. If Macnaghten wanted to send off an expedition, back the camels must come, perhaps two or three days' journey, to fulfil his august commands.

As to formation of magazines along the routes most generally traversed, Macnaghten would not hear of such a thing. Every winter he and Shah Shuja went, with an escort of one or two thousand men, from Kabul to pass the winter at Jalalabad; and it would have been a reasonable precaution, as well as a great convenience, to establish magazines at Jalalabad itself and at Gandamak, on the way to it. But Macnaghten scouted the bare idea of such a thing, as implying that

Afghanistan was a hostile country. Thus, in deciding as to the strength of an expedition, the military chiefs were confronted with a second great difficulty, namely, whether they were justified, for some object which they had no means of appraising aright, in hiring transport at enormous expense.

In the instance immediately before us, Broadfoot was aware that all the public transport-animals in Kabul had been sent to Zurmat; and one principal reason why he pressed Macnaghten to give information concerning the purpose of Monteith's march, was to ascertain whether he would be warranted in hiring transport to carry the tools of his sappers. But the political agents, though they poured out money like water in bribes and blackmail, would not condescend to such paltry details as this.

Thus the transport suffered terribly and unceasingly; and the men suffered not less. They had to march scores and even hundreds of miles into remote valleys, enduring hardship, privation and fatigue, only to find, very often, when they reached their destination, that the enemy, whom they were intended to frighten or chastise, had quietly decamped upon their approach, that there was nothing left to them but to march back again, and that all their labour had been for naught. The political agents were of course quite satisfied—they had made a "demonstration"—but the troops were thoroughly disgusted. It is well known that nothing is so ruinous to soldiers as to be worked, worried and harassed to no purpose; yet it was thus that Macnaghten and his underlings had treated those under his orders, ever since the departure of Keane.

★★★★★★

The British soldier's phrase describes the process more tersely and forcibly than any other, but unfortunately it cannot be written down in full. The one thing that he cannot stand is being "——d about."

★★★★★★

Of course, they had varied the process by occasionally leaving isolated posts in remote districts, far from any support; but this, at best, signified more work for transport and for escorts, and at worst disaster and annihilation.

The general consequence was, in every quarter outside the influence of Nott, a decline in the spirit and the discipline of the troops. They felt no confidence in their leaders. Elphinstone was so sick that he was no more than a cipher. Sale had mismanaged every operation that had been entrusted to him, and, though full of personal bravery, was utterly wanting in moral courage. Shelton, who had but just arrived, was generally hated. The senior officers next to them were bitterly hostile to the political agents, and resigned themselves, rather than have any communication with them, to dumb unintelligent, unquestioning and grudging obedience to their orders. They had a shrewder knowledge of the situation than was supposed. The political agents were by no means united among themselves, and did not conceal their opinions of each other.

Burnes, in particular, who was not on the best of terms with Macnaghten, had, as we have seen already, condemned the envoy's system, root and branch, and was anxious to show how much better he could manage things himself. To his credit, he assumed no Olympian majesty in his intercourse with his fellows, but was modest, affable, and therefore popular. And Burnes was a chatterer, flighty and unstable, but with occasional flashes of deep insight that were not lost upon his hearers. No officer of any professional knowledge could fail to note the extreme danger of the military situation, the weakness of the army scattered wide over an enormous area, and the utter insecurity of the communications. When men, who were in a position to know, added that there was general discontent with Macnaghten's rule in Afghanistan, the peril was naturally magnified in their minds. If matters came to the worst, where was the leader who could save the army?

And so there grew and waxed among all ranks a spirit of discouragement and even of despondency. Croaking was the rule, and one of the worst of the croakers was Grant, Elphinstone's chief staff-officer, an overbearing man who took up the attitude that it was useless to attempt anything, and, upon that ground, silenced all remonstrance and every suggestion. And so from headquarters the poison spread downward through channels that were only too well prepared to receive it; until from the commander-in-chief to the drummer there was but one desire, to get out of Afghanistan at any cost. There were officers with the troops—Henry Havelock of the Thirteenth and George Broadfoot, to name but two out of many—who, if they could have taken Elphinstone's place, would have revived confidence within twenty-four hours and discipline within three days; but they were mere majors and captains.

"The gentleman employed to command the army," to use Wellington's contemptuous phrase of Macnaghten, desired at the moment only a cipher as a military colleague. All was well. He had said it, and so it must be. But all was not well; and though it may be easy to turn a general into a cipher, it is not easy at a moment's notice to reconvert a cipher into a general. (Broadfoot's *Life of Major George Broadfoot*).

CHAPTER 7

Sale Forces the Khurd Kabul Pass

Pursuant to Macnaghten's order, Monteith marched on the 9th Oct. 1841, to Butkhak with the Thirty-Fifth Native Infantry, a squadron of the Fifth Cavalry, two guns and one hundred of Broadfoot's sappers. The camping-ground chosen for him was extremely ill-situated; but, having Macnaghten's assurance of a peaceable march to Jalalabad, he thought it not worth while to change it, though he took every precaution against surprise. At night he was suddenly attacked, and for a short time there was some confusion; but Monteith's dispositions were good, and he succeeded in beating off the enemy with some loss, though not before they had carried off a few camels and other plunder. Upon hearing this, Macnaghten, on the 10th, ordered Sale suddenly to move out to Butkhak with the Thirteenth and two to three hundred irregulars, and to clear the passes.

On the 12th, accordingly, Sale attacked and forced the Khurd Kabul pass—the more southerly of the two entrances to the defile—with little difficulty and no more than fifty casualties. He himself was wounded in the action, so it is not easy to say whether the next proceeding was due to Sale, who still accompanied the force in a litter, or to Dennie, who was next in command. In any case, Monteith with the Thirty-Fifth were left to encamp alone in the Khurd Kabul valley, while the rest of the force returned to Butkhak.

There is no need to dwell upon the viciousness of such a disposition; and, to make matters worse, there was attached to Monteith, on the usual terms, a political agent named Captain Macgregor, who, after the manner of his kind, cherished a profound belief in his powers of negotiation. From Macgregor the Ghilzais cunningly obtained permission for a body of so-called friendly Afghans to lodge themselves close to his quarters and virtually within the British encampment.

Sir Robert and Lady Sale

On the night of the 17th these amicable individuals fired a volley, which brought down a British officer and thirty men, as a signal to the tribesmen without; and the Ghilzais fell fiercely upon the camp. Monteith, a cool and resolute soldier, was quite equal to the occasion, and repulsed the enemy with some loss; but the Ghilzais managed to carry off eight camels, which was a sufficient encouragement to them, and a serious loss, in the circumstances, to the transport-department.

Then Sale awoke to his blunder; and, having obtained an additional battalion from Kabul, he marched away to join Monteith, which he did without difficulty or molestation on the 20th. He then drew additional camels from the capital, and, with his force now made up to respectable strength, marched eastward on the 22nd for Tezin. (H.M. 13th, 35th and 37th Bengal N.I., 1 squadron 5th Bengal Cavalry, 1 troop 2nd Cavalry, Abbott's battery, Backhouse's mountain-battery, Broadfoot's sappers, 200 Afghan irregular infantry).

The Ghilzais offered no opposition until the column issued from the mouth of the deep defile that opens on to the Tezin valley, when they were found assembled in some strength and seemingly inclined to make a stand. A few rounds of shrapnel sufficed to shift them, and the force moved into the plain with little further trouble. But someone, presumably Dennie, thought fit to push up a detachment, without adequate support, against parties of the enemy on the heights, with the result that the assailants went too far, found themselves overpowered by numbers and had to return with indecent haste. The casualties were not very heavy, though one officer of the Thirteenth was killed and two more officers were wounded; but it was not wholesome that even a few British soldiers should have run down for their lives into the plain with the Afghans in hot pursuit.

However, there was Sale in the valley with the fort and the possessions of a leading Ghilzai chief within his grasp; and the chief did not relish his presence. Sale gave orders for the attack on his principal fort next day, and all was in train for the operation when a messenger presented himself to Macgregor, tendering the submission of the chief and of his leading subordinates, and begging that his stronghold might be spared. Unwarned by the treacherous conduct of the Ghilzais to Monteith at Khurd Kabul, Macgregor readily entertained the overture, and persuaded Sale to defer the attack. Negotiations were begun, and continued for some days, with the result that on the 25th Macgregor agreed to restore to the chiefs their old scale of salary, or blackmail, and to make other concessions with which they professed themselves content.

Macgregor avowed himself a little doubtful of the good faith of the Ghilzais, but was anxious, seemingly, almost at any cost to get the troops out of the Tezin valley. He appears not to have reflected that the chiefs were even more solicitous for the same object; but it is difficult to realise all the various factors in the situation. For one thing, Sale had started with three to four thousand cattle along a route where forage was scarcely to be found, and with no arrangement made for feeding them. Providentially, two days' supply was discovered at Tezin, otherwise the unfortunate beasts must have starved; and it may have been this question of forage which made Macgregor so eager to come to terms.

On the other hand, this same forage might have been taken by force, and such capture would probably have been the heaviest blow that could have been dealt at the Ghilzais. In any case Macgregor decided to soothe the chiefs with bribes, and thereby gave them the funds that they needed to continue the insurrection. Macnaghten was not too well pleased with the agreement, for he had hoped that Sale would have given the insurgents a severe lesson; and yet he welcomed the settlement, however unsatisfactory, because he was frightened. (Durand; Broadfoot, *Career of Major Broadfoot*; Kaye, i.).

The Ghilzai rebellion had brought home to him for the first time that, in hill fighting, the regular troops were at a disadvantage. The Afghans, he wrote, were more agile, and their long matchlocks, or *jezails*, outranged the musket. The former of these two statements could not be disputed, and indeed the fact was nothing very novel nor startling. As to the inferiority of the musket to the *jezail*, that depended chiefly on the calibre of the latter weapon, some of which were so heavy that they were fired from rests and would throw a bullet eight hundred yards; but Sir Charles Napier claimed later to have proved that the musket was the superior weapon, and, even if it were not, the British artillery should have sufficed to redress any balance in its disfavour.

But in truth there seems to have been no warrant for this sudden panic about the musket beyond the ill-managed and unnecessary skirmish of a few score men with the Afghans on the 22nd of October. It is a fact that the muskets of the Thirteenth were worn out; and it is probable that Sale, had he looked for more than a peaceful march back to India, would have obtained leave to replace them with new weapons, of which there were plenty in store at Kabul. But men who have run away from the enemy generally seize the first excuse for their misbehaviour; and it is just possible that Sale may have made the most of this excuse from jealousy of his own regiments honour.

Still, as Wellington said, only proper management was needed to enable British troops to hold their own against any natives of any hills whatever. Macnaghten, on the other hand, countenanced the distrust of the musket, made it a pretext for continuing his old false policy of buying his enemies instead of fighting them, and thus contributed at once to the heartening of the enemy and the demoralisation of his own troops.

Nothing could at this juncture have been more fatal. The concession was truly construed by the Afghans as evidence of British weakness, and they quietly pursued their plans against the invaders with confidence. (*I.O.S.C.*, vol. 16 of 1841, Macnaghten to Indian government, Get. 26, 1841; Kaye, i. See Wellington's scathing memo, quoted in Kaye, i.).

Having reached Tezin, Sale, considering that his transport animals were insufficient for his needs, resolved to leave behind a part of his force and to continue his advance, taking all the transport with him. He therefore ordered the Thirty-Seventh Native Infantry, three companies of Broadfoot's sappers and three mountain-guns back to Kabar Jabar, between Tezin and Khurd Kabul, and there left them isolated, with three narrow defiles between them and Kabul, and with no means of movement—a proceeding which betrayed, not for the first time, his utter unfitness to command. Meanwhile, during the days wasted in negotiation, the Ghilzais had matured their preparations for resisting his passage through the two next defiles to eastward; but Sale had at least the good sense to attach little value to Macgregor's treaty with the Ghilzais, and eluded the ambush by moving over the high ground to the south. Had he possessed the sense to perceive it, he might have wheeled northward, engaged the Ghilzais with an impassable chasm in their rear, and annihilated them; but probably neither he nor Dennie knew the ground well enough to turn the opportunity to advantage.

Thus, having left Tezin on the 26th, he reached the valley of Jagdalak on the 29th, not without petty affairs with his rear-guard, but otherwise unmolested. From Jagdalak the road for three miles ascended a ravine, very trying for laden camels and gun-horses, and commanded by heights on each side, until the summit was reached from which began the long descent to Gandamak. At Gandamak itself was stationed a corps of Shah Shuja's irregular infantry, part of which might easily have been employed to seize the summit and hold it until Sale had traversed the defile of Jagdalak; but these troops could not move without the orders of Macnaghten; and so simple a matter of co-operation did not occur to "the gentleman who was employed to command the army."

Sale, for his part—or Dennie for him—took suitable measures for the protection of his march. Flanking-parties were detached both from the advanced guard and from the main body, with orders to hold the heights until the baggage had passed, and then to fall down and come on in rear of it; and the rear-guard was made up of four companies of infantry, two of them taken from the Thirteenth, two field-guns, three mountain-guns and a company of sappers—some four to five hundred men in all. The Ghilzais made such feeble opposition that the summit was easily won, and command of the pass and of the long descent to Gandamak was assured.

Thereupon, Dennie, (I suppose that Dennie was responsible; but the proceeding was equally characteristic of Sale, and the fault may have been Sale's), went forward quite happily with the main body of the column, leaving the baggage and rear-guard to take care of itself. The Ghilzais promptly attacked the latter with vigour. The four companies, finding themselves deserted and alone, were seized with panic and ran forward in confusion to get out of the pass, with the concealed Ghilzais firing into them from either flank, and the villagers bounding after them, knife in hand. There seemed every likelihood that the rear-guard and drivers would be cut to pieces, and that the whole of the baggage would be captured.

Half-a-dozen British officers, however, showed a bold front; a handful of Broadfoot's sappers stood nobly by him and checked the rush of the villagers; the fugitives of the rear-guard were rallied, and the arrival of reinforcements from the main body made everything secure. By nightfall the rear-guard had arrived safely at Surkhab; but the casualties amounted to over one hundred and twenty, among which were one British officer killed, besides four men of the Thirteenth, and three officers and forty-two men of the Thirteenth wounded. Furthermore, seventy camels were carried off, and much baggage was taken. Finally, for the second time within a week, both British and native Indian troops had run away from Afghans.

The whole affair was discreditable to the last degree to the chief commander. It may, indeed, be pleaded for him that the Ghilzais were bound by treaty not to attack; and it is possible that Macgregor may

Jagdalak

have intervened with ill-timed advice. But that an officer, who had made excellent and successful dispositions for forcing the pass, should ruin all by hurrying the main column away from his rear-guard, was unpardonable. (Durand; Broadfoot, *Career of Major Broadfoot*; Lady Sale's *Journal*).

On the following day Sale's column without further molestation marched into Gandamak, all ranks, with the exception of a few individual officers, feeling depressed and discouraged. During the next week not a word reached it from Kabul; but rumours came in of an outbreak at the capital, with contradictory accounts of the issue. On the 4th of November arrived definite news that a great chief in the vicinity had occupied a fort within four miles of the camp, and was about to raise the whole district in rebellion. Macgregor, who happened to be dining with Broadfoot and the artillery-officers, at their instigation went to Sale and urged him to attack at once, but returned at midnight to report that he had failed. The officers then sought out Havelock, who with great difficulty persuaded Sale to sanction an advance upon the hostile fort on the afternoon of the 5th. The Afghans fled at the first sight of the advanced guard; and, though they escaped with little loss, the incident had the best effect in restoring the moral spirit of Sale's troops, and lowering that of the enemy. But this was no thanks either to Sale or to Dennie, though it would have been hard to find two men of greater physical bravery.

CHAPTER 8

Crisis at Kabul

Meanwhile at Kabul the crisis had at last come. At the end of September, Henry Pottinger had arrived at Kabul from Kohistan to report that he considered a rising in that quarter to be certain, and to entreat for reinforcements. Macnaghten, with the Ghilzai insurrection heavy upon his back, could only answer that compliance was impossible; and the Kohistanis, taking courage from their own immunity and from the reports of Ghilzai success, nursed their projects for vengeance. On the night of the 1st of November a number of them came into Kabul, and there, meeting some of the Ghilzai insurgents and others of the disaffected, concerted with them their plans for the morrow. The troops at the moment were disposed as follows. Shelton was encamped on the Sia Sang hills, a mile and a half southeast of the cantonments and east of the Bala Hissar, with the Forty-Fourth Foot, half of the Fifty-Fourth Native Infantry, a battalion of the *Shah's* infantry, the Fifth Bengal Cavalry, and a battery of European horse-artillery.

In cantonments were the Fifth Bengal Native Infantry, three companies of Broadfoot's sappers, two troops of irregular horse and one field-battery. In the Bala Hissar, as guard to the *Shah*, were about eighteen hundred of his own troops, regular and irregular, and several guns. The supplies and stores were scattered about in various forts, as shall presently be described in detail; but the treasure, through unpardonable neglect or insane over-confidence, was kept in a house in the city, about nine hundred yards northwest of the Bala Hissar and approachable only through narrow streets, unless by following the southern skirt of the city. In another house close to the Treasury lived Burnes, who was hated as the man who had first brought the foreigners into Afghanistan, who had accompanied Sale in his punitive expedition to Kohistan, and who, above all, had made very free with the Afghan women. To kill Burnes and sack the Treasury appealed alike to Afghan vindictiveness and Afghan cupidity; and with this blow the insurgents had planned to open the revolt.

Accordingly, in the early hours of the 2nd of November, the rebels, having occupied the adjacent houses, opened fire upon Burnes's dwelling and the Treasury. Burnes sent a hurried note to inform Macnaghten, but, thinking that the attack was some petty riot, restrained the *sepoy* guard from returning the fire, and went out to harangue the mob. Very soon he and all with him were fighting desperately for their lives. Shah Shuja, hearing the sound of musketry, sent one of his regiments, known as Campbell's Hindustanis, with two guns under command of one of his sons, to quell the outbreak; but the foolish commander, trying to make his way through the narrow, tortuous streets, placed his troops at the mercy of the populace, which handled them very roughly.

The *Shah*, however, sent word to the envoy that all was well with Burnes, and Macnaghten seems not at first to have realised the danger. Shelton had at the first sound of firing got his men under arms, but as late as 10 a.m. he received a message from Macnaghten saying that all was quiet and bidding him stand fast. After waiting for an hour, Shelton sent Captain Sturt with a small escort to ascertain what was going on; and in half-an-hour a trooper returned to say that Sturt had been stabbed on entering the precincts of the palace, and that Shelton was to advance. He moved off at once, with the men that Elphinstone had at the outset ordered him to hold ready, to the Bala Hissar, and was met by a rude message from the *Shah* asking him why he had come.

Shelton, after waiting for another hour, sent another officer to obtain intelligence. In due time this officer reported that he had met fugitives from Campbell's regiment flying from the city into the Bala Hissar, who told him that they had been utterly cut up. Shelton sent down a company to cover their retreat, but though they brought their two guns out of the city, they were unable to get them into the citadel and left them under the ramparts, dismounted, where the fire from the citadel effectually prevented the Afghans from carrying them off, (Lady Sale's *Journal*, also republished by Leonaur as *Lady Sale's Afghanistan*).

Long before this—apparently by 9 a.m.—the guards at the Treasury and at Burnes's house had been overpowered, Burnes himself, with two other British officers, had been slain, and the treasure had been seized by the insurgents. Shelton has been much blamed for not

DEATH OF BURNES

acting with greater vigour, but he was deliberately kept idle in his camp until long after the mischief had been done; and it seems that he did recommend, though in vain, an immediate joint attack upon the city from the Bala Hissar and from cantonments, (Hough). Macnaghten himself appears to have taken long to realise the seriousness of the situation, and at first to have lost his head, for he and his wife left the residency and came into cantonments before 11 a.m. He is said to have called upon Elphinstone to act, but he took matters into his own hands when he ordered Shelton to stand fast. Elphinstone himself, who had expected to leave Kabul in company with Macnaghten on the 1st of November, was and knew himself to be unfit in body and mind to deal with any grave trouble. ("If anything were to turn up, I am unfit for it, done up body and mind, and I have told Lord Auckland so."—Broadfoot).

The only measures that he had taken were to send Shelton with about fourteen hundred men into the Bala Hissar, to order the rest of his troops from Sia Sang into cantonments, to mount guns on the rampart of the cantonments, and to recall the Thirty-Seventh Native Infantry from the dangerous situation in which it had been left by the stupidity of Sale.

Yet the attacks of the enemy had not been confined to Burnes's house and the Treasury. In a fort at the western end of the city were stored, under charge of Captain Colin Mackenzie, the supplies for the *Shah's* troops, where also were the quarters of Brigadier-General Anquetil, commandant of the *Shah's* regular forces. Within forty yards of it was another house, the residence of his brigade-major, Captain Troup, which was easily defensible against musketry; and seven hundred yards to south-west of these was a strong tower, which was occupied by Captain Trevor, and which could easily have been prepared for defence. The guard assigned to the fort and the brigade-major's house consisted of a native officer and thirty *sepoys*, but about one hundred and fifty of the *Shah's* irregular infantry were close by, and immediately to south of the fort lay the quarter of the Kizilbashis—Persians descended from colonists who had emigrated to Kabul at the time of Nadir Shah and were friendly to Shah Shuja and the British.

On the morning of the 2nd of November, Captain Mackenzie received warning of the insurrection and made ready to defend himself; but, while still engaged in his preparations, he was attacked by a large mob of armed Afghans. Not without difficulty he held his own until the afternoon, when, as ammunition was running short, he contrived to pass a message through to Trevor, who forwarded it at once to cantonments, asking at least for cartridges and, if possible, for reinforcements. Neither the one nor the other arrived, and Mackenzie was fain to make the best dispositions that he could for the night, conscious that the Afghans were undermining his defences, but powerless to prevent them. Yet the *Shah's* irregulars and the Kizilbash leaders had been ready, on the first sight of a British bayonet moving towards Mackenzie's fort, to strike in with him against the insurgents. (Eyre, *Kabul Insurrection of 1841-42*). Here, therefore, was one matter which demanded immediate action. Troops must be sent without delay to reinforce Mackenzie, and either to bring off the supplies of grain, or destroy them. There was another not less urgent.

The Commissariat fort, in which the victuals of the British troops had, with such fatuous carelessness, been lodged, was flanked, as has been told, to west by the *Shah's* garden and to northwest by the building known as Mohamed Sherif's fort. There was yet another fort, Mahmoud Khan's, about five hundred yards south of the south-eastern wall of the cantonments, which commanded the nearest road to the Bala Hissar. So far Elphinstone seemed to be divided in his mind whether to hold the Bala Hissar or the cantonments, for he had occupied both; but whatever his ultimate decision, it was imperative to seize at once and to hold, temporarily if not permanently, the *Shah's* garden and the three forts above named, for he had only three days' provisions within cantonments. The general was in a cruel position, for he had inherited all the blunders of Cotton and of Macnaghten, and the governor-general had cancelled his one effort to make them good.

Macnaghten, moreover, was still interfering, for he had prevented Elphinstone from occupying Mohamed Sherif's fort on the first day of the outbreak, (Kaye, ii.). But there was still time to make good this mistake by night; and then it could be decided whether to hold the cantonments or to move the entire force into the Bala Hissar. Meanwhile, the readiest remedy for all difficulties was to strike hard at the insurgents in Kabul itself.

Unfortunately, all was irresolution in the cantonments, as was natural seeing that there were two commanders. Moreover, Elphinstone, unable at the best of times to walk and rarely able even to ride, had sustained a severe fall from his horse on the 2nd, and had been much hurt and shaken. Remembering the stories of Buenos Ayres and Rosetta, he shrank from Shelton's proposal to attack the city from two

Two Arab followers of Burnes

sides, and threw himself upon the counsel of Macnaghten, (Kaye, ii.). Neither the one nor the other seems to have given a thought to Mackenzie, which might have given them the key to their subsequent operations by rallying the Kizilbashis to their side. At daybreak of the 3rd there was an alarm of the enemy approaching from the east. It turned out to be Major Griffiths with the detachment from Khurd Kabul. Though beset by Ghilzais on front, flanks and rear, he had fought his way through them, and reached the cantonments after twelve hours' march in perfect order, having lost not one scrap of baggage, suffered little more than thirty casualties, and shown conclusively that, under an officer of skill and resolution, the British had little to fear from the Afghans.

This was a welcome reinforcement, but Elphinstone allowed the whole morning to pass away in inactivity. The excitement among the population was very great, and the villagers from all sides were swarming into Kabul in such numbers that the road between cantonments and the city was barely passable. It was in such circumstances that at 3 p.m. of a November day Elphinstone detached two companies of *sepoys* and one of the Forty-Fourth, perhaps two hundred men, with two guns, under Major Swayne, to march to the Lahore or north-eastern gate of Kabul, and there co-operate with Shelton in an attack upon the city. Through the stupidity of Elphinstone's staff Swayne took the longest and most dangerous road, moving south-west past Mohamed Sherif's fort and the *Shah's* garden to the Kohistan gate.

Thus he encountered so galling a fire from both of these places and from Mahmoud Khan's fort, that, having lost an officer and several men, and seeing the whole road under the north side of the city to be held by the enemy, he returned to cantonments. If Elphinstone had sent two thousand men betimes in the morning, he might have accomplished something, but he was so apprehensive of an attack upon the cantonments, which were too extensive for his force to defend, that he took the fatal course of sparing only driblets of troops to take the offensive. On this same afternoon, however, he sent from cantonments to the Bala Hissar half a battalion of infantry, three mountain-guns and four more pieces of artillery, though of what service mountain-guns could be in the citadel, and why it was thought necessary to strengthen its garrison at all, it is hard to say. Macnaghten meanwhile wrote urgently to Nott to send him two battalions from Kandahar, and to Sale to march back immediately with his brigade to Kabul.

In the course of the forenoon of this day the insurgents seized

Captain Trevor's tower (though Trevor and his family contrived to escape), and with the fire of their *jezails* from the summit drove the defenders from the western face of Mackenzie's fort. All through the afternoon they pressed Mackenzie himself so closely, bringing up fuel to burn down his gate, that he had no alternative but to evacuate the fort under cover of night.

After a desperate personal encounter with a party of Afghans, he brought the survivors of his little force safe into cantonments. But the stores of grain were of course lost, representing some three weeks' rations, on half allowance, for the entire garrison. To discourage the troops still further, and to convince them of the incompetence of their leaders, there came in on this same day the news that a Kohistani regiment of the Shah's service had mutinied, murdered its two British officers, and was doubtless on its way from its station, twenty miles to north-west, to join the insurgents at Kabul.

The morning of the 4th brought with it a formidable menace. The enemy occupied in force the Shah's garden and Mohamed Sherif's fort, thereby effectually cutting off communication between the cantonments and the Commissariat fort, which last was held by Ensign Warren and eighty men. Elphinstone, evidently not in possession of his senses, ordered one company of *sepoys* and eleven camels laden with ammunition to go to Warren's relief. The party was beaten back, and their officer was killed. The general then directed two companies of the Forty-Fourth, perhaps one hundred men, to go out and bring back Warren and his garrison. They also were repulsed, with the loss of two officers and four men killed and three officers and sixteen men wounded. In the evening a third party, this time of the Fifth Cavalry, was sent out. They galloped boldly up to the gate of the *Shah's* garden, but found the gate shut in their faces, and were forced to return with eight troopers killed and fourteen badly wounded. The fatuity with which the lives of valuable officers and men were thus thrown away piecemeal is almost incredible; yet the facts are true.

Then Elphinstone's commissary rushed to him and pointed out that, if the Commissariat fort were given up, there would be sacrificed not only all the provisions of the force, but all the medical stores, rum and spare clothing, and that he knew not how further supplies could be obtained. Realising now, apparently for the first time, that the loss of his victuals would mean starvation, Elphinstone despatched orders to Warren to hold out to the last extremity. This message never reached Warren; but meanwhile he reported that the enemy were undermining one of his towers, that he could not prevent them, and that some of his men had already slipped away and escaped to cantonments. The answer returned was that he should be reinforced by two o'clock next morning.

At nine o'clock that evening there was a meeting of officers at Elphinstone's house, when Macnaghten urged that, unless Mohamed Sherif's fort were taken that very night, the Commissariat fort would be lost. It was very characteristic that the envoy, after forbidding the occupation of Mohamed Sherif's fort when it might have been effected without bloodshed, insisted upon it now at any sacrifice of life. Elphinstone hesitated. Spies were sent out; Sturt, who was lying prostrate with wounds that hardly allowed him to speak, was consulted; and at last, after hours of vacillation, troops—apparently two companies—were ordered to be ready at 4 a.m. to attack Mohamed Sherif's fort and to reinforce Warren.

It was past daylight before they could be collected, and just as they were about to march off, in came Warren with his garrison. Despairing of help, and expecting to be overwhelmed at any moment, for the enemy had set fire to the gate, he had knocked a hole in one of the walls, and crept back to cantonments. Now, therefore, all the supplies of the garrison of Kabul were in the enemy's hands, and there was left in the cantonment just one day's victuals.

The troops, of course, were furious. They knew that with proper management they could take the fort with ease, whereas many lives had been wasted with the result that there was now no prospect of food, and—a serious matter to the Europeans—absolute failure of rum. But if there was one thing that Elphinstone never lacked, it was councillors; and now Lieutenant Eyre approached him with a new plan for storming Mohamed Sherif's fort. Powder-bags were prepared to blow in the gate, two horse-artillery guns were told off to cover the advance of the storming-party; and at noon two companies of the Fifth Native Infantry, under Captain Swayne, moved out under cover of a wall towards the fort. The guns fired for twenty minutes; the infantry, without leaving their cover, expended the whole of their ammunition; and Elphinstone, who was watching the proceedings, recalled the entire party. Eyre, who was in charge of the two guns, complained of Swayne's unwillingness to rush forward with his men. It was perhaps discreditable, but after what had happened on the 4th of November it was not surprising.

On the morning of the 6th, Sturt, the only engineer with the force, having fretted himself almost into madness over the general mismanagement of affairs, staggered out of bed in his shirt and pyjamas to superintend a scientific attack on the fort by breach and assault. Starting at six o'clock, he managed to obtain the consent of Elphinstone and to get three nine-pounders and two heavy howitzers into position; and at ten, he opened fire.

At noon the storming-party—one company of the Forty-Fourth and two of *sepoys*, in all about one hundred and fifty men—made their rush and carried the fort without hesitation, though not without some loss. This method might perfectly well have been adopted from the first; but apparently no one had the brains, nor the energy, to employ it but an officer who had been terribly wounded four days earlier, and was still so weak that he could not put on his clothes, (Lady Sale's *Journal*). However, here was at least a little success, but Elphinstone could not be brought to follow it up. The Commissariat fort, which had been but half emptied by the enemy, was not recaptured.

The *Shah's* garden was shelled, and the insurgents were driven from it by a party of Colin Mackenzie's irregular infantry; but, being unsupported, Mackenzie was obliged to fall back with considerable loss. In the plain to the west of cantonments also a reconnoitring-party brought on engagement which gradually drew the whole of Elphinstone's cavalry into action against very superior numbers. More than one successful charge was headed by British officers with distinguished gallantry; but they were not adequately supported, and accomplished nothing permanent.

Elphinstone was particularly chary of his artillery, constantly sending out small parties with a single gun, though Lake had laid down in orders in 1806 that, where one gun was needed, two at least must always be employed, lest the one should be put out of action by growing too hot. Yet artillery was the arm which outranged all weapons of the Afghans; and tumultuous bands of tribesmen, mounted or afoot, could never stand many rounds of shrapnel in the open. But a man who used companies where he should have used battalions would naturally use single guns where he should have used batteries.

After the operations of the 6th the enemy were quiet for a day, having taken harder blows than they had given. But already Elphinstone was urging upon Macnaghten the expediency of coming to terms with the insurgents. Since the news of the mutiny of the Kohistani regiment, intelligence had come in that the Gurkha battalion at Charikar was closely beset, that most of its British officers had been killed, that the water-supply had been cut off, and in fact that its annihilation was practically inevitable. Macnaghten's sins were finding him out in terrible succession, and he had no resource but his old policy of bribing the Afghan chiefs, though he now added to this the new expedient of hiring assassins to make away with the most formidable of them. (Kaye, ii.).

It was all very pitiful, for the envoy was a brave man, and had he been a soldier, would have struck boldly and decisively; but unfortunately he did not know even his own business, and mismanaged diplomatic as disastrously as military affairs. By trying to buy off the hostility of one tribe after another, instead of securing the friendship of one only, he offered a premium to the sept that should prove itself most formidable, and kept them all waiting in expectation round Kabul.

On the 7th the enemy recovered themselves. They had found two British guns in the repairing shops, which, with the usual carelessness, had been set up in the city instead of in the Bala Hissar; and, having mounted them in Mahmoud Khan's fort, they opened fire upon the cantonment with such rude ammunition as they could improvise. On the 9th Macnaghten persuaded Elphinstone to recall Shelton from the Bala Hissar and entrust the future guidance of military affairs to him. Shelton came over accordingly, escorted by one of the Shah's regular battalions, a company of the Forty-Fourth and two guns, and brought a small supply of grain with him.

For the rest, the garrison in cantonments depended upon such provisions as Macnaghten, by means of liberal bribes, was able to get in from the village of Behmaru; and the whole question of the future military policy really turned upon the vital matter of supplies. More than one officer had already perceived that the design of the Afghans was to starve the British out. The stupendous imbecility of Elphinstone had given them every chance of prosecuting that design with success. It remained to be seen what decision an able-bodied officer of long and wide experience would take upon succeeding to this most undesirable command.

But the first difficulty was that Elphinstone, instead of putting himself on the sick list and effacing himself altogether, insisted upon remaining supreme. He would not allow Shelton even to change the position of a gun on the rampart of the cantonments; and, though he had ample stores of ammunition, he was possessed by so morbid a dread lest it should fail, that he forbade the sentries to fire at robbers and assassins who were doing their work within a dozen yards of them, (Mackenzie). But supposing that Elphinstone abdicated his powers, Macnaghten had no idea of parting with his own authority. The command therefore passed from the hands of an extremely inefficient duumvirate into those of a triumvirate, the third party being an extremely difficult, disagreeable, contradictious and obstinate man. But even he, as sole commander, would have been better than such a combination. The whole situation was complicated by the fact that Macnaghten looked every day for the arrival of Sale to put an end to his troubles, and was therefore disinclined to take any decisive step. But in any case the last state of the command at Kabul was worse than the first.

There was one principal question to be determined, namely, whether the British force should hold its ground at the capital or retreat. Macnaghten was strongly for the former course; and Sturt, from his sick-bed, had vehemently urged the withdrawal of all the troops into the Bala Hissar. To this the *Shah*, as always, objected, and consequently Macnaghten also, at any rate for the present. But though no one doubted the ability of the British to hold their own in the citadel against the attacks of any number of Afghans, there was no certainty about supplies of water, food, forage and fuel. The wells, it seems, barely sufficed for the present inmates of the Bala Hissar, and a small stream which supplemented them would certainly be cut off.

As to food, Elphinstone had sacrificed all that had been collected, and Macnaghten was keeping the garrison alive by bribing the villagers heavily to bring in grain in small quantities. But, even if the Commissariat fort had not been abandoned, the provisions therein would not have lasted beyond the end of January; and now it was at best doubtful whether the townsfolk would part with the victuals which they had laid up for the winter.

Of course it was always possible to use force; but to fight, especially in a barricaded town, for every day's rations during a period of months would wear away the numbers of the garrison very rapidly. As to forage, there was precisely the same difficulty. The animals were already weak and half-famished, and it was pretty certain that the vast majority of them must perish. As to fuel, there seem to have been no misgivings; but it was practically certain that in the Bala Hissar there was not sufficient shelter against the cold. Already, though the real winter had not begun, the *sepoys* in the citadel were succumbing to exposure, sixty men having gone into hospital within a week with pneumonia, which generally proved fatal. Moreover, there were no medical stores, the whole of them having been abandoned in the Commissariat fort. On the whole, therefore, though the only chance for the British to hold their ground was to move into the Bala Hissar, it should seem that even this course would have been hazardous.

It is true that with the coming of severe weather the tribes might have dispersed, though Macnaghten's system of bribes was admirably calculated to keep them assembled. It is possible, too, that the population of Kabul, overawed by the presence of a disciplined force in an impregnable position, might have sought reconciliation. But there was no reckoning upon this. The game was in their hands. They could starve the British out, if they wished, and there could be no question of the bitter and vindictive hatred which they nourished against the foreign invaders. For this was no ordinary rising of a few predatory tribes. For once the Afghans were united; and Mackeson and Macgregor, the political agents in the Khyber Pass, pronounced gravely and truly that there was no saying where the trouble might end.

It should seem, therefore, that the correct military measure was immediate retreat, before the snow should fall: and this was advocated practically by every senior officer. Elphinstone, utterly unnerved and exhausted, was for securing it by negotiation. Shelton, who had gone through the retreats from Sahagun and Burgos, would have treated it as an ordinary military operation, difficult perhaps, but perfectly practicable; and the more so since Sale would be able to give help from Gandamak. There was no occasion to retire further than to Jalalabad, which was halfway to Peshawar; and the force could advance again upon Kabul, if necessary, in the ensuing spring.

As to supplies, if enough could be collected to last through the winter at Kabul, it would be easy to raise enough for ten days' march. Any superfluous stores could be destroyed. The military reasons for such a retreat, indeed, seem to me to have been cogent and unanswerable; and, had the army alone been concerned, they might have prevailed. But the whole of Macnaghten's work was at stake, and, even if that had been abandoned as rotten, it was impossible for the army to leave the *Shah* behind. Moreover, not merely the Shah but the eight hundred members of his harem, their three or four thousand parasites, and their fifteen hundred camels must be brought away and fed; and this was a very serious matter. Retreat would have meant no discredit to the army, but it would have ruined Macnaghten and heaped shame upon Auckland.

Moreover, Macnaghten did not give Shelton credit for basing his advice upon purely military grounds. Shelton had made no secret of his longing to return to India, and he by no means stood alone. The senior officers, indeed, were almost without exception despondent, not concealing their misgivings that they would never see India again. They knew the extreme peril of their situation and the precarious nature of their communications. They had seen their men ruined in spirit and discipline by the vagaries of Macnaghten, and they had made up their minds that the army was to be sacrificed to the caprice of the political agents, with the governor-general at their head. That was one of the worst features in the prevailing discontent. The officers mistrusted the Supreme Government as thoroughly as they did Macnaghten; and unfortunately they had all too good reason.

The spirit of the whole force was bad, so bad that the finer and bolder among the young officers declined to share in it; but it was not inexplicable. Possibly Macnaghten reckoned that the veteran Shelton would revive the tone of the troops. If so, he was disappointed, for Shelton was not only the gloomiest but the most offensive of the prophets of evil; and Macnaghten no doubt set down Shelton's eagerness for a retreat to sheer perversity and love of obstruction. It would have been hard to find two men worse assorted to work together, for both were self-assertive, both were pompous, both were ill-tempered and neither was a gentleman.

On the morning of the 10th the enemy, both horse and foot, crowned the heights of Behmaru on the west, and of Sia Sang on the east, in great force, as if to threaten attack upon the cantonments on both fronts. Only those on the east, however, after some delay descended into the plain, and occupied all the forts upon that side; maintaining an annoying fire of sharpshooters from the Rika Bashi fort, seven hundred yards north-east of the north-eastern bastion of the cantonments. The British answered by a steady fire of shells from two howitzers and as many mortars, which was kept up for two hours with apparently no great effect.

Then Macnaghten, taking all responsibility upon himself, pressed Elphinstone to storm this fort; and at noon the Forty-Fourth, the Thirty-Seventh Native Infantry, one of the *Shah's* regular battalions, a party of irregular horse, and three light guns assembled at the eastern gate. A storming-party of two companies from each of the three battalions was told off; and Captain Bellew, Elphinstone's deputy quartermaster-general, ran forward with powder-bags to blow in the gate.

It seems strange that a staff-officer, who, presumably, had drawn out the scheme of operations, should not have ascertained first where the gate was, but Bellew only blew open a small wicket, so strait that but two or three men could enter abreast, and so low that they had to stoop to enter at all. The result was that the foremost of the stormers were easily shot down; but a few officers, with a handful of Europeans and *sepoys*, none the less forced their way in, and the Afghans at once fled headlong out of the gate on the opposite side of the fort. Just at this moment, however, a party of Afghan horse wheeled round the corner of the fort towards the wicket; the cry of "cavalry" was raised; a native bugler sounded the retire; and the storming-party, despite of the entreaties of their officers, took to their heels.

The Afghans returned to the attack in great numbers, and, in spite of a desperate resistance, cut down the few British within the fort, though one officer and a *sepoy*, finding a point of vantage, defended themselves with success. Meanwhile Shelton, perfectly calm and unmoved under a very hot fire, with great difficulty rallied the fugitives. The guns of the cantonments and a menace from the British cavalry sufficed to disperse the Afghan horse; and Shelton, though the men hesitated to follow him in a second trial, finally brought them forward to a third and successful assault. They found the solitary officer and a single *sepoy* still safe, with a heap of over thirty dead Afghans before them; and the enemy promptly evacuated the rest of the forts. Shelton then marched his force towards the Sia Sang heights, and opened fire from his two horse-artillery guns, whereupon the enemy speedily dispersed, and presently disappeared from sight.

The British casualties in this action, not including those of the Shah's battalion, exceeded one hundred, fully half of them being killed, and among them four European officers. (Eyre says 200 casualties, but Lady Sale's more exact figures seem to lower the number to 150). The whole affair was evidently ill-managed, and the only man who shone in it was Shelton, whose conduct seems to have excited general admiration and to have restored the confidence of the Forty-Fourth. A panic is a thing with which no commander can reckon, but, considering that the Afghan horse was plainly visible within a few hundred yards of the fort, it is not clear why a body of cavalry was not held in readiness to keep them at a distance.

According to one authority, (Lawrence, *Forty-Three Years in India*), who wrote many years after the event, Shelton was responsible for this, though the most unfriendly of contemporary chronicles say nothing of it. However, the British were heartened and the Afghans discouraged by the results of the day. The Rika Bashi fort and another, the Zulficar fort, outside the northern face of the Mission enclosure, were occupied. Four more were destroyed, and four days' supply of grain was gathered from them in all. Furthermore, for the next three days the enemy dared not show themselves. The Commissariat animals went far afield and brought in supplies and forage unmolested; and even a single officer walked three miles from the cantonment without seeing an enemy. Best of all, the Forty-Fourth regained their trust in Shelton. (Lawrence, *Forty-Three Years in India*. The account of the action is based on the narratives of Eyre and Lady Sale).

Little was done on the ensuing days beyond the bombardment of Mahmoud Khan's fort. Owing to the great extent of the cantonments the troops were already overworked; the spirit of enterprise was not strong in the military leaders; and, owing to the weakness of Elphinstone, discipline was steadily deteriorating. On the 13th the enemy again presented themselves in force on the Behmaru hills, and opened fire from two guns upon the cantonments.

At noon Macnaghten urged that a force should be sent out to dislodge them and capture the guns; and meeting, as usual, with objection from Elphinstone, he finally gave positive orders to that effect. Accordingly, at 3 p.m., Shelton was sent out with sixteen companies of infantry, four squadrons of horse, one horse-artillery gun and one mountain gun; (6 companies 44th, 6 companies 37th N.I., 4 companies *Shah's* infantry; 2 sq. 5th Bengal L.C., 2 sq. irregular horse), roughly speaking, about fourteen hundred infantry and three hundred and fifty cavalry. The advance was made in three columns, which seem to have raced each other for the hill, while the single horse-artillery gun—the only efficient piece with the force—was stuck fast in a water-course. The infantry pressed up the ascent, the Afghan horse standing firm on the summit, and poured in a volley at ten or twelve yards' range which did no execution whatever.

Thereupon a party of about fifty Afghans charged and drove one column in confusion to the foot of the hill, till the horse-artillery gun, coming up at last, tore the Afghan ranks with shrapnel and grape, and the British cavalry, charging in turn, drove the enemy again to the top of the hill. The British infantry, rallying, advanced once more; and the enemy fled, abandoning their two guns, one of which was spiked and the other brought in. Darkness forbade any pursuit, and the enemy took advantage of it to follow Shelton's people back to cantonments with much shouting and firing, but little, if any, real mischief.

✶✶✶✶✶✶

Lawrence says that if Shelton had pursued he might have entered Kabul on the backs of the fugitives and taken the city. But his animus for Macnaghten and against Shelton makes his judgement doubtful.

✶✶✶✶✶✶

The casualties in this skirmish seem not to have been very heavy, but they included two of the best officers of Elphinstone's staff, both of whom were severely wounded. It was not a good sign that such men should leave the general to do regimental duty on such an occasion. The harmlessness of the volley was another bad sign, pointing to the probability that the men's muskets had been loaded several hours—possibly even one or two days—before, and had been left lying against the rampart, where the powder had become damp, (See Lady Sale's *Journal*; Hough).

With proper discipline such a thing should have been impossible. It is difficult, too, to explain why more guns were not sent out, for, with skilful handling of these and of the cavalry, the enemy might have been driven from their cannon and severely punished. But nothing ordered by Macnaghten was kindly executed by Elphinstone and Shelton; though, if the general were bound to obey the envoy, he might just as well have sent out his troops earlier and laid his plans to strike a really telling blow.

On the 15th Major Eldred Pottinger and Lieutenant Haughton rode in, more dead than alive, to cantonments, to report that they and two Gurkhas were the only survivors of the garrison of Charikar and had themselves escaped by miracle. Both were wounded, Haughton so desperately that through a dreary ride of sixty miles he had been supported in the saddle by a man on each side. Here was another sacrifice—that of an entire battalion—to the ignorance of Macnaghten; and the fact was not lost upon the troops at Kabul. Then came tidings that Captain Woodburn, with one hundred and fifty of the Shah's infantry, had been treacherously inveigled into a fort near Ghazni, and that his entire party had been destroyed. Finally, on the 17th, came a rumour, confirmed by a letter on the 18th, that Sale, despite of the repeated orders of Macnaghten, had not marched for Kabul, but in the contrary direction for Jalalabad.

Our last sight of Sale was upon his arrival at Gandamak on the 30th of October. On the 5th of November rumours began to reach him of the rising at Kabul, but, all regular communication being cut off, it was not until the 10th that he received what seems to have been the last of Macnaghten's urgent appeals that he should return to the capital. Thereupon he called a council of war, which pronounced that obedience to the envoy's order was inadvisable, or, as Sale himself put it, impossible. His reasons were that he had three hundred wounded, not transport enough, owing to the desertion of his hired drivers, to carry one day's rations, no depots on the road, and ammunition sufficient for two days' fighting only, whereas he needed enough for six days.

It may be remarked that the number of the wounded, and the deficiency both of transport and of ammunition, were all due principally to Sale's own mismanagement in leaving his rear-guard to take care of itself, and enabling the enemy to wound men and capture camels and munitions as they would. Macnaghten had urged him to throw his wounded into some fort with a guard to protect them; but Sale pleaded that he had not provisions enough to feed both such a detachment for an uncertain period and his own men on their march to Kabul.

It is difficult to say whether or not he could have obeyed Macnaghten's order, if he had wished. Probably he could, though not without risk; and at least one critic has dealt with him sternly upon this assumption. But very certainly he did not wish; and it seems that Elphinstone was of the same mind, for he heartily applauded Sale's decision. (Mackenzie, i.; *I.O.S.C.*, vol. 18 of 1841, Macnaghten to Macgregor, Nov. 9; Sale to Mackeson and to Macnaghten, Nov. 11; Elphinstone to Sale, Nov. 28, 1841—"*Vous avez très bien fait)*." In these circumstances, it seems to me hard to blame Sale for not marching to Kabul.

But why Sale should have made for Jalalabad, a ruined fortress, without magazines and without military strength or importance, is not so easy to explain. He would have been quite as strong, quite as well off, and far more menacing at Gandamak. He would have threatened continually the passes to Kabul, kept a large portion of the Ghilzais inactively watching him, and struck misgiving and anxiety into all the host of the Afghans to the north. If he set himself diligently to collect supplies and transport, he might, as the wounded gradually recovered, have made a dash for Kabul after all, and at least, if Elphinstone decided ultimately to retreat, he might have facilitated the operation enormously.

But he evidently partook strongly of the general feeling that, the more nearly he approached to India, the better was his chance of quitting the detested Afghanistan for good. The force at Kabul or at Gandamak might be sacrificed by the Supreme Government, but hardly a brigade at Jalalabad. It is humiliating that such ideas should ever have occurred to a British general or to any British officer; but such was the pass to which the rule of Auckland, Macnaghten and the political element generally had brought the British Army. (Durand. See the account of the Council of War at Jalalabad in Broadfoot's *Career of Major Broadfoot*, and Shelton's comment in Lady Sale's *Journal*).

Here, then, was the situation at Kabul so far simplified. Sale's brigade was known to have moved away, and it was tolerably certain that no help could be forthcoming from Kandahar. As a matter of fact, Nott had, on receipt of Macnaghten's order, sent off two battalions towards Kabul, though unwillingly, for he felt sure that they would be stopped by snow between Ghazni and the capital; and he proved to be right, for the battalions were obliged to retrace their steps to Kandahar, having lost many of their transport-cattle through exposure. On the 19th, therefore, Macnaghten addressed to Elphinstone an official letter, asking him what he proposed to do.

He added that he himself thought it his duty to hold on to the cantonments for as long as possible, for a retreat would mean dishonour and much sacrifice of public property, and withdrawal into the Bala Hissar would be little less disastrous on every account than retreat. He advised, therefore, postponement of any decision for eight or ten days, during which "something might turn up in our favour". Meanwhile, the enemy remained inactive, and allowed supplies in small quantities, chiefly through the village of Behmaru, to be gathered into cantonments. This apathy puzzled the garrison, and probably encouraged Macnaghten, but it was not of long duration.

On the morning of the 22nd large bodies of Afghan horse and foot issued from the city, and moved to the summit of the Behmaru heights. Macnaghten thereupon urged Elphinstone to forestall the enemy in the occupation of the village, which lies at the eastern end; and a detachment of half a battalion of the Fifth Native Infantry, three troops of horse, and a single gun of the mountain-train, under Major Swayne, were sent out. On reaching the village, however, Swayne was greeted by a very sharp fire, and, putting his infantry under cover, kept up an useless fusillade upon the houses. Meanwhile a single horse-artillery gun, which had been despatched after him, unlimbered on the plain and played upon the summit of the ridge, offering, together with the cavalry drawn up in its rear, a very good target for the Afghan marksmen in the village. So matters went on for some five or six hours from the late forenoon until evening, when Shelton was sent out with the rest of the Fifth to bring Swayne's party in.

Later, a council of war was held at which it was determined, at Macnaghten's instance, that Shelton should on the following morning take the village by assault and hold the summit of the ridge against all attacks. It seems that the object was to establish a permanent post for the domination, if not for the actual occupation, of the village, and to that end to throw up a small stone fort, or *sangar*, on the crest of the height immediately above it. .

According to a good authority, (Lady Sale), high language was used by Shelton to Elphinstone in that council of war, though whether in reference to the general's conduct at large or to the projected operation in particular is not stated. As has already been told, sundry small parties of the British had already been stationed in forts outside the cantonments, thereby weakening the numbers at disposal to man the ramparts, and throwing additional duty upon men who were already overworked. These posts, however, were within musket-shot of the cantonments, whereas the projected redoubt on the Behmaru heights would be about eight hundred yards distant, that is to say, beyond effective range of a field-gun, and would therefore need a fairly strong garrison. The village of Behmaru itself lay on the north-eastern slope; and the upper houses commanded the Mission compound, which was within reach at any rate of the heavier Afghan *jezails*. This fact may not have been without its influence upon Macnaghten; but his chief motive in pressing for this operation was undoubtedly to give the Afghans, from whom he was buying supplies in the village, the excuse that their grain was taken from them by force.

At 2 a.m. of the 23rd Shelton sallied out in dead silence with six companies each of the Fifth and Thirty-Seventh Native Infantry, five of the Forty-fourth, one squadron of regular and two of irregular horse, and a single horse-artillery gun; altogether about nine hundred foot and three hundred and fifty cavalry, besides one hundred native sappers. The column made for a gorge which, running north and south, divides the Behmaru ridge into two distinct hills; the gun was dragged with great difficulty up the steep and rugged acclivity; and the whole moved to a knoll at the north-eastern extremity of the more easterly hill, which overhung the village. There was no moon; but watch-fires were visible in an open space among the buildings.

Upon these the gun opened fire with grape, whereupon the enemy fled to the houses and towers, from whence they discharged an answering fire of *jezails*. The British responded with their muskets, and this futile firing in the dark went on till dawn, when parties of the enemy were seen hurrying out of the village across the plain to a distant fort. Shelton then told off two companies of the Thirty-Seventh Native Infantry and a few of the Forty-fourth, under Major Swayne, to storm the village. Why Swayne, who belonged to the Fifth Native Infantry and had on a previous occasion showed himself backward in attack, was chosen to lead men of other regiments to this assault, is not clear; but he went to work in his usual fashion, leading his men to a small wicket, which he could not force, instead of to the main entrance. He then put his party under cover when he was himself shot through the neck, and several of his men were likewise shot down.

Before matters could go further, large bodies of men were seen streaming out of the city towards the scene of the conflict, and Shelton, recalling Swayne's detachment, made new dispositions. He had already posted a squadron of horse in the plain to south of the ridge to watch his flank; and he now left three companies of the Thirty-Seventh Native Infantry, under Major Kershaw, on the knoll overlooking the village, and moved the rest of his force with his gun southward to the brow of the gorge, where he drew it up in two lines of infantry, with the cavalry in rear, facing south. He seems at the same time to have sent a message to cantonments asking for reinforcements and for another gun.

No such message should have been necessary. The Afghans, in passing from Kabul to Behmaru, necessarily crossed the western front of the cantonments; and if Elphinstone had promptly sent out the strongest possible force of all three arms, he could have assailed them in flank, and brought on a general action under most advantageous conditions. It was, in fact, a great chance for righting the entire situation; but there seems to have been no one about Elphinstone who could force him to seize it.

The enemy now crowned the western hill of the ridge in masses, to the number (as was reckoned) of ten thousand, and pushed forward their sharpshooters to contend with the skirmishers posted by Shelton to watch the dead ground over the brow of the gorge. Gradually these crept round both of Shelton's flanks, so that he was compelled to double back the flank companies of both his lines, thus forming in each case three sides of a square. By 7 a.m. the pressure upon the skirmishers in front was already severe, and Shelton's single gun alone could retaliate, which it did with great effect, upon the masses of the enemy, until it grew too hot to be served any longer. So the action continued until past nine o'clock, the Afghans taking skilful advantage of every stone and hollow and ravine to pour bullets upon the whole of Shelton's array and to receive none in return. The troops became discouraged. They had been on foot already for ten hours; they had been for some days on half-rations; and there was no water on the hill. Thus they were weary, hungry and thirsty; and some, at any rate, of them had not been in the best of heart when they started.

The Fifth Native Infantry seems not to have been a good regiment; and their colonel, Oliver, though a very brave man, was one of the worst croakers in the force. He tried to lead some of his *sepoys* over the brow of the gorge to keep down the Afghan fire, but not a man would follow him; and it was only when he went down alone, saying that he at least would do his duty, that a bare dozen joined him for very shame. The apathy of their comrades in cantonments may well have contributed to the demoralisation of these men; but, though Shelton asked again and again for reinforcements and for another gun, not a man was sent to him.

It was not yet ten o'clock when a large body of Afghan cavalry, perhaps fifteen hundred strong, (Lady Sale, says from 3000 to 4000, and she had had some experience in judging of numbers; but I think it safer to halve her estimate), advanced along the plain to south of the heights, and drove Walker's single squadron to take refuge on the hill. They were checked by a few rounds of shrapnel, which did great execution and killed Abdulla Khan, one of their foremost leaders; but the withdrawal of Walker enabled the enemy to throw reinforcements into Behmaru and to threaten Shelton not only on the right flank but in rear. Shortly afterwards a party of Afghan fanatics, Ghazis, crept up to the very brow of the hill, drove back the British skirmishers and planted a flag within thirty yards of Shelton's first line of infantry. Shelton gave the word to fix bayonets and charge; but not a man would move.

The officers rushed to the front and flung stones at the Ghazis, who retorted with the same primitive missile; but still neither British nor *sepoys* would advance. Then a Ghazi rose, waving his sword over his head, and he and his fellows rushed on, drove Shelton's first line before them like sheep, cut down the gunners, who stood nobly by their piece, and captured the gun. The officers of the cavalry rode forward, calling to their men to charge, but not one of their troopers would move. Happily, the second line stood firm, the fugitives were with some difficulty rallied behind it, and then, singularly enough, the Ghazis, in their turn, were smitten with panic and ran back. The news of Abdulla Khan's death spread dismay among all ranks of the Afghans, who retired once more with some precipitation to the western hill, carrying off the limber and horses, but not the gun. The piece was therefore recovered, and the gunners reopened fire while the troops reoccupied their former ground.

To the spectators in cantonments the fight seemed now to be over, and Macnaghten went so far as to urge Elphinstone to pursue the flying Afghans into the city, (Lady Sale's *Journal*). The general refused, saying that it was a wild scheme and not feasible; and, as the enemy presently attempted unsuccessfully to intercept ammunition and a fresh limber that was on its way to Shelton, it is clear that they did not consider the action over. None the less, even thus late a counter-attack from cantonments—for Shelton's men were too much shaken and exhausted for any such movement—would have decided the day favourably; but Elphinstone sent out not a man. Colin Mackenzie, whom Shelton had taken on to his staff for the day, urged Shelton to retire to cantonments while the Afghans were still inactive; but Shelton refused, as it seems to me, rightly. He had, by his appeal for reinforcements, signified his inability to hold his own, and it was for Elphinstone to recall him if the general wished him to return.

Meanwhile the enemy reassembled in even greater numbers upon the southern hill, and, repeating their former tactics, advanced again to the attack. Soon after noon they had made such progress that Shelton ordered Kershaw to move up to his assistance. Kershaw, fully engaged with large bodies of the enemy by the village, in answer suggested rather that the brigadier should fall back to him as the surest way of securing a retreat. The first line was by this time wavering, and the sergeant in charge of the gun pressed for leave to retire upon Kershaw, which Shelton at last granted. With the retreat of the gun the Ghazis leaped to their feet, and made a rush which broke Shelton's shaken and enfeebled infantry; and all was panic. The men poured down the hill to the cantonments, a mere terrified rabble, with the Afghans in eager chase, and the gun was captured.

Poor, decrepit Elphinstone mounted his horse and rode out, vainly trying to restore order; for it seemed as if pursuers and pursued would enter the cantonments together. Two gallant officers with a small body of cavalry did something to save the fugitives; a party of native sharpshooters under Captain Trevor did something more, and the fire of some of the Shah's infantry from the Mission compound perhaps still more; but the real cause why Shelton's detachment escaped utter annihilation was that the foremost of the Afghan leaders, Osman Khan, voluntarily halted his followers and led them away.

With this crowning disgrace ended this most disgraceful day. Contemporary writers with one accord throw the blame of it upon Shelton, ascribing all misfortunes to his alleged tactical blunders. Shelton, on his side, spoke disparagingly of the bad spirit of the *sepoys* which, as he asserted, passed from them into the Forty-Fourth. There can be no doubt that both *sepoys* and Europeans behaved ill; but beyond the fact that Shelton had been openly despondent—which is by no means a thing to be readily condoned—it is unjust to hold him responsible for the disaster. The general deterioration in the tone and discipline of the troops had begun long before his arrival in Afghanistan, and was not due to him.

The really salient fact is this—that he was sent out with a weak force to an isolated position where he could be surrounded—was put forward, in fact, as though intended as a bait to lure the enemy into a general action; and that, when he actually was surrounded, no effort was made by his superior, who had plenty of men within less than a mile of the scene of action, to rescue him. To this may be added the one detail that, though the heavier of the Afghan *jezails* were known to outrange the musket, Shelton was provided, contrary to standing orders, with but one gun.

If additional proof were needed of the utter apathy and inefficiency which reigned within the cantonments it is to be discovered in the fact that, though ordnance-stores were abundant, the guns on the ramparts ran short of ammunition just at the moment when the Afghans were hunting Shelton's fugitives to the very walls. With such neglect and mismanagement it was hopeless to expect success in battle. It should seem that the Afghan tactics were well conceived, and skilfully and persistently executed; but Nott, in the place of Elphinstone, would have turned the day's fighting into a great and crushing victory.

The events of this day consummated the demoralisation of Elphinstone's force; and the *shah*, now thoroughly alarmed, wrote to Macnaghten, through one of the envoy's political subordinates, urging immediate retreat into the Bala Hissar. But the operation of moving all troops and stores from the cantonments in the face of an enemy flushed with triumph was declared both by Elphinstone and Shelton to be impossible, even if it could be pronounced expedient. It now appeared that fuel was so deficient in the citadel that the *sepoys* were dying of cold; (Kaye), and there was no prospect of obtaining more except by fighting for it.

On the 24th, however, a new opening offered itself to Macnaghten. The chief, Osman Khan, who had called his cavalry off from the pursuit on the previous day, wrote to him to recall this good service, and to suggest in a friendly way that the British should quietly evacuate the country. Elphinstone warmly supported the idea of entering into negotiations; and therewith all vigilance seems to have been more than ever relaxed. On the night of the 25th the enemy made an attempt to destroy the bridge over the Kabul River. Shelton had long since urged the construction of a small work to protect it. Sturt now advised that the Rika Bashi fort should be blown up and the garrison transferred to a small fort near the bridge. But nothing was done, though for a retreat the bridge was of vital importance.

On the 25th, when the Afghan negotiators came into cantonments, there was a still worse sign of demoralisation. Crowds of Afghans, armed to the teeth, swarmed round the ramparts with friendly gestures, crying out that all was settled; and the men of the Forty-fourth went out among them unarmed, shaking hands with them, and accepting presents of vegetables without the slightest check from their officers. Yet Afghan treachery had long been proverbial, and it was known that on this very day Mohamed Akbar Khan, a son of Dost Mohamed, had returned to Kabul in triumph with a following of some thousands of men. Where the carcase is, there will the vultures be gathered together; but there is no occasion for the carcase to welcome the vultures before life is extinct.

The terms proposed by the Afghans were so outrageously humiliating that on the 27th they were finally rejected, and on the 28th and 29th the British made some show of resuming hostilities by shelling the village of Behmaru, in order to cover the collection of grain. But the gathering in of supplies became more and more difficult, and the animals were dying fast from sheer starvation. Yet still Macnaghten remained sanguine of the success of his obscure intrigues. He declared that "prospects were brightening," and, when the Commissary adjured him to make up his mind to retreat while there were yet provisions to carry the army to Jalalabad, the envoy answered, "Let us wait two days longer, as something may turn up," (Kaye).

On the 1st of December the enemy made an attack on the citadel of the Bala Hissar, which was easily repulsed with considerable loss to the assailants; but there was no attempt to turn this success to account. On the 5th the Afghans burned, without molestation, the bridge over the Kabul River; and on the 6th they surprised the garrison of Mohamed Sherif's fort—forty men of the Forty-Fourth and sixty of the Thirty-Seventh Native Infantry—who seem to have been asleep, but at any rate had laid aside arms and accoutrements, and who took to their heels almost without firing a shot. Shelton paraded the fugitives to recapture the fort and so wipe away their disgrace, but after some hours of waiting in the cold they were dismissed, (Lady Sale's *Journal*).

The first snow had fallen on the 26th of November, and the weather was growing daily colder. Supplies failed in the cantonments and were only replenished by doles, gathered in with risk and difficulty from the Bala Hissar. On the 8th of December Macnaghten wrote officially to Elphinstone asking whether there were any resource now left but negotiation for peaceful retreat, and, having obtained his assent, met a number of tribal chiefs in conference on the 11th. He proposed that the British should evacuate Afghanistan and every post that they held in it, and return to India not only unmolested but with transport and supplies to be furnished to them by the Afghans; that Dost Mohamed and his fellow exiles should be restored to their own country, Shah Shuja abdicating his throne and remaining at Kabul, or retiring with the British to Ludhiana, as he might prefer; and that no British force should again enter Afghanistan without consent of the Afghan government.

The British were to evacuate their cantonments within three days, the chiefs meanwhile sending in supplies for their sustenance. The terms were accepted. Captain Trevor, one of Macnaghten's subordinates, was given over as hostage for Macnaghten's good faith; and the British looked forward to making their first march on the 14th. The Afghan chiefs had other ends in view.

Two days' delay were caused by Shah Shuja's hesitation whether to remain at Kabul, where the Durani chiefs wished to retain him for their own purposes, or to retire to India; but at last he decided upon the latter course. Meanwhile, the chiefs furnished to the cantonments no transport and only scanty supplies of victual, while a rabble of Afghan ruffians plundered and robbed all private traders within a dozen yards of the ramparts, the soldiers having orders not to fire upon them. On the 13th the troops were withdrawn from the Bala Hissar, but they had no time to load the grain that they had with them, and there was an ugly scene when, late in the evening, they at last emerged from the gate; for the Afghan chiefs seem to have laid some plot for entering the fortress as soon as the British had left it, and Shah Shuja, having some inkling of this, shut the gate hastily and fired indiscriminately on friend and foe.

The troops were kept waiting all night in bitter cold before the chief, Akbar Khan, dared to move them over the plain, though he finally led them into cantonments unmolested next morning. On that same day Elphinstone gave orders for the camp-followers to be armed with the spare muskets that he had in store, whereupon the wretched creatures rushed in and helped themselves not only to arms but to anything else that they could lay hands on. All discipline had vanished, thanks, primarily, to the weakness of the commander-in-chief, and latterly to lack of clothing and lack of fuel, sheer cold and sheer hunger.

The envoy now pressed for the promised transport and supplies. The chiefs retorted by first demanding the evacuation of the forts around the cantonments, which were duly yielded up on the afternoon of the 16th. Still the transport and supplies came not; and there was very good reason why they should not. Macnaghten was scattering money in all directions, offering bribes to all parties, after his usual fashion, and fairly inviting them to be dilatory in the hope of obtaining more. On the 18th a heavy fall of snow enabled the chiefs to put further pressure on the envoy. They extorted from him on the 19th an order for the evacuation of Ghazni, and on the 20th made a further demand for immediate surrender of the guns and ammunition, with the delivery of Shelton as a hostage into their hands.

On this latter day, Macnaghten received for the first time certain intelligence that Maclaren's brigade had been compelled by snow to return to Kandahar; so that the last hope, to which he had clung for so long, was gone. Lieutenant Sturt advised Elphinstone to break off the treaty and march for Jalalabad at once; but, on the contrary, one of the chiefs was invited on the 22nd to go over the ordnance-stores and make a selection from them. On that same evening Akbar Khan sent in proposals to Macnaghten that in return for a very large sum he, Akbar Khan, should join the British, rally the Ghilzais to them, seize the person of one of the leading chiefs, and enable the British to remain at Kabul until the spring, when they should return to India comfortably, leaving Shah Shuja still sovereign of Afghanistan, with Akbar Khan for his Prime Minister.

Death of Macnaghten

The whole scheme was so extravagant that only a desperate man could have been deluded by it, but Macnaghten, worried and harassed to death, eagerly accepted it. On the next day he went out with three companions and a very small escort to meet Akbar Khan and others in conference at a spot about six hundred yards from the cantonments. Armed Afghans crowded round them at once. Presently the envoy and all his companions were seized, and Macnaghten was shot down on the spot by Akbar Khan himself and cut to pieces by the fanatics who attended him. Captain Trevor shared his fate; and George Lawrence and Colin Mackenzie were carried off as prisoners. The scene was not distinctly visible from cantonments, though one officer was certain that he had seen Macnaghten fall, and the Afghans hacking at him. In any case, not a shot was fired, and not a man was even marched to the spot. There is no more ignoble passage in the history of the army.

On the 24th the chiefs held a discussion with their captives Lawrence and Mackenzie, and their hostages, Captain Connolly and another political officer; as the result of which the treaty was sent back to Elphinstone, with three additional clauses to the effect that the British should give up all their treasure, and all their guns but six, and that married men with their wives and families should be substituted for the existing hostages. It was also explained that Macnaghten had met his death because he had treacherously violated the treaty, which was unfortunately true. Unable to contemplate anything but peaceful withdrawal, Elphinstone begged Eldred Pottinger to assume the duties of Macnaghten.

Pottinger in vain tried to persuade the military leaders either to hold out in Kabul or to retreat. Messages had come in from Peshawar that reinforcements were arriving from India, and that Sale had gained a great success at Jalalabad; but Elphinstone would hear of nothing but negotiation. The terms were accepted, with some amendment in the matter of hostages. The sick and wounded were moved to the Bala Hissar, and every preparation was made for the march. But the chiefs had the game in their hands, and delayed the departure of the force from day to day, serving out only small quantities of supplies.

CHAPTER 9

The Retreat

The weather grew more and more severe. Snow lay thick on the ground. Fuel was so scarce that officers burned their furniture to cook their meals. At sunrise on the 3rd of January 1842 the thermometer was below zero of Fahrenheit; and even in an officer's quarters, with a blazing fire, rose to only eight degrees above freezing-point at noon. The Afghans judged that the time was come. They furnished a certain number of transport-animals, and informed Elphinstone that they would be ready on the 6th to escort him on his march from Kabul.

The force under his command is generally reckoned at four thousand five hundred fighting men, see list below.

★★★★★★

This is the estimate both of Eyre and of Lady Sale. Eyre's details are:

1 troop of Horse-artillery	90 men
H.M. 44th	600 ,,
5th Bengal Light Cavalry (2 sq.)	260 ,,
5th Shah's irregular horse	500 ,,
Other irregular cavalry	210 ,,
5th Bengal N.I	700 ,,
37th	600 ,,
54th ,,	650 ,,
Shah's troops	870 ,,
Sappers and Miners	20 ,,
	4500

I suspect these figures to be somewhat exaggerated. *Sepoy* battalions were always weak. The casualties since the 2nd of November had been considerable in action, and sickness had been very prevalent. Elphinstone stated his sick and wounded at from 600 to 700.

******

Of those barely seven hundred were Europeans, about two thousand were regular Bengal infantry, two hundred and fifty Bengal cavalry, and the remainder were irregular horse and Shah Shuja's troops of both arms. Added to these were from twelve to fifteen thousand followers, besides women and children, in themselves a serious, if not fatal, encumbrance. The order of march was as follows. The Forty-Fourth, Sappers and Miners, a squadron of irregular horse and three mountain-guns, composed the advanced guard, under Brigadier-General Anquetil. Then followed the main column, under Shelton, consisting of the European ladies with their escort, the invalids and sick, two horse-artillery guns, the Fifth Shah's Irregular Horse, the Thirty-Seventh Native Infantry with the treasure, and the Fifth Native Infantry with the baggage. The rear-guard, under Colonel Chambers, was made up of a battalion of the *Shah's* infantry, two squadrons of the Fifth Light Cavalry and four horse-artillery guns.

The conditions of the retreat were such that the only chance of extricating the force was to hustle it ruthlessly on, after the fashion of Soult and Massena in Portugal, without any real halt until it was clear of the Khurd Kabul pass, a distance of nineteen miles, and had reached Tezin, perhaps ten miles further on, where there would be no snow. To this end it was essential to use as many routes, to carry as little baggage and to make as early a start as possible. Shah Shuja had finally decided to stay at Kabul, so that one useless encumbrance at least was out of the way.

Now there are two passes which offer alternative routes to the Khurd Kabul; the Lataband, which runs on due east from Butkhak, and the Guldara, which turns eastward about six miles north of Kabul. Troops moving by the latter of these could have prevented the enemy from occupying the heights commanding the Khurd Kabul pass and thus have facilitated the passage of the main column through it, while the Lataband could have been used by some of the followers. No effort, however, was made to utilise either of these lateral passes. As to baggage, Shelton had been urgent that all that was not absolutely necessary should be left behind, both to free the column from impediments and to tempt the Afghans to remain behind and plunder.

Elphinstone spoke to the commanding officers, but none would consent to abandon their property, and he did not convert his recommendation into an order, as he should have done. It was not merely the possessions of the officers but their lives, and the lives of thousands of soldiers and followers, that were at stake. Lastly, instead of moving off at daylight, the troops were not roused until seven in the morning, preparatory to marching off at nine.

At that hour the advance guard left the cantonment through a cut that had been made in the eastern rampart, and traversed the few hundred yards to the Kabul river, where it came to a halt. Materials had been sent down for the construction of a temporary bridge, but this was not yet ready; and the column remained stationary on the bank in biting cold for more than an hour, though the men were bound to get their feet wet in the snow and could easily have forded the water.

Meanwhile, a message came from one of the chiefs that the march must be delayed, as his escort for the army was not yet ready; but matters had gone too far, and for once the behest was not obeyed. The Afghans also began swarming out of Behmaru, and, noticing that the Mission compound had been evacuated, forced their way into it and began the delightful work of pillage and destruction. The battalion stationed in the Mission compound was one of the Shah's, which had been told off as part of the rear-guard and need not therefore have left its post for hours; but it is impossible to divine what orders, if any, it may have received, or how far it may have thought fit to obey them.

Not until noon was the advanced guard clear of the bridge, leaving room for the main body to move in turn. Within a hundred and fifty yards of the ramparts the camels were in difficulties, descending and ascending the slippery banks to the bridge over the canal. There were two thousand of them, weak and half-starved, with a mob of followers swarming in utter confusion about them. The bridge over the river presently broke down, increasing the disorder, and the main column became a seething mass of men and animals which no efforts nor struggles could disentangle. The rear-guard, too weak to hold the cantonments, took up for its own safety a position outside them, and the Afghans burst in, exulting, to plunder and to burn. Every building was kindled, which at least gave light and some warmth as the day closed down; but meanwhile some of the Afghans lined the ramparts and opened fire upon the hapless rear-guard.

Two horse-artillery guns had to be spiked and abandoned, and an officer and fifty native troopers were killed outright before it could move off. Huge piles of the precious baggage of the officers were abandoned on the spot, and much of the rest was plundered before it had travelled far. Not until 2 a.m. of the 7th did the remnant of the rear-guard reach Elphinstone's bivouac, a bare five miles from Kabul. The whole length of those five miles was lined with camp-followers and *sepoys*, worn out with long starvation and overwork, who had sat down in the snow to die. The bivouac itself was a mere chaos of soldiers, followers, camels, bullocks, horses and baggage. There was no food for man or beast, no fuel, no shelter, nothing but the bitter invisible cloak of the frost above and around, and the snow underfoot. At daylight many, including one European officer, were found frozen to death; the Shah's infantry and sappers had vanished—who shall blame them?—and half of the *sepoys*, unfit for further work, and unable to hold their arms, had joined the mob of followers, who at the first streak of dawn struggled ahead, eager to return to India. No bugle was sounded; no order was given; but the advanced guard of *sepoys* moved off about 7.30, forcing their way through the mob, as best they could, to gain the front.

Armed Afghans, both horse and foot, hung about the flanks of the column, but for some time made no attack, and were supposed to be the escort furnished by the chiefs. Then suddenly they fell upon the rear-guard, now formed chiefly of the Forty-fourth, and clung to them closely despite of the fire of the mountain-guns. In order to avoid a block on the road these three pieces fetched a short compass apart without an escort, and were captured at once by a party of Afghans. Some of the Forty-Fourth charged and recaptured them, but the drivers had fled, and it was necessary to spike and abandon two of them. Anquetil sent forward a message to ask for reinforcements from the front, but these were unable to make their way through the press; and the Afghans, charging into the midst of what was left of the baggage-column, carried off much of the reserve of ammunition. And all the while men were dropping fast from wounds and weakness and cold, and animals as fast as the men. Two more horse-artillery guns were spiked and abandoned, the horses being powerless to drag them through the snow; and it seems that there was actually danger lest the column should be cut in twain through the centre and the whole of the rear should be destroyed.

On reaching Butkhak at 1 p.m., therefore, Elphinstone gave the order to halt, and sent back all the troops that could be spared, together with the two remaining guns, to extricate the rear-guard. The enemy had gathered by this time in great strength in the rear, and were threat-

THE RETREAT

ening an attack also on the right flank, which was parried by Shelton. Now, however, Mohamed Akbar Khan was found and approached by a political officer; and the chief declared that the force must halt at Butkhak until the following morning, and give hostages as a pledge not to advance beyond Tezin, until Sale, in compliance with an order sent to him after the signing of the treaty, should have evacuated Jalalabad. In return he undertook to supply food, forage and fuel for the troops. Elphinstone accepted the terms; the firing ceased; the rear shambled up in a disorderly mass; and the force settled down to another night of confusion, hunger, cold and misery. It had marched no greater distance than five miles, making ten miles in two days; and it should seem that only by thus restricting its progress could Mohamed Akbar Khan hope to bar its way at the further end of the pass.

Dawn of the 8th of January saw the fighting force reduced to a few hundred exhausted men. Many had perished outright; those that were alive were so much stiffened by cold that they could hardly move, and the troopers of the cavalry could not climb into their saddles without help. Very early the Afghans began to fire into the bivouac, but ran away directly when they saw the Forty-Fourth advance to attack; and the column began to thread the six miles of defile that bears the name of the Khurd Kabul. At the narrowest point fire was opened on the advanced guard, with which several English ladies were riding, and they hurried their horses forward in front of all. Thereupon, the crowd behind them, on coming under fire, likewise ran forward in panic, abandoning everything.

The rear-guard, consisting of the Thirty-Seventh Native Infantry and the Forty-Fourth, was heavily engaged from the first, but the *sepoys* were so utterly paralysed with the cold that they would make no effort to fight, and drifted slowly forward, allowing the Afghans to take from them their muskets and even their clothes. All the work, therefore, fell upon the Forty-fourth, who suffered heavily, but stood firm until their ammunition was nearly exhausted, and then forged their way forward to a position where Elphinstone was awaiting them with such few men as he could collect. One gun was abandoned in the pass, and the other was only brought into bivouac by the hands of the men, the horses being unable to drag it through the snow.

Many officers and men fell honourably on this day; and it was reckoned that five hundred soldiers and five times that number of followers perished in the Khurd Kabul pass. The night was worse than the two previous nights, for the snow fell from sunset until dawn, and the bivouac lay at an elevation of over seven thousand feet. The wounded lay or staggered about moaning, until the frost, cruelly merciful, put them slowly to their last sleep. Those that woke on the morning of the 9th marvelled to find that they were yet alive. With the first light most of the troops and all the camp-followers moved off without orders, but were presently stopped by Elphinstone's command. Mohamed Akbar had once again come forward, declaring that he would endeavour to furnish victuals, but meanwhile strongly recommending a halt until he could make arrangements for escorting the column with security. He also definitely engaged himself to take charge of the European ladies, their husbands and families, and of the wounded officers, and to bring them down under due protection a day's march in rear of the army.

Elphinstone and every soldier in the camp were by this time profoundly distrustful of all Afghan promises, but, yielding to the advice of the political officer, who urged that a mark of confidence in Mohamed Akbar would be for the good of the whole force, he gave his consent. The ladies were hurried off with such haste that only two of the wounded officers had time to join them; and the rest of the force remained halted in the snow.

The *Shah's* cavalry thereupon began to desert in whole bodies, and in company with large parties of Afghan horse remained hovering about the camp. The effective fighting-men were then paraded and were found to number from seven to eight hundred in all, two hundred and fifty of the Forty-Fourth, rather over four hundred *sepoys* and troopers of the Bengal Army, and about one hundred irregulars. Throughout the day the wretched mob of starving, shivering men waited in vain for the fuel and the food that never came; and night closed down upon them in misery and despair.

At daybreak the survivors once again struggled promiscuously to the front, the Europeans and a handful of troopers of the Fifth Native Cavalry being the only efficient men left. These appear to have maintained their discipline, and, being formed into an advanced guard, pushed their way through the staggering rabble ahead of them and marched on unopposed for a couple of miles until they reached a gorge, the heights of which upon one side were strongly occupied by the enemy. These at once opened fire, but the advanced guard forced their way through them, though with heavy loss, and halted five miles beyond to allow the rear to come up. But the helpless creatures behind them could offer no resistance, and the Afghans, after shooting them down for a time, rushed upon them with their knives and cut them down like sheep.

The last remnants of the *sepoys* were here destroyed, and the treasure and what remained of the baggage were taken. Terrified fugitives from the rear came up from time to time, and the followers still formed a considerable body; but the fighting force was reduced to about three hundred and fifty men, two-thirds of them Europeans of the Forty-Fourth and artillery, with a single twelve-pounder howitzer.

Once again Mohamed Akbar presented himself, professed that he had been unable to restrain the Ghilzais from attacking, and proposed that the fighting-men should lay down their arms and entrust themselves to be led under his protection to Jalalabad, leaving the followers to their fate. Elphinstone refused. The followers and the wounded were sent ahead, and the march was resumed down the steep descent of the Haft Kotal, Shelton with a small party of Europeans taking charge of the rear. At the foot of the hill was a narrow defile, and at the entrance to this the Afghans swooped down upon the helpless men at the head of the column and made an end of them.

The fighting soldiers then entered the gorge. For the whole three miles of its length the heights were lined with the enemy's sharpshooters, who threw their weight chiefly upon the rearguard. These were but a handful; their ammunition was scanty; the odds against them were terrific; but they had a leader in Shelton, who, with fiery energy and heedless courage, flew from group to group of his men, breathing his own gallantry into them, and heartening them against all odds, till at length, at 4 p.m., he brought his rear-guard proudly into the camping ground of the valley of Tezin. It was a great feat of arms, a great triumph of moral force, and much may be forgiven to Shelton for his supreme effort on this day.

There was no snow on the ground at Tezin, but the situation was not the less desperate. Twelve thousand soldiers and followers had been lost since the force had left Kabul, and fifteen European officers had fallen upon this day alone; but there still remained followers enough to imperil every movement. Elphinstone again sent an emissary to Mohamed Akbar in the faint hope of obtaining fair terms; but the only answer was a repetition of the proposal that the troops should surrender their arms, which was once more rejected. It was then resolved to make a night march to Jagdalak, a distance of twenty-two miles, in order, if possible, to traverse the dangerous pass of that name before the enemy could occupy it in strength. Similar energy at the outset might have saved a great part of the troops, and it is reasonable to suppose that this effort was due to Shelton.

At 7 p.m. the column moved off, spiking and abandoning its last gun, and for seven miles pursued its way unmolested, the main body of the Forty-Fourth leading the way, with a small party under Shelton bringing up the rear. Then a few shots were fired at the tail of the column, and the camp-followers, still from two to three thousand in number, rushed headlong to the front and became entangled with the advanced guard. Then a shot or two was fired at the front, and the senseless mob ran back again; and so they continued surging backward and forward, blocking up the road so that Shelton's party could hardly move on and the advanced guard could not march back to help it.

However, even so the foremost of the Forty-Fourth had traversed another six miles by dawn of the 11th, when they halted to allow the rear to close up. With the coming of the light the fighting became more serious, and from the halting-place to Jagdalak, a distance of nine or ten miles, the conflict was incessant, and the *jezails* of the Afghans very destructive. About 3 p.m. the advanced guard reached Jagdalak and took up a position behind some ruined walls on a height by the roadside. The officers extended themselves in line to make the front the more imposing; and the whole of the little body stood and cheered Shelton, as with indomitable courage and superhuman energy he thrust back the hordes of his pursuers, and foot by foot fought his way forward to his comrades.

Only a small remnant, perhaps two hundred men, were now left, and one and all were exhausted by hunger, fatigue and, even worse, by thirst. A stream ran near the foot of the hills, but to approach it was certain death. Even the chosen position was exposed to fire from three sides, the party being too weak to dislodge the enemy permanently from the heights above it. In despair the men swallowed the snow which lay on the ground, which of course aggravated rather than relieved their sufferings; and the only alleviation was the raw flesh of three bullocks, which had somehow been saved and were now slaughtered. This was served out, always under dropping fire from long range, and was ravenously swallowed.

Meanwhile, about 3.30 p.m., a message had come from Mohamed Akbar, requesting the presence of Captain Skinner, who, not abandoning hope, at once obeyed the summons, though manifestly at the risk of his life. Trusting that there would be a truce at least until his return, the weary troops threw themselves down to rest, but only to draw down on themselves volley after volley from the surrounding hills. Captain Bygrave, paymaster to the force, thereupon sallied out with fifteen men of the Forty-fourth and, charging up the slope, drove the Afghans into flight. For some time this little band held the ground that they had gained, until some of Mohamed Akbar's people caused the fire to cease, and the survivors of the column were left in comparative repose.

At 5 p.m. Skinner returned, requiring Elphinstone's immediate presence at a conference, and the delivery of Shelton and another officer as hostages for Sale's evacuation of Jalalabad. Elphinstone had no choice, as he conceived, but to comply; but the troops, though little disturbed during the night, saw the departure of Shelton with despair.

At 9 a.m. on the 12th the conference was held, and hours were spent in vain endeavours to conciliate the chiefs. Elphinstone begged to be sent back to his men, dwelling on the dishonour to himself of being denied the right of dying with them, but in vain. Mohamed Akbar was evidently bent on securing valuable hostages for the safety of Dost Mohamed and his fellow exiles. Meanwhile the Afghans crowned the heights as on the previous day, and kept up a steady, galling fire from dawn until dark. Very early Skinner, who had ridden out to meet an expected messenger from Mohamed Akbar, was brought in, mortally wounded by a skulking Ghilzai; and his fate confirmed the troops in their distrust of Afghan treachery. None the less, little handfuls of the Forty-Fourth, under various officers, sallied out time after time and drove the enemy off, though they were too weak in numbers to hold them permanently at a distance.

Night at length closed down; and at 7 p.m., despairing of Elphinstone's return, Anquetil, who was in command, decided to push on at all risks for Jalalabad. The sick and wounded were inevitably abandoned to their fate.

After traversing about a mile and a half, with little molestation, the column entered the Jagdalak pass, and the Ghilzais, now on the alert, at once closed in upon its rear. Still the troops struggled on through the three miles of the narrow defile until, near the summit, they came upon two strong barriers, or abatis, formed of branches of prickly oak, which blocked the whole breadth of the way. The advanced guard was checked while trying to force a way through these obstacles; the rear surged up to it; and the Afghans, after pouring volley after volley upon the mass, rushed in with their long knives to indiscriminate slaughter. Anquetil and eleven more officers fell in this struggle; but a single officer and a few men of the Forty-Fourth forced their way through both barriers and halted on the other side to allow stragglers to come up. The little body thus formed then gave three cheers and moved on in good order through the more open country beyond the pass.

Other officers, with or without a small following of men, came after them; and about a dozen, who were pretty well mounted, pushed ahead with such of the cavalry as was left, intent upon reaching Jalalabad. For seven miles more the remnant of the force pursued its way over pebbly paths, up and down steep ravines till, on descending the very steep declivity to the Surkhab River, they found the bridge held by the enemy. With great difficulty, for the stream was a roaring torrent, they forced a passage at a ford below the bridge, at the cost of an officer and several men of the Forty-Fourth killed, and pursued their way through the darkness to Gandamak. There were now remaining about twenty officers, of whom Major Griffiths was the senior, from fifty to seventy of the Forty-Fourth, about half of them armed, half-a-dozen artillerymen, four or five *sepoys* and three hundred followers. At Gandamak daylight, revealed the weakness of their numbers, and the enemy closed in upon them from all sides. They therefore left the road and took up a position on a height to defend themselves to the last.

Once again an attempt was made to parley with the enemy, and Griffiths actually descended the hill to confer with a chief. Several Afghans approached the British position in a friendly way, but, attempting to snatch their arms from the men, were driven off with the bayonet. The enemy then posted themselves on an adjacent hill and picked off officer after officer and man after man with unerring aim. Again and again parties rushed up to end the work with the knife and again and again they were driven back, until at last, with no ammunition left, and hardly a man unhurt, the little party was overwhelmed and exterminated. Captain Souter of the Forty-Fourth, who was wounded, and a few privates alone were spared, as also were Major Griffiths and his interpreter, who had been led off to a neighbouring fort.

Of the few officers who had ridden forward, six reached Fatehabad, the remainder having perished by the way. At Fatehabad the six waited, poor starving creatures, and ate bread which was brought to them by the peasants, thus giving time to the inhabitants to arm themselves and attack them. Two were killed on the spot, three more were overtaken and slain, and one only, Dr. Brydon, rode, desperately wounded, into Jalalabad. Of the two colours of the Forty-Fourth one was lost on the body of a quartermaster-sergeant, who had wound it round his waist and had afterwards fallen, and the other, likewise girt

Dr. Brydon,

about the waist of Captain Souter, was thus saved. Excepting Brydon and rather more than eighty officers and men, who had at different times passed into captivity of the Afghans, the force at Kabul had been annihilated.

There is no need to dwell upon the long chain of follies and imbecilities which brought about this final catastrophe; but it is necessary to emphasise the fact that the retreat, even though delayed, as it was delayed, until the snow was deep on the ground and the cold was intense, need not have been so disastrous, if it had been undertaken as a serious military operation. Apart from the feebleness of the supreme command, two causes mainly contributed to wreck it, namely, the vast number of followers and Elphinstone's unwillingness to go counter to the agreement with the Afghans. The chiefs pleaded that they were unable to restrain their people from attack, and this is very likely true, though they may not greatly have regretted their lack of authority in this matter. But a child could have seen from the first that the chiefs were merely playing with the British general, and he would have been fully justified in sweeping the treaty aside and acting as if the Afghans were open enemies. It is a grave reflection upon Cotton, as well as upon Elphinstone, and upon their staffs that no one seems to have taken the trouble to find out anything about the lateral defiles which supplement the main pass between Kabul and Jalalabad.

Much congestion might have been saved if these lateral passes had been utilised, and thereby rapid movement, rapid even to ruthlessness, which is of the essence of such retreats, might have been accomplished. The *sepoys*, paralysed as they were by cold, might no doubt have perished in great numbers, but the sense of quick progress towards India would have heartened them to make an effort. The followers, no doubt, would have dropped down by thousands, but even they would have been encouraged to extreme exertion. As to the Europeans, though the Forty-Fourth did not always shine in the actions around Kabul, yet from the moment of leaving Tezin, when the retreat assumed a really military character, the battalion recovered and behaved itself nobly.

A regiment which has been reduced through casualties to a tenth of its strength, and struggles on to the last as a formed body, as did the Forty-Fourth after forcing the barricades at Jagdalak, cannot be said to lack discipline or spirit. It seems to me beyond question that though his losses would doubtless have been very heavy, Elphinstone, with proper management and due exertion, could have brought certainly

Last Stand of the 44th

half, and perhaps more, of his fighting force into Jalalabad, and punished the Afghans severely in the process. The troops were not fairly treated by their commander. When, presumably at Shelton's instigation, he, so to speak, gave them their heads, on the 10th of January, they responded at once.

But it is idle to heap reproaches upon one whose misfortune it was to be a dying man and to resign his command too late. Fate spared poor Elphinstone nothing. Already worn out by disease, his pain and discomfort were increased by a wound received on the retreat; but even his bodily sufferings were as naught to his mental anguish over his sacrifice of his army. He lingered in captivity until the 23rd of April, when dysentery at last delivered him from his misery. It can only be said that he never attempted to blame any one but himself for the misfortunes that had come through his fault.

Shelton, after his release, was brought to a court-martial, less, to judge from the charges, because there was any idea of saddling the blame for the disaster upon him, than because it seemed advisable, according to the practice of the navy, to bring someone to trial for what was the equivalent of the loss of a small squadron of ships. Though hearsay evidence was, most irregularly, admitted against him, he was acquitted, and he remained in command of the Forty-Fourth. It was characteristic of his temper that, during his captivity, he was the one individual, male or female, who was not softened by the mental and bodily distress of Elphinstone; that he quarrelled with every one of his fellow prisoners except Colin Mackenzie, and that he gravely reproached even him for going before him in a general rush down the stairs when the house in which they were living was shaken about their ears by an earthquake, (Mackenzie, *Storms and Sunshine of a Soldier's Life*).

He met his end through a fall from his horse in a barrack-yard in Dublin in 1845; and it is said that thereupon the regiment turned out and gave three cheers. Yet the brightest figure in the retreat from Kabul is that of this little cantankerous man, with his right sleeve empty, ever at the point of greatest danger, watching every movement with untiring vigilance, securing every point of vantage, husbanding the strength of every man, inspiring every soul of the rear-guard with his own calm heroism, and foiling his fierce enemy with invincible energy and inexhaustible persistence. To so gallant a spirit surely much may be forgiven.

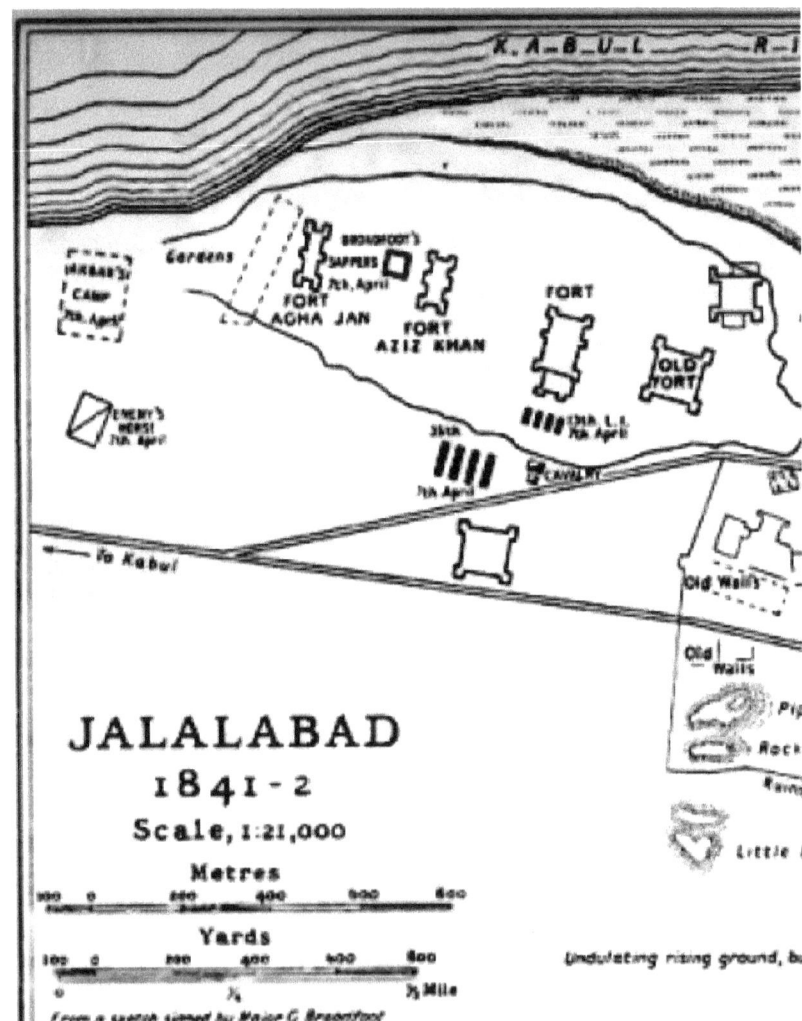

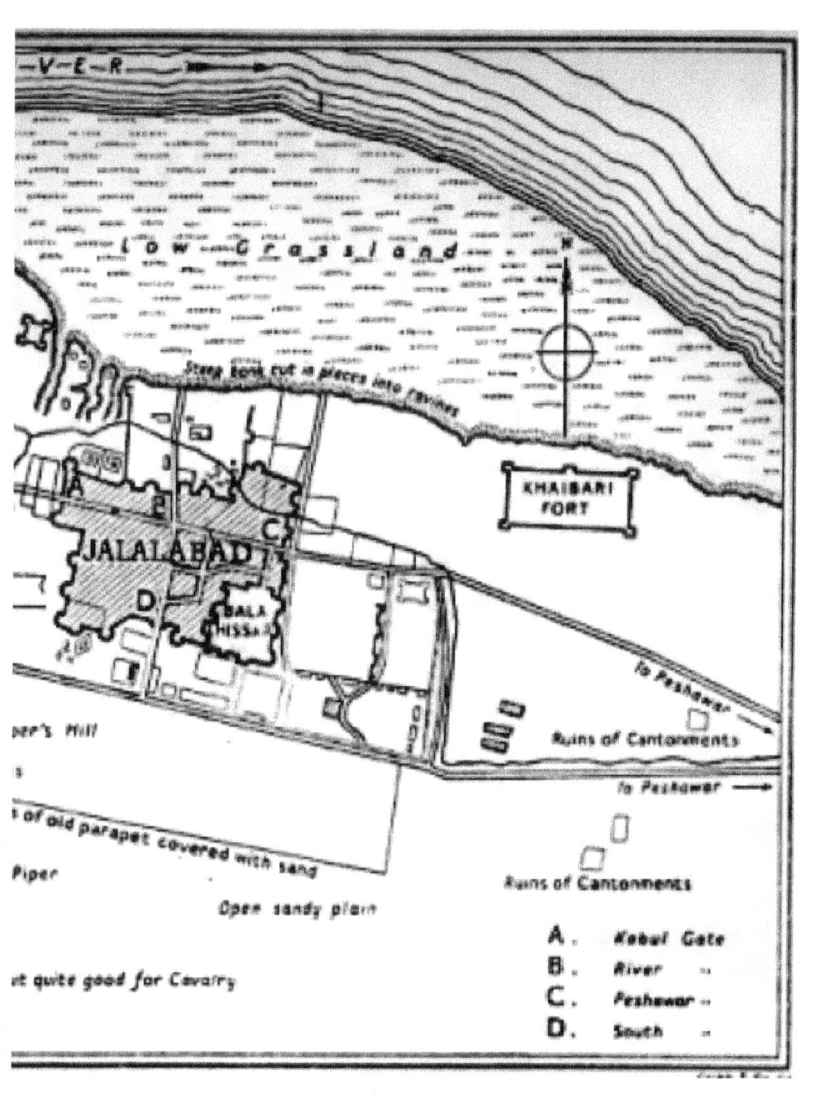

Chapter 10

Council of War at Jalalabad

It is now time to return to Sale, who, with his brigade, had reached Jalalabad on the 12th of November. The town lies on the south side of the Kabul River, and consisted then of an irregular quadrilateral enclosed within earthen walls, with thirty-two semi-circular bastions, and a citadel at the south-eastern angle, the entire perimeter being rather over two thousand yards. The defences were in a ruinous condition, and were closely surrounded on all sides by houses, gardens, enclosures, crumbling forts and old walls, which offered excellent cover to an enemy at close range.

The officers appointed by Sale to inspect the works upon his arrival reported unanimously that they were not defensible against a vigorous assault; but after some consultation it was decided to hold the town and repair the defences. Sale had with him only two days' supplies, but, as the whole population had fled, a few hours' search sufficed to discover provisions enough for several days, which relieved one great anxiety. More serious was the dearth of ammunition, the supply of which amounted to but one hundred and twenty rounds to each musket; but of this also enough was found in a mosque outside the town to furnish a small reserve.

At dawn of the 13th the Afghans swarmed round the south side and south-western angle and began firing at the sentries. The walls having no parapets, shelter was improvised for the sentinels by means of camel-saddles, and not until dusk did the enemy creep near enough to inflict a few casualties. Accordingly, at dawn of the 14th, Sale made a sortie with about seven hundred infantry, all the cavalry and two guns, under Colonel Monteith, who attacked the Afghans, about six thousand strong, on the hills opposite to the south-western angle and dispersed them with little difficulty, the enemy's casualties being about two hundred killed. This cleared the valley of the enemy for the present. More food and forage were secured in the outlying forts; the villagers daily brought in supplies; Macgregor succeeded in obtaining yet more victuals from the neighbouring chiefs; and altogether the danger of famine ceased to be pressing. It was a full week before the enemy showed again any aggressive spirit, and then they confined themselves to cutting off unwary grass-cutters and followers. This period was turned to full account in strengthening the defences.

On the 27th the enemy began to assemble again about a fort some two miles to west of Jalalabad; the villagers ceased to bring in supplies, and it was evident that the attack was about to be renewed. On the 1st of December the Afghans opened a heavy fire on the west side of the place, and Sale on that day made another sally and dispersed them with heavy loss, capturing also large quantities of food and fodder. Once again the villagers flocked into the town to sell flour, grain and vegetables, and the garrison was left practically unmolested for the next six weeks.

During this time authentic intelligence reached Sale on the 17th of December of the treaty made by Macnaghten, and on the 2nd of January of Macnaghten's murder; and on the 9th there arrived Elphinstone's order, sent in compliance with the treaty, for Sale to evacuate Jalalabad and retire to Peshawar. Sale decided that it would not be right to act upon such a document, and resolved to stand fast until further orders; a resolution which was not weakened by the arrival, on the 12th, of Dr. Brydon, giving by his mere presence the tidings of the destruction of the force at Kabul. But none the less Sale's nerve was evidently shaken, and unduly shaken. There was no difficulty about sending messages to and from Peshawar; and, though his ammunition was somewhat scanty, he could perfectly well have fought his way back to Peshawar, and that with no great difficulty. Yet, having shut himself up in Jalalabad, he had no idea except to call for all the forces of the Empire to come and extricate him.

By good fortune the agent on the north-western frontier, Mr. George Clerk, was a man of ability and energy, as also of great influence with the Sikhs. Having received information of the insurrection at Kabul, of the retreat of Sale to Jalalabad, and of the repeated attacks, successful and otherwise, upon the posts in the Khyber Pass, he urged the commander-in-chief, who was travelling through the north-west provinces, to hasten reinforcements to Peshawar. By the 27th of November four native regiments, with small detachments of cavalry and sappers, had crossed the Sutlej, the whole, numbering some forty-five

Jalalabad

hundred men, being under the command of Brigadier-General Wild. Simultaneously Clerk pressed the Sikhs also to strengthen their troops in Peshawar, and to give all possible help with men and guns to Captain Mackeson, the political agent at that place. Sir Jasper Nicolls, the commander in chief, authorised the advance of Wild to the relief of Sale, only on the condition that in Wild's judgement the operation could be executed with three of his four battalions, the other being employed in maintaining his communications with Peshawar.

By the end of the year Wild had reached his destination with the whole of his force, and there found a sea of troubles. The Sikh troops were mutinous, unwilling, and more than unwilling, to co-operate with the British, most of all in the Khyber Pass, and resolute to prevent the loan of any of their artillery to their allies. The British *sepoys* were infected by the example of their insubordination, and unfortunately found some pretext for it. The commander of the small detachment of native gunners had, without authority, paid them the additional allowance for service beyond the Indus.

The infantry claimed the same privilege, and on being refused displayed a disobedient spirit, which was not lessened even by the promise that they should receive their due later. Then Wild's camel-drivers refused to move beyond Peshawar. Then the Sikh troops, on receiving the order to advance to Jamrud, mutinously declined to stir. All these causes, added to shortage of ammunition, dearth of cavalry and lack of guns, led to delay; and the *sepoys*, who at first had been eager to march to the help of Sale, exchanged their former ardour for coolness, and began to share the terrors of the Sikhs and their taste for declining to obey all unwelcome orders, (*I.O.S.C.*, vol. 2 of 1842, Mackeson to Clerk, Jan. 8, 12, 1842).

However, Macgregor at Jalalabad pressed Wild to advance immediately to the relief of Sale; and most unfortunately the political agents, Mackeson and Henry Lawrence, joined their voices to Macgregor's. The danger in Afghanistan being by this time better apprehended in India, though the full truth was not yet known, a second brigade, under General McCaskill, had been ordered to march on Peshawar, and had crossed the Sutlej on the 4th of January. Wild, being satisfied that Sale was in no immediate danger, was rightly anxious to await this reinforcement before moving, but he allowed himself to be overruled by Mackeson and Lawrence. He had some excuse, for the post of Ali Masjid, which Mackeson's brother had maintained with great gallantry and resolution at the head of a weak garrison of Afghans, could not hold out much longer, and Mackeson begged to lead a column of two battalions of *sepoys* to its relief. Exaggerating the importance of Ali Masjid, and being, not without reason, apprehensive of the effect of its fall upon Sale, Wild consented; and it was arranged that Mackeson should advance with two battalions, followed by the Sikhs, if they would consent to do so, or if not, by the two remaining battalions.

Thanks to a bribe of a *lakh* and a half of *rupees*, the Sikhs had been persuaded to lend a couple of guns and a certain number of troops; but they declined to move in support of Mackeson, who accordingly advanced without them. Marching on the night of the 15th, Mackeson with great skill and daring outwitted the Afghans, and reached Ali Masjid unmolested with his troops. But a convoy of three hundred bullocks, laden with provisions to revictual the post, went astray, and only sixty of the animals reached their destination. This may have been due to carelessness, but is more probably to be ascribed to sheer cowardice on the part of the drivers, and to the sympathy which was extended to it by their escort of *sepoys*. Mackeson was therefore fain to put his force upon half-rations, and await the arrival of Wild to enable him to proceed to Jalalabad.

Wild, however, had his own difficulties. The Sikhs in his camp mutinied on the night of the 16th, and some time was lost before further preparations could be made. Even then men and officers worked reluctantly, and the camel-drivers deserted by scores, insomuch that, though Wild started on the night of the 18th, one quarter of the supplies which he was to take with him were still unloaded at daylight of the 19th, and the rear-guard did not move until 10 a.m. At the mouth of the pass the Afridis, seemingly in no great force, opened fire. The *sepoys* wasted much ammunition in shooting at the rocks; and presently the whole turned round and without orders marched back to Peshawar, leaving one gun abandoned on the ground. They were stopped, not without difficulty, both men and officers declaring it to be impossible to escort a convoy to Ali Masjid.

Wild summoned the officers and harangued them; and early in the morning of the 20th the *sepoys* again moved out towards the pass, only to give way once more with shameful and scandalous readiness. Wild himself was wounded and disabled early in the action; but the casualties of the entire force did not amount to forty; and the attempt failed chiefly because neither officers nor men would put their hearts into their work. Mackeson, after lingering at Ali Masjid until the 25th, was obliged to fight his way back to Peshawar unaided, and succeeded only at the cost of heavy loss. (*I.O.S.C.*, vol. 3 of 1842, Henry Lawrence to Clerk, Jan. 19; to Mackeson, Jan. 22; vol. 4 of 1842, Mackeson to Indian Government, Jan. 27; Memo of Henry Lawrence, Feb. 1, 1842).

The whole of these proceedings were foolish and unnecessary, and the Supreme Government rightly censured Mackeson and Lawrence for urging operations upon Wild, the inception and execution of which should have been left wholly to the military commander. Fortunately, this was the last interference of the political element with purely military matters, though it narrowly failed of being the most disastrous. The design of dividing Wild's force had been communicated to Sale at Jalalabad; where Broadfoot, divining at once that it must mean failure, had warned Sale, on the 13th, when the destruction of the Kabul force became known, that, unless he meant to defend Jalalabad to the last extremity, he must retreat to Peshawar at once.

Sale decided to stand fast, and therewith, despite of Broadfoot's urgent remonstrances, surrendered, or abandoned, the bulk of his transport-animals to the enemy. (This transaction is exceedingly obscure; but it is twice mentioned by Broadfoot and I have no doubt that it took place, probably because Sale shrank from the risk—very slight—of losses in obtaining forage for the beasts). When, however, the news of Wild's defeat came in, Sale held a council of war, the transactions of which are the most astonishing, and perhaps the most disgraceful, recorded in the annals of the army.

At the instance, apparently, of Macgregor the political agent, the entire body of the council, with the exception of Captain Backhouse of the artillery and Broadfoot, the acting engineer, declared for treating with the Afghan chiefs for the evacuation of Jalalabad, and for the escort of the garrison with safety and honour to Peshawar by Afghan troops. The chief argument used by Macgregor was that he knew the ways of men in high places, and that he was convinced that the Supreme Government, after Wild's failure, would abandon the garrison to its fate; and this seems to have been sufficient to satisfy every officer present except Broadfoot, who, single-handed, met the proposal with hot and righteous indignation. Every effort was made to cry him down, and the discussion seems to have lasted for several days, during which Broadfoot found a ready ally in Havelock and gradually persuaded others to his opinion.

Finally, all were converted except Sale and Macgregor, who, being left in a minority, were finally overruled. Yet Sale was known as

"Fighting Bob"; Macgregor was a man who would go on a mission to any Afghan chief unattended, carrying his life in his hand, and quite indifferent whether he had his throat cut or not; and Dennie, though old and eccentric, had without hesitation attacked the hordes of Dost Mohamed with a single battalion. The incident points the difference between physical and moral courage; but even more does it signalise the rottenness of the Indian administration and the relaxation of the moral fibre of all subject to its rule under the sovereignty of Auckland.

Meanwhile, the Supreme Government at Calcutta was still ignorant of what had happened at Kabul; but it was alive to the shortcomings of Elphinstone, and appointed General Pollock, an artillery officer of the Bengal Army who had distinguished himself in Burma, to supersede him, with full political as well as military control. On the 30th of January the news of Brydon's arrival at Jalalabad gave Auckland indisputable knowledge of the disaster at Kabul, and he hastened to assure to Pollock a force of ten thousand men at Peshawar, while Nicolls began collecting further regiments to take the place of those withdrawn from Ferozepore to the Afghan frontier. Frightened out of his senses, for the Madras Army was fully occupied with operations in China, Auckland summoned the Fiftieth Foot from Burma, and half of the Twenty-Second from Bombay to Karachi, gave orders for raising an additional company for every native infantry regiment in all three Presidencies, and begged for three more of the Queen's regiments from England. What he intended to do with all of these troops, when he got them, he was not very clear.

Sir Jasper Nicolls, who kept his head with great calmness throughout this critical time, summed up the situation coolly and clearly. There would, he said, be no difficulty in forcing a way to Kabul, and there was much to be said for doing so in order to make a display of power. But thirty-three thousand men had proved too few to overawe the tribes of Afghanistan, so that the country could not be held permanently, to say nothing of the difficulties of the climate and the long line of communication; and it was questionable whether an advance would have any great effect, if followed by a retirement, with what dignity soever, immediately afterwards.

Moreover, it was certain that the news of the reverse at Kabul would spread like wildfire from the Punjab to Burma, and therefore a force must be held in readiness to crush down a rising in any quarter. Nicolls, therefore, was not disposed for any renewal of the contest. Auckland, for his part, was hopelessly cowed and irresolute; and, as is the way of weak men, he sought to throw upon others the burden of decision.

In the first instance, therefore, Auckland ordered that Pollock, if it suited him, might give up Jalalabad after withdrawing Sale's brigade and concentrate again at Peshawar; but later, while more or less adhering to the policy of making no great effort against Kabul, he wished that this intention should be kept secret, obviously with the idea of changing it if it should be severely criticised. Mr. Clerk, further, was instructed that operations in advance of the Khyber should not be undertaken unless some unexpected turn in affairs should demand or encourage a forward movement, and that the Sikhs were to be informed accordingly, so that they might take their own measures for securing their western frontier.

But he was empowered at his discretion to delay the withdrawal of the British troops from Peshawar. Practically, the governor-general threw upon Clerk the responsibility of determining what should be done with Pollock's army. As regards Nott, Auckland's orders were equally vague. First, Nott was, in the event of the loss of Kabul, to instruct all detachments to fall back on their nearest supports and to take the garrison of Ghazni under his command, with a strong hint that he had better direct it to retreat.

Next Nott was to hold on to Kandahar in concentrated strength until further orders; and finally, after the fate of Elphinstone had been ascertained, Nott was bidden to use his own judgement to ensure the safety of his force and the honour of the British arms; and, if he decided to fall back on Quetta, he was to bring with him the garrisons of Kalat-i-Ghilzai and Ghazni. Evidently Auckland longed to awake one morning and find that Afghanistan had been evacuated, while carefully guarding himself against the possibility of being held answerable for the evacuation. (*I.O.S.C.,* vol. 2 of 1842, Gov.-gen. in Council to Nicolls, Jan. 28; vol. 3 of 1842, the same to Nicolls, Feb. 19; Indian government to Clerk and Nicolls, Feb. 10; vol. 4 of 1842, Indian government to Pollock, Feb. 24, 1842; Durand).

To Nott, for his part, the news of the rising at Kabul came as no surprise, and the reaction of the occurrences there soon made itself felt. On the morning of the 27th of December 1841, the senior regiment of Jan Baz horse mutinied, murdered its commander, Golding, and dispersed. The mutineers were pursued by other horse of Nott's garrison and some thirty or forty of them were cut down; but another body of Jan Baz horse mutinied on the same day; and the situation

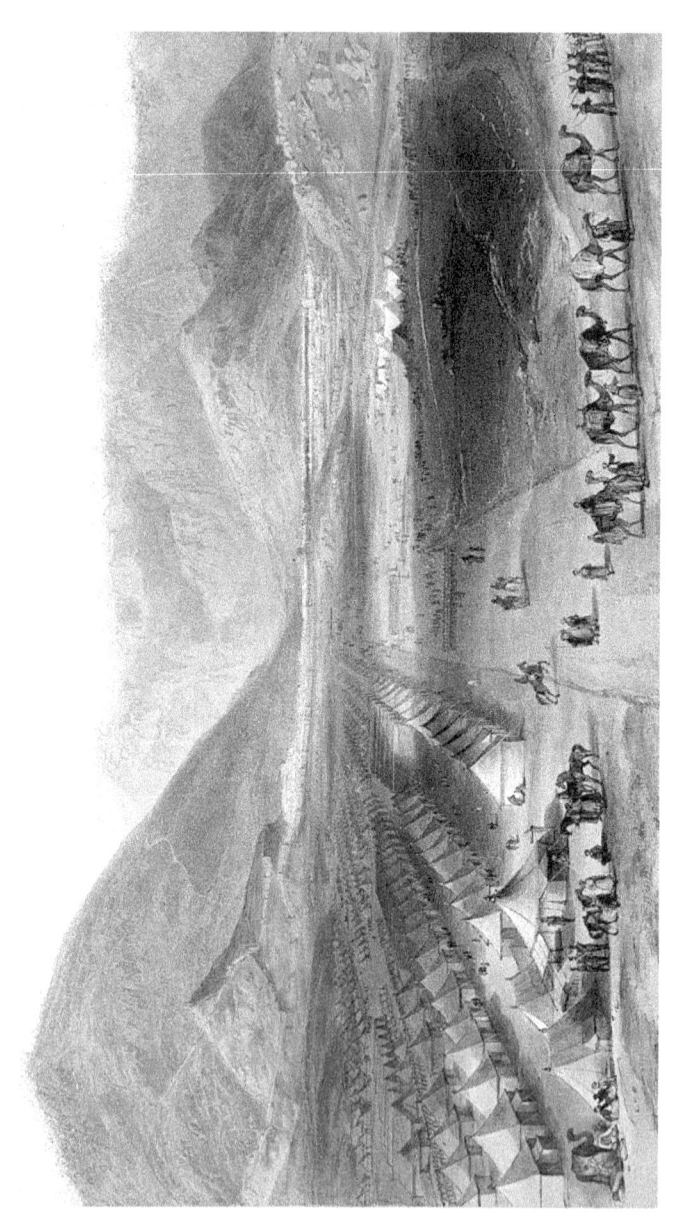

Pollock and his army at Kabul

was not pleasant. In the first week of January the insurrection in the Kandahar province was general, and the Durani chiefs, who had so far remained faithful, were expected daily to fall away from the British. Saftar Jang, a son of Shah Shuja, joined the insurgents, and Mohamed Akhtar, being reinforced from Kabul, advanced more and more closely upon Kandahar.

Rawlinson recommended negotiation with the leading chiefs for peaceful withdrawal of Nott's troops under the terms of a treaty. Nott flatly refused to consent to anything of the kind. Rawlinson then pressed him to sally out against the Afghans; but Nott, unwilling to venture his transport-camels at a distance during the severe weather, refused, to Rawlinson's great indignation, to fight except under the walls of Kandahar. He was still very imperfectly informed as to the progress of events at Kabul, and only learned of Macnaghten's death on the 30th of January, more than five weeks after the event. The general's comment was:

> Poor fellow, ... his system was always wrong. ... I fear that his three years' doings cannot be retrieved, and that our blood must flow for it.—*I.O.S.C.*, vol. 3 of 1842, Rawlinson to Hammersley, Jan. 8; vol. 4 of 1842, Rawlinson to Outram, Jan. 22, 1842; Stocqueler, *Life of Sir William Nott*, i.

In February Nott received from the Supreme Government the resolution of the 6th of January which placed both Pollock and himself in authority over all political agents; and Rawlinson was thenceforward subject to his orders. It was high time, for even so good an officer as Rawlinson had been writing to his brother agents in terms of intolerable disrespect because Nott had declined to obey his orders. As to his general policy, Nott was perfectly clear. It was, in his judgement, out of the question to think of withdrawing into India until September, since any movement into Sind before the end of the hot season would mean the destruction both of his army and of his transport.

It was, of course, possible that the junction of the victorious Afghans from Kabul with the insurgents about Kandahar might compel him to fall back to Quetta; and the Supreme Government, anticipating this contingency, had given orders for the advance of troops from Sind to the eastern end of the Khojak pass, to facilitate such a movement. But though hampered by want of cavalry, which disinclined him to take the offensive, so short of money that the pay of his men was three months in arrear, and deficient both in ammunition and medical stores, Nott had little doubt of his ability to hold Kandahar for as long as the Indian government might desire. He had a concentrated force of seventy-five hundred men of all descriptions, and he had laid up five months' reserve store of provisions. Finally, he was his own master, and could do as he pleased without reference to political agents.

Meanwhile, his immobility so far encouraged the insurgents that they drew very close to Kandahar, intercepting supplies from the neighbouring villages and plundering such chiefs as remained well disposed to the British. On the 7th of March, therefore, Nott sallied out with four thousand men, moving southwestward upon the enemy's camp at Panjwai, which was reached on the 8th and found to be deserted. Small parties of the enemy's horse alone were seen upon these two days, but on the 9th the main body, some twelve thousand strong, was encountered at Lakani, and Nott hoped for a general engagement. The Afghans, however, never permitted him to approach nearer than within cannon-shot, and drew off, leaving the British to bivouac for the night.

On the 10th Nott retired to Panjwai, once again meeting nothing but small bodies of cavalry; and, pursuing his way back to Kandahar on the 11th, learned that during his absence the enemy had on the 10th attacked Kandahar and had been repulsed.

Saftar Jang and Akhtar Khan had, in fact, executed a very skilful manoeuvre. Having drawn away Nott to Lakani they had doubled back to Kandahar on the night of the 9th, leaving sharp-shooters to fire a few shots into Nott's camp and keep it alarmed during the hours of darkness; and by the morning of the 10th they were seen in force round the city. The garrison was on the alert; all gates were shut, and all precautions were taken. After sunset a villager presented himself at the Herat gate with a donkey-load of faggots and asked for admission, which being refused, he threw down his faggots against the gate and went away.

At 8 p.m. a party of the enemy stole up to the gate, poured oil over the faggots and set fire to them. In this way the gate was speedily demolished, and the enemy then attacked with resolution. Happily the Commissary, who was on the spot, seeing the danger hastened to barricade the gateway with flour-bags. The Afghans surmounted this barrier, but were driven back, and after unsuccessful assaults, repeated at intervals for five hours, they finally abandoned the attempt, having suffered heavy loss.

The Afghan design had been to fire all of the gates and attack them simultaneously, but an officer of the Fortieth, observing faggots outside the citadel gate, when he closed it at sunset, removed them and so averted the danger. With a garrison of only twenty-five hundred men to a large perimeter, a simultaneous assault upon two of the gates would probably have caused the fall of Kandahar. Critics, wise after the event, blamed Nott for taking so large a force into the field and leaving so weak a garrison in the city; but if he had sallied out with a smaller force and suffered a reverse in the field, they would equally have censured him for leaving too many men behind the walls of the fortress. A general in Nott's position must take his choice of risks, and of two hazards Nott probably chose the less, (Neill, *Recollections of Four Years' Service in the East*; Stocqueler, i.).

The effect of his operations was not decisive, for, though the Afghan foot dispersed to their homes, their horse remained out in strength, cutting off all communications and intercepting all supplies. Dearth of forage, long troublesome, became so serious that on the 24th of March Nott was fain to send out Colonel Wymer with a brigade of infantry to secure the camels fresh grazing-ground, which, after a brisk little action with the Durani horse on the 25th, was, without further difficulty, accomplished. But apart from Kandahar itself, Nott was responsible also for the detachments at Kalat-i-Ghilzai and at Ghazni, as to the fate of which latter disquieting rumours were afloat. Ghazni, which was garrisoned by the Twenty-Seventh Native Infantry under Colonel Palmer, had in fact been invested on the 20th of November, and closely beleaguered since the 7th of December.

The inhabitants, undermining the walls, admitted their countrymen into the city, and the garrison was obliged to retire to the citadel. Short of fuel, though the thermometer stood below zero, short of provisions and constantly harassed by the Afghan sharp-shooters, Palmer held out until the 6th of March, when, being in difficulties even for water, he agreed to surrender on condition that the garrison should march out with colours, arms, ammunition and baggage, and be escorted to Peshawar. He marched out, accordingly, but his men were treacherously attacked on the following day, and, after defending themselves for nearly a fortnight with heavy loss, the survivors were swept into captivity. In Kalat-i-Ghilzai, on the other hand, the little garrison, though suffering extremity of hardship from cold and exposure, held its own gallantly without a thought of surrender.

Meanwhile, Brigadier-General England, who had succeeded Brooks in command of the Sind field-force, had reached Dadhar at the end of February, and received orders to assemble a strong force at Quetta in March, order to escort reinforcements, treasure and ammunition for the help of Nott through the Khojak pass. He himself marched from Dadhar on the 7th of March with such troops as were with him, (4 horse-artillery guns; 5 companies of the 41st Foot; 6 companies of N.I.; 100 Poonah Horse), and it was reckoned that by the end of the month he would have under his hand a battery of horse-artillery, two batteries of field-artillery, the Forty-First Foot, four battalions of *sepoys* and some four hundred native cavalry.

Arriving at Quetta on the 16th, England, being greatly in want of transport-animals, decided to advance into the valley of Pishin in the hope of obtaining more camels there, a measure which seems to have been approved, if not suggested, by the political agent Hammersley. On the 26th, accordingly, he moved out from Quetta, and early on the morning of the 28th he arrived at the entrance of a defile leading to the village of Haikalzai, where he came upon the enemy posted behind *sangars* and prepared to dispute his advance. England, therefore, ordered his guns to open fire, and attacked with the four light companies of his force, the remainder of the Forty-First following in support.

The Afghans seem to have allowed the light companies to approach within close range, when they poured in so destructive a fire that the assailants gave way, and fell back on the support, hotly pursued by the Afghan cavalry. The support formed square and repulsed the Afghan horse, and the light companies quickly rallied, ready for a fresh attempt. But England had suffered nearly one hundred casualties, seven-tenths of them among the Forty-First, and nothing would induce him to try another attack. He retired for the night three miles to north-east, and on the 29th retreated to Quetta, where he proceeded to throw up fortifications round the cantonments as though the whole country were upon him.

This was a foolish and most unnecessary little reverse. The object of England's advance was to escort treasure and ammunition to Nott at Kandahar, and to accomplish this purpose he had much better have waited at Quetta until the whole of his troops had joined him, so as to make success certain. There was no advantage whatever to be gained in moving nearer to the Khojak pass with a weak detachment, for he knew that Nott, anxious to keep his force together, would send no troops to meet him. In fact, he achieved nothing beyond throwing away lives to no purpose and shattering his own unsteady nerves. Nott was furious, and wrote him a stinging letter, telling him that his advance to Haikalzai and subsequent retreat to Quetta had done more injury to the Kandahar force than twenty thousand Afghans in the field; that the new fortifications of Quetta, requiring a garrison of fifteen hundred men, were absolutely useless, since the citadel, held by five hundred men, was ample for all purposes of defence; and, finally, that he would send out a brigade from Kandahar on the 25th of April, and expected England to meet him at Chaman, by the northern foot of the Khojak pass, without fail on the 1st of May. Nott might have added, if he had known it, that this reverse gave serious encouragement to the Amirs of Sind to turn against the British; but this unhappy expedition seemed to be doomed to mishandling by incompetent men, both civil and military, to the very end, (Stocqueler's *Life of Sir William Nott*, ii.; Kaye, ii.; *Parliamentary Papers*, Military Operations in Afghanistan, 1843).

Meanwhile, on the 5th of February, Pollock had arrived at Peshawar, where he found Wild's troops sunk in the lowest depths of demoralisation after their repulse. A thousand of them were in hospital, and the number of the invalids rose in a few days to eighteen hundred, sick hearts reacting upon sick bodies. The officers were little better than the men, and the spirit of the whole force was in the highest degree discreditable. In the circumstances it was impossible for Pollock to think yet of an advance through the Khyber Pass, for, even after the arrival of McCaskill's brigade, (9th Foot; 26th N.I.), which marched into Peshawar a day or two after him, he could count upon no more effective men than Wild had commanded a month before. The first and urgent matter was to raise the moral tone of the *sepoys*, which grew daily worse. Depression was turning to mutiny.

The four native battalions, which had been with Wild, positively refused to advance, and McCaskill's brigade had not been in camp forty-eight hours before emissaries from Wild's force were among them spreading disaffection. All this Pollock set himself at once to cure; and though Sale at Jalalabad was still shrieking for relief, Pollock, while lamenting his own inevitable inactivity, had the moral courage to stand fast until he had tempered the tool which he was presently to handle. Well he knew that any fresh military reverse might bring down Sikhs and Sindians and mountain tribes upon the whole line of the British communications.

Sale, for his part, remained strangely apathetic and unenterprising, though not really straitened, except in the matter of forage, having apparently no plans but to strengthen his fortifications and wait for the

Afghans to come and besiege him. On the 19th of February a great portion of the said fortifications was destroyed by an earthquake; but the enemy took no advantage of this piece of good fortune; and within five days the parapet had been rebuilt by strenuous labour, and the place was once again comparatively secure. On the 25th Mohamed Akbar camped within three miles of Jalalabad to westward, and by the 2nd of March he had extended his force round the eastern side also, more or less completing the investment of the place, and cutting off the supplies of food hitherto brought in by the villagers.

The Afghans also gave serious trouble to Sale's foragers, chiefly through Sale's own fault. He would never send out parties sufficiently strong to protect them; and, when the grass-cutters came running in before the threat of some little body of the enemy, Sale immediately ordered the covering troops to retire also, thus deliberately training his men daily to run away from a twentieth part of their own numbers. Happily, the Afghans were generally content with one demonstration of this kind every morning and then returned to their camp, whereupon the grass-cutters went out again without any protection at all and brought in a good supply. Had Sale shown any enterprise, he need never have been seriously troubled at all, but he seems to have been a man of stupidity so abnormal that he could neither think himself nor entertain the thoughts of others, (Broadfoot's *Career of George Broadfoot*; Seaton, *From Cadet to Colonel,* i.).

Within a month after the earthquake the fortifications were stronger than ever, but the enemy, growing bolder with Sale's timidity, on the 24th of March pressed the foragers so hard as to bring on a smart skirmish, in which Broadfoot was wounded. To diminish the more effectively Sale's supplies of forage, Akbar caused large flocks of sheep to be driven over the more distant foraging ground, so that the grass within range of Sale's guns might be exhausted by repeated cutting. Growing more confident through immunity the Afghans actually, on the 31st of March, pushed one flock within eight hundred yards of the walls, but Sale would not sanction any attempt to capture it; and it was only after hours of pestering that his officers at last persuaded him to sanction a sortie on the 1st of April.

The result was that nearly five hundred sheep were brought in at a cost of no more than one man killed and eight slightly wounded, a great encouragement to the half-starved garrison, and a neat little stroke at the enemy. Five days later news was brought in that Pollock had been repulsed in an attempt to force the Khyber Pass, and Akbar fired a royal salute in honour of the victory.

The story was, as shall be seen, a false one, but it gave Sale's officers a pretext for urging immediate, action upon him, so that by a march upon Dakka he might take the Khyberris in rear, while Pollock attacked them in front.

Accordingly, on the 7th April 1842, three columns of infantry, under Dennie, Monteith and Havelock, assembled at the west gate, and the artillery and cavalry at the south gate, with orders to march direct upon Akbar's camp, which extended from the Kabul River to the Kabul road, on the west of the city, to burn it and to capture his guns. Havelock, on the right, was to move northwestward to clear the ground by the river, Dennie in the centre, and Monteith on the left to advance due west direct upon the camp. Within half-a-mile of the west gate was a ruinous old fort which the enemy had patched up and occupied as an outpost with two or three hundred men. These fired upon Dennie's column as it advanced; and Sale at once halted the column, sent for his guns and ordered an immediate assault. There was no occasion for anything of the kind.

The fort was no impediment to the forward movement; and, if Akbar's main body were dispersed, its garrison was trapped and could be dealt with at leisure. But "Fighting Bob" had gained his name by persistently butting his head at stone walls, and was not to be turned from pursuing his one and only tactical idea. The assault was a complete failure. Dennie was killed, several men fell killed and wounded with him; the advance of the left column was delayed; and the whole mass of the Afghan horse swept down upon Havelock. Coolly forming square Havelock repulsed them with heavy loss, and Sale, presently awaking to his folly, abandoned the assault upon the fort and resumed the original plan of the advance.

The Afghans opened fire from their cannon with some small effect, but, not waiting for the infantry to close, fled away. Some, including the garrison of the fort, flung themselves into the river, which, being swollen and rapid, swallowed up many, and the rest followed the bank of the stream up the valley. Akbar's guns, some of them taken from Elphinstone, ammunition, plunder and provisions, all fell into Sale's hands, and by nightfall there was not an Afghan within eight miles of Jalalabad. The casualties did not exceed fourteen of all ranks killed and sixty-six wounded, and, but for Sale's criminal folly, should not have amounted to one-half of the number. The whole action is plain proof that if Sale had really deserved his name of a fighting soldier he need never have been beleaguered in Jalalabad at all.

Meanwhile, Pollock had on the 29th of March received the last reinforcements for which he was waiting, namely, a battery of Bengal horse-artillery and the Third Light Dragoons, and prepared to enter the Khyber Pass. On the 31st he moved to Jamrud, intending to advance on the next day; but the Sikh troops, which after much persuasion had been suffered by the authorities at Lahore to support him, were late in arriving. Heavy rain caused further delay; and the desertion of the camel-drivers up to the very last moment was a further serious embarrassment.

Pollock had appealed to his officers to reduce their baggage and followers to the very lowest that was possible, and had set the example by taking no more baggage-animals for himself than one camel and two mules; but sheer lack of cattle and drivers ensured that his force should not be over-encumbered. Not until the April. 5th of April was he able to begin his advance, and then always in a dispiriting atmosphere. The Sikhs were still terrified at the prospect of entering the defile; Avitabile averred that Pollock was marching to certain destruction; the *sepoys* of Wild's brigade were still deserting. There was much to shake the nerve of a commander unless he felt full confidence in himself, (Kaye, ii.).

Fortunately, Pollock knew his business, and was not a man to take fright at shadows. His dispositions were as follows. A column made up of four companies of the Ninth and eight companies of *sepoys*, under Colonel Taylor of the Ninth, were to clear the heights on the right of the pass; a second column similarly composed, with the addition of four hundred Afghan sharp-shooters, under Colonel Moseley, were to clear those on the left. When this should have been accomplished, four companies of the Ninth and eight of *sepoys*, drawn from both columns, were to descend the hills, ready to enter the pass with fourteen more companies of *sepoys* and ten guns, which were drawn up opposite the entrance. The rear-guard, under Brigadier-general McCaskill, was composed of seven squadrons of cavalry, three companies of infantry and five guns.

★★★★★★

The actual distribution of the troops was this:
Right flanking column: advance—2 cos. 9th Foot, 4 cos. 26th N.I.; rear—1½ cos. 9th, 4½ cos. 64th N.I.

Left flanking column: 4 cos. 9th Foot, 4 cos. each of 26th and 64th N.I., 400 *Jezailchees*.

Main column: 7 cos. 30th N.I., 7 cos. 53rd N.I., 10 guns.
Rear: 6 cos. 60th N.I., 6 cos. 33rd N.I.
Rear-guard: 2 guns H.-A., 3 guns F.-A., 2 squadrons H.M. 3rd L.D., 10th Bengal L.C., 2 troops of Irreg. Horse, 1 co. H.M. 9th Foot, 1 co. 6th N.I., 1 co. 60th N.I.

******

The troops moved off at 3 a.m. without call of bugle or beat of drum. The heights were covered with the enemy on both sides, waiting for the British in a body to enter the pass, across the mouth of which they had thrown up a barricade of huge stones, heavy branches and mud. To their surprise, they found the British ascending the hills to attack them, and they seem to have offered but a poor resistance, the steepness of the ground and the exhaustion of surmounting it being the chief difficulties that beset the assailants. Having cleared both flanks, the main column made its way through the barricade and pursued its march with little opposition to Ali Masjid.

No baggage was lost, and the rear-guard, which was not engaged at all, got into camp by 2 p.m. The casualties did not exceed fourteen killed and one hundred and twenty-one wounded and missing, and were confined almost entirely to the flanking-parties, the Ninth Foot alone bearing nearly one-third of the April, total losses. The enemy's dead and wounded were reckoned at the time to have amounted to eight or nine hundred, an estimate which should probably be divided by one-half.

Thus the dreaded pass was forced with little difficulty, and the Sikhs, who had hung back until success was assured, advanced by a parallel defile to Ali Masjid, and undertook to keep open Pollock's communications. Pollock meanwhile pursued his way on the 6th unmolested, despite of the unwieldy convoy with which he was encumbered for his own needs and those of Sale. The march appears to have been uneventful, and on the 16th of April Pollock's force reached Jalalabad, where he found Sale's troops better off, except in the matter of wine and beer, than his own. Thus the safety of the garrison was assured; but now the question arose what was to be done next; and Pollock wrote to the Supreme Government enumerating the difficulties that beset him. The contracts for his hired carriage-cattle extended only to their march to Jalalabad, upon arrival at which place the Commissary was pledged to return them to Peshawar. The animals remaining were too few to enable him to move freely about the country and live upon such supplies and forage as he could capture.

Moreover, for several marches between Jalalabad and Kabul no forage was obtainable. The establishment of depots along the line would eat up the entire force in garrisons. Even if transport-animals were more abundant, the conveyance of forage for them would so swell their numbers that the protection of the convoys would be impossible. The Afghans might, of course, be paid to lay up stores of forage for the army, but, if they played false, they could destroy it. He therefore judged an advance upon Kabul to be for the present unwarrantably hazardous. If the advance could have been made by Kandahar, success would have been certain.

Meanwhile, though it was impossible to advance, it was equally impossible to withdraw and leave Nott to be overwhelmed at Kandahar. Mackeson, at this same time, put the situation even more pithily to Nott. No force, he said, could conveniently protect more than fifteen days' supplies, besides its treasure, ammunition and baggage, through the passes. At present every village was deserted. By moving slowly and restoring confidence among the inhabitants, it might be possible eventually to reach Kabul; but at the moment it was out of the question, (*I.O.S.C.*, vol. 16 of 1842, Pollock to Indian government, April 20; Mackeson to Nott, April 18, 1842).

This letter from Pollock caused considerable disturbance to the Supreme Government. At the end of February Lord Ellenborough had taken over the governorship-general from Auckland, and on the 15th of March he had, in a general review of the situation, declared his intention of re-establishing the British military reputation by a signal blow at the Afghans, so as to prove to them that, if the army should ultimately evacuate Afghanistan, it was not from inability to maintain its position. It seems that copies of this document, which practically avowed the determination to withdraw from Afghanistan, were sent to the principal political agents; and it is certain that though Ellenborough flattered himself that he had preserved secrecy concerning the matter, and had "taken unusual measures to do so," it was, by the middle of May, the common talk of every cantonment in India and every village in Afghanistan.

Meanwhile, wishing to be nearer to the scene of action, Ellenborough left Calcutta for Allahabad on the 6th of April, and at Benares received the news of Pollock's arrival at Ali Masjid, of Sale's final success against Akbar Khan before Jalalabad, and of England's failure before Haikalzai and his subsequent retreat to Quetta. Therewith he seems to have made up his mind, in the language of commerce, to cut his losses, and to call back the army to the east bank of the Indus as soon as possible. On the 19th of April he sent orders to Nott to blow up the fortifications of Kalat-i-Ghilzai, withdraw the garrison, evacuate Kandahar, retreat to Quetta, and there remain until the heat should permit him to fall back to Sukkur.

On the same day he addressed the commander-in-chief, leaving it to him to decide where Pollock's force had best remain during the hot months until it also should be able to retire across the Indus. He still had hopes that the troops might have a chance of striking a severe blow at the Afghans, but doubted whether it were justifiable to push them forward again merely to revenge losses or redeem their military character. If new aggressive movements were deemed necessary, it would be for consideration whether the army should not be concentrated in one body and should not take up a new line of operations leading directly upon Ghazni. (Blue Book—papers relating to military operations in Afghanistan, 1843—; *I.O.S.C.*, vol. 10 of 1842, Ellenborough to Nicolls, May 14; vol. 17 of 1842, Nott to Indian government, March 24, 1842).

The impression left by these proceedings is that Ellenborough was an impulsive man. The idea of reinvading Afghanistan by a single line of operations was sound enough, but the withdrawal of Nott's force without any demonstration on the side of the Khyber to take pressure off him, to say the least, was ill-considered. However, Sir Jasper Nicolls on the 29th instructed Pollock to fall back from Jalalabad to Peshawar, authorising delay in the event of three contingencies only, namely, that the general should have initiated negotiations or operations for the recovery of the prisoners taken during Elphinstone's retreat, or that the Afghans should have moved out from Kabul to attack him.

Ten days later, however, Ellenborough, on the 28th of April, again addressed Pollock, conjecturing that the general might possibly have advanced and occupied Kabul, in which case it was still his opinion that the force should be withdrawn as soon as possible to positions within the Khyber Pass, from which communication with India would be easy. On the same day he wrote to Outram that he was taking measures to reinforce Nott's army as soon as it should reach the Indus, so as to render it thoroughly efficient in all arms.

The inference is that Ellenborough was intent rather on the practical objects of the navigation of the Indus and the overawing of the Amirs of Sind than on any further operations in Afghanistan, though his conjecture that Pollock might have advanced upon Kabul could certainly be construed as a hint that the general could do so without fear of reproof. It was, to say the least, a strange way of conveying instructions to a commander in the field; but yet more strange was the presumption of Ellenborough in thus scattering military orders broadcast without first consulting his military adviser, the commander-in-chief. (Blue Book, 1843).

Meanwhile England, in response to Nott's reproof, moved forward again from Quetta on the 26th April, with two battalions, two regiments of horse and a battery of horse-artillery, and on the 28th forced the position of Haikalzai with little difficulty or loss. On the 30th he entered the defile leading to the Khojak pass, halted the column, dismounted, called for a chair and sat down, apparently unable to nerve himself to move further. Nott, however, true to his promise had detached the Second, Sixteenth and Twenty-eighth Bengal Native Infantry, under Colonel Wymer, and these, clearing the pass with no great effort from the northern side, opened the way for England.

The two brigades then proceeded without any opposition to Kandahar, entering the city on the 10th of May; and Nott, now sure of money for the purchase of transport, announced to Pollock his intention of marching upon Kabul as early as possible. On the 17th Ellenborough's orders for his retreat burst upon him, to use Rawlinson's words, like a thunderclap. Nott, however, was too good a soldier to demur, but contented himself with saying that the operation would be most difficult, since the natives, being aware of the coming retreat, would now furnish neither supplies nor cattle, but, on the contrary, would employ every possible impediment and annoyance, (Kaye, ii.).

Pollock, as has been seen, found himself condemned to inaction from want of transport when he reached Jalalabad, and the relaxation of the old vigilance and excitement at once told upon the garrison. As the heat increased with the approach of summer, fever and dysentery increased likewise. On the 6th of May the second division of Pollock's force marched into Jalalabad, raising it to a strength of some fifteen thousand of all ranks; (see list below), and then sickness rapidly grew worse and worse.

★★★★★★

Cavalry Brigade:
H.M. 3rd Dragoons, 1st, 5th and 10th Bengal L.C., 3rd Irregular Horse, 2nd Regt. Shah Shuja's Horse.
1st Infantry Brigade:

H.M. 13th, 35th N.I., Broadfoot's Sappers and *Jezailchees*.
2nd Infantry Brigade:
H.M. 9th, 26th and 60th N.I., Sappers and Miners.
3rd Infantry Brigade:
30th, 53rd, 64th N.I.
4th Infantry Brigade:
H.M. 3 1st, 6th and 33rd N.I., Det. 6th Shah Shuja's Infantry.
3 batteries Horse-artillery, 1 battery Field-artillery, mountain battery.

******

Pollock was for the moment helpless. If he had been ordered at once to return from Jalalabad to Peshawar, he could have used his hired cattle for the purpose; but he had already sent them back when he received Nicolls's order to retire, and without them, or additional transport of some kind, he was not in a condition to obey. Moreover, with the carelessness habitual to Indian administration, a member of Nicolls's staff had privately imparted to a friend on Sale's staff the purport of his chief's instructions. The news at once became the common property of the force, and Pollock dreaded lest it should reach the Afghans also, who might then cease to bring in supplies and forage and so deal ruin to the expedition.

"These communications are very dangerous," he wrote to Nicolls; but in order to counteract their effect, he ordered Sale's brigade to Fatehabad, nineteen miles to west on the road to Kabul, to mark out a camp. So much enfeebled were the men that they only with difficulty crawled over this distance in three marches, in the first of which four men of the Thirteenth died of apoplexy. By sheer mismanagement, partly of the Commissariat department, partly of the governor-general, Pollock's column seemed likely to melt away until it should in its turn need a relieving column to extricate it. (Blue Book, 1843; *I.O.S.C.,* vol. 18 of 1842, Pollock to Nicolls, May 24, 1842; Seaton's *From Cadet to Colonel,* ii.).

A little later arrived Ellenborough's letter of the 28th of April, and Pollock seized the opportunity to interpret it as giving him discretionary powers. He represented that the British prisoners had not been released, that retirement would be construed as admission of defeat, that an advance on Kabul was for every reason politic, and that Nott should be directed to take part in it, since his withdrawal to Quetta must otherwise be very difficult. Moreover, he could find better climates than Peshawar within the pass itself. A few days later he wrote more explicitly to the Supreme Government urging that retirement must on every account be delayed until the hot weather was over. he wrote in effect:

> We must crown the heights all the way through the pass; it was difficult even in April to supply the troops employed on this duty, and it would be still more difficult now. In fact we could not furnish a continual supply of water, and without it the men cannot ascend precipitous mountains.

These are the little points that are overlooked by men who direct operations from a comfortable office hundreds of miles away, (Kaye, ii.; Blue Book; Pollock to Indian government, May 20, 25, 1842).

These letters were decisive. On the 1st of June the governor-general acknowledged that it was impossible for Pollock to withdraw before October, and expressed a hope that in the interval he might be able to strike a severe blow at the enemy. Nott also was informed that he likewise would not be expected to withdraw below the passes until the same month; and orders were issued for the collection in all quarters of camels and bullocks to enable the troops to move. It was reckoned that Pollock alone would require over fifty elephants, over five thousand camels and over four thousand bullocks, which, after the terrific waste of animals during the original march, might be difficult to supply; but, since he could not even return to India without them, Ellenborough pushed the business forward with all the energy—and this was not a little—that he could muster.(Blue Book, 1843).

At last, then, two months after the relief of Jalalabad, Ellenborough had made up his mind at least to equip Nott and Pollock with the means of moving at any rate in some direction, though in which direction, except sooner or later eastward, he would not commit himself to say. Nott, however, acting upon his first instructions to retire, on the 19th of May, detached a strong force of the Fortieth Foot, the Second, Sixteenth and Thirty-Eighth Native Infantry, with four or five squadrons of horse and ten guns, under Colonel Wymer, to bring away the garrison of Kalat-i-Ghilzai. The enemy took advantage of this division of his force with commendable promptitude.

On the 21st they attempted to carry Kalat-i-Ghilzai by escalade with four thousand men, but were beaten back with heavy loss by the garrison, whose casualties did not exceed six wounded, whereas the enemy left over one hundred dead bodies behind them. Another force of some eight thousand men under Akhtar Khan occupied some rocky hills within a mile of the walls of Kandahar, whereupon Nott, on the 29th, sallied out with about two thousand men and twelve guns, attacked them and drove them in confusion across the Arghandab, his own casualties amounting to no more than two killed and fifty wounded. In these circumstances, Wymer's task was an easy one; and the garrison of Kalat-i-Ghilzai, which had held out against cold and privation with indomitable spirit under the command of Captain Craigie, returned with Wymer safely on the 10th of June to Kandahar. (Blue Book; Neill).

Towards the end of June Pollock, having received a certain amount of transport, likewise began to bestir himself, and on the 27th sent Major Monteith with the Fourth Brigade to Pesh Bolak to chastise the tribes in the vicinity, which had given much trouble and were known to have appropriated much of the treasure taken from Elphinstone's force. The villagers had fled, so that there was no power of inflicting punishment except by destroying forts and fruit-trees. For the best part of a month Monteith marched from place to place engaged on this duty, meeting with no resistance until, on the 24th of July, he entered the Shinwari valley.

The Shinwaris, who held much of the plunder of Elphinstone's force and even one gun, had always been an ungovernable people, and Monteith, to make his power felt, made a progress through the valley destroying every fort. Once only, on the 26th of July, did the tribesmen attempt to stand in defence of one stronghold, but they were easily dispersed by shrapnel from a couple of guns, and by the advance of a few companies of the Thirty-First Foot, and of the Fifty-Second and Fifty-Third Native Infantry. Not even during a long retirement of over seven miles did they attempt seriously to molest the rear-guard, and Monteith, having done his work, returned on the 3rd of August to Jalalabad.

Meanwhile, by great exertions, Pollock had at last been equipped with a sufficiency of transport, and on the 4th of July Ellenborough wrote to him and to Nott that his resolution to withdraw the troops from Afghanistan held good, but that they might choose their own route, and that Nott might take that by Ghazni and Kabul in preference to that of Quetta, if he preferred it. The generals took the hint. August came before Pollock received a brief letter from Nott declaring his intention to move from Kandahar upon Kabul; and on the 20th of that month he marched his advanced guard to Gandamak. On the 24th he drove away some tribesmen some two miles ahead after a smart little engagement and returned to Gandamak, where his force was assembling by succession of brigades. On the 7th of September he resumed the advance with Sale's division, (3rd L.D., 1 squadron 1st L.C., 3 troops 3rd Irreg. Cav., H.M. 9th Foot and 13th L.I., 26th and 3 5th N.I.; 1 co. Sappers, Broadfoot's Sappers, 2 H.-A. guns, 6 light field guns, 3 mountain guns), and on the 8th encountered the Ghilzais in position commanding the road through the Jagdalak pass.

The tribesmen stood their ground against an accurate fire of shrapnel, but yielded to the attack of the Ninth, Thirteenth and Broadfoot's Sappers, and fled. A few brave men rallied at the summit of an almost inaccessible height, but with great difficulty and fatigue Pollock's men worked their way up to them and drove them also into flight. The casualties did not exceed sixty-four of all ranks killed and wounded.

The second division under McCaskill, which followed the first at the interval of a march, was harassed all day, and the rear-guard was continually and hotly engaged, but brought the cumbrous column of its transport safely through the pass without loss. Meanwhile, Pollock with the first division pushed on to Tezin, having ordered McCaskill to join him there by a forced march, since the enemy was reported to be ahead in strength. Little was gained by this order, for the second division, after a very trying day of constant encounter with the tribesmen, came into camp utterly exhausted, having destroyed over one hundred animals which were unable to carry their loads further.

Pollock, therefore, was obliged to halt on the 12th; and the enemy, gaining courage from his apparent hesitation, pressed so closely upon the picquets that it was necessary to drive them off by a counter-attack. On the 13th the advance was resumed, and the Afghans, under Akbar Khan, moved forward gallantly to meet the British. Pollock threw forward his European regiments to the attack, the Thirteenth on the right, the Ninth and Thirty-First on the left; and they quickly proved the truth of Wellington's assertion that they could meet any enemy, no matter whether outranged or not, with musket and bayonet.

The fight continued for the greater part of the day until the redcoats crowned the summit of the Haft Kotal, and the Afghans fled, having suffered heavily, leaving two guns and three standards in the hands of the victors. The casualties amounted to no more than thirty-two killed and one hundred and thirty wounded; and Pollock's success was decisive. On the 15th of September, he encamped on the racecourse at Kabul.

Nott, for his part, set his force in motion on the 8th of August, making short marches at first in order to distract the enemy from a column of five and a half battalions, cavalry and twelve guns, which was escorting guns and stores to Quetta. He himself retained two battalions of British and six of native infantry, one regiment of light cavalry, besides irregular horse, three batteries and the four siege-guns brought forward by Keane, see list following:

******

H.M. 40th and 41st Foot; 2nd, 16th, 38th, 42nd, 43rd Bengal N.L; 3rd Irreg. Infantry; 3rd Bombay L. Cav.; 2 regiments of Irreg. Horse; 1 troop of Bombay H.A.; 1 troop of the Shah's H.A.; 1 9-pounder battery, 4 1 8-pounders; detachment of Sappers.

******

No enemy was seen until the 28th of August, when the foolish precipitation of a cavalry officer brought on a small engagement in which Nott's cavalry was worsted, with a loss of some fifty killed and wounded. On the 30th an army, or rabble, of some twelve thousand men made some show of resistance at a point about forty miles southwest of Ghazni, but gave way after a short engagement, abandoning camp, baggage and guns. By the 4th of September Nott was before Ghazni and began to get his heavy cannon into position; but on the 6th he took peaceful possession of the place, which the enemy had evacuated during the previous night. The fortress was blown up; the sandal-wood gates were taken from the tomb of Sultan Mahmoud, in accordance with Ellenborough's instructions, and on the 10th the advance was continued upon Kabul. There was firing into the British camp upon most nights; but there was no serious resistance, beyond some slight skirmishing at Maidan, to impede Nott's progress to Kabul. On the 17th he encamped within four miles of the city.

There now remained no more to be accomplished but the recovery of the British prisoners, who meanwhile had practically been allowed to escape and were brought in by a detachment of Pollock's cavalry on the 17th. A detachment under General McCaskill was, however, pushed into Kohistan, where many hostile chiefs had taken refuge at Istaliff; and, the place having been taken by surprise, McCaskill pushed on unopposed to Charikar and ruined that fort. Pollock decided also to destroy the great bazaar at Kabul; and, this done, the army, on the 12th of October, began to leave Kabul on its return march to Peshawar, Pollock leading the way.

The tribesmen were on the watch to plunder, but due precaution was at first observed, the advanced guard detaching to every commanding height a picquet which held its post until the rearguard had passed, when it descended and formed in its rear, thus increasing the rear-guard continually to the end of the march. On the 1st of November, however, between Landi Khana and Ali Masjid, Sale made no such dispositions for the safety of his column, but pushed ahead by himself, as his way was, and left things to chance. The Khyberris saw their opportunity. One party of them engaged the rear-guard while another rushed into the baggage-column, carried off several score of mules and camels, and inflicted some loss upon the escort.

The second division under McCaskill being equally negligent was also attacked, and became involved in a serious affair, which cost numerous casualties, many transport-animals and two guns. The pieces were recovered a few days later by Nott, who brought up the rear. He likewise was continually harassed, but, handling his troops like a soldier, beat the enemy off and brought his column safely through the pass with no more than eighty-four casualties. Thus was accomplished the evacuation of Afghanistan, (See Diary of Lieut. Trower in *Journal of R.U.S.I.*, Nov. 1915; Blue Book).

That even to the end the tribesmen should have been able to wrest advantage from the British was most discreditable and very wrong. From stupid, unteachable old Sale nothing better, perhaps, was to be expected; but McCaskill was supposed to be a good officer and should not have been guilty of such a lapse. Nor is it easy to acquit Pollock of blame, for his force was not a large one, and he should have insisted upon proper conduct of the march by his subordinates. But everything in this wretched campaign was of a piece, and from beginning to end it brought nothing but disgrace.

Ellenborough, not without an eye to the effect of a display of strength upon the Sikhs, assembled a large force to receive the returning troops, welcomed them with pageantry and high honour, dubbed the garrison of Jalalabad "illustrious," exalted Sale as a hero, issued high-sounding proclamations, strove in every way to invest the final campaign with a halo of glory. All was in vain. The people of the East were not deceived; and the restoration of Dost Mohamed to the throne of Afghanistan was a confession of defeat.

Probably Ellenborough was right to endeavour to put a good face upon a bad business, though, in his effort, he need not have taken leave of his sense of the ridiculous. But his vacillation when he first took over the direction of affairs in Afghanistan, and the ambiguous terms in which he finally sanctioned the advance of Nott and Pollock to Kabul, leave an unpleasant taste in the mouth. His assertion that he was determined to save India, with an implication that no one else could, rings like a poor parody of Chatham's famous phrase, and suggests nervousness rather than commanding resolution and faith in his own will and ability. He was undoubtedly energetic, and for this he should receive every credit; but he interfered personally in a hundred matters which he should have left to subordinates, and when giving his orders to the troops had not the courtesy to inform, much less to consult, the commander-in-chief. (Kaye,ii.).

It may freely be admitted that he found a rotten system of administration in India; and it is possible that only his personal intervention could have hastened certain matters forward. But a great administrator is not one who does all the work himself. He is one who casts away bad instruments, chooses others more fitting, and sits Olympian, seeing that they do their task. He was, however, at least a great improvement upon Auckland.

Of the military commanders, Pollock deserves credit for restoring moral courage to a demoralised force, for waiting despite of Sale's cries until it was really fit to advance, and for enforcing a system of tactics which made an operation, supposed by the timid to be desperate, comparatively simple. That he accomplished this is a testimony to his possession both of nerve and of character. But he was not really an inspiring personality. He had not the gift of moulding his force into a really efficient military instrument, nor of making his will and his spirit dominant among all ranks; and his losses during his withdrawal through the Khyber Pass forbid us to rank him high among military commanders.

On the whole, Nott alone of the senior officers came out of the enterprise with credit. He was not a brilliant, but he was a sound man. He had at least one or two military principles to which he clung fast, first, to maintain discipline, and second, to keep his force together and never risk the employment of small detachments in isolation. These may sound elementary, but he was only able to maintain them at the cost of incessant conflict with the political agents; and that he did so maintain them is to his honour, for the struggle involved him in such quarrels with his civil superiors as almost daily to endanger his career. He had plenty of common sense and an inflexible will; but one has a feeling none the less that his outlook was narrow, that his limitations were many and close, and that the inflexible will could, and did, at times degenerate into mere mulish obstinacy.

As a Company's officer he was an aggressive champion of the worth of the *sepoy* and furiously jealous of the Queen's service, sentiments by no means unnatural, nor even dishonourable, in themselves, but liable to become unpleasant and even mischievous when carried to excess. And there was always danger of this with Nott, for he was both an umbrageous and a cantankerous man, ever on the watch for slights, quick to take offence and slow to accept conciliation. Thus he made things more difficult for himself than they would have been to one of more genial temper and with a livelier sense of the ridiculous. It must, however, be said for him that he entered upon his campaign under the shadow of a great personal sorrow; that he showed constancy, patience and determination in peculiarly trying circumstances, and proved himself to be an upright man and a good soldier.

But for his unfortunate temper it is probable that he and not Sale would have come down to posterity as the hero of this war; and then there would have been fewer instances of generals shutting themselves up in a fortress after making some false movement, and shrieking for the forces of the Empire to deliver them from the consequences of their own incompetence. This was one great evil which the Army inherited from this unhappy war; but it was as nothing to the evil which ultimately beset the British in India, not only through the loss of military reputation, but even more through the wanton alienation of the Afghans.

ALSO FROM LEONAUR
AVAILABLE IN SOFTCOVER OR HARDCOVER WITH DUST JACKET

THE FALL OF THE MOGHUL EMPIRE OF HINDUSTAN *by H. G. Keene*—By the beginning of the nineteenth century, as British and Indian armies under Lake and Wellesley dominated the scene, a little over half a century of conflict brought the Moghul Empire to its knees.

LADY SALE'S AFGHANISTAN *by Florentia Sale*—An Indomitable Victorian Lady's Account of the Retreat from Kabul During the First Afghan War.

THE CAMPAIGN OF MAGENTA AND SOLFERINO 1859 *by Harold Carmichael Wylly*—The Decisive Conflict for the Unification of Italy.

FRENCH'S CAVALRY CAMPAIGN *by J. G. Maydon*—A Special Correspondent's View of British Army Mounted Troops During the Boer War.

CAVALRY AT WATERLOO *by Sir Evelyn Wood*—British Mounted Troops During the Campaign of 1815.

THE SUBALTERN *by George Robert Gleig*—The Experiences of an Officer of the 85th Light Infantry During the Peninsular War.

NAPOLEON AT BAY, 1814 *by F. Loraine Petre*—The Campaigns to the Fall of the First Empire.

NAPOLEON AND THE CAMPAIGN OF 1806 *by Colonel Vachée*—The Napoleonic Method of Organisation and Command to the Battles of Jena & Auerstädt.

THE COMPLETE ADVENTURES IN THE CONNAUGHT RANGERS *by William Grattan*—The 88th Regiment during the Napoleonic Wars by a Serving Officer.

BUGLER AND OFFICER OF THE RIFLES *by William Green & Harry Smith*—With the 95th (Rifles) during the Peninsular & Waterloo Campaigns of the Napoleonic Wars.

NAPOLEONIC WAR STORIES *by Sir Arthur Quiller-Couch*—Tales of soldiers, spies, battles & sieges from the Peninsular & Waterloo campaigns.

CAPTAIN OF THE 95TH (RIFLES) *by Jonathan Leach*—An officer of Wellington's sharpshooters during the Peninsular, South of France and Waterloo campaigns of the Napoleonic wars.

RIFLEMAN COSTELLO *by Edward Costello*—The adventures of a soldier of the 95th (Rifles) in the Peninsular & Waterloo Campaigns of the Napoleonic wars.

AVAILABLE ONLINE AT **www.leonaur.com**
AND FROM ALL GOOD BOOK STORES

ALSO FROM LEONAUR
AVAILABLE IN SOFTCOVER OR HARDCOVER WITH DUST JACKET

ESCAPE FROM THE FRENCH by Edward Boys—A Young Royal Navy Midshipman's Adventures During the Napoleonic War.

THE VOYAGE OF H.M.S. PANDORA by Edward Edwards R. N. & George Hamilton, edited by Basil Thomson—In Pursuit of the Mutineers of the Bounty in the South Seas—1790-1791.

MEDUSA by J. B. Henry Savigny and Alexander Correard and Charlotte-Adélaïde Dard —Narrative of a Voyage to Senegal in 1816 & The Sufferings of the Picard Family After the Shipwreck of the Medusa.

THE SEA WAR OF 1812 VOLUME 1 by A. T. Mahan—A History of the Maritime Conflict.

THE SEA WAR OF 1812 VOLUME 2 by A. T. Mahan—A History of the Maritime Conflict.

WETHERELL OF H. M. S. HUSSAR by John Wetherell—The Recollections of an Ordinary Seaman of the Royal Navy During the Napoleonic Wars.

THE NAVAL BRIGADE IN NATAL by C. R. N. Burne—With the Guns of H. M. S. Terrible & H. M. S. Tartar during the Boer War 1899-1900.

THE VOYAGE OF H. M. S. BOUNTY by William Bligh—The True Story of an 18th Century Voyage of Exploration and Mutiny.

SHIPWRECK! by William Gilly—The Royal Navy's Disasters at Sea 1793-1849.

KING'S CUTTERS AND SMUGGLERS: 1700-1855 by E. Keble Chatterton—A unique period of maritime history-from the beginning of the eighteenth to the middle of the nineteenth century when British seamen risked all to smuggle valuable goods from wool to tea and spirits from and to the Continent.

CONFEDERATE BLOCKADE RUNNER by John Wilkinson—The Personal Recollections of an Officer of the Confederate Navy.

NAVAL BATTLES OF THE NAPOLEONIC WARS by W. H. Fitchett—Cape St. Vincent, the Nile, Cadiz, Copenhagen, Trafalgar & Others.

PRISONERS OF THE RED DESERT by R. S. Gwatkin-Williams—The Adventures of the Crew of the Tara During the First World War.

U-BOAT WAR 1914-1918 by James B. Connolly/Karl von Schenk—Two Contrasting Accounts from Both Sides of the Conflict at Sea During the Great War.

AVAILABLE ONLINE AT **www.leonaur.com**
AND FROM ALL GOOD BOOK STORES

www.ingramcontent.com/pod-product-compliance
Lightning Source LLC
Chambersburg PA
CBHW031623160426
43196CB00006B/254

SCÈNE V.

CLYTEMNESTRE, ÉLECTRE, IPHISE.

IPHISE.

Suivez-le, montrez-vous, ne craignez rien, parlez;
Portez les derniers coups dans les cœurs ébranlés.

ÉLECTRE.

Au nom de la nature achevez votre ouvrage;
De Clytemnestre enfin déployez le courage.
Volez, conduisez-nous.

CLYTEMNESTRE.

Mes filles, ces soldats
Me respectent à peine, et retiennent vos pas.
Demeurez; c'est à moi, dans ce moment si triste,
De répondre des jours et d'Oreste et d'Égisthe :
Je suis épouse et mère; et je veux à la fois,
Si j'en puis être digne, en remplir tous les droits.

(elle sort.)

SCÈNE VI.

ÉLECTRE, IPHISE.

IPHISE.

Ah! le dieu qui nous perd en sa rigueur persiste,
En défendant Oreste, elle ménage Égisthe.
Les cris de la pitié, du sang, et des remords,
Seront contre un tyran d'inutiles efforts.
Égisthe furieux, et brûlant de vengeance,
Consomme ses forfaits pour sa propre défense;
Il condamne, il est maître; il frappe, il faut périr.

ACTE V, SCÈNE VI.

ÉLECTRE.

Et j'ai pu le prier avant que de mourir !
Je descends dans la tombe avec cette infamie,
Avec le désespoir de m'être démentie !
J'ai supplié ce monstre et j'ai hâté ses coups.
Tout ce qui dut servir s'est tourné contre nous.
Que font tous ces amis dont se vantait Pammène ?
Ces peuples dont Égisthe a soulevé la haine ;
Ces dieux qui de mon frère armaient le bras vengeur,
Et qui lui défendaient de consoler sa sœur ;
Ces filles de la nuit, dont les mains infernales
Secouaient leurs flambeaux sous ces voûtes fatales ?
Quoi ! la nature entière, en ce jour de terreur,
Paraissait à ma voix s'armer en ma faveur ;
Et tout est pour Égisthe, et mon frère est sans vie ;
Et les dieux, les mortels, et l'enfer m'ont trahie !

SCÈNE VII.

ÉLECTRE, PYLADE, IPHISE.

ÉLECTRE.

En est-ce fait, Pylade ?

PYLADE.

Oui, tout est accompli,
Tout change ; Électre est libre, et le ciel obéi.

ÉLECTRE.

Comment ?

PYLADE.

Oreste règne, et c'est lui qui m'envoie.

IPHISE.

Justes dieux !

ÉLECTRE.
Je succombe à l'excès de ma joie.
Oreste! est-il possible?
PYLADE.
Oreste tout puissant
Va venger sa famille et le sang innocent.
ÉLECTRE.
Quel miracle a produit un destin si prospère?
PYLADE.
Son courage, son nom, le nom de votre père,
Le vôtre, vos vertus, l'excès de vos malheurs,
La pitié, la justice, un dieu qui parle aux cœurs.
Par les ordres d'Égisthe on amenait à peine,
Pour mourir avec nous, le fidèle Pammène;
Tout un peuple suivait, morne, glacé d'horreur;
J'entrevoyais sa rage à travers sa terreur;
La garde retenait leurs fureurs interdites.
Oreste se tournant vers ses fiers satellites,
Immolez, a-t-il dit, le dernier de vos rois;
L'osez-vous? A ces mots, au son de cette voix,
A ce front où brillait la majesté suprême,
Nous avons tous cru voir Agamemnon lui-même,
Qui, perçant du tombeau les gouffres éternels,
Revenait en ces lieux commander aux mortels.
Je parle : tout s'émeut ; l'amitié persuade ;
On respecte les nœuds d'Oreste et de Pylade :
Des soldats avançaient pour nous envelopper,
Ils ont levé le bras, et n'ont osé frapper :
Nous sommes entourés d'une foule attendrie ;
Le zèle s'enhardit, l'amour devient furie.
Dans les bras de ce peuple Oreste était porté.
Égisthe avec les siens d'un pas précipité

ole, croit le punir, arrive, et voit son maître.
'ai vu tout son orgueil à l'instant disparaître,
s esclaves le fuir, ses amis le quitter,
ans sa confusion ses soldats l'insulter.
jour d'un grand exemple ! ô justice suprême !
es fers que nous portions il est chargé lui-même.
a seule Clytemnestre accompagne ses pas,
e protège, l'arrache aux fureurs des soldats,
e jette au milieu d'eux, et d'un front intrépide
A la fureur commune enlève le perfide,
e tient entre ses bras, s'expose à tous les coups,
Et conjure son fils d'épargner son époux.
Oreste parle au peuple, il respecte sa mère ;
Il remplit les devoirs et de fils et de frère.
A peine délivré du fer de l'ennemi,
C'est un roi triomphant sur son trône affermi.

IPHISE.

Courons, venez orner ce triomphe d'un frère ;
Voyons Oreste heureux, et consolons ma mère.

ÉLECTRE.

Quel bonheur inouï, par les dieux envoyé !
Protecteur de mon sang, héros de l'amitié,
Venez.

PYLADE, *à sa suite.*

Brisez, amis, ces chaînes si cruelles ;
Fers, tombez de ses mains ; le sceptre est fait pour elles.
(*on lui ôte ses chaînes.*)

SCÈNE VIII.

ÉLECTRE, IPHISE, PYLADE, PAMMÈNE.

ÉLECTRE.

Ah ! Pammène, où trouver mon frère, mon vengeur ?
Pourquoi ne vient-il pas ?

PAMMÈNE.

Ce moment de terreur
Est destiné, madame, à ce grand sacrifice
Que la cendre d'un père attend de sa justice :
Tel est l'ordre qu'il suit. Cette tombe est l'autel
Où sa main doit verser le sang du criminel.
Daignez l'attendre ici, tandis qu'il venge un père.
Ce devoir redoutable est juste et nécessaire ;
Mais ce spectacle horrible aurait souillé vos yeux.
Vous connaissez les lois qu'Argos tient de ses dieux ;
Elles ne souffrent point que vos mains innocentes
Avant le temps prescrit pressent ses mains sanglantes.

IPHISE.

Mais que fait Clytemnestre en ces moments d'horreur ?
Voyons-la.

PAMMÈNE.

Clytemnestre, en proie à sa fureur.
De son indigne époux défend encor la vie ;
Elle oppose à son fils une main trop hardie.

ÉLECTRE.

Elle défend Égisthe.... elle de qui le bras
A sur Agamemnon.... Dieux, ne le souffrez pas !

PAMMÈNE.

On dit que dans ce trouble on voit les Euménides
Sourdes à la prière, et de meurtres avides,

ACTE V, SCÈNE VIII.

Ministres des arrêts prononcés par le sort,
Marcher autour d'Oreste, en appelant la mort.

IPHISE.

our terrible et sanglant, soyez un jour de grâce;
Terminez les malheurs attachés à ma race.
Ah, ma sœur! ah, Pylade! entendez-vous ces cris?

ÉLECTRE.

C'est ma mère!

PAMMÈNE.

Elle-même.

CLYTEMNESTRE, *derrière la scène.*

Arrête!

IPHISE.

Ciel!

CLYTEMNESTRE, *derrière la scène.*

Mon fils!

ÉLECTRE.

Il frappe Égisthe. Achève, et sois inexorable;
Venge-nous, venge-la; tranche un nœud si coupable;
Immole entre ses bras cet infâme assassin;
Frappe, dis-je.

CLYTEMNESTRE.

Mon fils!.... j'expire de ta main.

PYLADE.

O destinée!

IPHISE.

O crime!

ÉLECTRE.

Ah, trop malheureux frère!
Quel forfait a puni les forfaits de ma mère!
Jour à jamais affreux!

SCÈNE IX.

LES ACTEURS PRÉCÉDENTS, ORESTE.

ORESTE.

O terre, entr'ouvre-toi !
Clytemnestre, Tantale, Atrée, attendez-moi !
Je vous suis aux enfers, éternelles victimes ;
Je dispute avec vous de tourments et de crimes.

ÉLECTRE.

Qu'avez-vous fait, cruel ?

ORESTE.

Elle a voulu sauver....
Et les frappant tous deux.... Je ne puis achever.

ÉLECTRE.

Quoi ! de la main d'un fils ! quoi ! par ce coup funeste,
Vous....

ORESTE.

Non, ce n'est pas moi ; non, ce n'est point Oreste,
Un pouvoir effroyable a seul conduit mes coups :
Exécrable instrument d'un éternel courroux,
Banni de mon pays par le meurtre d'un père,
Banni du monde entier par celui de ma mère,
Patrie, états, parents, que je remplis d'effroi,
Innocence, amitié, tout est perdu pour moi !
Soleil, qu'épouvanta cette affreuse contrée,
Soleil, qui reculas pour le festin d'Atrée,
Tu luis encor pour moi, tu luis pour ces climats !
Dans l'éternelle nuit tu ne nous plonges pas !
Dieux, tyrans éternels, puissance impitoyable,
Dieux qui me punissez, qui m'avez fait coupable !

ACTE V, SCÈNE IX.

Eh bien, quel est l'exil que vous me destinez ?
Quel est le nouveau crime où vous me condamnez ?
Parlez.... Vous prononcez le nom de la Tauride ?
J'y cours, j'y vais trouver la prêtresse homicide,
Qui n'offre que du sang à des dieux en courroux,
A des dieux moins cruels, moins barbares que vous.

ÉLECTRE.

Demeurez : conjurez leur justice et leur haine.

PYLADE.

Je te suivrai partout où leur fureur t'entraîne.
Que l'amitié triomphe, en ce jour odieux,
Des malheurs des mortels, et du courroux des dieux !

FIN D'ORESTE.

L'ORPHELIN
DE LA CHINE,
TRAGÉDIE,

Représentée, pour la première fois, le 20 auguste 1755.

A MONSEIGNEUR LE MARÉCHAL DUC DE RICHELIEU,

PAIR DE FRANCE, PREMIER GENTILHOMME DE LA CHAMBRE DU ROI, COMMANDANT EN LANGUEDOC, L'UN DES QUARANTE DE L'ACADÉMIE.

Je voudrais, Monseigneur, vous présenter de beau marbre comme les Génois, et je n'ai que des figures chinoises à vous offrir. Ce petit ouvrage ne paraît pas fait pour vous; il n'y a aucun héros dans cette pièce qui ait réuni tous les suffrages par les agréments de son esprit, ni qui ait soutenu une république prête à succomber, ni qui ait imaginé de renverser une colonne anglaise avec quatre canons. Je sens mieux que personne le peu que je vous offre; mais tout se pardonne à un attachement de quarante années. On dira peut-être qu'au pied des Alpes, et vis-à-vis des neiges éternelles où je me suis retiré, et où je devais n'être que philosophe, j'ai succombé à la vanité d'imprimer que ce qu'il y a eu de plus brillant sur les bords de la Seine ne m'a jamais oublié. Cependant je n'ai consulté que mon cœur; il me conduit seul; il a toujours inspiré mes actions et mes paroles; il se trompe quelquefois, vous le savez, mais ce n'est pas après des épreuves si longues. Permettez donc que, si cette faible tragédie peut durer quelque temps après moi, on sache que l'auteur ne vous a pas été indifférent; permettez qu'on apprenne que, si votre oncle fonda des beaux arts en France, vous les avez soutenus dans leur décadence.

L'idée de cette tragédie me vint, il y a quelque temps, à la lecture de l'Orphelin de Tchao, tragédie chinoise, traduite par le P. Brémare, qu'on trouve dans le recueil que le P. du Halde a donné au public. Cette pièce chinoise fut composée au quatorzième siècle, sous la dynastie même de Gengis-Kan. C'est une nouvelle preuve que les vainqueurs tartares ne changèrent point les mœurs de la nation vaincue; ils protégèrent tous les arts établis à la Chine; ils adoptèrent toutes ses lois.

Voilà un grand exemple de la supériorité naturelle que donnent la raison et le génie sur la force aveugle et barbare; et les Tartares ont deux fois donné cet exemple. Car, lorsqu'ils ont conquis encore ce grand empire au commencement du siècle passé, ils se sont soumis une seconde fois à la sagesse des vaincus; et les deux peuples n'ont formé qu'une nation gouvernée par les plus anciennes lois du monde : évènement frappant, qui a été le premier but de mon ouvrage.

La tragédie chinoise, qui porte le nom de l'Orphelin, est tirée d'un recueil immense des pièces de théâtre de cette nation : elle cultivait depuis plus de trois mille ans cet art, inventé un peu plus tard par les Grecs, de faire des portraits vivants des actions des hommes, et d'établir de ces écoles de morale, où l'on enseigne la vertu en action et en dialogues. Le poëme dramatique ne fut donc long-temps en honneur que dans ce vaste pays de la Chine, séparé et ignoré du reste du monde, et dans la seule ville d'Athènes. Rome ne le cultiva qu'au bout de quatre cents années. Si vous le cherchez chez les Perses, chez les Indiens, qui passent pour des peuples inventeurs, vous ne l'y trouvez pas ; il n'y est jamais parvenu. L'Asie se contentait des fables de Pilpay et de Lokman, qui renferment toute la morale, et qui instruisent en allégories toutes les nations et tous les siècles.

Il semble qu'après avoir fait parler les animaux, il n'y eut qu'un pas à faire pour faire parler les hommes, pour les introduire sur la scène, pour former l'art dramatique; cependant ces peuples ingénieux ne s'en avisèrent jamais. On doit inférer de là que les Chinois, les Grecs et les Romains, sont les seuls peuples anciens qui aient connu le véritable esprit de la société. Rien, en effet, ne rend les hommes plus sociables, n'adoucit plus leurs mœurs, ne perfectionne plus leur raison, que de les rassembler pour leur faire goûter ensemble les plaisirs purs de l'esprit: aussi nous voyons qu'à peine Pierre le Grand eut policé la Russie, et bâti Pétersbourg, que les théâtres s'y sont établis. Plus l'Allemagne s'est perfectionnée, et plus nous l'avons vu adopter nos spectacles : le peu de pays où ils n'étaient pas reçus dans le siècle passé n'étaient pas mis au rang des pays civilisés.

L'Orphelin de Tchao est un monument précieux qui sert plus à faire connaître l'esprit de la Chine que toutes les relations qu'on a faites et qu'on fera jamais de ce vaste empire. Il est vrai que cette pièce est toute bar-

re en comparaison des bons ouvrages de
nos jours; mais aussi c'est un chef-d'œuvre,
si on le compare à nos pièces du quatorzième
siècle. Certainement nos troubadours, notre
bazoche, la société des enfants sans souci, et
de la mère-sotte, n'approchaient pas de l'auteur chinois. Il faut encore remarquer que
cette pièce est écrite dans la langue des mandarins, qui n'a point changé, et qu'à peine
entendons-nous la langue qu'on parlait du
temps de Louis XII et de Charles VIII.

On ne peut comparer l'Orphelin de Tchao
qu'aux tragédies françaises et espagnoles du
dix-septième siècle, qui ne laissent pas encore de plaire au-delà des Pyrénées et de la
mer. L'action de la pièce chinoise dure vingt-
cinq ans, comme dans les farces monstrueuses
de Shakespear et de Lopez de Vega, qu'on
a nommées tragédies; c'est un entassement
d'évènements incroyables. L'ennemi de la
maison de Tchao veut d'abord en faire périr
le chef, en lâchant sur lui un gros dogue,
qu'il fait croire être doué de l'instinct de découvrir les criminels, comme Jacques Ay-
mard, parmi nous, devinait les voleurs par
sa baguette. Ensuite il suppose un ordre de

l'empereur, et envoie à son ennemi une corde, du poison et un poignard. Il chante selon l'usage, et se coupe la gorge vertu de l'obéissance que tout homme sur terre doit de droit divin à un empereur la Chine. Le persécuteur fait mourir cents personnes de la maison de Tchao princesse veuve accouche de l'Orphelin dérobe cet enfant à la fureur de celui qui exterminé toute la maison, et qui veut en core faire périr au berceau le seul qui r Cet exterminateur ordonne qu'on égorge dans les villages d'alentour tous les enfants, afin que l'orphelin soit enveloppé dans la destruction générale.

On croit lire les Mille et une nuits en action et en scènes; mais, malgré l'incroyable, il y règne de l'intérêt; et, malgré la foule des évènements, tout est de la clarté la plus lumineuse: ce sont deux grands mérites en tout temps et chez toutes les nations; et ce mérite manque à beaucoup de nos pièces modernes. Il est vrai que la pièce chinoise n'a pas d'autres beautés: unité de temps et d'action, développements de sentiments, peinture des mœurs, éloquence, raison, passion, tout lui

anque; et cependant, comme je l'ai déjà
t, l'ouvrage est supérieur à tout ce que
ous faisions alors.

Comment les Chinois, qui au quatorième siècle, et si long-temps auparavant, avaient faire de meilleurs poëmes dramaques que tous les Européens, sont-ils restés oujours dans l'enfance grossière de l'art, tandis qu'à force de soins et de temps notre ation est parvenue à produire environ une ouzaine de pièces qui, si elles ne sont pas parfaites, sont pourtant fort au-dessus de tout ce que le reste de la terre a jamais produit en ce genre? Les Chinois, comme les autres Asiatiques, sont demeurés aux premiers éléments de la poésie, de l'éloquence, de la physique, de l'astronomie, de la peinture, connus par eux si long-temps avant nous. Il leur a été donné de commencer en tout plutôt que les autres peuples, pour ne faire ensuite aucun progrès. Ils ont ressemblé aux anciens Egyptiens, qui, ayant d'abord enseigné les Grecs, finirent par n'être pas capables d'être leurs disciples.

Ces Chinois chez qui nous avons voyagé à travers tant de périls, ces peuples de qui nous avons obtenu avec tant de peine la permission de leur apporter l'argent de l'Europe, et de venir les instruire, ne savent pas encore à quel point nous leur sommes supérieurs; ils ne sont pas assez avancés pour oser seulement vouloir nous imiter. Nous avons puisé dans leur histoire des sujets de tragédie, et ils ignorent si nous avons une histoire.

Le célèbre abbé Metastasio a pris pour sujet d'un de ses poëmes dramatiques le même sujet à peu près que moi, c'est-à-dire un orphelin échappé au carnage de sa maison, et il a puisé cette aventure dans une dynastie qui régnait neuf cents ans avant notre ère.

La tragédie chinoise de l'Orphelin de Tchao est tout un autre sujet. J'en ai choisi un tout différent encore des deux autres, et qui ne leur ressemble que par le nom. Je me suis arrêté à la grande époque de Gengis-Kan, et j'ai voulu peindre les mœurs des Tartares et des Chinois. Les aventures les plus intéressantes ne sont rien quand elles ne peignent pas les mœurs; et cette peinture, qui est un des plus grands secrets de l'art, n'est encore qu'un amusement frivole quand elle n'inspire pas la vertu.

J'ose dire que depuis la Henriade jusqu'à Zaire, et jusqu'à cette pièce chinoise, bonne ou mauvaise, tel a été toujours le principe qui m'a inspiré; et que, dans l'histoire du siècle de Louis XIV, j'ai célébré mon roi et ma patrie, sans flatter ni l'un ni l'autre. C'est dans un tel travail que j'ai consumé plus de quarante années. Mais voici ce que dit un auteur chinois traduit en espagnol par le célèbre Navarette :

« Si tu composes quelque ouvrage, ne le
« montre qu'à tes amis : crains le public et
« tes confrères : car on falsifiera, on empoi-
« sonnera ce que tu auras fait, et on t'impu-
« tera ce que tu n'auras pas fait. La calomnie,
« qui a cent trompettes, les fera sonner pour
« te perdre, tandis que la vérité, qui est
« muette, restera auprès de toi. Le célèbre
« Ming fut accusé d'avoir mal pensé du Tien
« et du Li, et de l'empereur Vang; on trouva
« le vieillard moribond qui achevait le pané-
« gyrique de Vang, et un hymne au Tien et
« au Li, etc. »

PERSONNAGES.

GENGIS-KAN, empereur tartare.
OCTAR, } guerriers tartares.
OSMAN,
ZAMTI, mandarin lettré.
IDAMÉ, femme de Zamti.
ASSÉLI, attachée à Idamé.
ÉTAN, attaché à Zamti.

La scène est dans un palais des mandarins, tient au palais impérial, dans la ville de C balu, aujourd'hui Pékin.

L'ORPHELIN DE LA CHINE,
TRAGÉDIE.

ACTE PREMIER.

SCÈNE I.
IDAMÉ, ASSÉLI.

IDAMÉ.

Se peut-il qu'en ce temps de désolation,
En ce jour de carnage et de destruction,
Quand ce palais sanglant, ouvert à des Tartares,
Tombe avec l'univers sous ces peuples barbares,
Dans cet amas affreux de publiques horreurs,
Il soit encor pour moi de nouvelles douleurs?

ASSÉLI.

Eh! qui n'éprouve, hélas! dans la perte commune,
Les tristes sentiments de sa propre infortune?
Qui de nous vers le ciel n'élève pas ses cris
Pour les jours d'un époux, ou d'un père, ou d'un fils?
Dans cette vaste enceinte, au Tartare inconnue,
Où le roi dérobait à la publique vue
Ce peuple désarmé de paisibles mortels,
Interprètes des lois, ministres des autels,
Vieillards, femmes, enfants, troupeau faible et timide,
Dont n'a point approché cette guerre homicide,

Nous ignorons encore à quelle atrocité
Le vainqueur insolent porte sa cruauté.
Nous entendons gronder la foudre et les tempêtes.
Le dernier coup approche, et vient frapper nos têtes.

IDAMÉ.

O fortune! ô pouvoir au-dessus de l'humain!
Chère et triste Asséli, sais-tu quelle est la main
Qui du Catai sanglant pressa le vaste empire,
Et qui s'appesantit sur tout ce qui respire?

ASSÉLI.

On nomme ce tyran du nom de roi des rois.
C'est ce fier Gengis-Kan, dont les affreux exploits
Font un vaste tombeau de la superbe Asie.
Octar, son lieutenant, déja, dans sa furie,
Porte au palais, dit-on, le fer et les flambeaux.
Le Catai passe enfin sous des maîtres nouveaux.
Cette ville, autrefois souveraine du monde,
Nage de tous côtés dans le sang qui l'inonde.
Voilà ce que cent voix, en sanglots superflus,
Ont appris dans ces lieux à mes sens éperdus.

IDAMÉ

Sais-tu que ce tyran de la terre interdite,
Sous qui de cet état la fin se précipite,
Ce destructeur des rois, de leur sang abreuvé,
Est un Scythe, un soldat dans la poudre élevé,
Un guerrier vagabond de ces déserts sauvages,
Climat qu'un ciel épais ne couvre que d'orages?
C'est lui qui, sur les siens briguant l'autorité,
Tantôt fort et puissant, tantôt persécuté,
Vint jadis à tes yeux, dans cette auguste ville,
Aux portes du palais demander un asile.
Son nom est Témugin; c'est t'en apprendre assez.

ACTE I, SCÈNE I.

ASSÉLI.

Quoi ! c'est lui dont les vœux vous furent adressés !
Quoi ! c'est ce fugitif, dont l'amour et l'hommage
A vos parents surpris parurent un outrage !
Lui qui traîne après lui tant de rois ses suivants,
Dont le nom seul impose au reste des vivants !

IDAMÉ.

C'est lui-même, Asséli : son superbe courage,
Sa future grandeur, brillaient sur son visage,
Tout semblait, je l'avoue, esclave auprès de lui ;
Et lorsque de la cour il mendiait l'appui,
Inconnu, fugitif, il ne parlait qu'en maître.
Il m'aimait ; et mon cœur s'en applaudit peut-être :
Peut-être qu'en secret je tirais vanité
D'adoucir ce lion dans mes fers arrêté,
De plier à nos mœurs cette grandeur sauvage,
D'instruire à nos vertus son féroce courage,
Et de le rendre enfin, grâces à ces liens,
Digne un jour d'être admis parmi nos citoyens.
Il eût servi l'état, qu'il détruit par la guerre :
Un refus a produit les malheurs de la terre.
De nos peuples jaloux tu connais la fierté.
De nos arts, de nos lois l'auguste antiquité,
Une religion de tout temps épurée,
De cent siècles de gloire une suite avérée,
Tout nous interdisait, dans nos préventions,
Une indigne alliance avec les nations.
Enfin un autre hymen, un plus saint nœud m'engage ;
Le vertueux Zamti mérita mon suffrage.
Qui l'eût cru, dans ces temps de paix et de bonheur,
Qu'un Scythe méprisé serait notre vainqueur ?
Voilà ce qui m'alarme, et qui me désespère.

J'ai refusé sa main; je suis épouse et mère :
Il ne pardonne pas : il se vit outrager;
Et l'univers sait trop s'il aime à se venger.
Étrange destinée, et revers incroyable !
Est-il possible, ô dieu, que ce peuple innombrable
Sous le glaive du Scythe expire sans combats,
Comme de vils troupeaux que l'on mène au trépas?

ASSÉLI.

Les Coréens, dit-on, rassemblaient une armée;
Mais nous ne savons rien que par la renommée,
Et tout nous abandonne aux mains des destructeurs.

IDAMÉ.

Que cette incertitude augmente mes douleurs !
J'ignore à quel excès parviennent nos misères,
Si l'empereur encore au palais de ses pères
A trouvé quelque asile, ou quelque défenseur,
Si la reine est tombée aux mains de l'oppresseur,
Si l'un et l'autre touche à son heure fatale.
Hélas! ce dernier fruit de leur foi conjugale,
Ce malheureux enfant, à nos soins confié,
Excite encor ma crainte, ainsi que ma pitié.
Mon époux aux palais porte un pied téméraire;
Une ombre de respect pour son saint ministère
Peut-être adoucira ces vainqueurs forcenés.
On dit que ces brigands aux meurtres acharnés
Qui remplissent de sang la terre intimidée,
Ont d'un dieu cependant conservé quelque idée;
Tant la nature même, en toute nation,
Grava l'Être suprême et la religion !
Mais je me flatte en vain qu'aucun respect les touche;
La crainte est dans mon cœur, et l'espoir dans ma bouche.
Je me meurs....

SCÈNE II.

IDAMÉ, ZAMTI, ASSÉLI.

IDAMÉ.

Est-ce vous, époux infortuné?
Notre sort sans retour est-il déterminé?
Hélas! qu'avez-vous vu?

ZAMTI.

Ce que je tremble à dire.
Le malheur est au comble; il n'est plus, cet empire:
Sous le glaive étranger j'ai vu tout abattu.
De quoi nous a servi d'adorer la vertu?
Nous étions vainement, dans une paix profonde,
Et les législateurs et l'exemple du monde;
Vainement par nos lois l'univers fut instruit:
La sagesse n'est rien; la force a tout détruit.
J'ai vu de ces brigands la horde hyperborée,
Par des fleuves de sang se frayant une entrée
Sur les corps entassés de nos frères mourants,
Portant partout le glaive et les feux dévorants.
Ils pénètrent en foule à la demeure auguste
Où de tous les humains le plus grand, le plus juste,
D'un front majestueux attendait le trépas.
La reine évanouie était entre ses bras.
De leurs nombreux enfants ceux en qui le courage
Commençait vainement à croître avec leur âge,
Et qui pouvaient mourir les armes à la main,
Étaient déja tombés sous le fer inhumain.
Il restait près de lui ceux dont la tendre enfance
N'avait que la faiblesse et des pleurs pour défense;
On les voyait encore autour de lui pressés,

Tremblants à ses genoux qu'ils tenaient embrassés;
J'entre par des détours inconnus au vulgaire;
J'approche en frémissant de ce malheureux père;
Je vois ces vils humains, ces monstres des déserts,
A notre auguste maître osant donner des fers;
Traîner dans son palais, d'une main sanguinaire,
Le père, les enfants, et leur mourante mère.

IDAMÉ.

C'est donc là leur destin! Quel changement, ô cieux!

ZAMTI.

Ce prince infortuné tourne vers moi les yeux;
Il m'appelle, il me dit, dans la langue sacrée
Du conquérant tartare et du peuple ignorée :
« Conserve au moins le jour au dernier de mes fils. »
Jugez si mes serments et mon cœur l'ont promis;
Jugez de mon devoir quelle est la voix pressante.
J'ai senti ranimer ma force languissante;
J'ai revolé vers vous. Les ravisseurs sanglants
Ont laissé le passage à mes pas chancelants;
Soit que dans les fureurs de leur horrible joie,
Au pillage acharnés, occupés de leur proie,
Leur superbe mépris ait détourné les yeux;
Soit que cet ornement d'un ministre des cieux,
Ce symbole sacré du grand dieu que j'adore,
A la férocité puisse imposer encore;
Soit qu'enfin ce grand dieu, dans ses profonds desseins,
Pour sauver cet enfant qu'il a mis dans mes mains,
Sur leurs yeux vigilants répandant un nuage,
Ait égaré leur vue, ou suspendu leur rage.

IDAMÉ.

Seigneur, il serait temps encor de le sauver;
Qu'il parte avec mon fils; je les puis enlever;

ACTE I, SCÈNE II.

e désespérons point, et préparons leur fuite;
De notre prompt départ qu'Étan ait la conduite.
Allons vers la Corée, au rivage des mers,
Aux lieux où l'océan ceint ce triste univers.
La terre a des déserts et des antres sauvages;
Portons-y ces enfants, tandis que les ravages
N'inondent point encor ces asiles sacrés,
Éloignés du vainqueur, et peut-être ignorés.
Allons; le temps est cher, et la plainte inutile.

ZAMTI.

Hélas! le fils des rois n'a pas même un asile!
J'attends les Coréens; ils viendront, mais trop tard:
Cependant la mort vole au pied de ce rempart.
Saisissons, s'il se peut, le moment favorable
De mettre en sûreté ce gage inviolable.

SCÈNE III.

ZAMTI, IDAMÉ, ASSELI, ÉTAN.

ZAMTI.

Étan, où courez-vous, interdit, consterné?

IDAMÉ.

Fuyons de ce séjour au Scythe abandonné.

ÉTAN.

Vous êtes observés, la fuite est impossible;
Autour de notre enceinte une garde terrible
Aux peuples consternés offre de toutes parts
Un rempart hérissé de piques et de dards.
Les vainqueurs ont parlé; l'esclavage en silence
Obéit à leurs voix dans cette ville immense;
Chacun reste immobile et de crainte et d'horreur
Depuis que sous le glaive est tombé l'empereur.

ZAMTI.

Il n'est donc plus!

IDAMÉ.

O cieux!

ÉTAN.

De ce nouveau carnage
Qui pourra retracer l'épouvantable image?
Son épouse, ses fils sanglants et déchirés....
O famille de dieux sur la terre adorés!
Que vous dirai-je? hélas! leurs têtes exposées
Du vainqueur insolent excitent les risées,
Tandis que leurs sujets, tremblant de murmurer,
Baissent des yeux mourants qui craignent de pleurer.
De nos honteux soldats les phalanges errantes
A genoux ont jeté leurs armes impuissantes.
Les vainqueurs fatigués dans nos murs asservis,
Lassés de leur victoire et de sang assouvis,
Publiant à la fin le terme du carnage,
Ont, au lieu de la mort, annoncé l'esclavage.
Mais d'un plus grand désastre on nous menace encor;
On prétend que ce roi des fiers enfants du Nord,
Gengis-Kan, que le ciel envoya pour détruire,
Dont les seuls lieutenants oppriment cet empire,
Dans nos murs autrefois inconnu, dédaigné,
Vient, toujours implacable, et toujours indigné,
Consommer sa colère et venger son injure.
Sa nation farouche est d'une autre nature
Que les tristes humains qu'enferment nos remparts:
Ils habitent des champs, des tentes et des chars;
Ils se croiroient gênés dans cette ville immense;
De nos arts, de nos lois la beauté les offense.

Ces brigands vont changer en d'éternels déserts
Les murs que si long-temps admira l'univers.

IDAMÉ.

Le vainqueur vient sans doute armé de la vengeance.
Dans mon obscurité j'avais quelque espérance ;
Je n'en ai plus. Les cieux, à nous nuire attachés,
Ont éclairé la nuit où nous étions cachés.
Trop heureux les mortels inconnus à leur maître !

ZAMTI.

Les nôtres sont tombés : le juste ciel peut-être
Voudra pour l'Orphelin signaler son pouvoir :
Veillons sur lui ; voilà notre premier devoir.
Que nous veut ce Tartare ?

IDAMÉ.

O ciel, prends ma défense.

SCÈNE IV.

ZAMTI, IDAMÉ, ASSÉLI, OCTAR, GARDES.

OCTAR.

Esclaves, écoutez ; que votre obéissance
Soit l'unique réponse aux ordres de ma voix.
Il reste encore un fils du dernier de vos rois ;
C'est vous qui l'élevez : votre soin téméraire
Nourrit un ennemi dont il faut se défaire.
Je vous ordonne, au nom du vainqueur des humains,
De remettre aujourd'hui cet enfant dans mes mains :
Je vais l'attendre : allez ; qu'on m'apporte ce gage.
Pour peu que vous tardiez, le sang et le carnage
Vont de mon maître encor signaler le courroux,
Et la destruction commencera par vous.
La nuit vient, le jour fuit ; vous, avant qu'il finisse,
Si vous aimez la vie, allez, qu'on obéisse.

SCÈNE V.

ZAMTI, IDAMÉ.

IDAMÉ.

Où sommes-nous réduits ? O monstres ! ô terreur !
Chaque instant fait éclore une nouvelle horreur,
Et produit des forfaits dont l'ame intimidée
Jusqu'à ce jour de sang n'avait point eu d'idée.
Vous ne répondez rien ; vos soupirs élancés
Au ciel qui nous accable en vain sont adressés.
Enfant de tant de rois, faut-il qu'on sacrifie
Aux ordres d'un soldat ton innocente vie ?

ZAMTI.

J'ai promis, j'ai juré de conserver ses jours.

IDAMÉ.

De quoi lui serviront vos malheureux secours ?
Qu'importent vos serments, vos stériles tendresses ?
Êtes-vous en état de tenir vos promesses ?
N'espérons plus.

ZAMTI.

Ah ciel ! Eh quoi ! vous voudriez
Voir du fils de mes rois les jours sacrifiés ?

IDAMÉ.

Non, je n'y puis penser sans des torrents de larmes,
Et si je n'étais mère, et si, dans mes alarmes,
Le ciel me permettait d'abréger un destin
Nécessaire à mon fils élevé dans mon sein,
Je vous dirais, mourons, et, lorsque tout succombe,
Sur les pas de nos rois descendons dans la tombe.

ZAMTI.

Après l'atrocité de leur indigne sort,
Qui pourrait redouter et refuser la mort ?

Le coupable la craint, le malheureux l'appelle,
Le brave la défie et marche au-devant d'elle ;
Le sage, qui l'attend, la reçoit sans regrets.

IDAMÉ.

Quels sont en me parlant vos sentiments secrets ?
Vous baissez vos regards, vos cheveux se hérissent,
Vous pâlissez, vos yeux de larmes se remplissent :
Mon cœur répond au vôtre ; il sent tous vos tourments.
Mais que résolvez-vous ?

ZAMTI.

    De garder mes serments.
Auprès de cet enfant allez, daignez m'attendre.

IDAMÉ.

Mes prières, mes cris pourront-ils le défendre ?

SCÈNE VI.

ZAMTI, ÉTAN.

ÉTAN.

Seigneur, votre pitié ne peut le conserver.
Ne songez qu'à l'état, que sa mort peut sauver :
Pour le salut du peuple il faut bien qu'il périsse.

ZAMTI.

Oui.... je vois qu'il faut faire un triste sacrifice.
Ecoute : cet empire est-il cher à tes yeux ?
Reconnais-tu ce dieu de la terre et des cieux,
Ce dieu que sans mélange annonçaient nos ancêtres,
Méconnu par le bonze, insulté par nos maîtres ?

ÉTAN.

Dans nos communs malheurs il est mon seul appui ;
Je pleure la patrie, et n'espère qu'en lui.

ZAMTI.

Jure ici par son nom, par sa toute-puissance,
Que tu conserveras dans l'éternel silence
Le secret qu'en ton sein je dois ensevelir.
Jure-moi que tes mains oseront accomplir
Ce que les intérêts et les lois de l'empire,
Mon devoir, et mon dieu, vont par moi te prescrire.

ÉTAN.

Je le jure; et je veux, dans ces murs désolés,
Voir nos malheurs communs sur moi seul assemblés,
Si, trahissant vos vœux, et démentant mon zèle,
Ou ma bouche, ou ma main, vous était infidèle.

ZAMTI.

Allons, il ne m'est plus permis de reculer.

ÉTAN.

De vos yeux attendris je vois des pleurs couler.
Hélas! de tant de maux les atteintes cruelles
Laissent donc place encore à des larmes nouvelles!

ZAMTI.

On a porté l'arrêt! rien ne peut le changer!

ÉTAN.

On presse; et cet enfant, qui vous est étranger....

ZAMTI.

Étranger! lui, mon roi!

ÉTAN.

Notre roi fut son père;
Je le sais, j'en frémis : parlez, que dois-je faire?

ZAMTI.

On compte ici mes pas; j'ai peu de liberté.
Sers-toi de la faveur de ton obscurité.
De ce dépôt sacré tu sais quel est l'asile :
Tu n'es point observé; l'accès t'en est facile.

ACTE I, SCÈNE VI.

achons pour quelque temps cet enfant précieux
aus le sein des tombeaux bâtis par ses aïeux.
ous remettrons bientôt au chef de la Corée
e tendre rejeton d'une tige adorée.
l peut ravir du moins à nos cruels vainqueurs
Ce malheureux enfant, l'objet de leurs terreurs ;
Il peut sauver mon roi. Je prends sur moi le reste.

ÉTAN.

Et que deviendrez-vous sans ce gage funeste ?
Que pourrez-vous répondre au vainqueur irrité ?

ZAMTI.

J'ai de quoi satisfaire à sa férocité.

ÉTAN.

Vous, seigneur ?

ZAMTI.

O nature ! ô devoir tyrannique !

ÉTAN.

Eh bien ?

ZAMTI.

Dans son berceau saisis mon fils unique.

ÉTAN.

Votre fils !

ZAMTI.

Songe au roi que tu dois conserver.
Prends mon fils.... que son sang.... je ne puis achever.

ÉTAN.

Ah ! que m'ordonnez-vous ?

ZAMTI.

Respecte ma tendresse ;
Respecte mon malheur, et surtout ma faiblesse :
N'oppose aucun obstacle à cet ordre sacré,
Et remplis ton devoir après l'avoir juré.

ÉTAN.

Vous m'avez arraché ce serment téméraire.
A quel devoir affreux me faut-il satisfaire ?
J'admire avec horreur ce dessein généreux ;
Mais si mon amitié....

ZAMTI.

C'en est trop, je le veux.
Je suis père ; et ce cœur qu'un tel arrêt déchire,
S'en est dit cent fois plus que tu ne peux m'en dire ;
J'ai fait taire le sang, fais taire l'amitié.
Pars.

ÉTAN.

Il faut obéir.

ZAMTI.

Laisse-moi, par pitié.

SCÈNE VII.

ZAMTI.

J'AI fait taire le sang ! Ah, trop malheureux père !
J'entends trop cette voix si fatale et si chère.
Ciel ! impose silence aux cris de ma douleur !
Mon épouse, mon fils, me déchirent le cœur.
De ce cœur effrayé cache-moi la blessure.
L'homme est trop faible, hélas ! pour dompter la nature :
Que peut-il par lui-même ? achève, soutiens-moi ;
Affermis la vertu prête à tomber sans toi.

FIN DU PREMIER ACTE.

ACTE SECOND.

SCÈNE I.

ZAMTI.

Étan auprès de moi tarde trop à se rendre :
Il faut que je lui parle ; et je crains de l'entendre.
Je tremble malgré moi de son fatal retour.
Ô mon fils ! mon cher fils ! as-tu perdu le jour ?
Aura-t-on consommé ce fatal sacrifice ?
Je n'ai pu de ma main te conduire au supplice ;
Je n'en eus pas la force : en ai-je assez au moins
Pour apprendre l'effet de mes funestes soins ?
En ai-je encore assez pour cacher mes alarmes ?

SCÈNE II.

ZAMTI, ÉTAN.

ZAMTI.

Viens, ami.... je t'entends.... je sais tout par tes larmes.

ÉTAN.

Votre malheureux fils....

ZAMTI.

   Arrête, parle-moi
De l'espoir de l'empire, et du fils de mon roi ;
Est-il en sûreté ?

ÉTAN.

   Les tombeaux de ses pères
Cachent à nos tyrans sa vie et ses misères.

Il vous devra des jours pour souffrir commencés.
Présent fatal peut-être !

ZAMTI.

Il vit : c'en est assez.
O vous, à qui je rends ces services fidèles !
O mes rois ! pardonnez mes larmes paternelles.

ÉTAN.

Osez-vous en ces lieux gémir en liberté ?

ZAMTI.

Où porter ma douleur et ma calamité ?
Et comment désormais soutenir les approches,
Le désespoir, les cris, les éternels reproches,
Les imprécations d'une mère en fureur ?
Encor si nous pouvions prolonger son erreur !

ÉTAN.

On a ravi son fils dans sa fatale absence :
A nos cruels vainqueurs on conduit son enfance ;
Et soudain j'ai volé pour donner mes secours
Au royal orphelin dont on poursuit les jours.

ZAMTI.

Ah ! du moins, cher Étan, si tu pouvais lui dire
Que nous avons livré l'héritier de l'empire,
Que j'ai caché mon fils, qu'il est en sûreté !
Imposons quelque temps à sa crédulité.
Hélas ! la vérité si souvent est cruelle !
On l'aime ; et les humains sont malheureux par elle.
Allons.... ciel ! elle-même approche de ces lieux ;
La douleur et la mort sont peintes dans ses yeux.

SCÈNE III.

ZAMTI, IDAMÉ.

IDAMÉ.

Qu'AI-JE vu ? Qu'a-t-on fait ? Barbare, est-il possible ?
L'avez-vous commandé ce sacrifice horrible ?
Non, je ne puis le croire; et le ciel irrité
N'a pas dans votre sein mis tant de cruauté.
Non, vous ne serez point plus dur et plus barbare
Que la loi du vainqueur, et le fer du Tartare.
Vous pleurez, malheureux !

ZAMTI.

Ah ! pleurez avec moi ;
Mais avec moi songez à sauver votre roi.

IDAMÉ.

Que j'immole mon fils !

ZAMTI.

Telle est notre misère :
Vous êtes citoyenne avant que d'être mère.

IDAMÉ.

Quoi ! sur toi la nature a si peu de pouvoir !

ZAMTI.

Elle n'en a que trop, mais moins que mon devoir ;
Et je dois plus au sang de mon malheureux maître,
Qu'à cet enfant obscur à qui j'ai donné l'être.

IDAMÉ.

Non, je ne connais point cette horrible vertu.
J'ai vu nos murs en cendre, et ce trône abattu,
J'ai pleuré de nos rois les disgrâces affreuses ;
Mais par quelles fureurs, encor plus douloureuses,
Veux-tu, de ton épouse avançant le trépas,
Livrer le sang d'un fils qu'on ne demande pas ?

Ces rois ensevelis, disparus dans la poudre,
Sont-ils pour toi des dieux dont tu craignes la foudre?
A ces dieux impuissants, dans la tombe endormis,
As-tu fait le serment d'assassiner ton fils ?
Hélas! grands et petits, et sujets, et monarques,
Distingués un moment par de frivoles marques,
Égaux par la nature, égaux par le malheur,
Tout mortel est chargé de sa propre douleur;
Sa peine lui suffit, et, dans ce grand naufrage,
Rassembler nos débris, voilà notre partage.
Où serais-je, grand dieu! si ma crédulité
Eût tombé dans le piège à mes pas présenté?
Auprès du fils des rois si j'étais demeurée,
La victime aux bourreaux allait être livrée;
Je cessais d'être mère, et le même couteau
Sur le corps de mon fils me plongeait au tombeau.
Grâces à mon amour, inquiète, troublée,
A ce fatal berceau l'instinct m'a rappelée.
J'ai vu porter mon fils à nos cruels vainqueurs;
Mes mains l'ont arraché des mains des ravisseurs.
Barbare, ils n'ont point eu ta fermeté cruelle;
J'en ai chargé soudain cette esclave fidèle,
Qui soutient de son lait ses misérables jours,
Ces jours qui périssaient sans moi, sans mon secours;
J'ai conservé le sang du fils et de la mère,
Et j'ose dire encor de son malheureux père.

ZAMTI.

Quoi! mon fils est vivant!

IDAMÉ.

Oui, rends grâces au ciel,
Malgré toi favorable à ton cœur paternel.
Repens-toi.

ACTE II, SCÈNE III.

ZAMTI.

Dieu des cieux, pardonnez cette joie,
Qui se mêle un moment aux pleurs où je me noie !
O ma chère Idamé ! ces moments seront courts :
Vainement de mon fils vous prolongiez les jours ;
Vainement vous cachiez cette fatale offrande :
Si nous ne donnons pas le sang qu'on nous demande,
Nos tyrans soupçonneux seront bientôt vengés ;
Nos citoyens tremblants, avec nous égorgés,
Vont payer de vos soins les efforts inutiles ;
De soldats entourés, nous n'avons plus d'asiles ;
Et mon fils, qu'au trépas vous croyez arracher,
A l'œil qui le poursuit ne peut plus se cacher.
Il faut subir son sort.

IDAMÉ.

Ah ! cher époux, demeure ;
Écoute-moi du moins.

ZAMTI.

Hélas...! il faut qu'il meure.

IDAMÉ.

Qu'il meure ! arrête, tremble, et crains mon désespoir ;
Crains sa mère.

ZAMTI.

Je crains de trahir mon devoir.
Abandonnez le vôtre ; abandonnez ma vie
Aux détestables mains d'un conquérant impie.
C'est mon sang qu'à Gengis il vous faut demander.
Allez, il n'aura pas de peine à l'accorder.
Dans le sang d'un époux trempez vos mains perfides ;
Allez : ce jour n'est fait que pour des parricides.
Rendez vains mes serments, sacrifiez nos lois,
Immolez votre époux, et le sang de vos rois.

IDAMÉ.

De mes rois! Va, te dis-je, ils n'ont rien à prétendre;
Je ne dois point mon sang en tribut à leur cendre;
Va; le nom de sujet n'est pas plus saint pour nous
Que ces noms si sacrés et de père et d'époux.
La nature et l'hymen, voilà les lois premières,
Les devoirs, les liens des nations entières :
Ces lois viennent des dieux; le reste est des humains.
Ne me fais point haïr le sang des souverains :
Oui, sauvons l'orphelin d'un vainqueur homicide;
Mais ne le sauvons pas au prix d'un parricide;
Que les jours de mon fils n'achètent point ses jours:
Loin de l'abandonner, je vole à son secours;
Je prends pitié de lui; prends pitié de toi-même,
De ton fils innocent, de sa mère qui t'aime.
Je ne menace plus, je tombe à tes genoux.
O père infortuné! cher et cruel époux!
Pour qui j'ai méprisé, tu t'en souviens peut-être,
Ce mortel qu'aujourd'hui le sort a fait ton maître;
Accorde-moi mon fils, accorde-moi ce sang
Que le plus pur amour a formé dans mon flanc,
Et ne résiste point au cri terrible et tendre
Qu'à tes sens désolés l'amour a fait entendre.

ZAMTI.

Ah! c'est trop abuser du charme et du pouvoir
Dont la nature et vous combattez mon devoir.
Trop faible épouse, hélas! si vous pouviez connaître...

IDAMÉ.

Je suis faible, oui, pardonne; une mère doit l'être!
Je n'aurai point de toi ce reproche à souffrir,
Quand il faudra te suivre, et qu'il faudra mourir.
Cher époux, si tu peux au vainqueur sanguinaire,

ACTE II, SCÈNE III.

A la place du fils, sacrifier la mère,
Je suis prête : Idamé ne se plaindra de rien ;
Et mon cœur est encore aussi grand que le tien.

ZAMTI.

Oui, j'en crois ta vertu.

SCÈNE IV.

ZAMTI, IDAMÉ, OCTAR, GARDES.

OCTAR.

Quoi ! vous osez reprendre
Ce dépôt que ma voix vous ordonna de rendre ?
Soldats, suivez leurs pas, et me répondez d'eux :
Saisissez cet enfant qu'ils cachent à mes yeux ;
Allez : votre empereur en ces lieux va paraître ;
Apportez la victime aux pieds de votre maître.
Soldats, veillez sur eux.

ZAMTI.

Je suis prêt d'obéir :
Vous aurez cet enfant.

IDAMÉ.

Je ne le puis souffrir ;
Non, vous ne l'obtiendrez, cruels, qu'avec ma vie.

OCTAR.

Qu'on fasse retirer cette femme hardie.
Voici votre empereur ; ayez soin d'empêcher
Que tous ces vils captifs osent en approcher.

SCÈNE V.

GENGIS, OCTAR, OSMAN, TROUPE DE GUERRIERS.

GENGIS.

On a poussé trop loin le droit de ma conquête.
Que le glaive se cache, et que la mort s'arrête :
Je veux que les vaincus respirent désormais.
J'envoyai la terreur, et j'apporte la paix :
La mort du fils des rois suffit à ma vengeance.
Étouffons dans son sang la fatale semence
Des complots éternels, et des rébellions
Qu'un fantôme de prince inspire aux nations.
Sa famille est éteinte : il vit ; il doit la suivre.
Je n'en veux qu'à des rois ; mes sujets doivent vivre.

Cessez de mutiler tous ces grands monuments,
Ces prodiges des arts consacrés par les temps ;
Respectez-les, ils sont le prix de mon courage :
Qu'on cesse de livrer aux flammes, au pillage,
Ces archives de lois, ce vaste amas d'écrits,
Tous ces fruits du génie, objets de vos mépris :
Si l'erreur les dicta, cette erreur m'est utile ;
Elle occupe ce peuple, et le rend plus docile.

Octar, je vous destine à porter mes drapeaux
Aux lieux où le soleil renaît du sein des eaux.

(à un de ses suivants.)

Vous, dans l'Inde soumise, humble dans sa défaite,
Soyez de mes décrets le fidèle interprète,
Tandis qu'en Occident je fais voler mes fils
Des murs de Samarcande aux bords du Tanaïs.
Sortez : demeure, Octar.

SCÈNE VI.

GENGIS, OCTAR.

GENGIS.

Eh bien ! pouvais-tu croire
Que le sort m'élevât à ce comble de gloire ?
Je foule aux pieds ce trône, et je règne en des lieux
Où mon front avili n'osa lever les yeux.
Voici donc ce palais, cette superbe ville
Où, caché dans la foule, et cherchant un asile,
J'essuyai les mépris qu'à l'abri du danger
L'orgueilleux citoyen prodigue à l'étranger :
On dédaignait un Scythe ; et la honte et l'outrage
De mes vœux mal conçus devinrent le partage ;
Une femme ici même a refusé la main
Sous qui, depuis cinq ans, tremble le genre humain.

OCTAR.

Quoi ! dans ce haut degré de gloire et de puissance,
Quand le monde à vos pieds se prosterne en silence,
D'un tel ressouvenir vous seriez occupé !

GENGIS.

Mon esprit, je l'avoue, en fut toujours frappé.
Des affronts attachés à mon humble fortune
C'est le seul dont je garde une idée importune.
Je n'eus que ce moment de faiblesse et d'erreur :
Je crus trouver ici le repos de mon cœur ;
Il n'est point dans l'éclat dont le sort m'environne :
La gloire le promet ; l'amour, dit-on, le donne.
J'en conserve un dépit trop indigne de moi ;
Mais au moins je voudrais qu'elle connût son roi ;

Que son œil entrevît, du sein de la bassesse,
De qui son imprudence outragea la tendresse ;
Qu'à l'aspect des grandeurs, qu'elle eût pu partager,
Son désespoir secret servît à me venger.

OCTAR.

Mon oreille, seigneur, était accoutumée
Aux cris de la victoire et de la renommée,
Au bruit des murs fumants renversés sous vos pas,
Et non à ces discours, que je ne conçois pas.

GENGIS.

Non, depuis qu'en ces lieux mon ame fut vaincue,
Depuis que ma fierté fut ainsi confondue,
Mon cœur s'est désormais défendu sans retour
Tous ces vils sentiments qu'ici l'on nomme amour.
Idamé, je l'avoue, en cette ame égarée
Fit une impression que j'avais ignorée.
Dans nos antres du Nord, dans nos stériles champs,
Il n'est point de beauté qui subjugue nos sens ;
De nos travaux grossiers les compagnes sauvages
Partageaient l'âpreté de nos mâles courages :
Un poison tout nouveau me surprit en ces lieux ;
La tranquille Idamé le portait dans ses yeux ;
Ses paroles, ses traits, respiraient l'art de plaire.
Je rends grâce au refus qui nourrit ma colère ;
Son mépris dissipa ce charme suborneur,
Ce charme inconcevable, et souverain du cœur.
Mon bonheur m'eût perdu ; mon ame toute entière
Se doit aux grands objets de ma vaste carrière.
J'ai subjugué le monde, et j'aurais soupiré !
Ce trait injurieux, dont je fus déchiré,
Ne rentrera jamais dans mon ame offensée ;
Je bannis sans regret cette lâche pensée :

Une femme sur moi n'aura point de pouvoir;
Je la veux oublier, je ne veux point la voir :
Qu'elle pleure à loisir sa fierté trop rebelle;
Octar, je vous défends que l'on s'informe d'elle.
OCTAR.
Vous avez en ces lieux des soins plus importants.
GENGIS.
Oui, je me souviens trop de tant d'égarements.

SCÈNE VII.
GENGIS, OCTAR, OSMAN.
OSMAN.
La victime, seigneur, allait être égorgée;
Une garde autour d'elle était déja rangée;
Mais un évènement, que je n'attendais pas,
Demande un nouvel ordre, et suspend son trépas :
Une femme éperdue, et de larmes baignée,
Arrive, tend les bras à la garde indignée;
Et nous surprenant tous par ses cris forcenés,
Arrêtez! c'est mon fils que vous assassinez!
C'est mon fils! on vous trompe au choix de la victime.
Le désespoir affreux qui parle et qui l'anime,
Ses yeux, son front, sa voix, ses sanglots, ses clameurs,
Sa fureur intrépide au milieu de ses pleurs,
Tout semblait annoncer, par ce grand caractère,
Le cri de la nature, et le cœur d'une mère.
Cependant son époux devant nous appelé,
Non moins éperdu qu'elle, et non moins accablé,
Mais sombre et recueilli dans sa douleur funeste,
De nos rois, a-t-il dit, voilà ce qui nous reste;
Frappez : voilà le sang que vous me demandez.

De larmes en parlant ses yeux sont inondés.
Cette femme à ces mots d'un froid mortel saisie,
Long-temps sans mouvement, sans couleur, et sans vie,
Ouvrant enfin les yeux, d'horreur appesantis,
Dès qu'elle a pu parler a réclamé son fils :
Le mensonge n'a point des douleurs si sincères ;
On ne versa jamais de larmes plus amères.
On doute, on examine, et je reviens confus
Demander à vos pieds vos ordres absolus.

GENGIS.

Je saurai démêler un pareil artifice ;
Et qui m'a pu tromper est sûr de son supplice.
Ce peuple de vaincus prétend-il m'aveugler ?
Et veut-on que le sang recommence à couler ?

OCTAR.

Cette femme ne peut tromper votre prudence :
Du fils de l'empereur elle a conduit l'enfance ;
Aux enfants de son maître on s'attache aisément ;
Le danger, le malheur ajoute au sentiment ;
Le fanatisme alors égale la nature ;
Et sa douleur si vraie ajoute à l'imposture.
Bientôt, de son secret perçant l'obscurité,
Vos yeux sur cette nuit répandront la clarté.

GENGIS.

Quelle est donc cette femme ?

OCTAR.

On dit qu'elle est unie
A l'un de ces lettrés que respectait l'Asie,
Qui, trop enorgueillis du faste de leurs lois,
Sur leur vain tribunal osaient braver cent rois.
Leur foule est innombrable : ils sont tous dans les chaînes ;
Ils connaîtront enfin des lois plus souveraines :

ACTE II, SCÈNE VII.

Zamti, c'est là le nom de cet esclave altier
Qui veillait sur l'enfant qu'on doit sacrifier.

GENGIS.

Allez interroger ce couple condamnable ;
Tirez la vérité de leur bouche coupable ,
Que nos guerriers surtout, à leurs postes fixés,
Veillent dans tous les lieux où je les ai placés ;
Qu'aucun d'eux ne s'écarte. On parle de surprise ;
Les Coréens, dit-on, tentent quelque entreprise ;
Vers les rives du fleuve on a vu des soldats.
Nous saurons quels mortels s'avancent au trépas,
Et si l'on veut forcer les enfants de la guerre
A porter le carnage aux bornes de la terre.

FIN DU SECOND ACTE.

ACTE TROISIÈME.

SCÈNE I.

GENGIS, OCTAR, OSMAN, TROUPE DE GUERRIERS.

GENGIS

A-t-on de ces captifs éclairci l'imposture ?
A-t-on connu leur crime et vengé mon injure ?
Ce rejeton des rois à leur garde commis
Entre les mains d'Octar est-il enfin remis ?

OSMAN.

Il cherche à pénétrer dans ce sombre mystère.
A l'aspect des tourments, ce mandarin sévère
Persiste en sa réponse avec tranquillité ;
Il semble sur son front porter la vérité :
Son épouse en tremblant nous répond par des larmes ;
Sa plainte, sa douleur augmente encor ses charmes.
De pitié malgré nous nos cœurs étaient surpris,
Et nous nous étonnions de nous voir attendris :
Jamais rien de si beau ne frappa notre vue.
Seigneur, le croiriez-vous ? cette femme éperdue
A vos sacrés genoux demande à se jeter.
« Que le vainqueur des rois daigne enfin m'écouter :
« Il pourra d'un enfant protéger l'innocence ;
« Malgré ses cruautés j'espère en sa clémence :
« Puisqu'il est tout-puissant, il sera généreux ;
« Pourrait-il rebuter les pleurs des malheureux ? »
C'est ainsi qu'elle parle ; et j'ai dû lui promettre
Qu'à vos pieds en ces lieux vous daignerez l'admettre.

GENGIS.

De ce mystère enfin je dois être éclairci,
(*à sa suite.*)
Oui, qu'elle vienne : allez, et qu'on l'amène ici.
Qu'elle ne pense pas que par de vaines plaintes,
Des soupirs affectés, et quelques larmes feintes,
Aux yeux d'un conquérant on puisse en imposer :
Les femmes de ces lieux ne peuvent m'abuser ;
Je n'ai que trop connu leurs larmes infidèles,
Et mon cœur dès long-temps s'est affermi contre elles.
Elle cherche un honneur dont dépendra son sort ;
Et vouloir me tromper, c'est demander la mort.

OSMAN.

Voilà cette captive à vos pieds amenée.

GENGIS.

Que vois-je ? est-il possible ? ô ciel ! ô destinée !
Ne me trompé-je point ? est-ce un songe, une erreur ?
C'est Idamé ! c'est elle ! et mes sens.....

SCÈNE II.

GENGIS, IDAMÉ, OCTAR, OSMAN, GARDES.

IDAMÉ.

Ah ! seigneur,
Tranchez les tristes jours d'une femme éperdue;
Vous devez vous venger, je m'y suis attendue ;
Mais, seigneur, épargnez un enfant innocent.

GENGIS.

Rassurez-vous ; sortez de cet effroi pressant.....
Ma surprise, madame, est égale à la vôtre.....
Le destin qui fait tout nous trompa l'un et l'autre.

Les temps sont bien changés : mais si l'ordre des cieux
D'un habitant du Nord, méprisable à vos yeux,
A fait un conquérant sous qui tremble l'Asie,
Ne craignez rien pour vous ; votre empereur oublie
Les affronts qu'en ces lieux essuya Témugin.
J'immole à ma victoire, à mon trône, au destin,
Le dernier rejeton d'une race ennemie :
Le repos de l'état me demande sa vie :
Il faut qu'entre mes mains ce dépôt soit livré.
Votre cœur sur un fils doit être rassuré ;
Je le prends sous ma garde.

IDAMÉ.
A peine je respire.

GENGIS.
Mais de la vérité, madame, il faut m'instruire :
Quel indigne artifice ose-t-on m'opposer ?
De vous, de votre époux, qui prétend m'imposer ?

IDAMÉ.
Ah ! des infortunés épargnez la misère.

GENGIS.
Vous savez si je dois haïr ce téméraire.

IDAMÉ.
Vous, seigneur !

GENGIS.
J'en dis trop, et plus que je ne veux.

IDAMÉ.
Ah ! rendez-moi, seigneur, un enfant malheureux :
Vous me l'avez promis ; sa grâce est prononcée.

GENGIS.
Sa grâce est dans vos mains ; ma gloire est offensée,
Mes ordres méprisés, mon pouvoir avili ;
En un mot vous savez jusqu'où je suis trahi.

C'est peu de m'enlever le sang que je demande,
De me désobéir alors que je commande ;
Vous êtes dès long-temps instruite à m'outrager ;
Ce n'est pas d'aujourd'hui que je dois me venger.
Votre époux !.... ce seul nom le rend assez coupable.
Quel est donc ce mortel pour vous si respectable,
Qui sous ses lois, madame, a pu vous captiver ?
Quel est cet insolent qui pense me braver ?
Qu'il vienne.

IDAMÉ.

Mon époux, vertueux et fidèle,
Objet infortuné de ma douleur mortelle,
Servit son dieu, son roi, rendit mes jours heureux.

GENGIS.

Qui!... lui? mais depuis quand formâtes-vous ces nœuds?

IDAMÉ.

Depuis que loin de nous le sort, qui vous seconde,
Eut entraîné vos pas pour le malheur du monde.

GENGIS.

J'entends ; depuis le jour que je fus outragé,
Depuis que de vous deux je dus être vengé,
Depuis que vos climats ont mérité ma haine.

SCÈNE III.

GENGIS, OCTAR, OSMAN, *d'un côté* ; IDAMÉ, ZAMTI, *de l'autre*, GARDES.

GENGIS.

PARLE ; as-tu satisfait à ma loi souveraine ?
As-tu mis dans mes mains le fils de l'empereur ?

ZAMTI.

J'ai rempli mon devoir, c'en est fait ; oui, seigneur.

GENGIS.

Tu sais si je punis la fraude et l'insolence :
Tu sais que rien n'échappe aux coups de ma vengeance;
Que si le fils des rois par toi m'est enlevé,
Malgré ton imposture, il sera retrouvé;
Que son trépas certain va suivre ton supplice.

(à ses gardes.)

Mais je veux bien le croire. Allez, et qu'on saisisse
L'enfant que cet esclave a remis en vos mains.
Frappez.

ZAMTI.

Malheureux père !

IDAMÉ.

Arrêtez, inhumains !
Ah ! seigneur, est-ce ainsi que la pitié vous presse ?
Est-ce ainsi qu'un vainqueur sait tenir sa promesse ?

GENGIS.

Est-ce ainsi qu'on m'abuse, et qu'on croit me jouer ?
C'en est trop; écoutez, il faut tout m'avouer.
Sur cet enfant, madame, expliquez-vous sur l'heure,
Instruisez-moi de tout, répondez, ou qu'il meure.

IDAMÉ.

Eh bien ! mon fils l'emporte : et si, dans mon malheur,
L'aveu que la nature arrache à ma douleur
Est encore à vos yeux une offense nouvelle ;
S'il faut toujours du sang à votre ame cruelle,
Frappez ce triste cœur qui cède à son effroi,
Et sauvez un mortel plus généreux que moi.
Seigneur, il est trop vrai que notre auguste maître,
Qui, sans vos seuls exploits, n'eût point cessé de l'être,
A remis à mes mains, aux mains de mon époux,
Ce dépôt respectable à tout autre qu'à vous.

Seigneur, assez d'horreurs suivaient votre victoire;
Assez de cruautés ternissaient tant de gloire;
Dans des fleuves de sang tant d'innocents plongés,
L'empereur et sa femme, et cinq fils égorgés,
Le fer de tous côtés dévastant cet empire,
Tous ces champs de carnage auraient dû vous suffire.
Un barbare en ces lieux est venu demander
Ce dépôt précieux que j'aurais dû garder,
Ce fils de tant de rois, notre unique espérance.
A cet ordre terrible, à cette violence,
Mon époux, inflexible en sa fidélité,
N'a vu que son devoir, et n'a point hésité :
Il a livré son fils. La nature outragée
Vainement déchirait son ame partagée ;
Il imposait silence à ses cris douloureux.
Vous deviez ignorer ce sacrifice affreux :
J'ai dû plus respecter sa fermeté sévère ;
Je devais l'imiter : mais enfin je suis mère ;
Mon ame est au-dessous d'un si cruel effort ;
Je n'ai pu de mon fils consentir à la mort.
Hélas ! au désespoir que j'ai trop fait paraître,
Une mère aisément pouvait se reconnaître.
Voyez de cet enfant le père confondu,
Qui ne vous a trahi qu'à force de vertu :
L'un n'attend son salut que de son innocence ;
Et l'autre est respectable alors qu'il vous offense.
Ne punissez que moi, qui trahis à la fois
Et l'époux que j'admire, et le sang de mes rois.
Digne époux ! digne objet de toute ma tendresse !
La pitié maternelle est ma seule faiblesse :
Mon sort suivra le tien ; je meurs, si tu péris ;
Pardonne-moi du moins d'avoir sauvé ton fils.

ZAMTI.

Je t'ai tout pardonné, je n'ai plus à me plaindre.
Pour le sang de mon roi je n'ai plus rien à craindre;
Ses jours sont assurés.

GENGIS.

Traître, ils ne le sont pas :
Va réparer ton crime, ou subir ton trépas.

ZAMTI.

Le crime est d'obéir à des ordres injustes.
La souveraine voix de mes maîtres augustes
Du sein de leurs tombeaux parle plus haut que toi :
Tu fus notre vainqueur, et tu n'es pas mon roi;
Si j'étais ton sujet, je te serais fidèle.
Arrache-moi la vie, et respecte mon zèle :
Je t'ai livré mon fils, j'ai pu te l'immoler;
Penses-tu que pour moi je puisse encor trembler?

GENGIS.

Qu'on l'ôte de mes yeux.

IDAMÉ.

Ah! daignez....

GENGIS.

Qu'on l'entraîne

IDAMÉ.

Non, n'accablez que moi des traits de votre haine.
Cruel! qui m'aurait dit que j'aurais par vos coups
Perdu mon empereur, mon fils, et mon époux?
Quoi! votre ame jamais ne peut-être amollie?

GENGIS.

Allez, suivez l'époux à qui le sort vous lie.
Est-ce à vous de prétendre encore à me toucher?
Et quel droit avez-vous de me rien reprocher?

ACTE III, SCÈNE III.

IDAMÉ.

Ah! je l'avais prévu, je n'ai plus d'espérance.

GENGIS.

Allez, dis-je, Idamé : si jamais la clémence
Dans mon cœur malgré moi pouvait encore entrer,
Vous sentez quels affronts il faudrait réparer.

SCÈNE IV.

GENGIS, OCTAR.

GENGIS.

D'où vient que je gémis? d'où vient que je balance?
Quel dieu parlait en elle et prenait sa défense?
Est-il dans les vertus, est-il dans la beauté
Un pouvoir au-dessus de mon autorité?
Ah! demeurez, Octar; je me crains, je m'ignore :
Il me faut un ami, je n'en eus point encore;
Mon cœur en a besoin.

OCTAR.

Puisqu'il faut vous parler,
S'il est des ennemis qu'on vous doive immoler,
Si vous voulez couper d'une race odieuse,
Dans ses derniers rameaux, la tige dangereuse,
Précipitez sa perte; il faut que la rigueur,
Trop nécessaire appui du trône d'un vainqueur,
Frappe sans intervalle un coup sûr et rapide :
C'est un torrent qui passe en son cours homicide;
Le temps ramène l'ordre et la tranquillité;
Le peuple se façonne à la docilité;
De ses premiers malheurs l'image est affaiblie;
Bientôt il les pardonne, et même il les oublie.
Mais lorsque goutte à goutte on fait couler le sang,

Qu'on ferme avec lenteur, et qu'on rouvre le flanc,
Que les jours renaissants ramènent le carnage,
Le désespoir tient lieu de force et de courage,
Et fait d'un peuple faible un peuple d'ennemis,
D'autant plus dangereux qu'ils étaient plus soumis.

GENGIS.

Quoi! c'est cette Idamé? quoi! c'est là cette esclave?
Quoi! l'hymen l'a soumise au mortel qui me brave?

OCTAR.

Je conçois que pour elle il n'est point de pitié;
Vous ne lui devez plus que votre inimitié.
Cet amour, dites-vous, qui vous toucha pour elle,
Fut d'un feu passager la légère étincelle :
Ses imprudents refus, la colère, et le temps,
En ont éteint dans vous les restes languissants;
Elle n'est à vos yeux qu'une femme coupable,
D'un criminel obscur épouse méprisable.

GENGIS.

Il en sera puni ; je le dois, je le veux :
Ce n'est pas avec lui que je suis généreux.
Moi, laisser respirer un vaincu que j'abhorre!
Un esclave! un rival!

OCTAR.

    Pourquoi vit-il encore?
Vous êtes tout-puissant, et n'êtes point vengé!

GENGIS.

Juste ciel! à ce point mon cœur serait changé!
C'est ici que ce cœur connaîtrait les alarmes,
Vaincu par la beauté, désarmé par les larmes,
Dévorant mon dépit et mes soupirs honteux!
Moi, rival d'un esclave, et d'un esclave heureux!

ACTE III, SCENE IV.

Je souffre qu'il respire, et cependant on l'aime !
Je respecte Idamé jusqu'en son époux même ;
Je crains de la blesser en enfonçant mes coups
Dans le cœur détesté de cet indigne époux.
Est-il bien vrai que j'aime ? est-ce moi qui soupire ?
Qu'est-ce donc que l'amour ? a-t-il donc tant d'empire ?

OCTAR.

Je n'appris qu'à combattre, à marcher sous vos lois ;
Mes chars et mes coursiers, mes flèches, mon carquois,
Voilà mes passions et ma seule science :
Des caprices du cœur j'ai peu d'intelligence ;
Je connais seulement la victoire et nos mœurs :
Les captives toujours ont suivi leurs vainqueurs ;
Cette délicatesse importune, étrangère,
Dément votre fortune et votre caractère.
Et qu'importe pour vous qu'une esclave de plus
Attende en gémissant vos ordres absolus ?

GENGIS.

Qui connaît mieux que moi jusqu'où va ma puissance ?
Je puis, je le sais trop, user de violence ;
Mais quel bonheur honteux, cruel, empoisonné,
D'assujettir un cœur qui ne s'est point donné,
De ne voir en des yeux, dont on sent les atteintes,
Qu'un nuage de pleurs et d'éternelles craintes,
Et de ne posséder, dans sa funeste ardeur,
Qu'une esclave tremblante à qui l'on fait horreur !
Les monstres des forêts qu'habitent nos Tartares
Ont des jours plus sereins, des amours moins barbares.
Enfin il faut tout dire ; Idamé prit sur moi
Un secret ascendant qui m'imposait la loi.
Je tremble que mon cœur aujourd'hui s'en souvienne ;
J'en étais indigné ; son ame eut sur la mienne,

Et sur mon caractère, et sur ma volonté,
Un empire plus sûr, et plus illimité,
Que je n'en ai reçu des mains de la victoire
Sur cent rois détrônés, accablés de ma gloire :
Voilà ce qui tantôt excitait mon dépit.
Je la veux pour jamais chasser de mon esprit ;
Je me rends tout entier à ma grandeur suprême ;
Je l'oublie : elle arrive ; elle triomphe, et j'aime.

SCÈNE V.

GENGIS, OCTAR, OSMAN.

GENGIS.

Eh bien ! que résout-elle ? et que m'apprenez-vous ?

OSMAN.

Elle est prête à périr auprès de son époux
Plutôt que découvrir l'asile impénétrable
Où leurs soins ont caché cet enfant misérable ;
Ils jurent d'affronter le plus cruel trépas.
Son époux la retient tremblante entre ses bras ;
Il soutient sa constance, il l'exhorte au supplice :
Ils demandent tous deux que la mort les unisse.
Tout un peuple autour d'eux pleure et frémit d'effroi.

GENGIS.

Idamé, dites-vous, attend la mort de moi ?
Ah ! rassurez son ame, et faites-lui connaître
Que ses jours sont sacrés, qu'ils sont chers à son maître.
C'en est assez ; volez.

SCÈNE VI.

GENGIS, OCTAR.

OCTAR.

Quels ordres donnez-vous
Sur cet enfant des rois qu'on dérobe à nos coups ?

GENGIS.

Aucun.

OCTAR.

Vous commandiez que notre vigilance
Aux mains d'Idamé même enlevât son enfance.

GENGIS.

Qu'on attende.

OCTAR.

On pourrait....

GENGIS.

Il ne peut m'échapper.

OCTAR.

Peut-être elle vous trompe.

GENGIS.

Elle ne peut tromper.

OCTAR.

Voulez-vous de ses rois conserver ce qui reste ?

GENGIS.

Je veux qu'Idamé vive ; ordonne tout le reste.
Va la trouver. Mais non, cher Octar, hâte-toi
De forcer son époux à fléchir sous ma loi :
C'est peu de cet enfant, c'est peu de son supplice ;
Il faut bien qu'il me fasse un plus grand sacrifice.

OCTAR.

Lui ?

GENGIS.

Sans doute; oui, lui-même.

OCTAR.

Et quel est votre espoir?

GENGIS.

De domter Idamé, de l'aimer, de la voir,
D'être aimé de l'ingrate, ou de me venger d'elle,
De la punir. Tu vois ma faiblesse nouvelle :
Emporté, malgré moi, par de contraires vœux,
Je frémis, et j'ignore encor ce que je veux.

FIN DU TROISIÈME ACTE.

ACTE QUATRIÈME.

SCÈNE I.

GENGIS, TROUPE DE GUERRIERS TARTARES.

GENGIS.

Ainsi la liberté, le repos, et la paix,
Ce but de mes travaux me fuira pour jamais ?
Je ne puis être à moi ! D'aujourd'hui je commence
A sentir tout le poids de ma triste puissance :
Je cherchais Idamé ; je ne vois près de moi
Que ces chefs importuns qui fatiguent leur roi.
(à sa suite.)
Allez : au pied des murs hâtez-vous de vous rendre ;
L'insolent Coréen ne pourra nous surprendre.
Ils ont proclamé roi cet enfant malheureux,
Et, sa tête à la main, je marcherai contre eux.
Pour la dernière fois que Zamti m'obéisse :
J'ai trop de cet enfant différé le supplice.
(il reste seul.)
Allez. Ces soins cruels, à mon sort attachés,
Gênent trop mes esprits d'un autre soin touchés :
Ce peuple à contenir, ces vainqueurs à conduire,
Des périls à prévoir, des complots à détruire ;
Que tout pèse à mon cœur en secret tourmenté !
Ah ! je fus plus heureux dans mon obscurité.

SCÈNE II.

GENGIS, OCTAR.

GENGIS.

Eh bien ! vous avez vu ce mandarin farouche ?

OCTAR.

Nul péril ne l'émeut, nul respect ne le touche.
Seigneur, en votre nom j'ai rougi de parler
A ce vil ennemi qu'il fallait immoler ;
D'un œil d'indifférence il a vu le supplice ;
Il répète les noms de devoir, de justice ;
Il brave la victoire : on dirait que sa voix
Du haut d'un tribunal nous dicte ici des lois.
Confondez avec lui son épouse rebelle ;
Ne vous abaissez point à soupirer pour elle ;
Et détournez les yeux de ce couple proscrit,
Qui vous ose braver quand la terre obéit.

GENGIS

Non, je ne reviens point encor de ma surprise :
Quels sont donc ces humains que mon bonheur maîtrise ?
Quels sont ces sentiments, qu'au fond de nos climats
Nous ignorions encore, et ne soupçonnions pas ?
A son roi, qui n'est plus, immolant la nature,
L'un voit périr son fils sans crainte et sans murmure ;
L'autre pour son époux est prête à s'immoler :
Rien ne peut les fléchir, rien ne les fait trembler.
Que dis-je ? si j'arrête une vue attentive
Sur cette nation désolée et captive,
Malgré moi je l'admire en lui donnant des fers :
Je vois que ses travaux ont instruit l'univers ;

ACTE IV, SCÈNE II.

ois un peuple antique, industrieux, immense.
rois sur la sagesse ont fondé leur puissance,
leurs voisins soumis heureux législateurs,
uvernant sans conquête, et régnant par les mœurs.
ciel ne nous donna que la force en partage ;
s arts sont les combats, détruire est notre ouvrage.
! de quoi m'ont servi tant de succès divers ?
el fruit me revient-il des pleurs de l'univers ?
us rougissons de sang le char de la victoire.
ut-être qu'en effet il est une autre gloire :
u cœur est en secret jaloux de leurs vertus ;
, vainqueur, je voudrais égaler les vaincus.

OCTAR.

uvez-vous de ce peuple admirer la faiblesse ?
uel mérite ont des arts enfants de la mollesse,
ui n'ont pu les sauver des fers et de la mort ?
e faible est destiné pour servir le plus fort :
out cède sur la terre aux travaux, au courage ;
ais c'est vous qui cédez, qui souffrez un outrage,
ous qui tendez les mains, malgré votre courroux,
je ne sais quels fers inconnus parmi nous ;
ous qui vous exposez à la plainte importune
e ceux dont la valeur a fait votre fortune.
es braves compagnons de vos travaux passés
erront-ils tant d'honneurs par l'amour effacés ?
eur grand cœur s'en indigne, et leurs fronts en rougissent :
eurs clameurs jusqu'à vous par ma voix retentissent ;
e vous parle en leur nom comme au nom de l'état.
xcusez un Tartare, excusez un soldat
Blanchi sous le harnois et dans votre service,
Qui ne peut supporter un amoureux caprice,
Et qui montre la gloire à vos yeux éblouis.

GENGIS.

Que l'on cherche Idamé.

OCTAR.

Vous voulez....

GENGIS.

Obéis:
De ton zèle hardi réprime la rudesse;
Je veux que mes sujets respectent ma faiblesse.

SCÈNE III.

GENGIS.

A mon sort à la fin je ne puis résister;
Le ciel me la destine; il n'en faut point douter.
Qu'ai-je fait, après tout, dans ma grandeur suprême?
J'ai fait des malheureux, et je le suis moi-même;
Et de tous ces mortels attachés à mon rang,
Avides de combats, prodigues de leur sang,
Un seul a-t-il jamais, arrêtant ma pensée,
Dissipé les chagrins de mon ame oppressée?
Tant d'états subjugués ont-ils rempli mon cœur?
Ce cœur, lassé de tout, demandait une erreur
Qui pût de mes ennuis chasser la nuit profonde,
Et qui me consolât sur le trône du monde.
Par ses tristes conseils Octar m'a révolté :
Je ne vois près de moi qu'un tas ensanglanté
De monstres affamés et d'assassins sauvages,
Disciplinés au meurtre, et formés aux ravages;
Ils sont nés pour la guerre, et non pas pour ma cour;
Je les prends en horreur, en connaissant l'amour :
Qu'ils combattent sous moi, qu'ils meurent à ma suite;
Mais qu'ils n'osent jamais juger de ma conduite.
Idamé ne vient point.... c'est elle, je la voi.

SCÈNE IV.

GENGIS, IDAMÉ.

IDAMÉ.

Quoi ! vous voulez jouir encor de mon effroi ?
Ah ! seigneur, épargnez une femme, une mère :
Ne rougissez-vous pas d'accabler ma misère ?

GENGIS.

Cessez à vos frayeurs de vous abandonner :
Votre époux peut se rendre, on peut lui pardonner ;
J'ai déjà suspendu l'effet de ma vengeance,
Et mon cœur pour vous seule a connu la clémence.
Peut-être ce n'est pas sans un ordre des cieux
Que mes prospérités m'ont conduit à vos yeux ;
Peut-être le destin voulut vous faire naître
Pour fléchir un vainqueur, pour captiver un maître,
Pour adoucir en moi cette âpre dureté
Des climats où mon sort en naissant m'a jeté.
Vous m'entendez, je règne, et vous pourriez reprendre
Un pouvoir que sur moi vous deviez peu prétendre.
Le divorce, en un mot, par mes lois est permis ;
Et le vainqueur du monde à vous seule est soumis.
S'il vous fut odieux, le trône a quelques charmes ;
Et le bandeau des rois peut essuyer des larmes.
L'intérêt de l'état et de vos citoyens
Vous presse autant que moi de former ces liens.
Ce langage, sans doute, a de quoi vous surprendre :
Sur les débris fumants des trônes mis en cendre,
Le destructeur des rois dans la poudre oubliés
Semblait n'être plus fait pour se voir à vos pieds :

Mais sachez qu'en ces lieux votre foi fut trompée;
Par un rival indigne elle fut usurpée :
Vous la devez, madame, au vainqueur des humains;
Témugin vient à vous vingt sceptres dans les mains.
Vous baissez vos regards, et je ne puis comprendre
Dans vos yeux interdits ce que je dois attendre :
Oubliez mon pouvoir, oubliez ma fierté;
Pesez vos intérêts, parlez en liberté.

IDAMÉ.

A tant de changements tour à tour condamnée,
Je ne le cèle point, vous m'avez étonnée :
Je vais, si je le puis, reprendre mes esprits;
Et, quand je répondrai, vous serez plus surpris.
Il vous souvient du temps et de la vie obscure
Où le ciel enfermait votre grandeur future;
L'effroi des nations n'était que Témugin;
L'univers n'était pas, seigneur, en votre main :
Elle étoit pure alors, et me fut présentée :
Apprenez qu'en ce temps je l'aurais acceptée.

GENGIS.

Ciel! que m'avez-vous dit? ô ciel! vous m'aimeriez!
Vous!

IDAMÉ.

J'ai dit que ces vœux, que vous me présentiez,
N'auraient point révolté mon ame assujettie,
Si les sages mortels à qui j'ai dû la vie
N'avaient fait à mon cœur un contraire devoir.
De nos parents sur nous vous savez le pouvoir;
Du Dieu que nous servons ils sont la vive image;
Nous leur obéissons en tout temps, en tout âge.
Cet empire détruit, qui dut être immortel,
Seigneur, était fondé sur le droit paternel,

Sur la foi de l'hymen, sur l'honneur, la justice,
Le respect des serments ; et, s'il faut qu'il périsse,
Si le sort l'abandonne à vos heureux forfaits,
L'esprit qui l'anima ne périra jamais.
Vos destins sont changés, mais le mien ne peut l'être.

GENGIS.

Quoi ! vous m'auriez aimé !

IDAMÉ.

C'est à vous de connaître
Que ce serait encore une raison de plus
Pour n'attendre de moi qu'un éternel refus.
Mon hymen est un nœud formé par le ciel même :
Mon époux m'est sacré ; je dirai plus, je l'aime.
Je le préfère à vous, au trône, à vos grandeurs.
Pardonnez mon aveu, mais respectez nos mœurs.
Ne pensez pas non plus que je mette ma gloire
A remporter sur vous cette illustre victoire,
A braver un vainqueur, à tirer vanité
De ces justes refus qui ne m'ont point coûté :
Je remplis mon devoir, et je me rends justice ;
Je ne fais point valoir un pareil sacrifice.
Portez ailleurs les dons que vous me proposez,
Détachez-vous d'un cœur qui les a méprisés :
Et, puisqu'il faut toujours qu'Idamé vous implore,
Permettez qu'à jamais mon époux les ignore.
De ce faible triomphe il serait moins flatté
Qu'indigné de l'outrage à ma fidélité.

GENGIS.

Il sait mes sentiments, madame ; il faut les suivre :
Il s'y conformera, s'il aime encore à vivre.

IDAMÉ.

Il en est incapable ; et si dans les tourments

Voltaire. Théâtre. 4.

La douleur égarait ses nobles sentiments,
Si son ame vaincue avait quelque mollesse,
Mon devoir et ma foi soutiendraient sa faiblesse;
De son cœur chancelant je deviendrais l'appui
En attestant des nœuds déshonorés par lui.

GENGIS.

Ce que je viens d'entendre, ô dieux! est-il croyable?
Quoi! lorsqu'envers vous-même il s'est rendu coupable,
Lorsque sa cruauté, par un barbare effort,
Vous arrachant un fils, l'a conduit à la mort.

IDAMÉ.

Il eut une vertu, seigneur, que je révère :
Il pensait en héros, je n'agissais qu'en mère;
Et, si j'étais injuste assez pour le haïr,
Je me respecte assez pour ne le point trahir.

GENGIS.

Tout m'étonne dans vous, mais aussi tout m'outrage :
J'adore avec dépit cet excès de courage;
Je vous aime encor plus quand vous me résistez;
Vous subjuguez mon cœur, et vous le révoltez.
Redoutez-moi; sachez que, malgré ma faiblesse,
Ma fureur peut aller plus loin que ma tendresse.

IDAMÉ.

Je sais qu'ici tout tremble ou périt par vos coups :
Les lois vivent encore, et l'emportent sur vous.

GENGIS.

Les lois! il n'en est plus : quelle erreur obstinée
Ose les alléguer contre ma destinée?
Il n'est ici de lois que celles de mon cœur,
Celles d'un souverain, d'un Scythe, d'un vainqueur :
Les lois que vous suivez m'ont été trop fatales...
Oui, lorsque dans ces lieux nos fortunes égales,

ACTE IV, SCÈNE IV.

Nos sentiments, nos cœurs l'un vers l'autre emportés,
(Car je le crois ainsi malgré vos cruautés)
Quand tout nous unissait, vos lois, que je déteste,
Ordonnèrent ma honte et votre hymen funeste.
Je les anéantis, je parle, c'est assez :
Imitez l'univers, madame, obéissez.
Vos mœurs que vous vantez, vos usages austères,
Sont un crime à mes yeux, quand ils me sont contraires.
Mes ordres sont donnés, et votre indigne époux
Doit remettre en mes mains votre empereur et vous :
Leurs jours me répondront de votre obéissance.
Pensez-y ; vous savez jusqu'où va ma vengeance ;
Et songez à quel prix vous pouvez désarmer
Un maître qui vous aime, et qui rougit d'aimer.

SCÈNE V.

IDAMÉ, ASSÉLI.

IDAMÉ.

Il me faut donc choisir leur perte ou l'infamie !
O pur sang de mes rois ! ô moitié de ma vie !
Cher époux, dans mes mains quand je tiens votre sort,
Ma voix sans balancer vous condamne à la mort.

ASSÉLI.

Ah ! reprenez plutôt cet empire suprême
Qu'aux beautés, aux vertus, attacha le ciel même ;
Ce pouvoir, qui soumit ce Scythe furieux
Aux lois de la raison qu'il lisait dans vos yeux.
Long-temps accoutumée à dompter sa colère,
Que ne pouvez-vous point puisque vous savez plaire ?

IDAMÉ.

Dans l'état où je suis c'est un malheur de plus.

ASSÉLI.

Vous seule adouciriez le destin des vaincus :
Dans nos calamités, le ciel, qui vous seconde,
Veut vous opposer seule à ce tyran du monde :
Vous avez vu tantôt son courage irrité
Se dépouiller pour vous de sa férocité.
Il aurait dû cent fois, il devrait même encore
Perdre dans votre époux un rival qu'il abhorre ;
Zamti pourtant respire après l'avoir bravé ;
A son épouse encore il n'est point enlevé.
On vous respecte en lui ; ce vainqueur sanguinaire
Sur les débris du monde a craint de vous déplaire.
Enfin souvenez-vous que dans ces mêmes lieux
Il sentit, le premier, le pouvoir de vos yeux :
Son amour autrefois fut pur et légitime.

IDAMÉ.

Arrête ; il ne l'est plus ; y penser est un crime.

SCÈNE VI.

ZAMTI, IDAMÉ, ASSÉLI.

IDAMÉ.

Ah ! dans ton infortune, et dans mon désespoir,
Suis-je encor ton épouse, et peux-tu me revoir ?

ZAMTI.

On le veut : du tyran tel est l'ordre funeste ;
Je dois à ses fureurs ce moment qui me reste.

IDAMÉ.

On t'a dit à quel prix ce tyran daigne enfin
Sauver tes tristes jours, et ceux de l'orphelin ?

ZAMTI.

Ne parlons pas des miens, laissons notre infortune.
Un citoyen n'est rien dans la perte commune ;

ACTE IV, SCÈNE VI.

Il doit s'anéantir. Idamé, souviens-toi
Que mon devoir unique est de sauver mon roi ;
Nous lui devions nos jours, nos services, notre être,
Tout jusqu'au sang d'un fils qui naquit pour son maître.
Mais l'honneur est un bien que nous ne devons pas.
Cependant l'orphelin n'attend que le trépas ;
Mes soins l'ont enfermé dans ces asiles sombres
Où des rois ses aïeux on révère les ombres ;
La mort, si nous tardons, l'y dévore avec eux.
En vain des Coréens le prince généreux
Attend ce cher dépôt que lui promit mon zèle.
Étan, de son salut ce ministre fidèle,
Étan, ainsi que moi, se voit chargé de fers.
Toi seule à l'orphelin restes dans l'univers ;
C'est à toi maintenant de conserver sa vie,
Et ton fils, et ta gloire à mon honneur unie.

IDAMÉ.

Ordonne ; que veux-tu ? que faut-il ?

ZAMTI.

      M'oublier,
Vivre pour ton pays, lui tout sacrifier.
Ma mort, en éteignant les flambeaux d'hyménée,
Est un arrêt des cieux qui fait ta destinée.
Il n'est plus d'autres soins ni d'autres lois pour nous :
L'honneur d'être fidèle aux cendres d'un époux
Ne saurait balancer une gloire plus belle.
C'est au prince, à l'état qu'il faut être fidèle.
Remplissons de nos rois les ordres absolus ;
Je leur donnai mon fils, je leur donne encor plus.
Libre par mon trépas, enchaîne ce Tartare ;
Éteins sur mon tombeau les foudres du barbare :
Je commence à sentir la mort avec horreur

Quand ma mort t'abandonne à cet usurpateur;
Je fais en frémissant ce sacrifice impie;
Mais mon devoir l'épure, et mon trépas l'expie;
Il était nécessaire autant qu'il est affreux.
Idamé, sers de mère à ton roi malheureux;
Règne; que ton roi vive, et que ton époux meure;
Règne, dis-je, à ce prix : oui, je le veux....

IDAMÉ.

Demeure.

Me connais-tu ? veux-tu que ce funeste rang
Soit le prix de ma honte, et le prix de ton sang ?
Penses-tu que je sois moins épouse que mère ?
Tu t'abuses, cruel; et ta vertu sévère
A commis contre moi deux crimes en un jour,
Qui font frémir tous deux la nature et l'amour.
Barbare envers ton fils, et plus envers moi-même,
Ne te souvient-il plus qui je suis, et qui t'aime ?
Crois-moi; dans nos malheurs il est un sort plus beau,
Un plus noble chemin pour descendre au tombeau.
Soit amour, soit mépris, le tyran qui m'offense,
Sur moi, sur mes desseins, n'est pas en défiance :
Dans ces remparts fumants, et de sang abreuvés,
Je suis libre, et mes pas ne sont point observés ;
Le chef des Coréens s'ouvre un secret passage
Non loin de ces tombeaux, où ce précieux gage
A l'œil qui le poursuit fut caché par tes mains :
De ces tombeaux sacrés je sais tous les chemins ;
Je cours y ranimer sa languissante vie,
Le rendre aux défenseurs armés pour la patrie,
Le porter en mes bras dans leurs rangs belliqueux
Comme un présent d'un dieu qui combat avec eux.
Nous mourrons, je le sais, mais tout couverts de gloire

Nous laisserons de nous une illustre mémoire.
Mettons nos noms obscurs au rang des plus grands noms,
Et juge si mon cœur a suivi tes leçons.

ZAMTI.

Tu l'inspires, grand dieu ! que ton bras la soutienne !
Idamé, ta vertu l'emporte sur la mienne ;
Toi seule as mérité que les cieux attendris
Daignent sauver par toi ton prince et ton pays.

FIN DU QUATRIÈME ACTE.

ACTE CINQUIÈME.

SCÈNE I.
IDAMÉ, ASSÉLI.

ASSÉLI.

Quoi! rien n'a résisté! tout a fui sans retour!
Quoi! je vous vois deux fois sa captive en un jour!
Fallait-il affronter ce conquérant sauvage?
Sur les faibles mortels il a trop d'avantage.
Une femme, un enfant, des guerriers sans vertu!
Que pouviez-vous? hélas!

IDAMÉ.

              J'ai fait ce que j'ai dû.
Tremblante pour mon fils, sans force, inanimée,
J'ai porté dans mes bras l'empereur à l'armée.
Son aspect a d'abord animé les soldats :
Mais Gengis a marché; la mort suivait ses pas ;
Et des enfants du Nord la horde ensanglantée
Aux fers dont je sortais m'a soudain rejetée.
C'en est fait.

ASSÉLI.

        Ainsi donc ce malheureux enfant
Retombe entre ses mains, et meurt presque en naissant :
Votre époux avec lui termine sa carrière.

IDAMÉ.

L'un et l'autre bientôt voit son heure dernière.
Si l'arrêt de la mort n'est point porté contre eux,
C'est pour leur préparer des tourments plus affreux.

ACTE V, SCENE I.

Mon fils, ce fils si cher, va les suivre peut-être.
Devant ce fier vainqueur il m'a fallu paraître;
Tout fumant de carnage, il m'a fait appeler,
Pour jouir de mon trouble, et pour mieux m'accabler.
Ses regards inspiraient l'horreur et l'épouvante.
Vingt fois il a levé sa main toute sanglante
Sur le fils de mes rois, sur mon fils malheureux.
Je me suis en tremblant jetée au-devant d'eux;
Tout en pleurs, à ses pieds je me suis prosternée;
Mais lui me repoussant d'une main forcénée,
La menace à la bouche, et détournant les yeux,
Il est sorti pensif, et rentré furieux;
Et s'adressant aux siens d'une voix oppressée,
Il leur criait vengeance, et changeait de pensée;
Tandis qu'autour de lui ses barbares soldats
Semblaient lui demander l'ordre de mon trépas.

ASSÉLI.

Pensez-vous qu'il donnât un ordre si funeste?
Il laisse vivre encor votre époux, qu'il déteste;
L'orphelin aux bourreaux n'est point abandonné.
Daignez demander grâce, et tout est pardonné.

IDAMÉ.

Non, ce féroce amour est tourné tout en rage.
Ah! si tu l'avais vu redoubler mon outrage,
M'assurer de sa haine, insulter à mes pleurs!

ASSÉLI.

Et vous doutez encor d'asservir ses fureurs?
Ce lion subjugué qui rugit dans sa chaîne,
S'il ne vous aimait pas, parlerait moins de haine.

IDAMÉ.

Qu'il m'aime ou me haïsse, il est temps d'achever
Des jours que sans horreur je ne puis conserver.

ASSÉLI.

Ah ! que résolvez-vous ?

IDAMÉ.

Quand le ciel en colère
De ceux qu'il persécute a comblé la misère,
Il les soutient souvent dans le sein des douleurs,
Et leur donne un courage égal à leurs malheurs.
J'ai pris dans l'horreur même où je suis parvenue
Une force nouvelle à mon cœur inconnue.
Va, je ne craindrai plus ce vainqueur des humains ;
Je dépendrai de moi : mon sort est dans mes mains.

ASSÉLI.

Mais ce fils, cet objet de crainte et de tendresse,
L'abandonnerez-vous ?

IDAMÉ.

Tu me rends ma faiblesse,
Tu me perces le cœur. Ah ! sacrifice affreux !
Que n'avais-je point fait pour ce fils malheureux !
Mais Gengis, après tout, dans sa grandeur altière,
Environné de rois couchés dans la poussière,
Ne recherchera point un enfant ignoré
Parmi les malheureux dans la foule égaré ;
Ou peut-être il verra d'un regard moins sévère
Cet enfant innocent dont il aima la mère :
A cet espoir au moins mon triste cœur se rend ;
C'est une illusion que j'embrasse en mourant.
Haïra-t-il ma cendre, après m'avoir aimée ?
Dans la nuit de la tombe en serai-je opprimée ?
Poursuivra-t-il mon fils ?

SCÈNE II.

IDAMÉ, ASSÉLI, OCTAR.

OCTAR.

IDAME, demeurez :
Attendez l'empereur en ces lieux retirés.
(à sa suite.)
Veillez sur ces enfants ; et vous à cette porte,
Tartares, empêchez qu'aucun n'entre & ne sorte.
(à Asséli.)
Eloignez-vous.

IDAMÉ.

Seigneur, il veut encor me voir !
J'obéis, il le faut, je cède à son pouvoir.
Si j'obtenais du moins, avant de voir un maître,
Qu'un moment à mes yeux mon époux pût paraître,
Peut-être du vainqueur les esprits ramenés
Rendraient enfin justice à deux infortunés.
Je sens que je hasarde une prière vaine :
La victoire est chez vous implacable, inhumaine ;
Mais enfin la pitié, seigneur, en vos climats,
Est-elle un sentiment qu'on ne connaisse pas ?
Et ne puis-je implorer votre voix favorable ?

OCTAR.

Quand l'arrêt est porté, qui conseille est coupable.
Vous n'êtes plus ici sous vos antiques rois,
Qui laissent désarmer la rigueur de leurs lois.
D'autres temps, d'autres mœurs : ici règnent les armes ;
Nous ne connaissons point les prières, les larmes.
On commande, et la terre écoute avec terreur,
Demeurez, attendez l'ordre de l'empereur.

SCÈNE III.

IDAMÉ.

Dieu des infortunés, qui voyez mon outrage,
Dans ces extrémités soutenez mon courage ;
Versez du haut des cieux, dans ce cœur consterné,
Les vertus de l'époux que vous m'avez donné.

SCÈNE IV.

GENGIS, IDAMÉ.

GENGIS.

Non, je n'ai point assez déployé ma colère,
Assez humilié votre orgueil téméraire,
Assez fait de reproche aux infidélités
Dont votre ingratitude a payé mes bontés.
Vous n'avez pas conçu l'excès de votre crime,
Ni tout votre danger, ni l'horreur qui m'anime,
Vous, que j'avais aimée, et que je dus haïr,
Vous, qui me trahissiez, et que je dois punir.

IDAMÉ.

Ne punissez que moi ; c'est la grâce dernière
Que j'ose demander à la main meurtrière
Dont j'espérais en vain fléchir la cruauté.
Éteignez dans mon sang votre inhumanité.
Vengez-vous d'une femme à son devoir fidèle ;
Finissez ses tourments.

GENGIS.
    Je ne le puis, cruelle ;
Les miens sont plus affreux, je les veux terminer.
Je viens pour vous punir, je puis tout pardonner.

ACTE V, SCÈNE IV.

Moi, pardonner ! à vous ! non, craignez ma vengeance :
Je tiens le fils des rois, le vôtre, en ma puissance.
De votre indigne époux je ne vous parle pas ;
Depuis que vous l'aimez, je lui dois le trépas :
Il me trahit, me brave, il ose être rebelle.
Mille morts punissaient sa fraude criminelle :
Vous retenez mon bras, et j'en suis indigné ;
Oui, jusqu'à ce moment le traître est épargné.
Mais je ne prétends plus supplier ma captive.
Il le faut oublier, si vous voulez qu'il vive.
Rien n'excuse à présent votre cœur obstiné :
Il n'est plus votre époux, puisqu'il est condamné ;
Il a péri pour vous : votre chaîne odieuse
Va se rompre à jamais par une mort honteuse.
C'est vous qui m'y forcez ; et je ne conçois pas
Le scrupule insensé qui le livre au trépas.
Tout couvert de son sang, je devais sur sa cendre
A mes vœux absolus vous forcer de vous rendre ;
Mais sachez qu'un barbare, un Scythe, un destructeur,
A quelques sentiments dignes de votre cœur.
Le destin, croyez-moi, nous devait l'un à l'autre ;
Et mon ame a l'orgueil de régner sur la vôtre.
Abjurez votre hymen, et dans le même temps
Je place votre fils au rang de mes enfants.
Vous tenez dans vos mains plus d'une destinée ;
Du rejeton des rois l'enfance condamnée,
Votre époux, qu'à la mort un mot peut arracher,
Les honneurs les plus hauts tout prêts à le chercher,
Le destin de son fils, le vôtre, le mien même,
Tout dépendra de vous, puisqu'enfin je vous aime.
Oui, je vous aime encor ; mais ne présumez pas
D'armer contre mes vœux l'orgueil de vos appas ;

Gardez-vous d'insulter à l'excès de faiblesse
Que déja mon courroux reproche à ma tendresse.
C'est un danger pour vous que l'aveu que je fais :
Tremblez de mon amour, tremblez de mes bienfaits.
Mon ame à la vengeance est trop accoutumée ;
Et je vous punirais de vous avoir aimée.
Pardonnez : je menace encore en soupirant ;
Achevez d'adoucir ce courroux qui se rend :
Vous ferez d'un seul mot le sort de cet empire ;
Mais ce mot important, madame, il faut le dire :
Prononcez sans tarder, sans feinte, sans détour,
Si je vous dois enfin ma haine ou mon amour.

IDAMÉ.

L'une et l'autre aujourd'hui serait trop condamnable ;
Votre haine est injuste et votre amour coupable ;
Cet amour est indigne et de vous et de moi :
Vous me devez justice ; et, si vous êtes roi,
Je la veux, je l'attends pour moi contre vous-même.
Je suis loin de braver votre grandeur suprême ;
Je la rappelle en vous, lorsque vous l'oubliez ;
Et vous-même en secret vous me justifiez.

GENGIS.

Eh bien ! vous le voulez ; vous choisissez ma haine,
Vous l'aurez ; et déja je la retiens à peine :
Je ne vous connais plus ; et mon juste courroux
Me rend la cruauté que j'oubliais pour vous.
Votre époux, votre prince, et votre fils, cruelle,
Vont payer de leur sang votre fierté rebelle.
Ce mot que je voulais les a tous condamnés.
C'en est fait, et c'est vous qui les assassinez.

IDAMÉ.

Barbare !

ACTE V, SCÈNE IV.

GENGIS.

Je le suis ; j'allais cesser de l'être :
Vous aviez un amant, vous n'avez plus qu'un maître
Un ennemi sanglant, féroce, sans pitié,
Dont la haine est égale à votre inimitié.

IDAMÉ.

Eh bien ! je tombe aux pieds de ce maître sévère :
Le ciel l'a fait mon roi ; seigneur, je le révère :
Je demande à genoux une grâce de lui.

GENGIS.

Inhumaine, est-ce à vous d'en attendre aujourd'hui ?
Levez-vous : je suis prêt encore à vous entendre.
Pourrai-je me flatter d'un sentiment plus tendre ?
Que voulez-vous ? parlez.

IDAMÉ.

   Seigneur, qu'il soit permis
Qu'en secret mon époux près de moi soit admis,
Que je lui parle.

GENGIS.

 Vous !

IDAMÉ.

  Écoutez ma prière.
Cet entretien sera ma ressource dernière :
Vous jugerez après si j'ai dû résister.

GENGIS.

Non, ce n'était pas lui qu'il fallait consulter :
Mais je veux bien encor souffrir cette entrevue.
Je crois qu'à la raison son ame enfin rendue
N'osera plus prétendre à cet honneur fatal
De me désobéir, et d'être mon rival.
Il m'enleva son prince, il vous a possédée.
Que de crimes ! Sa grâce est encore accordée :

Qu'il la tienne de vous, qu'il vous doive son sort;
Présentez à ses yeux le divorce ou la mort :
Oui ; j'y consens. Octar, veillez à cette porte.
Vous, suivez-moi. Quel soin m'abaisse et me transporte!
Faut-il encore aimer ? est-ce là mon destin ?

(il sort.)

IDAMÉ.

Je renais, et je sens s'affermir dans mon sein
Cette intrépidité dont je doutais encore.

SCÈNE V.

ZAMTI, IDAMÉ.

IDAMÉ.

O toi, qui me tiens lieu de ce ciel que j'implore,
Mortel plus respectable et plus grand à mes yeux
Que tous ces conquérants dont l'homme a fait des dieux;
L'horreur de nos destins ne t'est que trop connue;
La mesure est comblée, et notre heure est venue.

ZAMTI.

Je le sais.

IDAMÉ.

   C'est en vain que tu voulus deux fois
Sauver le rejeton de nos malheureux rois.

ZAMTI.

Il n'y faut plus penser, l'espérance est perdue ;
De tes devoirs sacrés tu remplis l'étendue :
Je mourrai consolé.

IDAMÉ.

   Que deviendra mon fils ?
Pardonne encor ce mot à mes sens attendris,
Pardonne à ces soupirs ; ne vois que mon courage.

ACTE V, SCÈNE V.

ZAMTI.

Nos rois sont au tombeau, tout est dans l'esclavage.
Va, crois-moi, ne plaignons que les infortunés
Qu'à respirer encor le ciel a condamnés.

IDAMÉ.

La mort la plus honteuse est ce qu'on te prépare.

ZAMTI.

Sans doute; et j'attendais les ordres du barbare:
Ils ont tardé long-temps.

IDAMÉ.

Eh bien! écoute-moi:
Ne saurons-nous mourir que par l'ordre d'un roi?
Les taureaux aux autels tombent en sacrifice;
Les criminels tremblants sont traînés au supplice;
Les mortels généreux disposent de leur sort:
Pourquoi des mains d'un maître attendre ici la mort?
L'homme était-il donc né pour tant de dépendance?
De nos voisins altiers imitons la constance;
De la nature humaine ils soutiennent les droits,
Vivent libres chez eux, et meurent à leur choix;
Un affront leur suffit pour sortir de la vie,
Et plus que le néant ils craignent l'infamie.
Le hardi Japonais n'attend pas qu'au cercueil
Un despote insolent le plonge d'un coup-d'œil.
Nous avons enseigné ces braves insulaires;
Apprenons d'eux enfin des vertus nécessaires;
Sachons mourir comme eux.

ZAMTI.

Je t'approuve, et je crois
Que le malheur extrême est au-dessus des lois.
J'avais déja conçu tes desseins magnanimes,

Mais seuls et désarmés, esclaves et victimes,
Courbés sous nos tyrans, nous attendons leurs coups.

IDAMÉ, *en tirant un poignard.*

Tiens, sois libre avec moi ; frappe, et délivre-nous.

ZAMTI.

Ciel !

IDAMÉ.

Déchire ce sein, ce cœur qu'on déshonore.
J'ai tremblé que ma main, mal affermie encore,
Ne portât sur moi-même un coup mal assuré.
Enfonce dans ce cœur un bras moins égaré ;
Immole avec courage une épouse fidèle ;
Tout couvert de mon sang, tombe et meurs auprès d'elle ;
Qu'à mes derniers moments j'embrasse mon époux ;
Que le tyran le voie, et qu'il en soit jaloux.

ZAMTI.

Grâce au ciel, jusqu'au bout ta vertu persévère ;
Voilà de ton amour la marque la plus chère.
Digne épouse, reçois mes éternels adieux ;
Donne ce glaive, donne, et détourne les yeux.

IDAMÉ, *en lui donnant le poignard.*

Tiens, commence par moi ; tu le dois : tu balances !

ZAMTI.

Je ne puis.

IDAMÉ.

Je le veux.

ZAMTI.

Je frémis.

IDAMÉ.

Tu m'offenses.

Frappe, et tourne sur toi tes bras ensanglantés.

ZAMTI.

Eh bien ! imite-moi.

IDAMÉ, *lui saisissant le bras.*
Frappe, dis-je...

SCÈNE VI.

GENGIS, OCTAR, IDAMÉ, ZAMTI, GARDES.

GENGIS, *accompagné de ses gardes, et désarmant Zamti.*

ARRÊTEZ,
Arrêtez, malheureux ! O ciel ! qu'alliez-vous faire ?

IDAMÉ.

Nous délivrer de toi, finir notre misère,
A tant d'atrocités dérober notre sort.

ZAMTI.

Veux-tu nous envier jusques à notre mort ?

GENGIS.

Oui.... Dieu, maître des rois, à qui mon cœur s'adresse,
Témoin de mes affronts, témoin de ma faiblesse,
Toi qui mis à mes pieds tant d'états, tant de rois,
Deviendrai-je à la fin digne de mes exploits ?
Tu m'outrages, Zamti ; tu l'emportes encore
Dans un cœur né pour moi, dans un cœur que j'adore.
Ton épouse à mes yeux, victime de sa foi,
Veut mourir de ta main plutôt que d'être à moi.
Vous apprendrez tous deux à souffrir mon empire,
Peut-être à faire plus.

IDAMÉ.

Que prétends-tu nous dire ?

ZAMTI.

Quel est ce nouveau trait de l'inhumanité ?

IDAMÉ.

D'où vient que notre arrêt n'est pas encor porté ?

GENGIS.

Il va l'être, madame, et vous allez l'apprendre.
Vous me rendiez justice, et je vais vous la rendre.
A peine dans ces lieux je crois ce que j'ai vu :
Tous deux je vous admire, et vous m'avez vaincu.
Je rougis, sur le trône où m'a mis la victoire,
D'être au-dessous de vous au milieu de ma gloire.
En vain par mes exploits j'ai su me signaler ;
Vous m'avez avili : je veux vous égaler.
J'ignorais qu'un mortel pût se domter lui-même ;
Je l'apprends ; je vous dois cette gloire suprême :
Jouissez de l'honneur d'avoir pu me changer.
Je viens vous réunir ; je viens vous protéger.
Veillez, heureux époux, sur l'innocente vie
De l'enfant de vos rois, que ma main vous confie ;
Par le droit des combats j'en pouvais disposer ;
Je vous remets ce droit, dont j'allais abuser.
Croyez qu'à cet enfant, heureux dans sa misère,
Ainsi qu'à votre fils, je tiendrai lieu de père.
Vous verrez si l'on peut se fier à ma foi.
Je fus un conquérant, vous m'avez fait un roi.

(à Zamti.)

Soyez ici des lois l'interprète suprême ;
Rendez leur ministère aussi saint que vous-même ;
Enseignez la raison, la justice, et les mœurs.
Que les peuples vaincus gouvernent les vainqueurs.
Que la sagesse règne, et préside au courage ;
Triomphez de la force, elle vous doit hommage :
J'en donnerai l'exemple, et votre souverain
Se soumet à vos lois les armes à la main.

IDAMÉ.
Ciel! que viens-je d'entendre? Hélas! puis-je vous croire?
ZAMTI.
Êtes-vous digne enfin, seigneur, de votre gloire?
Ah! vous ferez aimer votre joug aux vaincus.
IDAMÉ.
Qui peut vous inspirer ce dessein?
GENGIS.
     Vos vertus.

FIN DE L'ORPHELIN DE LA CHINE.

TANCRÈDE,

TRAGÉDIE,

Représentée, pour la première fois, le 3 septembre 1760.

A MADAME LA MARQUISE
DE POMPADOUR.

Madame,

Toutes les épîtres dédicatoires ne sont pas de lâches flatteries, toutes ne sont pas dictées par l'intérêt; celle que vous reçûtes de M. Crébillon, mon confrère à l'académie, et mon premier maître dans un art que j'ai toujours aimé, fut un monument de sa reconnaissance; le mien durera moins, mais il est aussi juste. J'ai vu dès votre enfance les grâces et les talents se développer; j'ai reçu de vous, dans tous les temps, des témoignages d'une bonté toujours égale. Si quelque censeur pouvait désapprouver l'hommage que je vous rends, ce ne pourrait être qu'un cœur né ingrat. Je vous dois beaucoup, Madame, et je dois le dire. J'ose encore plus, j'ose vous remercier publiquement du bien que vous avez fait à un très grand nombre de véritables gens de lettres, de grands artistes, d'hommes de mérite en plus d'un genre.

Les cabales sont affreuses, je le sais ; la littérature en sera toujours troublée, ainsi que tous les autres états de la vie. On calomniera toujours les gens de lettres comme les gens en place; et j'avouerai que l'horreur pour ces cabales m'a fait prendre le parti de la retraite, qui seule m'a rendu heureux. Mais j'avoue en même temps que vous n'avez jamais écouté aucune de ces petites factions, que jamais vous ne reçûtes d'impression de l'imposture secrète qui blesse sourdement le mérite, ni de l'imposture publique qui l'attaque insolemment. Vous avez fait du bien avec discernement, parce que vous avez jugé par vous-même ; aussi je n'ai connu ni aucun homme de lettres, ni aucune personne sans prévention, qui ne rendît justice à votre caractère, non seulement en public, mais dans les conversations particulières, où l'on blâme beaucoup plus qu'on ne loue. Croyez, Madame, que c'est quelque chose que le suffrage de ceux qui savent penser.

De tous les arts que nous cultivons en France, l'art de la tragédie n'est pas cel qui mérite le moins l'attention publique; car il faut avouer que c'est celui dans lequel les Français se sont le plus distingués. C'est d'ailleurs, au théâtre seul que la nation se rassemble; c'est là que l'esprit et le goût de la jeunesse se forment : les étrangers y viennent apprendre notre langue; nulle mauvaise maxime n'y est tolérée, et nul sentiment estimable n'y est débité sans être applaudi ; c'est une école toujours subsistante de poésie et de vertu.

La tragédie n'est pas encore peut-être tout-à-fait ce qu'elle doit être; supérieure à celle d'Athènes en plusieurs endroits, il lui manque ce grand appareil que les magistrats d'Athènes savaient lui donner.

Permettez-moi, Madame, en vous dédiant une tragédie, de m'étendre sur cet art des Sophocle et des Euripide. Je sais que toute la pompe de l'appareil ne vaut pas une pensée sublime, ou un sentiment; de même que la parure n'est presque rien sans la beauté. Je sais bien que ce n'est pas un grand mérite de parler aux yeux; mais j'ose être sûr que le sublime et le touchant portent un coup beaucoup plus sensible, quand ils sont soutenus d'un appareil convenable, et qu'il faut frapper l'ame et les yeux à la fois. Ce sera le partage des génies qui viendront après nous. J'aurai du moins encouragé ceux qui me feront oublier.

C'est dans cet esprit, Madame, que je dessinai la faible esquisse que je soumets à vos lumières. Je la crayonnai dès que je sus que le théâtre de Paris était changé, et devenait un vrai spectacle. Des jeunes gens de beaucoup de talent la représentèrent avec moi sur un petit théâtre que je fis faire à la campagne. Quoique ce théâtre fût extrêmement étroit, les acteurs ne furent point gênés; tout fut exécuté facilement; ces boucliers, ces devises, ces armes qu'on suspendait dans la lice, faisaient un effet qui redoublait l'intérêt, parce que cette décoration, cette action devenait une partie de l'intrigue. Il eût fallu que la pièce eût joint à cet avantage celui d'être écrite avec plus de chaleur, que j'eusse pu éviter les longs récits, que les vers eussent été faits avec plus de soin. Mais le temps où nous nous étions proposé de nous donner ce divertissement ne permettait pas de délai; la pièce fut faite et apprise en deux mois.

Mes amis me mandent que les comédiens de Paris ne l'ont représentée que parce qu'il en courait une grande quantité de copies infidèles. Il a donc fallu la laisser paraître avec tous les défauts que je n'ai pu corriger : mais ces défauts même instruiront ceux qui voudront travailler dans le même goût.

Il y a encore dans cette pièce une autre nouveauté qui me paraît mériter d'être perfectionnée ; elle est écrite en vers croisés. Cette sorte de poésie sauve l'uniformité de la rime ; mais aussi ce genre d'écrire est dangereux, car tout a son écueil. Ces grands tableaux, que les anciens regardaient comme une partie essentielle de la tragédie, peuvent aisément nuire au théâtre de France, en le réduisant à n'être presque qu'une vaine décoration ; et la sorte de vers que j'ai employés dans Tancrède approche peut-être trop de la prose. Ainsi il pourrait arriver qu'en voulant perfectionner la scène française, on la gâterait entièrement. Il se peut qu'on y ajoute un mérite qui lui manque, il se peut qu'on la corrompe.

J'insiste seulement sur une chose, c'est la variété dont on a besoin dans une ville immense, la seule de la terre qui ait jamais eu des spectacles tous les jours. Tant que nous saurons maintenir par cette variété le mérite de notre scène, ce talent nous rendra toujours agréables aux autres peuples; c'est ce qui fait que des personnes de la plus haute distinction représentent souvent nos ouvrages dramatiques, en Allemagne, en Italie, qu'on les traduit même en Angleterre, tandis que nous voyons dans nos provinces des salles de spectacles magnifiques, comme on voyait des cirques dans toutes les provinces romaines; preuve incontestable du goût qui subsiste parmi nous, et preuve de nos ressources dans les temps les plus difficiles. C'est en vain que plusieurs de nos compatriotes s'efforcent d'annoncer notre décadence en tout genre. Je ne suis pas de l'avis de ceux qui, au sortir du spectacle, dans un souper délicieux, dans le sein du luxe et du plaisir, disent gaiement que tout est perdu; je suis assez près d'une ville de province, aussi peuplée que Rome moderne, et beaucoup plus opulente, qui entretient plus de quarante mille ouvriers, et qui vient de construire en même temps le plus bel hôpital du royaume, et le plus beau théâtre. De bonne foi, tout cela existerait-il si les campagnes ne produisaient que des ronces?

J'ai choisi pour mon habitation un des moins bons terrains qui soient en France; cependant rien ne nous y manque : le pays est orné de maisons qu'on eût regardées autrefois comme trop belles; le pauvre qui veut s'occuper y cesse d'être pauvre; cette petite province est devenue un jardin riant. Il vaut mieux, sans doute, fertiliser sa terre, que de se plaindre à Paris de la stérilité de sa terre.

Me voilà, Madame, un peu loin de Tancrède : j'abuse du droit de mon âge, j'abuse de vos moments, je tombe dans les digressions, je dis peu en beaucoup de paroles. Ce n'est pas là le caractère de votre esprit; mais je serais plus diffus si je m'abandonnais aux sentiments de ma reconnaissance. Recevez avec votre bonté ordinaire, Madame, mon attachement et mon respect, que rien ne peut altérer jamais.

PERSONNAGES.

ARGIRE,
TANCRÈDE,
ORBASSAN, } chevaliers.
LOREDAN,
CATANE,
ALDAMON, soldat.
AMÉNAÏDE, fille d'Argire.
FANIE, suivante d'Aménaïde.
PLUSIEURS CHEVALIERS, assistant au conseil.
ÉCUYERS, SOLDATS, PEUPLE.

La scène est à Syracuse, d'abord dans le palais d'Argire et dans une salle du conseil, ensuite dans la place publique sur laquelle cette salle est construite. L'époque de l'action est de l'année 1005. Les Sarrasins d'Afrique avaient conquis toute la Sicile au neuvième siècle; Syracuse avait secoué leur joug. Des gentilshommes normands commencèrent à s'établir vers Salerne, dans la Pouille. Les empereurs grecs possédaient Messine; les Arabes tenaient Palerme et Agrigente.

TANCRÈDE,
TRAGÉDIE.

ACTE PREMIER.

SCÈNE I.

ASSEMBLÉE DES CHEVALIERS RANGÉS EN DEMI-CERCLE.

ARGIRE.

Illustres chevaliers, vengeurs de la Sicile,
Qui daignez, par égard au déclin de mes ans,
Vous assembler chez moi pour chasser nos tyrans,
Et former un état triomphant et tranquille ;
Syracuse en ses murs a gémi trop long-temps
Des desseins avortés d'un courage inutile.
Il est temps de marcher à ces fiers Musulmans ;
Il est temps de sauver d'un naufrage funeste
Le plus grand de nos biens, le plus cher qui nous reste,
Le droit le plus sacré des mortels généreux,
La liberté : c'est là que tendent tous nos vœux.
Deux puissants ennemis de notre république,
Des droits des nations, du bonheur des humains,
Les Césars de Byzance, et les fiers Sarrasins,
Nous menacent encor de leur joug tyrannique.
Ces despotes altiers, partageant l'univers,
Se disputent l'honneur de nous donner des fers.
Le Grec a sous ses lois les peuples de Messine ;
Le hardi Solamir insolemment domine

Sur les fertiles champs couronnés par l'Etna,
Dans les murs d'Agrigente, aux campagnes d'Enna;
Et tout de Syracuse annonçait la ruine.
Mais nos communs tyrans, l'un de l'autre jaloux,
Armés pour nous détruire, ont combattu pour nous;
Ils ont perdu leur force en disputant leur proie.
A notre liberté le ciel ouvre une voie;
Le moment est propice, il en faut profiter.
La grandeur musulmane est à son dernier âge;
On commence en Europe à la moins redouter.
Dans la France un Martel, en Espagne un Pélage,
Le grand Léon [1] dans Rome, armé d'un saint courage,
Nous ont assez appris comme on peut la domter.

---

[1] Par le grand Léon, M. de Voltaire entend Léon IV, et non le pape Léon I, connu dans les cloîtres sous le nom de saint Léon, de Léon le grand. Ce saint Léon est le premier pape qui ait approuvé le supplice des hérétiques. Il dit dans ses lettres que le tyran Maxime, en punissant de mort Priscillien, a rendu un grand service à l'église; et il poursuivit avec violence ce qui restait de priscillianistes en Espagne. Les légendaires racontent qu'un jour une femme lui ayant baisé la main, il sentit un mouvement de concupiscence; qu'en conséquence il se coupa la main. Mais la vierge la lui rendit quelques jours après, afin qu'il pût célébrer la messe. C'est depuis ce temps qu'on baise les pieds du pape, attendu que, le pied étant enveloppé dans une pantoufle, le saint-père court moins de risque d'être obligé de se le couper. On sent bien que ce n'est pas à ce pape que M. de Voltaire a pu donner le nom de Grand. D'ailleurs saint Léon vivait plusieurs siècles avant l'époque où la tragédie de Tancrède est placée.

Je sais qu'aux factions Syracuse livrée
N'a qu'une liberté faible et mal assurée.
Je ne veux point ici vous rappeler ces temps
Où nous tournions sur nous nos armes criminelles,
Où l'état répandait le sang de ses enfants.
Étouffons dans l'oubli nos indignes querelles.
Orbassan, qu'il ne soit qu'un parti parmi nous,
Celui du bien public, et du salut de tous.
Que de notre union l'état puisse renaître;
Et, si de nos égaux nous fûmes trop jaloux,
Vivons et périssons sans avoir eu de maître.

ORBASSAN.

Argire, il est trop vrai que les divisions
Ont régné trop long-temps entre nos deux maisons :
L'état en fut troublé; Syracuse n'aspire
Qu'à voir les Orbassans unis au sang d'Argire.
Aujourd'hui l'un par l'autre il faut nous protéger.
En citoyen zélé j'accepte votre fille ;
Je servirai l'état, vous, et votre famille ;
Et, du pied des autels où je vais m'engager,
Je marche à Solamir, et je cours vous venger.
Mais ce n'est pas assez de combattre le Maure;
Sur d'autres ennemis il faut jeter les yeux :
Il fut d'autres tyrans non moins pernicieux,
Que peut-être un vil peuple ose chérir encore.
De quel droit les Français, portant partout leurs pas,
Se sont-ils établis dans nos riches climats ?
De quel droit un Coucy [1] vint-il dans Syracuse,
Des rives de la Seine aux bords de l'Aréthuse ?

---

[1] Un seigneur de Coucy s'établit en Sicile, du temps de Charles-le-Chauve.

D'abord modeste et simple, il voulut nous servir;
Bientôt fier et superbe, il se fit obéir.
Sa race accumulant d'immenses héritages,
Et d'un peuple ébloui maîtrisant les suffrages,
Osa sur ma famille élever sa grandeur.
Nous l'en avons punie, et, malgré sa faveur,
Nous voyons ses enfants bannis de nos rivages.
Tancrède [1], un rejeton de ce sang dangereux,
Des murs de Syracuse éloigné dès l'enfance,
A servi, nous dit-on, les Césars de Byzance;
Il est fier, outragé, sans doute valeureux;
Il doit haïr nos lois, il cherche la vengeance.
Tout Français est à craindre : on voit même en nos jours
Trois simples écuyers [2], sans bien et sans secours,
Sortis des flancs glacés de l'humide Neustrie, [3]
Aux champs [4] apuliens se faire une patrie;
Et n'ayant pour tout droit que celui des combats,
Chasser les possesseurs, et fonder des états.
Grecs, Arabes, Français, Germains, tout nous dévore;
Et nos champs, malheureux par leur fécondité,
Appellent l'avarice et la rapacité
Des brigands du Midi, du Nord, et de l'Aurore.
Nous devons nous défendre ensemble et nous venger.
J'ai vu plus d'une fois Syracuse trahie;
Maintenons notre loi, que rien ne doit changer;

---

[1] Ce n'est pas Tancrède de Hauteville, qui n'alla en
Italie que quelque temps après.

[2] Les premiers normands qui passèrent dans la Pouille,
Drogon, Bateric, et Ripostel.

[3] La Normandie.

[4] Le pays de Naples.

Elle condamne à perdre et l'honneur et la vie.
Quiconque entretiendrait avec nos ennemis
Un commerce secret, fatal à son pays.
A l'infidélité l'indulgence encourage.
On ne doit épargner ni le sexe ni l'âge.
Venise ne fonda sa fière autorité
Que sur la défiance et la sévérité :
Imitons sa sagesse en perdant les coupables.

LORÉDAN.

Quelle honte en effet, dans nos jours déplorables,
Que Solamir, un Maure, un chef des Musulmans,
Dans la Sicile encore ait tant de partisans!
Que partout dans cette île et guerrière et chrétienne,
Que même parmi nous Solamir entretienne
Des sujets corrompus vendus à ses bienfaits!
Tantôt chez les Césars occupé de nous nuire,
Tantôt dans Syracuse ayant su s'introduire,
Nous préparant la guerre, et nous offrant la paix,
Et pour nous désunir soigneux de nous séduire!
Un sexe dangereux, dont les faibles esprits
D'un peuple encor plus faible attirent les hommages,
Toujours des nouveautés et des héros épris,
A ce Maure imposant prodigua ses suffrages.
Combien de citoyens aujourd'hui prévenus
Pour ces arts séduisants [1] que l'Arabe cultive!
Arts trop pernicieux, dont l'éclat les captive,
A nos vrais chevaliers noblement inconnus.
Que notre art soit de vaincre, et je n'en veux point d'autre,

---

[1] En ce temps les Arabes cultivaient seuls les sciences en Occident; et ce sont eux qui fondèrent l'école de Salerne.

J'espère en ma valeur, j'attends tout de la vôtre;
Et j'approuve surtout cette sévérité
Vengeresse des lois et de la liberté.
Pour détruire l'Espagne il a suffi d'un traître [1] :
Il en fut parmi nous; chaque jour en voit naître.
Mettons un frein terrible à l'infidélité;
Au salut de l'état que toute pitié cède;
Combattons Solamir, et proscrivons Tancrède.
Tancrède, né d'un sang parmi nous détesté,
Est plus à craindre encor pour notre liberté.
Dans le dernier conseil un décret juste et sage
Dans les mains d'Orbassan remit son héritage,
Pour confondre à jamais nos ennemis cachés,
A ce nom de Tancrède en secret attachés;
Du vaillant Orbassan c'est le juste partage,
Sa dot, sa récompense.

CATANE.

Oui, nous y souscrivons.
Que Tancrède, s'il veut, soit puissant à Byzance;
Qu'une cour odieuse honore sa vaillance;
Il n'a rien à prétendre aux lieux où nous vivons.
Tancrède, en se donnant un maître despotique,
A renoncé lui-même à nos sacrés remparts :
Plus de retour pour lui; l'esclave des Césars
Ne doit rien posséder dans une république.
Orbassan de nos lois est le plus ferme appui,
Et l'état, qu'il soutient, ne pouvait moins pour lui;
Tel est mon sentiment.

ARGIRE.

Je vois en lui mon gendre;

---

[1] Le comte Julien, ou l'archevêque Opas.

Ma fille m'est bien chère, il est vrai ; mais enfin
Je n'aurais point pour eux dépouillé l'orphelin :
Vous savez qu'à regret on m'y vit condescendre.
LORÉDAN.
Blâmez-vous le sénat ?
ARGIRE.
Non ; je hais la rigueur ;
Mais toujours à la loi je fus prêt à me rendre,
Et l'intérêt commun l'emporta dans mon cœur.
ORBASSAN.
Ces biens sont à l'état, l'état seul doit les prendre.
Je n'ai point recherché cette faible faveur.
ARGIRE.
N'en parlons plus : hâtons cet heureux hyménée ;
Qu'il amène demain la brillante journée
Où ce chef arrogant d'un peuple destructeur,
Solamir, à la fin, doit connaître un vainqueur.
Votre rival en tout, il osa bien prétendre,
En nous offrant la paix, à devenir mon gendre [1] ;
Il pensait m'honorer par cet hymen fatal.
Allez.... dans tous les temps triomphez d'un rival :
Mes amis, soyons prêts...., ma faiblesse et mon âge
Ne me permettent plus l'honneur de commander ;
A mon gendre Orbassan vous daignez l'accorder.
Vous suivre est pour mes ans un assez beau partage ;
Je serai près de vous ; j'aurai cet avantage ;

---

[1] Il était très commun de marier des chrétiennes à des musulmans ; et Abdalise, le fils de Musa, conquérant de l'Espagne, épousa la fille du roi Rodrigue. Cet exemple fut imité dans tous les pays où les Arabes portèrent leurs armes victorieuses.

Je sentirai mon cœur encor se ranimer ;
Mes yeux seront témoins de votre fier courage,
Et vous auront vu vaincre avant de se fermer.

LORÉDAN.

Nous combattrons sous vous, seigneur, nous osons croire
Que ce jour, quel qu'il soit, nous sera glorieux ;
Nous nous promettons tous l'honneur de la victoire,
Ou l'honneur consolant de mourir à vos yeux.

SCÈNE II.

ARGIRE, ORBASSAN.

ARGIRE.

Eh bien ! brave Orbassan, suis-je enfin votre père ?
Tous vos ressentiments sont-ils bien effacés ?
Pourrai-je en vous d'un fils trouver le caractère ?
Dois-je compter sur vous ?

ORBASSAN.

Je vous l'ai dit assez :
J'aime l'état, Argire ; il nous réconcilie.
Cet hymen nous rapproche, et la raison nous lie ;
Mais le nœud qui nous joint n'eût point été formé,
Si dans notre querelle, à jamais assoupie,
Mon cœur qui vous hait ne vous eût estimé.
L'amour peut avoir part à ma nouvelle chaîne ;
Mais un si noble hymen ne sera point le fruit
D'un feu né d'un instant, qu'un autre instant détruit,
Que suit l'indifférence, et trop souvent la haine.
Ce cœur, que la patrie appelle aux champs de Mars,
Ne sait point soupirer au milieu des hasards.
Mon hymen a pour but l'honneur de vous complaire,
Notre union naissante, à tous deux nécessaire,

La splendeur de l'état, votre intérêt, le mien ;
Devant de tels objets l'amour a peu de charmes.
Il pourra resserrer un si noble lien ;
Mais sa voix doit ici se taire au bruit des armes.

ARGIRE.

J'estime en un soldat cette mâle fierté ;
Mais la franchise plaît, et non l'austérité.
J'espère que bientôt ma chère Aménaïde
Pourra fléchir en vous ce courage rigide.
C'est peu d'être un guerrier ; la modeste douceur
Donne un prix aux vertus, et sied à la valeur.
Vous sentez que ma fille au sortir de l'enfance,
Dans nos temps orageux de trouble et de malheur,
Par sa mère élevée à la cour de Byzance,
Pourrait s'effaroucher de ce sévère accueil,
Qui tient de la rudesse, et ressemble à l'orgueil.
Pardonnez aux avis d'un vieillard et d'un père.

ORBASSAN.

Vous-même pardonnez à mon humeur austère :
Élevé dans nos camps, je préférai toujours
A ce mérite faux des politesses vaines,
A cet art de flatter, à cet esprit des cours,
La grossière vertu des mœurs républicaines :
Mais je sais respecter la naissance et le rang
D'un estimable objet formé de votre sang ;
Je prétends par mes soins mériter qu'elle m'aime,
Vous regarder en elle, et m'honorer moi-même.

ARGIRE.

Par mon ordre en ces lieux elle avance vers vous.

SCÈNE III.

ARGIRE, ORBASSAN, AMÉNAÏDE.

ARGIRE.

Le bien de cet état, les voix de Syracuse,
Votre père, le ciel, vous donnent un époux;
Leurs ordres réunis ne souffrent point d'excuse.
Ce noble chevalier, qui se rejoint à moi,
Aujourd'hui par ma bouche a reçu votre foi.
Vous connaissez son nom, son rang, sa renommée;
Puissant dans Syracuse, il commande l'armée :
Tous les droits de Tancrède entre ses mains remis....

AMÉNAÏDE, *à part.*

De Tancrède !

ARGIRE.

À mes yeux sont le moins digne prix
Qui relève l'éclat d'une telle alliance.

ORBASSAN.

Elle m'honore assez, seigneur; et sa présence
Rend plus cher à mon cœur le don que je reçois.
Puissé-je, en méritant vos bontés et son choix,
Du bonheur de tous trois confirmer l'espérance !

AMÉNAÏDE.

Mon père, en tous les temps je sais que votre cœur
Sentit tous mes chagrins, et voulut mon bonheur.
Votre choix me destine un héros en partage ;
Et quand ces longs débats qui troublèrent vos jours,
Grâce à votre sagesse, ont terminé leur cours,
Du nœud qui vous rejoint votre fille est le gage ;
D'une telle union je conçois l'avantage.

Orbassan permettra que ce cœur étonné,
Qu'opprima dès l'enfance un sort toujours contraire,
Par ce changement même au trouble abandonné,
Se recueille un moment dans le sein de son père.

ORBASSAN.

Vous le devez, madame ; et, loin de m'opposer
A de tels sentiments, dignes de mon estime,
Loin de vous détourner d'un soin si légitime,
Des droits que j'ai sur vous je craindrais d'abuser.
J'ai quitté nos guerriers, je revole à leur tête :
C'est peu d'un tel hymen, il le faut mériter ;
La victoire en rend digne ; et j'ose me flatter
Que bientôt des lauriers en orneront la fête.

SCÈNE IV.

ARGIRE, AMÉNAIDE.

ARGIRE.

Vous semblez interdite ; et vos yeux pleins d'effroi,
De larmes obscurcis, se détournent de moi.
Vos soupirs étouffés semblent me faire injure :
La bouche obéit mal lorsque le cœur murmure.

AMÉNAÏDE.

Seigneur, je l'avouerai, je ne m'attendais pas
Qu'après tant de malheurs, et de si longs débats,
Le parti d'Orbassan dût être un jour le vôtre ;
Que mes tremblantes mains uniraient l'un et l'autre,
Et que votre ennemi dût passer dans mes bras.
Je n'oublierai jamais que la guerre civile
Dans vos propres foyers vous priva d'un asile ;
Que ma mere, à regret évitant le danger,

Chercha loin de nos murs un rivage étranger ;
Que des bras paternels avec elle arrachée,
A ses tristes destins dans Byzance attachée,
J'ai partagé long-temps les maux qu'elle a soufferts.
Au sortir du berceau j'ai connu les revers :
J'appris sous une mère, abandonnée, errante,
A supporter l'exil et le sort des proscrits,
L'accueil impérieux d'une cour arrogante,
Et la fausse pitié, pire que les mépris.
Dans un sort avili noblement élevée,
De ma mère bientôt cruellement privée,
Je me vis seule au monde, en proie à mon effroi,
Roseau faible et tremblant, n'ayant d'appui que moi.
Votre destin changea. Syracuse en alarmes
Vous remit dans vos biens, vous rendit vos honneurs,
Se reposa sur vous du destin de ses armes,
Et de ses murs sanglants repoussa ses vainqueurs.
Dans le sein paternel je me vis rappelée ;
Un malheur inouï m'en avait exilée :
Peut-être j'y reviens pour un malheur nouveau.
Vos mains de mon hymen allument le flambeau ;
Je sais quel intérêt, quel espoir vous anime ;
Mais de vos ennemis je me vis la victime.
Je suis enfin la vôtre ; et ce jour dangereux
Peut-être de nos jours sera le plus affreux.

ARGIRE.

Il sera fortuné, c'est à vous de m'en croire.
Je vous aime, ma fille, et j'aime votre gloire.
On a trop murmuré quand ce fier Solamir,
Pour le prix de la paix qu'il venait nous offrir,
Osa me proposer de l'accepter pour gendre ;
Je vous donne au héros qui marche contre lui,

Au plus grand des guerriers armés pour nous défendre,
Autrefois mon émule, à présent notre appui.

AMÉNAÏDE.

Quel appui ! vous vantez sa superbe fortune ;
Mes vœux plus modérés la voudraient plus commune :
Je voudrais qu'un héros si fier et si puissant
N'eût point, pour s'agrandir, dépouillé l'innocent.

ARGIRE.

Du conseil, il est vrai, la prudence sévère
Veut punir dans Tancrède une race étrangère :
Elle abusa long-temps de son autorité ;
Elle a trop d'ennemis.

AMÉNAÏDE.

Seigneur, ou je m'abuse,
Ou Tancrède est encore aimé dans Syracuse.

ARGIRE.

Nous rendons tous justice à son cœur indomté ;
Sa valeur a, dit-on, subjugué l'Illyrie ;
Mais plus il a servi sous l'aigle des Césars,
Moins il doit espérer de revoir sa patrie :
Il est par un décret chassé de nos remparts.

AMÉNAÏDE.

Pour jamais ! lui ? Tancrède ?

ARGIRE.

Oui, l'on craint sa présence ;
Et si vous l'avez vu dans les murs de Byzance,
Vous savez qu'il nous hait.

AMÉNAÏDE.

Je ne le croyais pas.
Ma mère avait pensé qu'il pouvait être encore
L'appui de Syracuse et le vainqueur du Maure ;

Et lorsque dans ces lieux des citoyens ingrats
Pour ce fier Orbassan contre vous s'animèrent,
Qu'ils ravirent vos biens, et qu'ils vous opprimèrent,
Tancrède aurait pour vous affronté le trépas.
C'est tout ce que j'ai su.

ARGIRE.

C'est trop, Aménaïde :
Rendez-vous aux conseils d'un père qui vous guide ;
Conformez-vous au temps, conformez-vous aux lieux :
Solamir, et Tancrède, et la cour de Byzance,
Sont tous également en horreur à nos yeux.
Votre bonheur dépend de votre complaisance.
J'ai pendant soixante ans combattu pour l'état ;
Je le servis injuste, et le chéris ingrat :
Je dois penser ainsi jusqu'à ma dernière heure.
Prenez mes sentiments ; et, devant que je meure,
Consolez mes vieux ans dont vous faites l'espoir.
Je suis prêt à finir une vie orageuse :
La vôtre doit couler sous les lois du devoir ;
Et je mourrai content si vous vivez heureuse.

AMÉNAÏDE.

Ah, seigneur ! croyez-moi, parlez moins de bonheur.
Je ne regrette point la cour d'un empereur.
Je vous ai consacré mes sentiments, ma vie ;
Mais, pour en disposer, attendez quelques jours.
Au crédit d'Orbassan trop d'intérêt vous lie :
Ce crédit si vanté doit-il durer toujours ?
Il peut tomber ; tout change ; et ce héros peut-être
S'est trop tôt déclaré votre gendre et mon maître.

ARGIRE.

Comment ? que dites-vous ?

AMÉNAÏDE.

Cette témérité
Vous offense peut-être, et vous semble une injure.
Je sais que dans les cours mon sexe plus flatté
Dans votre république a moins de liberté :
A Byzance on le sert ; ici la loi plus dure
Veut de l'obéissance, et défend le murmure.
Les Musulmans altiers, trop long-temps vos vainqueurs,
Ont changé la Sicile, ont endurci vos mœurs :
Mais qui peut altérer vos bontés paternelles ?

ARGIRE.

Vous seule, vous, ma fille, en abusant trop d'elles.
De tout ce que j'entends mon esprit est confus :
J'ai permis vos délais, mais non pas vos refus.
La loi ne peut plus rompre un nœud si légitime :
La parole est donnée ; y manquer est un crime.
Vous me l'avez bien dit, je suis né malheureux :
Jamais aucun succès n'a couronné mes vœux.
Tous les jours de ma vie ont été des orages.
Dieu puissant ! détournez ces funestes présages ;
Et puisse Aménaïde, en formant ces liens,
Se préparer des jours moins tristes que les miens !

SCÈNE V.

AMÉNAIDE.

Tancrède, cher amant ! moi, j'aurais la faiblesse
De trahir mes serments pour ton persécuteur !
Plus cruelle que lui, perfide avec bassesse,
Partageant ta dépouille avec cet oppresseur,
Je pourrais....

SCÈNE VI.

AMÉNAÏDE, FANIE.

AMÉNAÏDE.

Viens approche, ô ma chère Fanie!
Vois le trait détesté qui m'arrache la vie.
Orbassan par mon père est nommé mon époux.

FANIE.

Je sens combien cet ordre est douloureux pour vous.
J'ai vu vos sentiments, j'en ai connu la force.
Le sort n'eut point de traits, la cour n'eut point d'amorce,
Qui pussent arrêter ou détourner vos pas,
Quand la route par vous fut une fois choisie.
Votre cœur s'est donné, c'est pour toute la vie.
Tancrède et Solamir, touchés de vos appas,
Dans la cour des Césars en secret soupirèrent :
Mais celui que vos yeux justement distinguèrent,
Qui seul obtint vos vœux, qui sut les mériter,
En sera toujours digne; et, puisque dans Byzance,
Sur le fier Solamir il eut la préférence,
Orbassan dans ces lieux ne pourra l'emporter :
Votre ame est trop constante.

AMÉNAÏDE.

Ah! tu n'en peux douter.
On dépouille Tancrède, on l'exile, on l'outrage :
C'est le sort d'un héros d'être persécuté;
Je sens que c'est le mien de l'aimer davantage.
Écoute : dans ces murs Tancrède est regretté;
Le peuple le chérit.

FANIE.

Banni dans son enfance,

ACTE I, SCÈNE VI.

De son père oublié les fastueux amis
Ont bientôt à son sort abandonné le fils.
Peu de cœurs comme vous tiennent contre l'absence.
A leurs seuls intérêts les grands sont attachés.
Le peuple est plus sensible.

AMÉNAÏDE.
Il est aussi plus juste.

FANIE.
Mais il est asservi : nos amis sont cachés ;
Aucun n'ose parler pour ce proscrit auguste.
Un sénat tyrannique est ici tout puissant.

AMÉNAÏDE.
Oui, je sais qu'il peut tout quand Tancrède est absent.

FANIE.
S'il pouvait se montrer, j'espérerais encore ;
Mais il est loin de vous.

AMÉNAÏDE.
Juste ciel, je t'implore !

(à Fanie.)

Je me confie à toi. Tancrède n'est pas loin ;
Et quand de l'écarter on prend l'indigne soin,
Lorsque la tyrannie au comble est parvenue,
Il est temps qu'il paraisse, et qu'on tremble à sa vue.
Tancrède est dans Messine.

FANIE.
Est-il vrai ? justes cieux !
Et cet indigne hymen est formé sous ses yeux !

AMÉNAÏDE.
Il ne le sera pas.... non, Fanie ; et peut-être
Mes oppresseurs et moi nous n'aurons plus qu'un maître.
Viens.... je t'apprendrai tout.... mais il faut tout oser ?
Le joug est trop honteux ; ma main doit le briser

La persécution enhardit ma faiblesse.
Le trahir est un crime, obéir est bassesse.
S'il vient, c'est pour moi seule, et je l'ai mérité ?
Et moi, timide esclave à son tyran promise,
Victime malheureuse indignement soumise,
Je mettrais mon devoir dans l'infidélité !
Non, l'amour à mon sexe inspire le courage :
C'est à moi de hâter ce fortuné retour ;
Et s'il est des dangers que ma crainte envisage,
Ces dangers me sont chers, ils naissent de l'amour.

FIN DU PREMIER ACTE.

ACTE SECOND.

SCÈNE I.

AMÉNAÏDE.

Où porté-je mes pas ?... d'où vient que je frissonne ?
Moi, des remords ?... qui, moi ? le crime seul les donne...
Ma cause est juste... O cieux ! protégez mes desseins !
(*à Fanie qui entre.*)
Allons, rassurons-nous... Suis-je en tout obéie ?

FANIE.

Votre esclave est parti; la lettre est dans ses mains.

AMÉNAÏDE.

Il est maître, il est vrai, du secret de ma vie ;
Mais je connais son zèle : il m'a toujours servie.
On doit tout quelquefois aux derniers des humains.
Né d'aïeux musulmans chez les Syracusains,
Instruit dans les deux lois, et dans les deux langages,
Du camp des Sarrasins il connaît les passages,
Et des monts de l'Etna les plus secrets chemins.
C'est lui qui découvrit, par une course utile,
Que Tancrède en secret a revu la Sicile ;
C'est lui par qui le ciel veut changer mes destins.
Ma lettre, par ses soins remise aux mains d'un Maure,
Dans Messine demain doit être avant l'aurore.
Des Maures et des Grecs les besoins mutuels
Ont toujours conservé, dans cette longue guerre,
Une correspondance à tous deux nécessaire,
Tant la nature unit les malheureux mortels !

FANIE.

Ce pas est dangereux ; mais le nom de Tancrède,
Ce nom si redoutable à qui tout autre cède,
Et qu'ici nos tyrans ont toujours en horreur,
Ce beau nom que l'amour grava dans votre cœur,
N'est point dans cette lettre à Tancrède adressée.
Si vous l'avez toujours présent à la pensée,
Vous avez su du moins le taire en écrivant.
Au camp des Sarrasins votre lettre portée
Vainement serait lue, ou serait arrêtée.
Enfin, jamais l'amour ne fut moins imprudent,
Ne sut mieux se voiler dans l'ombre du mystère,
Et ne fut plus hardi sans être téméraire.
Je ne puis cependant vous cacher mon effroi.

AMÉNAÏDE.

Le ciel jusqu'à présent semble veiller sur moi ;
Il ramène Tancrède, et tu veux que je tremble ?

FANIE.

Hélas ! qu'en d'autres lieux sa bonté vous rassemble.
La haine et l'intérêt s'arment trop contre lui :
Tout son parti se taît ; qui sera son appui ?

AMÉNAÏDE.

Sa gloire. Qu'il se montre, il deviendra le maître.
Un héros qu'on opprime attendrit tous les cœurs ;
Il les anime tous, quand il vient à paraître.

FANIE.

Son rival est à craindre.

AMÉNAÏDE.

     Ah ! combats ces terreurs,
Et ne m'en donne point. Souviens-toi que ma mère
Nous unit l'un et l'autre à ses derniers moments ;
Que Tancrède est à moi ; qu'aucune loi contraire

Ne peut rien sur nos vœux et sur nos sentiments.
Hélas! nous regrettions cette île si funeste.
Dans le sein de la gloire et des murs des Césars;
Vers ces champs trop aimés qu'aujourd'hui je déteste,
Nous tournions tristement nos avides regards.
J'étais loin de penser que le sort qui m'obsède
Me gardât pour époux l'oppresseur de Tancrède,
Et que j'aurais pour dot l'exécrable présent
Des biens qu'un ravisseur enlève à mon amant.
Il faut l'instruire au moins d'une telle injustice;
Qu'il apprenne de moi sa perte et mon supplice;
Qu'il hâte son retour et défende ses droits.
Pour venger un héros je fais ce que je dois.
Ah! si je le pouvais, j'en ferais davantage.
J'aime, je crains un père, et respecte son âge;
Mais je voudrais armer nos peuples soulevés
Contre cet Orbassan qui nous a captivés.
D'un brave chevalier sa conduite est indigne:
Intéressé, cruel, il prétend à l'honneur!
Il croit d'un peuple libre être le protecteur!
Il ordonne ma honte, et mon père la signe!
Et je dois la subir, et je dois me livrer
Au maître impérieux qui pense m'honorer!
Hélas! dans Syracuse on hait la tyrannie;
Mais la plus exécrable et la plus impunie,
Est celle qui commande et la haine et l'amour,
Et qui veut nous forcer de changer en un jour.
Le sort en est jeté.

FANIE.
Vous aviez paru craindre.
AMÉNAÏDE.
Je ne crains plus.

FANIE.

          On dit qu'un arrêt redouté
Contre Tancrède même est aujourd'hui porté :
Il y va de la vie à qui le veut enfreindre.

AMÉNAÏDE.

Je le sais : mon esprit en fut épouvanté :
Mais l'amour est bien faible alors qu'il est timide.
J'adore, tu le sais, un héros intrépide ;
Comme lui je dois l'être.

FANIE.

              Une loi de rigueur
Contre vous, après tout, serait-elle écoutée ?
Pour effrayer le peuple elle paraît dictée.

AMÉNAÏDE.

Elle attaque Tancrède ; elle me fait horreur.
Que cette loi jalouse est digne de nos maîtres !
Ce n'était point ainsi que ses braves ancêtres,
Ces généreux Français, ces illustres vainqueurs,
Subjugaient l'Italie, et conquéraient des cœurs.
On aimait leur franchise, on redoutait leurs armes ;
Des soupçons n'entraient point dans leurs esprits altiers.
L'honneur avait uni tous ces grands chevaliers :
Chez les seuls ennemis ils portaient les alarmes,
Et le peuple, amoureux de leur autorité,
Combattait pour leur gloire et pour sa liberté.
Ils abaissaient les Grecs, ils triomphaient du Maure.
Aujourd'hui je ne vois qu'un sénat ombrageux,
Toujours en défiance, et toujours orageux,
Qui lui-même se craint, et que le peuple abhorre.
Je ne sais si mon cœur est trop plein de ses feux ;
Trop de prévention peut-être me possède ;
Mais je ne puis souffrir ce qui n'est pas Tancrède :

La foule des humains n'existe point pour moi;
Son nom seul en ces lieux dissipe mon effroi,
Et tous ses ennemis irritent ma colère.

SCÈNE II.

AMÉNAÏDE, FANIE, *sur le devant*; ARGIRE, LES CHEVALIERS, *au fond.*

ARGIRE.

Chevaliers.... je succombe à cet excès d'horreur.
Ah! j'espérais du moins mourir sans déshonneur.
(*à sa fille, avec des sanglots mêlés de colère.*)
Retirez-vous.... sortez.

AMÉNAÏDE.

Qu'entends-je? vous, mon père!

ARGIRE.

Moi, ton père!... est-ce à toi de prononcer ce nom,
Quand tu trahis ton sang, ton pays, ta maison?

AMÉNAÏDE, *faisant un pas, appuyée sur Fanie.*
Je suis perdue!...

ARGIRE.

Arrête.... ah, trop chère victime!
Qu'as-tu fait?...

AMÉNAÏDE, *pleurant.*
Nos malheurs....

ARGIRE.

Pleures-tu sur ton crime?

AMÉNAÏDE.

Je n'en ai point commis.

ARGIRE.

Quoi! tu démens ton seing?

AMÉNAÏDE.

Non....

ARGIRE.

Tu vois que le crime est écrit de ta main.
Tout sert à m'accabler, tout sert à te confondre.
Ma fille !... il est donc vrai ?... tu n'oses me répondre.
Laisse au moins dans le doute un père au désespoir.
J'ai vécu trop long-temps.... Qu'as-tu fait ?...

AMÉNAÏDE.

Mon devoir.
Aviez-vous fait le vôtre ?

ARGIRE.

Ah ! c'en est trop, cruelle !
Oses-tu te vanter d'être si criminelle ?
Laisse-moi, malheureuse ; ôte-toi de ces lieux :
Va, sors.... une autre main saura fermer mes yeux.

AMÉNAÏDE *sort presque évanouie entre les bras de Fanie.*

Je me meurs.

SCÈNE III.

ARGIRE, LES CHEVALIERS.

ARGIRE.

Mes amis, dans une telle injure....
Après son aveu même.... après ce crime affreux....
Excusez d'un vieillard les sanglots douloureux....
Je dois tout à l'état.... mais tout à la nature.
Vous n'exigerez pas qu'un père malheureux
A vos sévères voix mêle sa voix tremblante.
Aménaïde, hélas ! ne peut être innocente ;

ACTE II, SCÈNE III.

Mais signer à la fois mon opprobre et sa mort,
Vous ne le voulez pas.... c'est un barbare effort :
La nature en frémit, et j'en suis incapable.

LORÉDAN.

Nous plaignons tous, seigneur, un père respectable ;
Nous sentons sa blessure, et craignons de l'aigrir :
Mais vous-même avez vu cette lettre coupable ;
L'esclave la portait au camp de Solamir ;
Auprès de ce camp même on a surpris le traître,
Et l'insolent Arabe a pu le voir punir.
Ses odieux desseins n'ont que trop su paraître.
L'état était perdu. Nos dangers, nos serments,
Ne souffrent point de nous de vains ménagements :
Les lois n'écoutent point la pitié paternelle ;
L'état parle, il suffit.

ARGIRE.

Seigneur, je vous entends.
Je sais ce qu'on prépare à cette criminelle.
Mais elle était ma fille.... et voilà son époux....
Je cède à ma douleur.... je m'abandonne à vous....
Il ne me reste plus qu'à mourir avant elle.

(il sort.)

SCÈNE IV.

LES CHEVALIERS.

CATANE.

Déja de la saisir l'ordre est donné par nous.
Sans doute il est affreux de voir tant de noblesse,
Les grâces, les attraits, la plus tendre jeunesse,
L'espoir de deux maisons, le destin le plus beau,
Par le dernier supplice enfermés au tombeau.

Mais telle est parmi nous la loi de l'hyménée;
C'est la religion lâchement profanée,
C'est la patrie enfin que nous devons venger.
L'infidèle en nos murs appelle l'étranger !
La Grèce et la Sicile ont vu des citoyennes,
Renonçant à leur gloire, au titre de chrétiennes,
Abandonner nos lois pour ces fiers Musulmans,
Vainqueurs de tous côtés, et partout nos tyrans :
Mais que d'un chevalier la fille respectée,
  (à Orbassan.)
Sur le point d'être à vous, et marchant à l'autel,
Exécute un complot si lâche et si cruel !
De ce crime nouveau Syracuse infectée
Veut de notre justice un exemple éternel.

    LORÉDAN.

Je l'avoue en tremblant; sa mort est légitime :
Plus sa race est illustre, et plus grand est le crime.
On sait de Solamir l'espoir ambitieux;
On connaît ses desseins, son amour téméraire,
Ce malheureux talent de tromper et de plaire,
D'imposer aux esprits, et d'éblouir les yeux.
C'est à lui que s'adresse un écrit si funeste,
Régnez dans nos états : ces mots trop odieux
Nous révèlent assez un complot manifeste.
Pour l'honneur d'Orbassan je supprime le reste;
Il nous ferait rougir. Quel est le chevalier
Qui daignera jamais, suivant l'antique usage,
Pour ce coupable objet signaler son courage,
Et hasarder sa gloire à le justifier ?

    CATANE.

Orbassan, comme vous nous sentons votre injure;
Nous allons l'effacer au milieu des combats.

ACTE II, SCÈNE IV.

Le crime rompt l'hymen : oubliez la parjure.
Son supplice vous venge, et ne vous flétrit pas.

ORBASSAN.

Il me consterne, au moins.... et coupable ou fidèle,
Sa main me fut promise.... On approche.... C'est elle
Qu'au séjour des forfaits conduisent des soldats!...
Cette honte m'indigne autant qu'elle m'offense :
Laissez-moi lui parler.

SCÈNE V.

LES CHEVALIERS, *sur le devant*; AMÉNAÏDE *au fond, entourée de gardes.*

AMÉNAÏDE.

O céleste puissance,
Ne m'abandonne point dans ces moments affreux.
Grand Dieu ! vous connaissez l'objet de tous mes vœux;
Vous connaissez mon cœur ; est-il donc si coupable ?

CATANE.

Vous voulez voir encor cet objet condamnable ?

ORBASSAN.

Oui, je le veux.

CATANE.

Sortons. Parlez-lui ; mais songez
Que les lois, les autels, l'honneur, sont outragés :
Syracuse à regret exige une victime.

ORBASSAN.

Je le sais comme vous : un même soin m'anime.
Éloignez-vous, soldats.

SCÈNE VI.

AMÉNAÏDE, ORBASSAN.

AMÉNAÏDE.

Qu'osez-vous attenter ?
A mes derniers moments venez-vous insulter ?

ORBASSAN.

Ma fierté jusque-là ne peut être avilie.
Je vous donnais ma main, je vous avais choisie ;
Peut-être l'amour même avait dicté ce choix.
Je ne sais si mon cœur s'en souviendrait encore,
Ou s'il est indigné d'avoir connu ses lois ;
Mais il ne peut souffrir ce qui le déshonore.
Je ne veux point penser qu'Orbassan soit trahi
Pour un chef étranger, pour un chef ennemi,
Pour un de ces tyrans que notre culte abhorre :
Ce crime est trop indigne ; il est trop inouï :
Et pour vous, pour l'état, et surtout pour ma gloire,
Je veux fermer les yeux, et prétends ne rien croire.
Syracuse aujourd'hui voit en moi votre époux :
Ce titre me suffit ; je me respecte en vous ;
Ma gloire est offensée, et je prends sa défense.
Les lois des chevaliers ordonnent ces combats ;
Le jugement de Dieu [1] dépend de notre bras :
C'est le glaive qui juge et qui fait l'innocence.
Je suis prêt.

AMÉNAÏDE.

Vous ?

---

[1] On sait assez qu'on appelait ces combats *le jugement de Dieu*.

ACTE II, SCÈNE VI.

ORBASSAN.
Moi seul; et j'ose me flatter
(D'après cette démarche, après cette entreprise
Qu'aux yeux de tout guerrier mon honneur autorise),
Un cœur qui m'était dû me saura mériter.
Je n'examine point si votre ame surprise
Ou par mes ennemis, ou par un séducteur,
Un moment aveuglée eut un moment d'erreur,
Si votre aversion fuyait mon hyménée.
Les bienfaits peuvent tout sur une ame bien née;
La vertu s'affermit par un remords heureux.
Je suis sûr, en un mot, de l'honneur de tous deux.
Mais ce n'est point assez : j'ai le droit de prétendre
(Soit fierté, soit amour) un sentiment plus tendre.
Les lois veulent ici des serments solennels ;
J'en exige un de vous, non tel que la contrainte
En dicte à la faiblesse, en impose à la crainte,
Qu'en se trompant soi-même on prodigue aux autels :
A ma franchise altière il faut parler sans feinte :
Prononcez. Mon cœur s'ouvre, et mon bras est armé.
Je puis mourir pour vous ; mais je dois être aimé.

AMÉNAÏDE.
Dans l'abîme effroyable où je suis descendue,
A peine avec horreur à moi-même rendue,
Cet effort généreux, que je n'attendais pas,
Porte le dernier coup à mon ame éperdue,
Et me plonge au tombeau qui s'ouvrait sous mes pas.
Vous me forcez, seigneur, à la reconnaissance ;
Et, tout près du sépulcre où l'on va m'enfermer,
Mon dernier sentiment est de vous estimer.
Connaissez-moi ; sachez que mon cœur vous offense ;
Mais je n'ai point trahi ma gloire et mon pays :

Je ne vous trahis point; je n'avais rien promis.
Mon âme envers la vôtre est assez criminelle;
Sachez qu'elle est ingrate, et non pas infidèle.....
Je ne peux vous aimer; je ne peux, à ce prix,
Accepter un combat pour ma cause entrepris.
Je sais de votre loi la dureté barbare,
Celle de mes tyrans, la mort qu'on me prépare.
Je ne me vante point du fastueux effort
De voir, sans m'alarmer, les apprêts de ma mort....
Je regrette la vie.... elle dut m'être chère.
Je pleure mon destin, je gémis sur mon père;
Mais, malgré ma faiblesse, et malgré mon effroi,
Je ne puis vous tromper; n'attendez rien de moi.
Je vous parais coupable après un tel outrage;
Mais ce cœur, croyez-moi, le serait davantage,
Si jusqu'à vous complaire il pouvait s'oublier.
Je ne veux (pardonnez à ce triste langage)
De vous pour mon époux, ni pour mon chevalier.
J'ai prononcé; jugez, et vengez votre offense.

ORBASSAN.

Je me borne, madame, à venger mon pays,
A dédaigner l'audace, à braver le mépris,
A l'oublier. Mon bras prenait votre défense :
Mais, quitte envers ma gloire, aussi bien qu'envers vous,
Je ne suis plus qu'un juge à son devoir fidèle,
Soumis à la loi seule, insensible comme elle,
Et qui ne doit sentir ni regrets ni courroux.

SCÈNE VII.

AMÉNAÏDE, SOLDATS, *dans l'enfoncement.*

AMÉNAÏDE.

J'AI donc dicté l'arrêt.... et je me sacrifie!
O toi, seul des humains qui méritas ma foi,
Toi, pour qui je mourrai, pour qui j'aimais la vie,
Je suis donc condamnée.... Oui, je le suis pour toi;
Allons... je l'ai voulu... Mais tant d'ignominie,
Mais un père accablé, dont les jours vont finir!
Des liens, des bourreaux.... ces apprêts d'infamie!
O mort! affreuse mort! puis-je vous soutenir?
Tourments, trépas honteux... tout mon courage cède...
Non, il n'est point de honte en mourant pour Tancrède,
On peut m'ôter le jour, et non pas me punir.
Quoi! je meurs en coupable!... un père, une patrie!
Je les servais tous deux, et tous deux m'ont flétrie!
Et je n'aurai pour moi, dans ces moments d'horreur,
Que mon seul témoignage, et la voix de mon cœur!
(*à Fanie qui entre.*)
Quels moments pour Tancrède! O ma chère Fanie!
(*Fanie lui baise la main en pleurant, et Aménaïde
l'embrasse.*)
La douceur de te voir ne m'est donc point ravie!

FANIE.

Que ne puis-je avant vous expirer en ces lieux!

AMÉNAÏDE.

Ah!... je vois s'avancer ces monstres odieux....
(*Les gardes qui étaient dans le fond s'avancent pour
l'emmener.*)
Porte un jour au héros à qui j'étais unie

Mes derniers sentiments, et mes derniers adieux,
Fanie.... il apprendra si je mourus fidèle.
Je coûterai du moins des larmes à ses yeux;
Je ne meurs que pour lui.... ma mort est moins cruelle.

FIN DU SECOND ACTE.

ACTE TROISIÈME.

SCÈNE I.

TANCRÈDE, *suivi de deux écuyers qui portent sa lance, son écu, etc.;* ALDAMON.

TANCRÈDE.

A tous les cœurs bien nés que la patrie est chère!
Qu'avec ravissement je revois ce séjour!
Cher et brave Aldamon, digne ami de mon père,
C'est toi dont l'heureux zèle a servi mon retour.
Que Tancrède est heureux! que ce jour m'est prospère!
Tout mon sort est changé. Cher ami, je te dois
Plus que je n'ose dire, et plus que tu ne crois.

ALDAMON.

Seigneur, c'est trop vanter mes services vulgaires,
Et c'est trop relever un sort tel que le mien;
Je ne suis qu'un soldat, un simple citoyen...

TANCRÈDE.

Je le suis comme vous : les citoyens sont frères.

ALDAMON.

Deux ans dans l'Orient sous vous j'ai combattu;
Je vous vis effacer l'éclat de vos ancêtres;
J'admirai d'assez près votre haute vertu;
C'est-là mon seul mérite. Elevé par mes maîtres,
Né dans votre maison, je vous suis asservi.
Je dois...

TANCRÈDE.

Vous ne devez être que mon ami.

Voilà donc ces remparts que je voulais défendre,
Ces murs toujours sacrés pour le cœur le plus tendre,
Ces murs qui m'ont vu naître, et dont je suis banni!
Apprends-moi dans quels lieux respire Aménaïde.

ALDAMON.

Dans ce palais antique où son père réside;
Cette place y conduit : plus loin vous contemplez
Ce tribunal auguste, où l'on voit assemblés
Ces vaillants chevaliers, ce sénat intrépide,
Qui font les lois du peuple, et combattent pour lui,
Et qui vaincraient toujours le musulman perfide,
S'ils ne s'étaient privés de leur plus grand appui.
Voilà leurs boucliers, leurs lances, leurs devises,
Dont la pompe guerrière annonce aux nations
La splendeur de leurs faits, leurs nobles entreprises.
Votre nom seul ici manquait à ces grands noms.

TANCRÈDE.

Que ce nom soit caché, puisqu'on le persécute;
Peut-être en d'autres lieux il est célèbre assez.

(*à ses écuyers.*)

Vous, qu'on suspende ici mes chiffres effacés;
Aux fureurs des partis qu'ils ne soient plus en butte;
Que mes armes sans faste, emblême des douleurs,
Telles que je les porte au milieu des batailles,
Ce simple bouclier, ce casque sans couleurs,
Soient attachés sans pompe à ces tristes murailles.

(*les écuyers suspendent ses armes aux places vides, au milieu des autres trophées.*)

Conservez ma devise, elle est chère à mon cœur;
Elle a dans mes combats soutenu ma vaillance;
Elle a conduit mes pas et fait mon espérance;
Les mots en sont sacrés; c'est *l'amour et l'honneur.*

ACTE III, SCÈNE I.

Lorsque les chevaliers descendront dans la place,
Vous direz qu'un guerrier qui veut être inconnu,
Pour les suivre au combat dans leurs murs est venu,
Et qu'à les imiter il borne son audace.
   (à Aldamon.)
Quel est leur chef, ami ?

ALDAMON.
            Ce fut depuis trois ans,
Comme vous l'avez su, le respectable Argire.

TANCRÈDE, à part.
Père d'Aménaïde !..

ALDAMON.
            On le vit trop long-temps
Succomber au parti dont nous craignons l'empire.
Il reprit à la fin sa juste autorité :
On respecte son rang, son nom, sa probité ;
Mais l'âge l'affaiblit. Orbassan lui succède.

TANCRÈDE.
Orbassan ! l'ennemi, l'oppresseur de Tancrède !
Ami, quel est le bruit répandu dans ces lieux ?
Ah ! parle, est-il bien vrai que cet audacieux
D'un père trop facile ait surpris la faiblesse,
Que de son alliance il ait eu la promesse,
Que sur Aménaïde il ait levé les yeux,
Qu'il ait osé prétendre à s'unir avec elle ?

ALDAMON.
Hier confusément j'en appris la nouvelle.
Pour moi, loin de la ville, établi dans ce fort
Où je vous ai reçu, grâce à mon heureux sort,
A mon poste attaché, j'avouerai que j'ignore
Ce qu'on a fait depuis dans ces murs que j'abhorre ;
On vous y persécute, ils sont affreux pour moi.

TANCRÈDE.

Cher ami, tout mon cœur s'abandonne à ta foi;
Cours chez Aménaïde, et parais devant elle;
Dis-lui qu'un inconnu, brûlant du plus beau zèle
Pour l'honneur de son sang, pour son auguste nom,
Pour les prospérités de sa noble maison,
Attaché dès l'enfance à sa mère, à sa race,
D'un entretien secret lui demande la grâce.

ALDAMON.

Seigneur, dans sa maison j'eus toujours quelque accès;
On y voit avec joie, on accueille, on honore
Tous ceux qu'à votre nom le zèle attache encore.
Plût au ciel qu'on eût vu le pur sang des Français
Uni dans la Sicile au noble sang d'Argire !
Quel que soit le dessein, seigneur, qui vous inspire,
Puisque vous m'envoyez, je réponds du succès.

SCÈNE II.

TANCRÈDE; SES ÉCUYERS, *au fond.*

TANCRÈDE.

Il sera favorable; et ce ciel qui me guide,
Ce ciel qui me ramène aux pieds d'Aménaïde,
Et qui dans tous les temps accorda sa faveur
Au véritable amour, au véritable honneur,
Ce ciel qui m'a conduit dans les tentes du Maure,
Parmi mes ennemis soutient ma cause encore.
Aménaïde m'aime, et son cœur me répond
Que le mien dans ces lieux ne peut craindre un affront.
Loin du camp des Césars, et loin de l'Illyrie,
Je viens enfin pour elle au sein de ma patrie,
De ma patrie ingrate, et qui, dans mon malheur,

Après Aménaïde est si chère à mon cœur!
J'arrive : un autre ici l'obtiendrait de son père !
Et sa fille à ce point aurait pu me trahir !
Quel est cet Orbassan ? quel est ce téméraire ?
Quels sont donc les exploits dont il doit s'applaudir ?
Qu'a-t-il fait de si grand qui le puisse enhardir
A demander un prix qu'on doit à la vaillance ;
Qui des plus grands héros serait la récompense ;
Qui m'appartient, du moins par les droits de l'amour ?
Avant de me l'ôter, il m'ôtera le jour.
Après mon trépas même elle serait fidèle.
L'oppresseur de mon sang ne peut régner sur elle.
Oui, ton cœur m'est connu, je n'en redoute rien,
Ma chère Aménaïde, il est tel que le mien,
Incapable d'effroi, de crainte, et d'inconstance.

SCÈNE III.

TANCRÈDE, ALDAMON.

TANCRÈDE.

Ah ! trop heureux ami, tu sors de sa présence :
Tu vois tous mes transports ; allons, conduis mes pas.

ALDAMON.

Vers ces funestes lieux, seigneur, n'avancez pas.

TANCRÈDE.

Que me dis-tu ? les pleurs inondent ton visage !

ALDAMON.

Ah ! fuyez pour jamais ce malheureux rivage ;
Après les attentats que ce jour a produits,
Je n'y puis demeurer tout obscur que je suis.

TANCRÈDE

Comment ?

ALDAMON.

Portez ailleurs ce courage sublime :
La gloire vous attend aux tentes des Césars ;
Elle n'est point pour vous dans ces affreux remparts ;
Fuyez ; vous n'y verriez que la honte et le crime.

TANCRÈDE.

De quels traits inouïs viens-tu percer mon cœur ?
Qu'as-tu vu ? que t'a dit, que fait Aménaïde ?

ALDAMON.

J'ai trop vu vos desseins.... Oubliez-la, seigneur.

TANCRÈDE.

Ciel ! Orbassan l'emporte ! Orbassan ! la perfide !
L'ennemi de son père, et mon persécuteur !

ALDAMON.

Son père a ce matin signé cet hyménée ;
Et la pompe fatale en était ordonnée....

TANCRÈDE.

Et je serais témoin de cet excès d'horreur !

ALDAMON.

Votre dépouille ici leur fut abandonnée ;
Vos biens étaient sa dot. Un rival odieux,
Seigneur, vous enlevait le bien de vos aïeux.

TANCRÈDE.

Le lâche ! il m'enlevait ce qu'un héros méprise.
Aménaïde, ô ciel ! en ses mains est remise ?
Elle est à lui ?

ALDAMON.

Seigneur, ce sont les moindres coups
Que le ciel irrité vient de lancer sur vous.

TANCRÈDE.

Achève donc, cruel, de m'arracher la vie ;
Achève.... parle.... hélas !

ACTE III, SCÈNE III.

ALDAMON.
Elle allait être unie
Au fier persécuteur de vos jours glorieux ;
Le flambeau de l'hymen s'allumait en ces lieux,
Lorsqu'on a reconnu quelle est sa perfidie :
C'est peu d'avoir changé, d'avoir trompé vos vœux,
L'infidèle, seigneur, vous trahissait tous deux.

TANCRÈDE.
Pour qui ?

ALDAMON.
Pour une main étrangère, ennemie,
Pour l'oppresseur altier de notre nation,
Pour Solamir.

TANCRÈDE.
O ciel ! ô trop funeste nom !
Solamir !... Dans Byzance il soupira pour elle :
Mais il fut dédaigné, mais je fus son vainqueur ;
Elle n'a pu trahir ses serments et mon cœur ;
Tant d'horreur n'entre point dans une ame si belle ;
Elle en est incapable.

ALDAMON.
A regret j'ai parlé ;
Mais ce secret horrible est partout révélé.

TANCRÈDE
Écoute : je connais l'envie et l'imposture :
Eh ! quel cœur généreux échappe à leur injure !
Proscrit dès mon berceau, nourri dans le malheur,
Moi toujours éprouvé, moi qui suis mon ouvrage,
Qui d'états en états ai porté mon courage,
Qui partout de l'envie ai senti la fureur,
Depuis que je suis né, j'ai vu la calomnie
Exhaler les venins de sa bouche impunie

Chez les républicains, comme à la cour des rois.
Argire fut long-temps accusé par sa voix;
Il souffrit comme moi : cher ami, je m'abuse,
Ou ce monstre odieux règne dans Syracuse;
Ses serpents sont nourris de ces mortels poisons
Que dans les cœurs trompés jettent les factions.
De l'esprit de parti je sais quelle est la rage :
L'auguste Aménaïde en éprouve l'outrage.
Entrons : je veux la voir, l'entendre, et m'éclairer.

ALDAMON.

Ah! seigneur, arrêtez : il faut donc tout vous dire;
On l'arrache des bras du malheureux Argire;
Elle est aux fers.

TANCRÈDE.

Qu'entends-je?

ALDAMON.

Et l'on va la livrer,
Dans cette place même, au plus affreux supplice.

TANCRÈDE.

Aménaïde!

ALDAMON.

Hélas! si c'est une justice,
Elle est bien odieuse; on ose en murmurer,
On pleure; mais, seigneur, on se borne à pleurer.

TANCRÈDE.

Aménaïde! ô cieux!... crois-moi, ce sacrifice,
Cet horrible attentat ne s'achèvera pas.

ALDAMON.

Le peuple au tribunal précipite ses pas :
Il la plaint, il gémit, en la nommant perfide;
Et d'un cruel spectacle indignement avide,

ACTE III, SCÈNE III.

Turbulent, curieux avec compassion,
Il s'agite en tumulte autour de la prison.
Étrange empressement de voir des misérables!
On hâte en gémissant ces moments formidables.
Ces portiques, ces lieux que vous voyez déserts,
De nombreux citoyens seront bientôt couverts.
Éloignez-vous, venez.

TANCRÈDE.
    Quel vieillard vénérable
Sort d'un temple en tremblant, les yeux baignés de pleurs?
Ses suivants consternés imitent ses douleurs.

ALDAMON.
C'est Argire, seigneur, c'est le malheureux père....

TANCRÈDE.
Retire-toi.... surtout ne me découvre pas.
Que je le plains!

SCÈNE IV.

ARGIRE, *dans un des côtés de la scène*; TANCRÈDE, *sur le devant*; ALDAMON, *loin de lui, dans l'enfoncement*.

ARGIRE.
O ciel! avance mon trépas.
O mort! viens me frapper; c'est ma seule prière.

TANCRÈDE.
Noble Argire, excusez un de ces chevaliers
Qui, contre le croissant déployant leur bannière,
Dans de si saints combats vont chercher des lauriers.
Vous voyez le moins grand de ces dignes guerriers.
Je venais.... Pardonnez.... dans l'état où vous êtes,
Si je mêle à vos pleurs mes larmes indiscrètes.

ARGIRE.

Ah ! vous êtes le seul qui m'osiez consoler ;
Tout le reste me fuit, ou cherche à m'accabler.
Vous-même pardonnez à mon désordre extrême.
A qui parlé-je ? hélas !

TANCRÈDE.

Je suis un étranger,
Plein de respect pour vous, touché comme vous-même,
Honteux, et frémissant de vous interroger ;
Malheureux comme vous.... Ah ! par pitié... de grâce,
Une seconde fois excusez tant d'audace.
Est-il vrai ?... votre fille...! est-il possible ?...

ARGIRE.

Hélas !
Il est trop vrai, bientôt on la mène au trépas.

TANCRÈDE.

Elle est coupable ?

ARGIRE, *avec des soupirs et des pleurs.*

Elle est.... la honte de son père.

TANCRÈDE.

Votre fille !... Seigneur, nourri loin de ces lieux,
Je pensais, sur le bruit de son nom glorieux,
Que si la vertu même habitait sur la terre,
Le cœur d'Aménaïde était son sanctuaire.
Elle est coupable ! ô jour ! ô détestables bords !
Jour à jamais affreux !

ARGIRE.

Ce qui me désespère,
Ce qui creuse ma tombe, et ce qui chez les morts
Avec plus d'amertume encor me fait descendre,
C'est qu'elle aime son crime, et qu'elle est sans remords.
Aussi nul chevalier ne cherche à la défendre :

Ils ont en gémissant signé l'arrêt mortel;
Et, malgré notre usage antique et solennel,
Si vanté dans l'Europe, et si cher au courage,
De défendre en champ clos le sexe qu'on outrage,
Celle qui fut ma fille à mes yeux va périr
Sans trouver un guerrier qui l'ose secourir.
Ma douleur s'en accroît, ma honte s'en augmente;
Tout frémit, tout se tait, aucun ne se présente.

TANCRÈDE.

Il s'en présentera; gardez-vous d'en douter.

ARGIRE.

De quel espoir, seigneur, daignez-vous me flatter?

TANCRÈDE.

Il s'en présentera, non pas pour votre fille,
Elle est loin d'y prétendre et de le mériter,
Mais pour l'honneur sacré de sa noble famille,
Pour vous, pour votre gloire, et pour votre vertu.

ARGIRE.

Vous rendez quelque vie à ce cœur abattu.
Eh! qui pour nous défendre entrera dans la lice?
Nous sommes en horreur, on est glacé d'effroi;
Qui daignera me tendre une main protectrice?
Je n'ose m'en flatter.... Qui combattra?

TANCRÈDE.

Qui? moi.
Moi, dis-je; et, si le ciel seconde ma vaillance,
Je demande de vous, seigneur, pour récompense,
De partir à l'instant sans être retenu,
Sans voir Aménaïde, et sans être connu.

ARGIRE.

Ah! seigneur, c'est le ciel, c'est Dieu qui vous envoie;
Mon cœur triste et flétri ne peut goûter de joie;

Mais je sens que j'expire avec moins de douleur.
Ah! ne puis-je savoir à qui, dans mon malheur,
Je dois tant de respect et de reconnaissance?
Tout annonce à mes yeux votre haute naissance;
Hélas! qui vois-je en vous?

TANCRÈDE.

Vous voyez un vengeur.

SCÈNE V.

ORBASSAN, ARGIRE, TANCRÈDE, CHEVALIERS, SUITE.

ORBASSAN, *à Argire.*

L'ÉTAT est en danger; songeons à lui, seigneur.
Nous prétendions demain sortir de nos murailles;
Nous sommes prévenus. Ceux qui nous ont trahis
Sans doute avertissaient nos cruels ennemis.
Solamir veut tenter le destin des batailles;
Nous marcherons à lui. Vous, si vous m'en croyez,
Dérobez à vos yeux un spectacle funeste,
Insupportable, horrible à nos sens effrayés.

ARGIRE.

Il suffit, Orbassan; tout l'espoir qui me reste
C'est d'aller expirer au milieu des combats.
(montrant Tancrède.)
Ce brave chevalier y guidera mes pas;
Et, malgré les horreurs dont ma race est flétrie,
Je périrai du moins en servant ma patrie.

ORBASSAN.

Des sentiments si grands sont bien dignes de vous.
Allez aux musulmans porter vos derniers coups;

Mais, avant tout, fuyez cet appareil barbare,
Si peu fait pour vos yeux, et déja qu'on prépare.
On approche.

ARGIRE.

Ah ! grand Dieu !

ORBASSAN.

Les regards paternels
Doivent se détourner de ces objets cruels.
Ma place me retient, et mon devoir sévère
Veut qu'ici je contienne un peuple téméraire :
L'inexorable loi ne sait rien ménager ;
Tout horrible qu'elle est, je la dois protéger.
Mais vous, qui n'avez point cet affreux ministère,
Qui peut vous retenir, et qui peut vous forcer
A voir couler le sang que la loi va verser ?
On vient ; éloignez-vous.

TANCRÈDE, à *Argire*.

Non, demeurez, mon père.

ORBASSAN.

Et qui donc êtes-vous ?

TANCRÈDE.

Votre ennemi, seigneur,
L'ami de ce vieillard, peut-être son vengeur,
Peut-être autant que vous à l'état nécessaire.

SCÈNE VI.

La scène s'ouvre : on voit AMÉNAIDE, *au milieu des gardes ;* LES CHEVALIERS, LE PEUPLE, *remplissent la place.*

ARGIRE, à *Tancrède*.

GÉNÉREUX inconnu, daignez me soutenir ;
Cachez-moi ces objets.... c'est ma fille elle-même.

20.

TANCRÈDE.
Quels moments pour tous trois !
AMÉNAÏDE.
O justice suprême !
Toi qui vois le passé, le présent, l'avenir,
Tu lis seule en mon cœur, toi seule es équitable ;
Des profanes humains la foule impitoyable
Parle et juge en aveugle, et condamne au hasard.
Chevaliers, citoyens, vous qui tous avez part
Au sanguinaire arrêt porté contre ma vie,
Ce n'est pas devant vous que je me justifie ;
Que ce ciel qui m'entend juge entre vous et moi,
Organes odieux d'un jugement inique,
Oui, je vous outrageais, j'ai trahi votre loi ;
Je l'avais en horreur, elle était tyrannique.
Oui, j'offensais un père, il a forcé mes vœux ;
J'offensais Orbassan, qui, fier et rigoureux,
Prétendait sur mon ame une injuste puissance.
Citoyens, si la mort est due à mon offense,
Frappez ; mais écoutez ; sachez tout mon malheur :
Qui va répondre à Dieu parle aux hommes sans peur.
Et vous, mon père, et vous, témoin de mon supplice,
Qui ne deviez pas l'être, et de qui la justice
(apercevant Tancrède.)
Aurait pu.... Ciel ! ô ciel ! qui vois-je à ses côtés ?
Est-ce lui....? je me meurs.
(elle tombe évanouie entre les gardes.)
TANCRÈDE.
Ah ! ma seule présence
Est pour elle un reproche ! il n'importe.... Arrêtez,
Ministres de la mort, suspendez la vengeance ;
Arrêtez, citoyens, j'entreprends sa défense,

Je suis son chevalier : ce père infortuné,
Prêt à mourir comme elle, et non moins condamné,
Daigne avouer mon bras propice à l'innocence.
Que la seule valeur rende ici des arrêts,
Des dignes chevaliers c'est le plus beau partage ;
Que l'on ouvre la lice à l'honneur, au courage ;
Que les juges du camp fassent tous les apprêts.
Toi, superbe Orbassan, c'est toi que je défie ;
Viens mourir de mes mains ou m'arracher la vie ;
Tes exploits et ton nom ne sont pas sans éclat ;
Tu commandes ici, je veux t'en croire digne :
Je jette devant toi le gage du combat.

(*il jette son gantelet sur la scène.*)

L'oses-tu relever ?

ORBASSAN.

Ton arrogance insigne
Ne mériterait pas qu'on te fît cet honneur.

(*Il fait signe à son écuyer de ramasser le gage de bataille.*)

Je le fais à moi-même ; et, consultant mon cœur,
Respectant ce vieillard qui daigne ici t'admettre,
Je veux bien avec toi descendre à me commettre,
Et daigner te punir de m'oser défier.
Quel est ton rang, ton nom ? ce simple bouclier
Semble nous annoncer peu de marques de gloire.

TANCRÈDE.

Peut-être il en aura des mains de la victoire.
Pour mon nom, je le tais, et tel est mon dessein ;
Mais je te l'apprendrai les armes à la main.
Marchons.

ORBASSAN.

Qu'à l'instant même on ouvre la barrière ;

Qu'Aménaïde ici ne soit plus prisonnière
Jusqu'à l'évènement de ce léger combat.
Vous, sachez, compagnons, qu'en quittant la carrière,
Je marche à votre tête, et je défends l'état.
D'un combat singulier la gloire est périssable;
Mais servir la patrie est l'honneur véritable.

TANCRÈDE.

Viens; et vous, chevaliers, j'espère qu'aujourd'hui
L'état sera sauvé par d'autres que par lui.

SCÈNE VII.

ARGIRE, *sur le devant*; AMÉNAIDE, *au fond, à qui l'on a ôté les fers.*

AMÉNAÏDE, *revenant à elle.*

Ciel! que deviendra-t-il? si l'on sait sa naissance,
Il est perdu.

ARGIRE.

Ma fille.....

AMÉNAÏDE, *appuyée sur Fanie, et se retournant vers son père.*

Ah! que me voulez-vous?
Vous m'avez condamnée.

ARGIRE.

O destins en courroux!
Voulez-vous, ô mon Dieu qui prenez sa défense,
Ou pardonner sa faute, ou venger l'innocence?
Quels bienfaits à mes yeux daignez-vous accorder?
Est-ce justice ou grâce? ah! je tremble et j'espère.
Qu'as-tu fait? et comment dois-je te regarder!
Avec quels yeux, hélas?

ACTE III, SCÈNE VII.

AMÉNAÏDE.

Avec les yeux d'un père.
Votre fille est encore au bord de son tombeau.
Je ne sais si le ciel me sera favorable :
Rien n'est changé, je suis encor sous le couteau.
Tremblez moins pour ma gloire, elle est inaltérable;
Mais, si vous êtes père, ôtez-moi de ces lieux;
Dérobez votre fille accablée, expirante,
A tout cet appareil, à la foule insultante
Qui sur mon infortune arrête ici ses yeux,
Observe mes affronts, et contemple des larmes,
Dont la cause est si belle.... et qu'on ne connaît pas.

ARGIRE.

Viens; mes tremblantes mains rassureront tes pas.
Ciel, de son défenseur favorisez les armes,
Ou d'un malheureux père avancez le trépas!

FIN DU TROISIÈME ACTE.

ACTE QUATRIÈME.

SCÈNE I.

TANCRÈDE, LORÉDAN, CHEVALIERS.

Marche guerrière : on porte les armes de Tancrède devant lui.

LORÉDAN.

Seigneur, votre victoire est illustre et fatale :
Vous nous avez privés d'un brave chevalier,
Dont le cœur à l'état se livrait tout entier,
Et de qui la valeur fut à la vôtre égale ;
Ne pouvons-nous savoir votre nom, votre sort ?

TANCRÈDE, *dans l'attitude d'un homme pensif et affligé.*

Orbassan ne l'a su qu'en recevant la mort ;
Il emporte au tombeau mon secret et ma haine.
De mon sort malheureux ne soyez point en peine ;
Si je puis vous servir, qu'importe qui je sois ?

LORÉDAN.

Demeurez ignoré, puisque vous voulez l'être ;
Mais que votre vertu se fasse ici connaître
Par un courage utile et de dignes exploits.
Les drapeaux du croissant dans nos champs vont paraître ;
Défendez avec nous notre culte et nos lois ;
Voyez dans Solamir un plus grand adversaire :
Nous perdons notre appui, mais vous le remplacez.
Rendez-nous le héros que vous nous ravissez ;
Le vainqueur d'Orbassan nous devient nécessaire.
Solamir vous attend.

TANCRÈDE.

Oui, je vous ai promis
De marcher avec vous contre vos ennemis ;
Je tiendrai ma parole : et Solamir peut-être
Est plus mon ennemi que celui de l'état.
Je le hais plus que vous : mais, quoi qu'il en puisse être,
Sachez que je suis prêt pour ce nouveau combat.

CATANE.

Nous attendons beaucoup d'une telle vaillance ;
Attendez tout aussi de la reconnaissance
Que devra Syracuse à votre illustre bras.

TANCRÈDE.

Il n'en est point pour moi, je n'en exige pas ;
Je n'en veux point, seigneur ; et cette triste enceinte
N'a rien qui désormais soit l'objet de mes vœux.
Si je verse mon sang, si je meurs malheureux,
Je ne prétends ici récompense, ni plainte ;
Ni gloire, ni pitié. Je ferai mon devoir ;
Solamir me verra, c'est-là tout mon espoir.

LORÉDAN.

C'est celui de l'état ; déja le temps nous presse.
Ne songeons qu'à l'objet qui tous nous intéresse,
A la victoire ; et vous, qui l'allez partager,
Vous serez averti quand il faudra vous rendre
Au poste où l'ennemi croit bientôt nous surprendre.
Dans le sang musulman tout prêts à nous plonger,
Tout autre sentiment nous doit être étranger.
Ne pensons, croyez-moi, qu'à servir la patrie.

(les chevaliers sortent.)

TANCRÈDE.

Qu'elle en soit digne ou non, je lui donne ma vie.

SCÈNE II.

TANCRÈDE, ALDAMON.

ALDAMON.

Ils ne connaissent pas quel trait envenimé
Est caché dans ce cœur trop noble et trop charmé.
Mais, malgré vos douleurs, et malgré votre outrage,
Ne remplirez-vous pas l'indispensable usage
De paraître en vainqueur aux yeux de la beauté
Qui vous doit son honneur, ses jours, sa liberté,
Et de lui présenter de vos mains triomphantes
D'Orbassan terrassé les dépouilles sanglantes ?

TANCRÈDE.

Non, sans doute, Aldamon, je ne la verrai pas.

ALDAMON.

Eh quoi ! pour la servir vous cherchiez le trépas,
Et vous fuyez loin d'elle ?

TANCRÈDE.

    Et son cœur le mérite.

ALDAMON.

Je vois trop à quel point son crime vous irrite;
Mais pour ce crime, enfin, vous avez combattu.

TANCRÈDE.

Oui, j'ai tout fait pour elle, il est vrai, je l'ai dû.
Je n'ai pu, cher ami, malgré sa perfidie,
Supporter ni sa mort ni son ignominie ;
Et, l'eussé-je aimé moins, comment l'abandonner ?
J'ai dû sauver ses jours, et non lui pardonner.
Qu'elle vive, il suffit, et que Tancrède expire.
Elle regrettera l'amant qu'elle a trahi,
Le cœur qu'elle a perdu, ce cœur qu'elle déchire....
A quel excès, ô ciel ! je lui fus asservi !

ACTE IV, SCÈNE II.

Pouvais-je craindre, hélas! de la trouver parjure?
Je pensais adorer la vertu la plus pure,
Je croyais les serments, les autels moins sacrés
Qu'une simple promesse, un mot d'Aménaïde....

ALDAMON.

Tout est-il en ces lieux ou barbare ou perfide?
A la proscription vos jours furent livrés;
La loi vous persécute, et l'amour vous outrage.
Eh bien! s'il est ainsi, fuyons de ce rivage:
Je vous suis au combat; je vous suis pour jamais,
Loin de ces murs affreux, trop souillés de forfaits.

TANCRÈDE.

Quel charme, dans son crime, à mes esprits rappelle
L'image des vertus que je crus voir en elle!
Toi, qui me fais descendre avec tant de tourment
Dans l'horreur du tombeau dont je t'ai délivrée,
Odieuse coupable.... et peut-être adorée!
Toi, qui fais mon destin jusqu'au dernier moment;
Ah! s'il était possible, ah! si tu pouvais être
Ce que mes yeux trompés t'ont vu toujours paraître!
Non, ce n'est qu'en mourant que je puis l'oublier;
Ma faiblesse est affreuse.... il la faut expier,
Il faut périr.... mourons, sans nous occuper d'elle.

ALDAMON.

Elle vous a paru tantôt moins criminelle.
L'univers, disiez-vous, au mensonge est livré;
La calomnie y règne.

TANCRÈDE.
Ah! tout est avéré,
Tout est approfondi dans cet affreux mystère:
Solamir en ces lieux adora ses attraits;
Il demanda sa main pour le prix de la paix.

Voltaire. Théâtre. 4.

Hélas ! l'eût-il osé, s'il n'avait pas su plaire ?
Ils sont d'intelligence. En vain j'ai cru mon cœur,
En vain j'avais douté ; je dois en croire un père :
Le père le plus tendre est son accusateur :
Il condamne sa fille ; elle-même s'accuse ;
Enfin mes yeux l'ont vu ce billet plein d'horreur :
« Puissiez-vous vivre en maître au sein de Syracuse,
« Et régner dans nos murs, ainsi que dans mon cœur ! »
Mon malheur est certain.

ALDAMON.

Que ce grand cœur l'oublie,
Qu'il dédaigne une ingrate à ce point avilie.

TANCRÈDE.

Et, pour comble d'horreur, elle a cru s'honorer !
Au plus grand des humains elle a cru se livrer !
Que cette idée encor m'accable et m'humilie !
L'Arabe impérieux domine en Italie ;
Et le sexe imprudent, que tant d'éclat séduit,
Ce sexe à l'esclavage en leurs états réduit,
Frappé de ce respect que des vainqueurs impriment,
Se livre par faiblesse aux maîtres qui l'oppriment !
Il nous trahit pour eux, nous, son servile appui,
Qui vivons à ses pieds, et qui mourons pour lui !
Ma fierté suffirait, dans une telle injure,
Pour détester ma vie, et pour fuir la parjure.

SCÈNE III.

TANCRÈDE, ALDAMON, PLUSIEURS CHEVALIERS.

CATANE.

Nos chevaliers sont prêts ; le temps est précieux.

TANCRÈDE.

Oui, j'en ai trop perdu : je m'arrache à ces lieux ;
Je vous suis, c'en est fait.

SCÈNE IV.

TANCRÈDE, AMÉNAIDE, ALDAMON, FANIE.
CHEVALIERS.

AMÉNAÏDE, *arrivant avec précipitation.*

O mon dieu tutélaire !
Maître de mon destin, j'embrasse vos genoux.
(*Tancrède la relève, mais en se détournant.*)
Ce n'est point m'abaisser ; et mon malheureux père
A vos pieds, comme moi, va tomber devant vous.
Pourquoi nous dérober votre auguste présence ?
Qui pourra condamner ma juste impatience ?
Je m'arrache à ses bras.... mais ne puis-je, seigneur,
Me permettre ma joie, et montrer tout mon cœur ?
Je n'ose vous nommer.... et vous baissez la vue....
Ne puis-je vous revoir, en cet affreux séjour,
Qu'au milieu des bourreaux qui m'arrachaient le jour ?
Vous êtes consterné.... mon ame est confondue ;
Je crains de vous parler.... quelle contrainte, hélas !
Vous détournez les yeux.... vous ne m'écoutez pas.

TANCRÈDE, *d'une voix entrecoupée.*

Retournez.... consolez ce vieillard que j'honore ;
D'autres soins plus pressants me rappellent encore.
Envers vous, envers lui, j'ai rempli mon devoir,
J'en ai reçu le prix.... je n'ai point d'autre espoir ;
Trop de reconnaissance est un fardeau peut-être ;
Mon cœur vous en dégage.... et le vôtre est le maître
De pouvoir à son gré disposer de son sort.
Vivez heureuse.... et moi, je vais chercher la mort.

SCÈNE V.

AMÉNAIDE, FANIE.

AMÉNAÏDE.

Veillé-je ? et du tombeau suis-je en effet sortie ?
Est-il vrai que le ciel m'ait rendue à la vie ?
Ce jour, ce triste jour, éclaire-t-il mes yeux ?
Ce que je viens d'entendre, ô ma chère Fanie,
Est un arrêt de mort plus dur, plus odieux,
Plus affreux que les lois qui m'avaient condamnée.

FANIE.

L'un et l'autre est horrible à mon ame étonnée.

AMÉNAÏDE.

Est-ce Tancrède, ô ciel ! qui vient de me parler ?
As-tu vu sa froideur altière, avilissante,
Ce courroux dédaigneux dont il m'ose accabler ?
Fanie, avec horreur il voyait son amante !
Il m'arrache à la mort, et c'est pour m'immoler !
Qu'ai-je donc fait, Tancrède ? ai-je pu vous déplaire ?

FANIE.

Il est vrai que son front respirait la colère,

ACTE IV, SCÈNE V.

Sa voix entrecoupée affectait des froideurs ;
Il détournait les yeux, mais il cachait ses pleurs.

AMÉNAÏDE.

Il me rebute, il fuit, me renonce, et m'outrage !
Quel changement affreux a formé cet orage ?
Que veut-il ? quelle offense excite son courroux ?
De qui dans l'univers peut-il être jaloux ?
Oui, je lui dois la vie, et c'est toute ma gloire.
Seul objet de mes vœux, il est mon seul appui.
Je mourais, je le sais, sans lui, sans sa victoire ;
Mais s'il sauva mes jours, je les perdais pour lui.

FANIE.

Il le peut ignorer ; la voix publique entraîne ;
Même en s'en défiant, on lui résiste à peine.
Cet esclave, sa mort, ce billet malheureux,
Le nom de Solamir, l'éclat de sa vaillance,
L'offre de son hymen, l'audace de ses feux,
Tout parlait contre vous, jusqu'à votre silence,
Ce silence si fier, si grand, si généreux,
Qui dérobait Tancrède à l'injuste vengeance
De vos communs tyrans armés contre vous deux.
Quels yeux pouvaient percer ce voile ténébreux ?
Le préjugé l'emporte, et l'on croit l'apparence.

AMÉNAÏDE.

Lui, me croire coupable !

FANIE.

Ah ! s'il peut s'abuser,
Excusez un amant.

AMÉNAÏDE, *reprenant sa fierté et ses forces.*

Rien ne peut l'excuser....
Quand l'univers entier m'accuserait d'un crime,
Sur son jugement seul un grand homme appuyé

A l'univers séduit oppose son estime;
Il aura donc pour moi combattu par pitié !
Cet opprobre est affreux, et j'en suis accablée.
Hélas ! mourant pour lui, je mourais consolée ;
Et c'est lui qui m'outrage et m'ose soupçonner !
C'en est fait, je ne veux jamais lui pardonner ;
Ses bienfaits sont toujours présents à ma pensée,
Ils resteront gravés dans mon ame offensée ;
Mais, s'il a pu me croire indigne de sa foi,
C'est lui qui pour jamais est indigne de moi.
Ah ! de tous mes affronts c'est le plus grand peut-être.

FANIE.

Mais il ne connaît pas....

AMÉNAÏDE.

Il devait me connaître ;
Il devait respecter un cœur tel que le mien ;
Il devait présumer qu'il était impossible
Que jamais je trahisse un si noble lien.
Ce cœur est aussi fier que son bras invincible ;
Ce cœur était en tout aussi grand que le sien,
Moins soupçonneux, sans doute, et surtout plus sensible.
Je renonce à Tancrède, au reste des mortels ;
Ils sont faux ou méchants, ils sont faibles, cruels,
Ou trompeurs, ou trompés ; et ma douleur profonde,
En oubliant Tancrède, oubliera tout le monde.

SCÈNE VI.

ARGIRE, AMÉNAIDE, SUITE.

ARGIRE, *soutenu par ses écuyers.*

MES amis, avancez, sans plaindre mes tourments :
On va combattre ; allons, guidez mes pas tremblants.

ACTE IV, SCÈNE VI.

Ne pourrai-je embrasser ce héros tutélaire ?
Ah ! ne puis-je savoir qui t'a sauvé le jour ?

AMÉNAÏDE, *plongée dans sa douleur, appuyée d'une main sur Fanie, et se tournant à moitié vers son père.*

Un mortel autrefois digne de mon amour,
Un héros en ces lieux opprimé par mon père,
Que je n'osais nommer, que vous avez proscrit,
Le seul et cher objet de ce fatal écrit,
Le dernier rejeton d'une famille auguste,
Le plus grand des humains, hélas ! le plus injuste ;
En un mot, c'est Tancrède.

ARGIRE.
O ciel ! que m'as-tu dit ?

AMÉNAÏDE.
Ce que ne peut cacher la douleur qui m'égare,
Ce que je vous confie en craignant tout pour lui.

ARGIRE.
Lui, Tancrède !

AMÉNAÏDE.
Et quel autre eût été mon appui ?

ARGIRE.
Tancrède qu'opprima notre sénat barbare ?

AMÉNAÏDE.
Oui, lui-même.

ARGIRE.
Et pour nous il fait tout aujourd'hui.
Nous lui ravissions tout, biens, dignités, patrie,
Et c'est lui qui pour nous vient prodiguer sa vie !
O juges malheureux, qui dans nos faibles mains
Tenons aveuglément le glaive et la balance ;
Combien nos jugements sont injustes et vains,

Et combien nous égare une fausse prudence!
Que nous étions ingrats! que nous étions tyrans!

AMÉNAÏDE.

Je puis me plaindre à vous, je le sais.... mais, mon père,
Votre vertu se fait des reproches si grands,
Que mon cœur désolé tremble de vous en faire;
Je les dois à Tancrède.

ARGIRE.

A lui par qui je vis,
A qui je dois tes jours?

AMÉNAÏDE.

Ils sont trop avilis,
Ils sont trop malheureux. C'est en vous que j'espère;
Réparez tant d'horreurs et tant de cruauté;
Ah! rendez-moi l'honneur que vous m'avez ôté.
Le vainqueur d'Orbassan n'a sauvé que ma vie;
Venez, que votre voix parle et me justifie.

ARGIRE.

Sans doute, je le dois.

AMÉNAÏDE.

Je vole sur vos pas.

ARGIRE.

Demeure.

AMÉNAÏDE.

Moi rester! je vous suis aux combats.
J'ai vu la mort de près, et je l'ai vue horrible;
Croyez qu'aux champs d'honneur elle est bien moins terrible
Qu'à l'indigne échafaud où vous me conduisiez.
Seigneur, il n'est plus temps que vous me refusiez :
J'ai quelques droits sur vous; mon malheur me les donne.
Faudra-t-il que deux fois mon père m'abandonne?

ACTE IV, SCÈNE VI.

ARGIRE.

Ma fille, je n'ai plus d'autorité sur toi ;
J'en avais abusé, je dois l'avoir perdue.
Mais quel est ce dessein qui me glace d'effroi ?
Crains les égarements de ton ame éperdue.
Ce n'est point en ces lieux, comme en d'autres climats,
Où le sexe, élevé loin d'une triste gêne,
Marche avec les héros, et s'en distingue à peine :
Et nos mœurs et nos lois ne le permettent pas.

AMÉNAÏDE.

Quelles lois ! quelles mœurs indignes et cruelles !
Sachez qu'en ce moment je suis au-dessus d'elles ;
Sachez que, dans ce jour d'injustice et d'horreur,
Je n'écoute plus rien que la loi de mon cœur.
Quoi ! ces affreuses lois, dont le poids vous opprime,
Auront pris dans vos bras votre sang pour victime !
Elles auront permis qu'aux yeux des citoyens
Votre fille ait paru dans d'infâmes liens,
Et ne permettront pas qu'aux champs de la victoire
J'accompagne mon père et défende ma gloire !
Et le sexe en ces lieux, conduit aux échafauds,
Ne pourra se montrer qu'au milieu des bourreaux !
L'injustice à la fin produit l'indépendance.
Vous frémissez, mon père ; ah ! vous deviez frémir
Quand, de vos ennemis caressant l'insolence,
Au superbe Orbassan vous pûtes vous unir
Contre le seul mortel qui prend votre défense,
Quand vous m'avez forcée à vous désobéir.

ARGIRE.

Va, c'est trop accabler un père déplorable :
N'abuse point du droit de me trouver coupable ;
Je le suis, je le sens, je me suis condamné.

Ménage ma douleur ; et si ton cœur encore
D'un père au désespoir ne s'est point détourné,
Laisse-moi seul mourir par les flèches du Maure.
Je vais joindre Tancrède, et tu n'en peux douter.
Vous, observez ses pas.

SCÈNE VII.

AMÉNAIDE.

Qui pourra m'arrêter ?
Tancrède, qui me hais, et qui m'as outragée,
Qui m'oses mépriser après m'avoir vengée,
Oui, je veux à tes yeux combattre et t'imiter ;
Des traits sur toi lancés affronter la tempête,
En recevoir les coups..... en garantir ta tête ;
Te rendre à tes côtés tout ce que je te dois ;
Punir ton injustice en expirant pour toi ;
Surpasser, s'il se peut, ta rigueur inhumaine ;
Mourante entre tes bras, t'accabler de ma haine,
De ma haine trop juste, et laisser, à ma mort,
Dans ton cœur qui m'aima le poignard du remord,
L'éternel repentir d'un crime irréparable,
Et l'amour que j'abjure, et l'horreur qui m'accable.

FIN DU QUATRIÈME ACTE.

ACTE CINQUIÈME.

SCÈNE I.

LES CHEVALIERS ET LEURS ÉCUYERS, *l'épée à la main* ; DES SOLDATS, *portant des trophées* ; LE PEUPLE, *dans le fond.*

LORÉDAN.

Allez et préparez les chants de la victoire,
Peuple, au dieu des combats prodiguez votre encens ;
C'est lui qui nous fait vaincre, à lui seul est la gloire !
S'il ne conduit nos coups, nos bras sont impuissants.
Il a brisé les traits, il a rompu les pièges
Dont nous environnaient ces brigands sacrilèges ;
De cent peuples vaincus dominateurs cruels.
Sur leurs corps tout sanglants érigez vos trophées ;
Et foulant à vos pieds leurs fureurs étouffées,
Des trésors du Croissant ornez nos saints autels.
Que l'Espagne opprimée, et l'Italie en cendre,
L'Égypte terrassée, et la Syrie aux fers,
Apprennent aujourd'hui comme on peut se défendre
Contre ces fiers tyrans, l'effroi de l'univers.
C'est à nous maintenant de consoler Argire ;
Que le bonheur public apaise ses douleurs ;
Puissions-nous voir en lui, malgré tous ses malheurs,
L'homme d'état heureux quand le père soupire !

Mais pourquoi ce guerrier, ce héros inconnu,
A qui l'on doit, dit-on, le succès de nos armes,
Avec nos chevaliers n'est-il point revenu ?
Ce triomphe à ses yeux a-t-il si peu de charmes ?

Croit-il de ses exploits que nous soyons jaloux ?
Nous sommes assez grands pour être sans envie.
Veut-il fuir Syracuse après l'avoir servie ?
   (à Catane.)
Seigneur, il a long-temps combattu près de vous ;
D'où vient qu'ayant voulu courir notre fortune
Il ne partage point l'allégresse commune ?
    CATANE.
Apprenez-en la cause, et daignez m'écouter.
Quand du chemin d'Etna vous fermiez le passage,
Placé loin de vos yeux, j'étais vers le rivage
Où nos fiers ennemis osaient nous résister ;
Je l'ai vu courir seul et se précipiter.
Nous étions étonnés qu'il n'eût point ce courage
Inaltérable et calme au milieu du carnage,
Cette vertu d'un chef, et ce don d'un grand cœur :
Un désespoir affreux égarait sa valeur ;
Sa voix entrecoupée et son regard farouche
Annonçaient la douleur qui troublait ses esprits.
Il appelait souvent Solamir à grands cris ;
Le nom d'Aménaïde échappait de sa bouche ;
Il la nommait parjure, et, malgré ses fureurs,
De ses yeux enflammés j'ai vu tomber des pleurs.
Il cherchait à mourir ; et, toujours invincible,
Plus il s'abandonnait, plus il était terrible.
Tout cédait à nos coups, et surtout à son bras ;
Nous revenions vers vous conduits par la victoire ;
Mais lui, les yeux baissés, insensible à sa gloire,
Morne, triste, abattu, regrettant le trépas,
Il appelle en pleurant Aldamon qui s'avance ;
Il l'embrasse, il lui parle, et loin de nous s'élance
Aussi rapidement qu'il avait combattu.

ACTE V, SCÈNE I.

C'est pour jamais, dit-il. Ces mots nous laissent croire
Que ce grand chevalier, si digne de mémoire,
Veut être à Syracuse à jamais inconnu.
Nul ne peut soupçonner le dessein qui le guide.
Mais dans le même instant je vois Aménaïde,
Je la vois éperdue au milieu des soldats,
La mort dans les regards, pâle, défigurée;
Elle appelle Tancrède, elle vole égarée :
Son père en gémissant suit à peine ses pas;
Il ramène avec nous Aménaïde en larmes;
C'est Tancrède, dit-il, ce héros dont les armes
Ont étonné nos yeux par de si grands exploits,
Ce vengeur de l'état, vengeur d'Aménaïde,
C'est lui que ce matin, d'une commune voix,
Nous déclarions rebelle, et nous nommions perfide;
C'est ce même Tancrède exilé par nos lois.
Amis, que faut-il faire, et quel parti nous reste?

LORÉDAN.

Il n'en est qu'un pour nous, celui du repentir;
Persister dans sa faute est horrible et funeste :
Un grand homme opprimé doit nous faire rougir.
On condamna souvent la vertu, le mérite;
Mais quand ils sont connus, il les faut honorer.

SCÈNE II.

LES CHEVALIERS, ARGIRE; AMÉNAIDE, *dans l'enfoncement, soutenue par ses femmes.*

ARGIRE, *arrivant avec précipitation.*

Il les faut secourir, il les faut délivrer.
Tancrède est en péril, trop de zèle l'excite :
Tancrède s'est lancé parmi les ennemis,

Contre lui ramenés, contre lui seul unis.
Hélas! j'accuse en vain mon âge qui me glace:
O vous, de qui la force est égale à l'audace,
Vous qui du faix des ans n'êtes point affaiblis,
Courez-tous, dissipez ma crainte impatiente,
Courez; rendez Tancrède à ma fille innocente.

LORÉDAN.

C'est nous en dire trop : le temps est cher, volons;
Secourons sa valeur qui devient imprudente,
Et cet emportement que nous désapprouvons.

SCÈNE III.

ARGIRE, AMÉNAIDE.

ARGIRE.

O ciel! tu prends pitié d'un père qui t'adore;
Tu m'as rendu ma fille, et tu me rends encore
L'heureux libérateur qui nous a tous vengés.

(Aménaïde entre.)

Ma fille, un juste espoir dans nos cœurs doit renaître.
J'ai causé tes malheurs, je les ai partagés;
Je les termine enfin : Tancrède va paraître.
Ne puis-je consoler tes esprits affligés?

AMÉNAÏDE.

Je me consolerai, quand je verrai Tancrède,
Quand ce fatal objet de l'horreur qui m'obsède
Aura plus de justice, et sera sans danger,
Quand j'apprendrai de vous qu'il vit sans m'outrager,
Et lorsque ses remords expieront mes injures.

ARGIRE.

Je ressens ton état; sans doute, il doit t'aigrir.
On n'essuya jamais des épreuves plus dures.

ACTE V, SCÈNE III.

Je sais ce qu'il en coûte, et qu'il est des blessures
Dont un cœur généreux peut rarement guérir :
La cicatrice en reste, il est vrai ; mais, ma fille,
Nous avons vu Tancrède en ces lieux abhorré ;
Apprends qu'il est chéri, glorieux, honoré :
Sur toi-même il répand tout l'éclat dont il brille.
Après ce qu'il a fait, il veut nous faire voir,
Par l'excès de sa gloire, et de tant de services,
L'excès où ses rivaux portaient leurs injustices.
Le vulgaire est content, s'il remplit son devoir :
Il faut plus au héros, il faut que sa vaillance
Aille au-delà du terme et de notre espérance.
C'est ce que fait Tancrède ; il passe notre espoir.
Il te verra constante, il te sera fidèle.
Le peuple en ta faveur s'élève et s'attendrit :
Tancrède va sortir de son erreur cruelle ;
Pour éclairer ses yeux, pour calmer son esprit,
Il ne faudra qu'un mot.

AMÉNAÏDE.

Et ce mot n'est pas dit.
Que m'importe à présent ce peuple et son outrage,
Et sa faveur crédule, et sa pitié volage,
Et la publique voix que je n'entendrai pas ?
D'un seul mortel, d'un seul dépend ma renommée.
Sachez que votre fille aime mieux le trépas
Que de vivre un moment sans en être estimée.
Sachez (il faut enfin m'en vanter devant vous)
Que dans mon bienfaiteur j'adorais mon époux.
Ma mère au lit de mort a reçu nos promesses ;
Sa dernière prière a béni nos tendresses :
Elle joignit nos mains, qui fermèrent ses yeux.
Nous jurâmes par elle, à la face des cieux,

Par ses mânes, par vous, vous, trop malheureux père,
De nous aimer en vous, d'être unis pour vous plaire,
De former nos liens dans vos bras paternels!
Seigneur.... les échafauds ont été nos autels.
Mon amant, mon époux cherche un trépas funeste;
Et l'horreur de ma honte est tout ce qui me reste.
Voilà mon sort.

ARGIRE.

Eh bien! ce sort est réparé,
Et nous obtiendrons plus que tu n'as espéré.

AMÉNAÏDE.

Je crains tout.

SCÈNE IV.
ARGIRE, AMÉNAÏDE, FANIE.

FANIE.

Partagez l'allégresse publique,
Jouissez plus que nous de ce prodige unique.
Tancrède a combattu; Tancrède a dissipé
Le reste d'une armée au carnage échappé.
Solamir est tombé sous cette main terrible,
Victime dévouée à notre état vengé,
Au bonheur d'un pays qui devient invincible,
Surtout à votre nom qu'on avait outragé.
La prompte renommée en répand la nouvelle;
Ce peuple, ivre de joie, et volant après lui,
Le nomme son héros, sa gloire, son appui,
Parle même du trône où sa vertu l'appelle.
Un seul de nos guerriers, seigneur, l'avait suivi;
C'est ce même Aldamon qui sous vous a servi.
Lui seul a partagé ses exploits incroyables;
Et quand nos chevaliers, dans un danger si grand,

ACTE V, SCÈNE IV.

Lui sont venus offrir leurs armes secourables;
Tancrède avait tout fait, il était triomphant.
Entendez-vous ces cris qui vantent sa vaillance?
On l'élève au-dessus des héros de la France,
Des Rolands, des Lisois, dont il est descendu.
Venez de mille mains couronner sa vertu,
Venez voir ce triomphe, et recevoir l'hommage
Que vous avez de lui trop long-temps attendu.
Tout vous rit, tout vous sert, tout venge votre outrage;
Et Tancrède à vos vœux est pour jamais rendu.

AMÉNAÏDE.

Ah! je respire enfin; mon cœur connaît la joie.
Ah! mon père, adorons le ciel qui me renvoie,
Par ces coups inouis, tout ce que j'ai perdu.
De combien de tourments sa bonté nous délivre!
Ce n'est qu'en ce moment que je commence à vivre.
Mon bonheur est au comble; hélas! il m'est bien dû.
Je veux tout oublier; pardonnez-moi mes plaintes,
Mes reproches amers, et mes frivoles craintes.
Oppresseurs de Tancrède, ennemis, citoyens,
Soyez tous à ses pieds, il va tomber aux miens.

ARGIRE.

Oui, le ciel pour jamais daigne essuyer nos larmes.
Je me trompe, ou je vois le fidèle Aldamon,
Qui suivait seul Tancrède, et secondait ses armes;
C'est lui, c'est ce guerrier si cher à ma maison.
De nos prospérités la nouvelle est certaine :
Mais d'où vient que vers nous il se traîne avec peine?
Est-il blessé? ses yeux annoncent la douleur.

SCÈNE V.

ARGIRE, AMÉNAÏDE, ALDAMON, FANIE.

AMÉNAÏDE.

Parlez, cher Aldamon, Tancrède est donc vainqueur ?

ALDAMON.

Sans doute il l'est, madame.

AMÉNAÏDE.

A ces chants d'allégresse,
A ces voix que j'entends, il s'avance en ces lieux ?

ALDAMON.

Ces chants vont se changer en des cris de tristesse.

AMÉNAÏDE.

Qu'entends-je ? Ah, malheureuse !

ALDAMON.

Un jour si glorieux
Est le dernier des jours de ce héros fidèle.

AMÉNAÏDE.

Il est mort !

ALDAMON.

La lumière éclaire encor ses yeux ;
Mais il est expirant d'une atteinte mortelle.
Je vous apporte ici de funestes adieux.
Cette lettre fatale, et de son sang tracée,
Doit vous apprendre, hélas ! sa dernière pensée.
Je m'acquitte en tremblant de cet affreux devoir.

ARGIRE.

O jour de l'infortune ! ô jour du désespoir !

AMÉNAÏDE, *revenant à elle.*

Donnez-moi mon arrêt, il me défend de vivre ;
Il m'est cher.... O Tancrède ! ô maître de mon sort !
Ton ordre, quel qu'il soit, est l'ordre de te suivre ;
J'obéirai.... Donnez votre lettre et la mort.

ACTE V, SCÈNE V.

ALDAMON.

Lisez donc ; pardonnez ce triste ministère.

AMÉNAÏDE.

O mes yeux ! lirez-vous ce sanglant caractère ?
Le pourrai-je ? Il le faut.... c'est mon dernier effort!
(elle lit.)
« Je ne pouvais survivre à votre perfidie ;
« Je meurs dans les combats, mais je meurs par vos coups.
« J'aurais voulu, cruelle, en m'exposant pour vous,
« Vous avoir conservé la gloire avec la vie.... »
Eh bien, mon père !
(elle se rejette dans les bras de Fanie.)

ARGIRE.

Enfin, les destins désormais
Ont assouvi leur haine, ont épuisé leurs traits :
Nous voilà maintenant sans espoir et sans crainte.
Ton état et le mien ne permet plus la plainte.
Ma chère Aménaïde ! avant que de quitter
Ce jour, ce monde affreux que je dois détester,
Que j'apprenne du moins à ma triste patrie
Les honneurs qu'on devait à ta vertu trahie ;
Que, dans l'horrible excès de ma confusion,
J'apprenne à l'univers à respecter ton nom.

AMÉNAÏDE.

Eh ! que fait l'univers à ma douleur profonde ?
Que me fait ma patrie et le reste du monde ?
Tancrède meurt.

ARGIRE.

Je cède aux coups qui m'ont frappé.

AMÉNAÏDE.

Tancrède meurt ! ô ciel ! sans être détrompé !
Vous en êtes la cause.... Ah ! devant qu'il expire...
Que vois-je ? mes tyrans !

SCÈNE VI.

LORÉDAN, CHEVALIERS, SUITE, AMÉNAÏDE, ARGIRE, FANIE, ALDAMON; TANCRÈDE, *dans le fond, porté par des soldats.*

LORÉDAN.

O malheureux Argire !
O fille infortunée ! on conduit devant vous
Ce brave chevalier percé de nobles coups.
Il a trop écouté son aveugle furie ;
Il a voulu mourir, mais il meurt en héros.
De ce sang précieux, versé pour la patrie,
Nos secours empressés ont suspendu les flots.
Cette ame, qu'enflammait un courage intrépide,
Semble encor s'arrêter pour voir Aménaïde ;
Il la nomme ; les pleurs coulent de tous les yeux,
Et d'un juste remords je ne puis me défendre.

Pendant qu'il parle on approche lentement Tancrède vers Aménaïde, presque évanouie entre les bras de ses femmes ; elle se débarrasse précipitamment des femmes qui la soutiennent, et se retournant avec horreur vers Lorédan, dit :

AMÉNAÏDE.

Barbares, laissez-là vos remords odieux.
(puis courant à Tancrède, et se jetant à ses pieds.)
Tancrède, cher amant, trop cruel et trop tendre,
Dans nos derniers instants, hélas ! peux-tu m'entendre ?
Tes yeux appesantis peuvent-ils me revoir ?
Hélas ! reconnais-moi, connais mon désespoir.
Dans le même tombeau souffre au moins ton épouse ;
C'est là le seul honneur dont mon ame est jalouse.
Ce nom sacré m'est dû ; tu me l'avais promis :

ACTE V, SCÈNE VI.

Ne sois point plus cruel que tous nos ennemis ;
Honore d'un regard ton épouse fidèle.....
(*il la regarde.*)
C'est donc là le dernier que tu jettes sur elle !...
De ton cœur généreux son cœur est-il haï ?
Peux-tu me soupçonner ?

TANCRÈDE, *se soulevant un peu.*

Ah ! vous m'avez trahi !

AMÉNAÏDE.

Qui ! moi ? Tancrède !

ARGIRE, *se jetant aussi à genoux de l'autre côté, et embrassant Tancrède, puis se relevant.*

Hélas ! ma fille infortunée,
Pour t'avoir trop aimé, fut par nous condamnée,
Et nous la punissions de te garder sa foi.
Nous fûmes tous cruels envers elle, envers toi.
Nos lois, nos chevaliers, un tribunal auguste,
Nous avons failli tous ; elle seule était juste.
Son écrit malheureux qui nous avait armés,
Cet écrit fut pour toi, pour le héros qu'elle aime.
Cruellement trompé, je t'ai trompé moi-même.

TANCRÈDE.

Aménaïde... ô ciel ! est-il vrai ? vous m'aimez !

AMÉNAÏDE.

Va, j'aurais en effet mérité mon supplice,
Ce supplice honteux, dont tu m'as su tirer,
Si j'avais un moment cessé de t'adorer,
Si mon cœur eût commis cette horrible injustice.

TANCRÈDE, *en reprenant un peu de force, et élevant la voix.*

Vous m'aimez ! ô bonheur plus grand que mes revers !
Je sens trop qu'à ce mot je regrette la vie.

J'ai mérité la mort, j'ai cru la calomnie.
Ma vie était horrible, hélas! et je la perds
Quand un mot de ta bouche allait la rendre heureuse!

AMÉNAÏDE.

Ce n'est donc, juste Dieu! que dans cette heure affreuse,
Ce n'est qu'en le perdant que j'ai pu lui parler!
Ah, Tancrède!

TANCRÈDE.

Vos pleurs devraient me consoler;
Mais il faut vous quitter; ma mort est douloureuse!
Je sens qu'elle s'approche. Argire, écoutez-moi :
Voilà le digne objet qui me donna sa foi;
Voilà de nos soupçons la victime innocente :
A sa tremblante main joignez ma main sanglante ;
Que j'emporte au tombeau le nom de son époux.
Soyez mon père.

ARGIRE, *prenant leurs mains.*

Hélas! mon cher fils, puissiez-vous
Vivre encore adoré d'une épouse chérie!

TANCRÈDE.

J'ai vécu pour venger ma femme et ma patrie ;
J'expire entre leurs bras, digne de toutes deux,
De toutes deux aimé.... j'ai rempli tous mes vœux...
Ma chère Aménaïde!....

AMÉNAÏDE.

Eh bien!

TANCRÈDE.

Gardez de suivre
Ce malheureux amant.... et jurez-moi de vivre...,
(*il retombe.*)

CATANE.

Il expire... et nos cœurs, de regrets pénétrés..
Qui l'ont connu trop tard....

AMÉNAÏDE, *se jetant sur le corps de Tancrède.*
                    Il meurt, et vous pleurez...
Vous, cruels, vous, tyrans, qui lui coûtez la vie !
            (*elle se relève et marche.*)
Que l'enfer engloutisse, et vous, et ma patrie,
Et ce sénat barbare, et ces horribles droits
D'égorger l'innocence avec le fer des lois !
Que ne puis-je expirer dans Syracuse en poudre,
Sur vos corps tout sanglants écrasés par la foudre !
        (*elle se rejette sur le corps de Tancrède.*)
Tancrède ! cher Tancrède !
            (*elle se relève en fureur.*)
                    Il meurt, et vous vivez ?
Vous vivez, je le suis... je l'entends, il m'appelle...
Il se rejoint à moi dans la nuit éternelle.
Je vous laisse aux tourments qui vous sont réservés.
        (*elle tombe dans les bras de Fanie.*)

ARGIRE.

Ah, ma fille !
    AMÉNAÏDE, *égarée, et le repoussant.*
            Arrêtez... vous n'êtes point mon père ;
Votre cœur n'en eut point le sacré caractère :
Vous fûtes leur complice... Ah ! pardonnez, hélas !
Je meurs en vous aimant... j'expire entre tes bras,
Cher Tancrède...
            (*elle tombe à côté de lui.*)

ARGIRE.

        O ma fille ! ô ma chère Fanie !
Qu'avant ma mort, hélas ! on la rende à la vie.

FIN DE TANCRÈDE.

TABLE

DES PIÈCES CONTENUES DANS CE VOLUME.

ORESTE, TRAGÉDIE.
Épître à la duchesse du Maine............ Pag. 3
Texte d'ORESTE........................ 23
L'ORPHELIN DE LA CHINE, TRAGÉDIE.
Épître dédicatoire au maréchal de Richelieu. 101
Texte de l'ORPHELIN DE LA CHINE..... 111
TANCRÈDE, TRAGÉDIE.
Épître dédicatoire à la marquise de Pompadour, 181
Texte de TANCRÈDE.................... 183

FIN DE LA TABLE DU QUATRIÈME ET DERNIER VOLUME.

www.ingramcontent.com/pod-product-compliance
Lightning Source LLC
Chambersburg PA
CBHW050336170426
43200CB00009BA/1611